Science, Explanation, and Rationality

Carl G. Hempel (1905–1997)
Photograph by Jan Hempel (1985)

Science,
Explanation,
and Rationality _____

Aspects of the Philosophy of Carl G. Hempel

Edited by
JAMES H. FETZER

UNIVERSITY PRESS

2000

OXFORD

UNIVERSITY PRESS

Oxford New York
Athens Auckland Bangkok Bogotá Buenos Aires Calcutta
Cape Town Chennai Dar es Salaam Delhi Florence Hong Kong Istanbul
Karachi Kuala Lumpur Madrid Melbourne Mexico City Mumbai
Nairobi Paris São Paulo Shanghai Singapore Taipei Tokyo Toronto Warsaw

and associated companies in
Berlin Ibadan

Library of Congress Cataloging-in-Publication Data
Science, explanation, and rationality : aspects of the philosophy
of Carl G. Hempel/edited by James H. Fetzer.
   p. cm.
Includes bibliographical references and indexes.
ISBN 0-19-512137-6
1. Hempel, Carl Gustav, 1905–   I. Fetzer, James H., 1940–
B945.H454 S35 2000
191—dc21   99–087642

9 8 7 6 5 4 3 2 1

Printed in the United States of America
on acid-free paper

TO *PETER*
in memoriam

Editor's Preface

Although Carl G. Hempel was not unusually prolific by some standards (his bibliography reports 112 publications, including a few short monographs and an anthology of twelve articles), his influence was immense. At least twelve of his papers were instant classics, which not only exerted profound influence upon professional philosophers of science but spawned dozens and dozens of critical commentaries and learned replies. His influence upon teaching was similarly enormous. His *Philosophy of Natural Science,* for example, became the instant text of choice for introductory courses worldwide. Page for page, his achievements were stunning. And as a human being, he was exemplary. As a philosopher, as a teacher, and as a human being, "Peter" was a paradigm.

This volume complements *The Philosophy of Carl G. Hempel,* which reprints many of his most important articles on the central problems of philosophy of science, before and after his *Aspects of Scientific Explanation.* Authors of very high caliber, many of whom number among his former students, were invited to contribute, and their responses have been extremely gratifying. The pieces appearing here attest to the extraordinary stimulation and influence his work has exercised for more than half a century. I cannot imagine a more beneficial result than that this collection might contribute to preserving and perpetuating his contributions far into the twenty-first century. For a discipline that some of us are inclined to believe has lost its way, these studies should help in its rediscovery.

All of the essays collected here were prepared especially for this book—with one exception: Wesley C. Salmon's piece, "The Spirit of Logical Empiricism: Carl G. Hempel's Role in Twentieth-Century Philosophy of Science," which was published in *Philosophy of Science* 66 (1999), pp. 333–50. Nevertheless, that is as it should be. Many of Hempel's most important publications appeared in *Philosophy of Science.* His influence upon the profession during the twentieth century was unparalleled. It is altogether fitting that this author, whose own contributions to many of the same subjects, including explanation, were exceeded only by those of Hempel, should be invited to have the last word—especially when, as in the case of the present volume, the last word reflects what may prove to be a new beginning.

Duluth, Minnesota   J. H. F.
August 1999

Contents

Part IV: Theories and Predictions

Part V: Explanations of Behavior

Part VI: Scientific Rationality

Contributors

PETER ACHINSTEIN, Professor of Philosophy at Johns Hopkins University, received his B.A. in 1956 and his Ph.D. in 1961, both from Harvard University, where he was a student of Hempel during the 1953–54 academic year. The author of *Concepts of Science* (1968), *Law and Explanation* (1970), *The Nature of Explanation* (1983), and *Particles and Waves* (1991, Lakatos Award), he is currently completing a new work entitled *The Book of Evidence*.

WILLIAM H. DRAY, Emeritus Professor of Philosophy at the University of Ottowa, has held visiting appointments at Harvard, Stanford, Ohio State, and Duke Universities and at the Case Institute. His books include *Laws and Explanation in History* (1957), *Philosophy of History* (1964), *Perspectives on History* (1980), *On History and Philosophers of History* (1989), and *History as Reenactment* (1995). With W. J. van der Dussen, he recently edited a collection of philosophical manuscripts of R. G. Collingwood.

JAMES H. FETZER, McKnight University Professor at the University of Minnesota, Duluth, has published twenty books, including *Scientific Knowledge* (1981), *AI: Its Scope and Limits* (1990), *Philosophy of Science* (1993), and *Philosophy and Cognitive Science* (2nd ed., 1996). A recipient of the Medal of the University of Helsinki (1990), his undergraduate thesis for Carl G. Hempel won The Dickinson Prize (1962). He is the Editor of *Minds and Machines* and the Series Editor of *Studies in Cognitive Systems*.

MICHAEL FRIEDMAN, Ruth N. Halls Professor of Arts and Humanities, Professor of Philosophy and of History and Philosophy of Science at Indiana University, earned his Ph.D. at Princeton in 1973. Author of *Foundations of Space-Time Theories* (1983, Matchette Prize and Lakatos Award), *Kant and the Exact Sciences* (1992), and *Reconsidering Logical Positivism* (1999), he has served as President of the American Philosophical Assocation (Central Division) and of the Philosophy of Science Association.

RISTO HILPINEN, Professor of Philosophy at the University of Miami, has also held visiting appointments at other universities in the United States, Australia, Austria, and Finland. An editor of *Synthese*, he has edited several books and has published more than one hundred papers in epistemology, philosophy of science, deontoic logic, and the philosophy of Charles S. Peirce. From 1983 to 1991, he served as Secretary for the Division of Logic, Methodology, and Philosophy of Science of the International Union of History and Philosophy of Science.

JAAKKO HINTIKKA, Professor of Philosophy at Boston University, has authored over thirty books that have appeared in ten languages and has published more than three hundred scholarly papers. He is the principal architect of game-theoretical semantics and of the interrogatory approach to inquiry and an architect of epistemic logic, distributive normal-forms, and possible-worlds semantics. His many distinctions include a John Locke Lectureship at Oxford (1964), Wihuri International Prize (1976), Guggenheim Fellowship (1979–80), and Immanuel Kant Lectureship at Stanford (1985).

PAUL W. HUMPHREYS, Professor of Philosophy at the University of Virginia, has written extensively on the nature of explanation and is the author of *The Chances of Explanation* (Princeton 1989). His other research interests include mathematical modeling, especially computational modeling, in the natural and social sciences; probability theory; emergent phenomena; and the nature of contemporary empiricism. Currently completing a book on these topics, entitled *Extending Ourselves*, he is the Series Editor of Oxford Studies in the Philosophy of Science.

PHILIP KITCHER, Professor of Philosophy at Columbia University, earned his Ph.D. from Princeton University. He is the author of several books and many articles on topics in the philosophy of science. His writings include *The Nature of Mathematical Knowledge* (1983) and *The Advancement of Science* (1993), and numerous essays on scientific explanation. With Wesley Salmon, he also co-edited *Minnesota Studies in the Philosophy of Science*, Vol. XIII (1989), on scientific explanation, a volume that was dedicated to Peter Hempel.

HENRY E. KYBURG, JR. Burbank Professor of Philosophy and Computer Science at the University of Rochester, has authored or edited more than a dozen books on probability, induction, and the philosophy of science, including *Probability and the Logic of Rational Belief* (1964) and *The Logic of Statistical Inference* (1974). Best known for discovering "the lottery paradox," he has been active in the foundations of statistics as well as in epistemology. He is associated with the Institute for Human and Machine Cognition in Pensacola, Florida.

ILKKA NIINILUOTO, Professor of Theoretical Philosophy at the University of Helsinki, studied mathematics and philosophy there as an undergraduate. His dissertation explored the role of theoretical concepts in inductive inference, while his work since then has encompassed inductive logic, verisimilitude, theory change, the logic of explanation, and verisimilitude; and, more recently, philosophical logic, philosophy of technology, and philosophy of culture. His latest books include *Is Science Progressive?* (1984), *Truthlikeness* (1987), and *Critical Scientific Realism* (1999).

ROBERT NOZICK, Pellegrino University Professor at Harvard University, earned his Ph.D. with Carl G. Hempel at Princeton University in 1963. The author of *Anarchy State and Utopia* (1977, National Book Award), *Philosophical Explanations* (1981, Ralph Waldo Emerson Award), *The Examined Life* (1990), *The Nature of Rationality* (1993), and *Socratic Puzzles* (1997), he is a Fellow of the American Academy of Arts and Sciences and a Corresponding Fellow of the Brjtish Academy and has served as President of the American Philosophical Association (Eastern Division).

WESLEY C. SALMON has served as President of the International Union of History and Philosophy of Science (1998–99) and of its Division of Logic, Methodology, and Philosophy of Science (1996–99). He is also Past President of the Philosophy of Science Association and of the American Philosophical Association (Pacific Division). He has written extensively on Hempel's theory of explanation. His most recent books are *Scientific Explanation and the Causal Stucture of the World* (1984) and *Causality and Explanation* (1998).

FREDERICK SUPPE, Professor of Philosophy and Distinguished Scholar-Teacher at the University of Maryland, chairs its Program in the History and Philosophy of Science. His books include *The Structure of Scientific Theories* (1974) and *The Semantic Conception of Theories and Scientific Realism* (1989). He has published over one hundred articles and is well known for his investigations of models and theories in science, especially for his contributions to the development of the semantic conception.

Editor's Introduction

Carl Gustav Hempel (known as "Peter" by his friends) received his Ph.D. *summa cum laude* from the University of Berlin in 1934, with a dissertation on the logical form and empirical testability of probability hypotheses about limiting frequencies (see the appendix to this essay).[1] He studied under Hans Reichenbach, who was abruptly dismissed in 1933 after Adolf Hitler became the Chancellor of Germany, and completed this work with the Gestalt psychologist Wolfgang Koehler and the philosopher Nicholi Hartman, whose principal contributions were in ethics. In his "Intellectual Autobiography" hereafter, Hempel describes the oral examination as "a very amiable conversation about some broad philosophical questions" and how he appreciated their considerate and thoughtful attitude.

In a discursive curriculum vitae dated December 6, 1938, Hempel stated that he had been born at Eden near Berlin on January 8, 1905, and that he had studied mathematics, physics, chemistry, psychology, and philosophy (which he listed first) at the universities of Göttingen, Heidelberg, and Berlin.[2] In 1929, he passed scientific examinations for high school teachers in mathematics, physics, and philosophy. (When Hempel taught at Princeton, interestingly, its graduate programs ranked first nationally in mathematics, physics, and philosophy.) In preparation for becoming a high school teacher, he took two years of pedagogical training—"which was very systematic and very intense"—that may have contributed to his admirable classroom success.

The Early Years

Under the influence of David Hilbert and Paul Bernays, Hempel took a special interest in symbolic logic and the foundations of mathematics. Later, during the course of his studies with Reichenbach, he was "initiated into the application of symbolic logic to the theory of science," for which he would become renowned (including his formal studies of induction and confirmation, his precise accounts of the structure of deductive and inductive models of scientific explanation, and his exacting analyses of scientific theories and of concept formation in scientific language). When he first encountered Rudolf Carnap's *Pseudoproblems in Philosophy* (1928b) and *The Logical Structure of the World* (1928a), he was greatly impressed and thought they held the key to all philosophical problems.

With Reichenbach's encouragement, he traveled to the University of Vienna for the 1929–30 academic year, where he studied with Carnap, Moritz Schlick, and Friedrich Waismann. He had contact with Otto Neurath, Herbert Feigl, and Hans Hahn, who were also members of this "Vienna Circle," and with Ludwig Wittgenstein, who was not.[3] In his "Intellectual Autobiography," Hempel discusses these exchanges, including conversations with Felix Kaufmann, who advocated a quasi-intuitionist position on the foundations of mathematics, where *intuitionism* insists on immediately intelligible constructions as the only acceptable methodology, which entails a rejection of basic parts of set theory, of unrestricted use of the law of excluded middle, and of indirect proofs (Church 1959).

As Michael Friedman explains in Chapter 1, among the controversial issues debated by the members of this group was the nature of a language that would be suitable as the foundation of science. This debate was focused upon *protocol sentences* (or "basic sentences") as sentences that formulate the results of observations or perceptions, which serve as the basis for confirming and disconfirming other sentences. Thus, some philosophers maintain that basic sentences should be restricted to the (intersubjectively) observable properties of observable entities, while others suppose that they ought to be limited to those describing (subjective) perceptions of individual subjects as perceivers (Carnap 1959). Hempel appropriately sided with intersubjectivity.

Indeed, in *Fundamentals of Concept Formation in Empirical Science* (1952), Hempel suggests that the choice between a *phenomenalistic* language (of sense data and perceptions, such as "looks-brighter-than," "appears-to-be-blue," and so on) and a *physicalistic* language (of objects and their properties, such as "is brighter than," "is blue," and such) is not amenable to definitive solution, but that, as Karl Popper had remarked, *the intersubjectivity of science*—which requires "that all statements of empirical science be capable of test by reference to evidence that is public, i.e., which can be secured by different observers and does not depend essentially upon the observer" (Hempel 1952, p. 22)—is promoted by reliance on physicalistic language. As Friedman establishes, this debate was philosophically intense, logically complex, and varied in its methodological ramifications.

After returning to Berlin and completing his Ph.D., Hempel decided that he should get out of Germany and accepted an invitation from Paul Oppenheim to come to Brussels, where they collaborated from 1934 to 1937. (Indeed, their collaboration, although intermittent, would endure far longer, initially focusing upon the concept of type relative to taxonomy but later encompassing studies of the logic of confirmation and of the logic of explanation.) Hempel spent the academic year 1937–38 at the University of Chicago as Carnap's research associate, where he assisted Carnap with his seminar and presented lectures of his own on probability and induction. In 1938, he returned to Brussels and completed research with Oppenheim on the logic of confirmation, which would later appear as "A Definition of 'Degree of Confirmation'" (Hempel and Oppenheim 1945).

Coming to America

Hempel taught summer and evening courses at City University, New York, in 1939–40, remaining in the United States and eventually becoming a naturalized citizen. From 1940 to 1948, he served as instructor and then assistant professor at Queen's College, New York. During this interval, some of the most important of his early papers appeared, including "The Function of General Laws in History" (1942), "A Purely Syntactical Definition of Confirmation" (1943), "Studies in the Logic of Confirmation" (1945c), "Geometry and Empirical Science" (1945a), "On the Nature of Mathematical Truth" (1945b), and (with Paul Oppenheim) "Studies in the Logic of Explanation" (1948). Most scholars' lifetime productivity cannot compare with Hempel's at this time—some would swap for his of 1945 alone!

These publications dramatically illustrate the clarity and illumination of the application of symbolic logic to the theory of science that became Hempel's trademark. "Studies in the Logic of Confirmation" (1945c), for example, explained that, if the generalization "All ravens are black" is translated as a logically unrestricted material conditional, then on the plausible assumption that hypotheses are *confirmed* by instances that satisfy their antecedents and their consequents, *disconfirmed* by instances that satisfy their antecedents but not their consequents, and *neither* confirmed *nor* disconfirmed by non-instances of their antecedents, then, if logically equivalent sentences are confirmed by the same instances, observations of white shoes must evidentially confirm the hypothesis "All ravens are black."

This puzzling predicament, which is known as "the paradox of confirmation," remains a subject of controversy to this day. Indeed, several of the essays in this book address this problem in one form or another, either in relation to induction and probability or relative to the theory of explanation. Even Hempel's less formal papers, such as "Geometry and Empirical Science" (1945a), became minor classics for their combination of depth of content with pellucid prose, which, in this instance, drew a clear and careful distinction between *pure* and *applied* mathematics, explaining that a *formal calculus* must be combined with an empirical interpretation to produce a *scientific theory*, which alters its epistemic and its ontic status from certain-but-vacuous to informative-but-fallible.

Similarly, "On the Nature of Mathematical Truth" (1945b), addressed one of Hempel's enduring interests.[4] As Jaakko Hintikka, explains in chapter 2, Hempel defines and defends logicism as an alternative to intuitionism, where *logicism* embraces the theses that mathematical concepts can be defined on the basis of logical ones, mathematical reasoning is reducible to logical reasoning, and logical reasoning is tautological (true necessarily, but contentless). Hintikka suggests that, even though certain aspects of Hempel's position have proven to be problematical, especially his appeal to tautologies, recent developments tend to vindicate the central tenets of his position and suggest that logicism remains a defensible foundation for pure mathematics.

Even Hempel's more informal papers, such as "The Function of General Laws in History" (1942) and the informal-to-semiformal introductory parts of "Studies in the Logic of Explanation" (1948)—the formal parts of which, I suspect, most philosophers have never read—have exerted influence far beyond the confines of the profession. William Dray, for example, focuses in chapter 9 on issues that were already raised in Hempel (1942) and elaborated in several articles published during the 1960s, including the nature of causal explanation and the character of narrative explanation in history. Those familiar with the debate Hempel ignited in 1942 may be astonished to discover the intensity of the continuing controversy, which Dray's critical discussion vividly displays.

Coming to Yale

Hempel's first wife, Eva Ahrends, died in 1944, not long after giving birth to their only child, Peter Andrew. Two years later, Hempel married Diane Perlow and, in 1948, accepted an appointment as associate professor at Yale, where their daughter, Miranda Toby Anne, was born in 1949. He would remain at Yale until 1955. While his publications in these years were relatively few in number, they were very influential. "Problems and Changes in the Empiricist Criterion of Meaning" (1950) and "The Concept of Cognitive Significance: A Reconsideration" (1951) were public declarations of the theoretical indefensibility of *logical positivism* and the necessity for a more sophisticated approach toward understanding the logic and language of science, which has become known as *logical empiricism*.

Logical positivism, in its classic guise, represented the intersection of three theses about knowledge, namely: the analytic/synthetic distinction, the observational/theoretical distinction, and the verifiability criterion of cognitive significance.[5] In these articles, which were merged into his "Empiricist Criteria of Cognitive Significance: Problems and Changes" for inclusion in Hempel (1965c), he explained the consequences of these conditions for the language of science—including that existential generalizations are verifiable but not falsifiable, while universal generalizations are falsifiable but not verifiable, while statements of mixed quantification are neither—which thus renders sentences that formulate general laws, perhaps the most basic scientific claims, cognitively insignificant.

In *Fundamentals of Concept Formation in Empirical Science* (1952), Hempel elaborated upon criticisms of the analytic/synthetic distinction that were rooted in Carnap's "Testability and Meaning" (1936–37), for example, and W. V. O. Quine's "Two Dogmas of Empiricism" (1951). Carnap introduced the method of reduction sentences to cope with problems in formally defining dispositional predicates on the basis of *extensional logic*, while Quine attacked the legitimacy of the presumption that such a distinction exists to be drawn. Hempel was decidedly more pessimistic about overcoming these problems than was Carnap, who expected that they would be resolved with the development of *intensional languages* of greater power than merely truth-functional languages, to which Hempel always remained committed.

Logical empiricism thus represented the continuation of the search for methods and techniques that would insure the cognitive significance of hypotheses and theories in science, but now recognizing that the issue was far more subtle and complex than had been recognized. Thus, Hempel (1965b) proposed that cognitive significance should be acknowledged to be "a matter of degree" in relation to multiple criteria, including the clarity and precision of the language in which a hypothesis or theory is formulated, its systematic (explanatory and predictive) power relative to the phenomena of interest, its degree of confirmation on the basis of the available relevant empirical evidence, and the formal simplicity, economy, or elegance with which these effects were attained, which thereby repositioned the movement.

The Princeton Period

In 1955, after a semester's visit, Hempel accepted an appointment as the Stuart Professor of Philosophy at Princeton, where he would remain until his mandatory retirement in 1973 at the age of sixty-eight but continue to teach as a lecturer until 1975. During these two decades, Hempel's work dominated the philosophy of science, by virtue not only of his choice of problems but also his methodological sophistication. His magnificent achievements during this interval included "The Theoretician's Dilemma" (1958), "Inductive Inconsistencies" (1962c), "Deductive-Nomological vs. Statistical Explanation" (1962a), "Explanation in Science and in History" (1962b), "Rational Action" (1962d), and the anthology *Aspects of Scientific Explanation* (1965c), including "Empiricist Criteria of Cognitive Significance" (1965b) and the extremely impressive 165-page study "Aspects of Scientific Explanation" (1965a).

Hempel did not neglect his pedagogical obligations during this period, publishing a Prentice-Hall textbook, *Philosophy of Natural Science* (1966a), that would become the most widely used introduction to philosophy of science not only in this country but in nations around the world. It would eventually be translated into ten languages: Japanese, 1967; Italian and Polish, 1968; Swedish, 1969; Portuguese and Dutch, 1970; French, 1972; Spanish, 1973; German, 1974; and Chinese, 1986. Yet Hempel continued his production of important articles, including "Recent Problems of Induction" (1966b), "Maximal Specificity and Lawlikeness in Probabilistic Explanation" (1968), and a series of studies of the structure of and of relations between scientific theories, which include Hempel (1969a, 1969b, 1970, 1973a).

It should come as no surprise, therefore, that several of the contributions to this book examine aspects of the work Hempel was publishing at this time. In chapter 3 Henry Kyburg explores one of the most fundamental questions about inductive reasoning within scientific contexts, namely: whether such arguments simply confer *measures of evidential support* upon hypotheses or actually warrant *their acceptance as true*. While enthusiam for subjective Bayesian accounts suggest that calculations concerning degrees of uncertainty are sufficient, the theory of errors of measurement and other studies support acceptance. Kyburg considers the arguments pro and con, concluding that science requires uncertain inferences in addition to inferences about uncertainty.[6]

Risto Hilpinen, in chapter 4, investigates Hempel's contributions to the study of the problem of induction, which Hempel divided into two distinct problems, namely: *the characterization problem*, which involves the characterization of inductive procedures; and *the justification problem*, which involves the justification of inductive reasoning. Without an adequate answer to the first, he maintained, the second could not be significantly raised. Thus, his discussions of the *paradoxes of confirmation* and of *inductive inconsistencies* are directed toward the characterization problem as logically prior to the justification problem. Hilpinen explores many facets of Hempel's studies, including his investigations of measures of inductive acceptance based upon considerations of epistemic utility.

My own contribution, chapter 5, attempts to clarify and illuminate the covering-law model of *deductive-nomological explanation* by an examination of several kinds of paradoxes of explanation that arise as counterparts to the paradoxes of confirmation. It turns out that there is more to nomic explainability than *nomic expectability*, where, even though Hempel's conditions reflect the logical structure of important forms of scientific reasoning, they are not strong enough to insure that the explanans-premises of an argument are *nomically responsible* for the occurrence of their explanandum-conclusion. Hempel's account can be reconstituted within an intensional framework, where degrees of nomic expectability play a crucial role in relating explanations to predictions and inference.

Ilkka Niiniluoto in chapter 6 pursues the problem of the statistical ambiguity of inductive explanations with an historical dimension. As he explains, Hempel was aware that his model of *deductive-nomological* explanation had been anticipated by John Stuart Mill in the mid-nineteenth century. In "Four Decades of Scientific Explanation" (Salmon 1989), Salmon asserts that Hempel (1962a) is "the first attempt by any philosopher to give a systematic characterization of probabilistic or statistical explanation," which Niiniluoto regards as unfair to Charles S. Peirce, who had done so a century earlier. He suggests Hempel's achievement was convincing his contemporaries that *inductive-probabilistic* arguments, when applied with a suitable requirement of maximal specificity, can serve as explanations as well as predictions.

Peter Achinstein in chapter 7, addresses one of the most contentious aspects of Hempel's work on explanation, which, in its strongest version (Hempel and Oppenheim 1948), maintains that *every adequate scientific explanation is potentially predictive*, and that *every adequate scientific prediction is potentially explanatory*. He suggests that inferences from samples to samples, such as inferences to the outcome of the 101st toss with a coin based upon outcomes of the first one hundred tosses, which do not require laws, might be assimilated by explanatory connections between them. Achinstein also remarks that arguments that assign low probabilities to their conclusions may be explanatory yet do not support corresponding predictions. He concludes, quite reasonably, that sometimes an adequate explanation will be potentially predictive and sometimes not, while raising objections to theories that appeal to "chances" or causal propensities.

Philip Kitcher in chapter 10 takes as his point of departure Hempel (1962d), where Hempel advances an account of *rational action* that is intended to explicate the normative (or "critical") use of the notion but also to display how this notion can figure in explanations of human behavior. Hempel was concerned to understand how an agent with *specific preferences* and *specific beliefs* should carry them into action. Kitcher situates Hempel's approach within a general normative framework, arguing that consideration of a broad range of cases suggests that human actions frequently reflect the influence of *heuristics* that often yield rewarding outcomes. He therefore recommends an alternative approach to rationality—or "reasonableness"—that integrates norms of action with many aspects of psychology into a more realistic model.

Paul Humphreys suggests in chapter 11 that there are two broad types of scientific understanding, analytic and synthetic, and that Hempel's account falls into the synthetic category. The important issue underlying the symmetry thesis is a difference in epistemic states between an *explanatory* why-questioner and an *epistemic* why-questioner. Knowing the explanandum phenomenon often provides crucial information for understanding by means of analysis. Construing analysis in the *material* mode, rather than in the *linguistic* mode, is essential to properly appreciate analytic understanding. This framework supports the view that understanding does not require the specification of causal processes, that understanding is possible without explanation, that laws are unnecessary for explanation or for understanding, and that analysis provides epistemic unification.

The Pittsburgh Years

In 1977, Hempel departed Princeton for the University of Pittsburgh, where he was warmly received and appointed as University Professor. Although this was the twilight of his professional career, he continued to produce important articles, including several reflections on the nature of scientific methodology and scientific rationality, which were motivated by the emergence of the *descriptive-sociological* approach represented by Thomas S. Kuhn and Paul Feyerabend, as opposed to the *analytical-normative* approach exemplified by Reichenbach and especially Carnap. He presented various versions of these papers, among which "Scientific Rationality: Normative vs. Descriptive Construals" (1979) and "Valuation and Objectivity in Science" (1983) are especially important, while continuing to pursue his interest in induction with "Turns in the Evolution of the Problem of Induction" (1981).

Robert Nozick in chapter 12 addresses the issues involved in the ongoing debate between naturalized and nonnaturalized (descriptive and normative) conceptions of science, where the work of the sociologists of science, such as Barry Barnes and David Bloor, represents a more radical position than that defined by Feyerabend and Kuhn. Nozick begins by identifying objections to the logical empiricist conception—that isolated sentences are not subject to refutation on their own; that theories are not abandoned unless a better alternative is available; that theories can be rendered immune from refutation by ad hoc modifications; that observations are typically theory-laden; that there are no specific rules or algorithms for theory acceptance; and that a great deal of scientific research takes place as normal science within various paradigms.

These complications have produced two reactions, a radical reaction that holds that science is not objective *because of* these conditions and a defensive reaction that science can be objective *in spite of* these conditions. In Nozick's view, Hempel's response has been thoughtful and open-minded, acknowledging that desiderata for theory acceptance are not precisely defined or clearly weighted relative to one another, where he views the objectivity of scientific inquiry as requiring that "scientific procedures," including theory choice, should not be determined by idiosyncratic personalities and individual preferences. Hempel thus endorses a more relaxed conception of scientific inquiry, where scientific procedures do not dictate theory choice in all situations and where somewhat vague and imprecise factors may influence them, so long as they are not subjective and idiosyncratic.

Back to Princeton

It bears notice that, even after his retirement from Pittsburgh in 1985, when he returned to Princeton, Hempel continued his philosophical research for nearly another decade. Some of the articles he published after departing from Pitt were major revisions of previous positions. Most strikingly, in "Provisoes: A Problem Concerning the Inferential Function of Scientific Theories" (1988b) and "Limits of a Deductive Construal of of the Function of Scientific Theories" (1988a), Hempel reconsidered the logical properties of *deductive predictions* on the basis of theories, when the range of relevant conditions that affect the phenomena of interest may include theoretical, dispositional, and observational properties whose presence or absence might or might not be explicitly encompassed by that theory.

Hempel attached considerable significance to his work on provisos, which is clearly understandable when its consequences, which Hempel lucidly explained, are understood. If the inferential application of scientific theories presupposes the values of variables that are not even logically required by that theory, then (1) the falsification of a theory is more complex than is commonly assumed, (2) programs for the elimination of theoretical terms from the language of science are illusory, (3) the instrumentalistic conception of theories as mere calculating devices loses any plausibility, and (4) the notion of the empirical content of a scientific theory is far more problematical than has usually been supposed. It should be astonishing that work of this profundity and originality was published when its author was in his mid-eighties and had retired not once, but actually twice![7]

Frederick Suppe in chapter 8 thus investigates the theoretical signifiance of "provisos" that specify the presence or absence of other relevant conditions, situating Hempel's studies within the context of his work on theories, including "The Theoretician's Dilemma" (1958), which established that theories have the function of *inductive* systematization as well as *deductive* systematization, and a series of studies moving away from the standard conception of scientific theories as *formal calculi* supplemented by *empirical interpretations* that he had long advocated to a revised conception (Hempel 1969a, 1970, and 1973a), where scientific theories consist of *internal principles* and *bridge principles*, a view that initially appeared in *Philosophy of Natural Science* (1966a, pp. 72–5).

Suppe suggests that this transition was motivated by the demise of the observational/theoretical distinction, which could no longer sustain the elements required to clearly separate *theoretical hypotheses* and *correspondence rules* from empirical consequences. He contends that the problem of provisos reflects the status of laws in physics as *counterfactual idealizations*, whose conditions of application may seldom if ever be realized. Classical mechanics, for example, assumes that bodies are exclusively under the influence of gravitational forces, which precludes the possible influence of electromagnetic forces. Suppe believes that *experimental inquiries* of specific kinds can establish whether specific systems satisfy the conditions under which those laws apply. He concludes that the problem can be resolved by abandoning the mistaken supposition that theories must ground their own provisos.

Hempel's last reflections on philosophy and science, which likewise appeared after his return to Princeton, are of considerable interest. "Science, Induction and Truth" (1985), for example, reviews the character of scientific knowledge, beginning with the distinction between *pure* and *applied* mathematics. Hempel explains why observational findings cannot, strictly speaking, verify or falsify hypotheses or theories yet can confirm or disconfirm them, but only provided they are understood to apply in conjunction with "a huge set of other premises." He reviews multiple desiderata for the appraisal of hypotheses and theories, emphasizing that, while they may be difficult to formalize, that does not make theory choice in science *subjective*. And he explains why, although science aims at the discovery of true hypotheses and theories, its resources are restricted to establishing comprehensive, systematic, and elegant "pictures of the world" that may be epistemically optimal, in this sense, but whose truth is a property science cannot guarantee. Even the reliability of observations requires empirical study.

And in "On the Cognitive Status and the Rationale of Scientific Methodology" (1988c), Hempel confronts the underlying question: Is the methodology of science to be viewed as a descriptive study of actual scientific research or as a quasi-normative discipine aimed at formulating the standards of rational scientific inquiry? Even if those standards are regarded as *conventions*, they are not arbitrary but require *justification*, where the justificatory reasons for adopting them include empirical claims about actual scientific practice. He discusses the views of Carnap, Popper, and Kuhn, offering evidence for concluding that neither approach is purely descriptive and neither is purely normative. Both support a conception of science according to which the bearing of given evidence on hypotheses always remains open to critical appraisal on the basis of normative standards.

The collection concludes with Wesley C. Salmon's essay, which surveys the development of logical empiricism from its roots in logical postivism, with special attention to Hempel's work on explanation. The early work of Carnap and Reichenbach sets the stage for Hempel's appearance, where "The Theoretician's Dilemma" (1958), in Salmon's view, already provides a powerful argument for the existence of theoretical objects and properties. As he observes, the dominant attitude of scientifically oriented philosophers and philosophically minded scientists at the beginning of the twentieth century was that *explanation lies beyond the scope of science*, which can describe how things happen but never explain why. Yet as the century draws to a close, even Nobel laureates extol the discovery of natural laws and the explanations they provide as *the greatest contribution science can supply*.

In Salmon's estimation, this profound difference in outlook, which approximates an exchange in worldviews, was due to at least two factors, namely: the scientific development of *quantum mechanics*, which made appeals to nonobservable things scientifically respectable, and the philosophical development of *the covering-law models*. The probabilistic (or "indeterministic") character of quantum phenomena, no doubt, made the introduction of Hempel's inductive-statistical model at least as important as his deductive-nomological model, even though its difficulties may even now remain partially unresolved. Nevertheless, in advancing a general conception of the nature of scientific explanation, Hempel contributed one of the most significant philosophical achievements of the twentieth century, whose influence is destined to endure.

A Personal Note

As a Princeton undergraduate (Class of 1962), I had the great good fortune to participate in Hempel's senior seminar and subsequently compose a thesis on the explanation of human behavior for him. Whenever he returned our written work, it was accompanied by handwritten notes on separate pages correlated with numerals penciled *very lightly* in the margins. His suggestions often converted ill-formed or pedestrian observations into penetrating remarks in lucid prose, greatly enhancing the interest and value of the original. No doubt he wrote those numerals as he did in case we wanted to erase them; I am sure, he never knew that for us, his students, they were our papers' most precious parts.

When I solicited his advice, Hempel encouraged me to pursue graduate study with Wesley Salmon at Indiana University, not because he was a follower but because he was Hempel's strongest critic. As Hempel's former colleagues have observed,

> [a]lthough he had many students—he attracted the best around at the time—he did not spawn a herd of doctrinal disciples. What students took from him was a passion for clarity and a devotion to rational argument as the sole means of progress. (Benacerraf and Jeffrey 1998, p. 149)

He cared more about getting the right solution than whether his solution was right—and he was genuinely open-minded about alternatives. Carl G. Hempel was not only immensely gifted intellectually but also the most admirable human being that I or his other students, colleagues, and friends have been honored to have known.

The death of Carnap, who had influenced Hempel profoundly and whom he admired beyond measure, in 1970 at the age of seventy-nine, must have been difficult for Hempel to endure. In his "Homage to Rudolf Carnap" (1971), he recounted how Carnap had visited two political prisoners in Mexico City in January 1970 and how one of their wives gave him some small cards on which Carnap wrote some words of admiration for the fortitude, tenacity, and stoic equanimity with which they were enduring their difficult fate and their devotion to their calling. Hempel concluded, "The words we are saying tonight are words that we would like to write on little cards for Carnap; alas, it is too late to give them to him." Alas, he captured precisely how those of us who knew and who loved him feel today about "Peter."

Appendix

In his "Intellectual Autobiography" in this book, Hempel notes that statistical probability hypotheses are neither verifiable nor falsifiable, which raises questions of their empirical testability, which he attempted to resolve in his dissertation. Hempel (1934) proposes that a *sentence* asserts as much as the set of all its test implications, of which every empirical hypothesis has infinitely many. For finite sets of relevant tests, a *statistical probability hypothesis* asserts that, in those cases, the relative frequency for an outcome in each sample should fall within a fixed interval of its hypothetical value, an interval whose breadth decreases with increasing length of the statistical sequence. Therefore, "a probability statement refers to the relative frequency of an event in a series of experiments of arbitrary finite length."

He argues that the traditional interpretation of the "law of large numbers" in its customary formulation (by means of limits in transfinite sequences) has no testable consequences, but that it appears to aim at "the condition of the approximate constancy of the relative frequencies," where his *finitization* program would appear to infuse it with appropriate empirical content. He also observes that, for any domain in which this finitization obtains (where arbitrarily longer sequences of trials yield successively less and less diverging values), the theorems of *general physical probability theory* advanced by Reichenbach are satisfied. Hempel's dissertation thus effects an "operationalization" of statistical probability hypotheses on the basis of confirmation by successive replications involving (more or less) random sampling.

Although this approach does not solve the *single case* problem of making probabililty values meaningful for singular events, it provides an explication of statistical probabilities as *short run* relative frequencies, which are empirically testable, as an alternative to conceptions of *long run* limiting frequencies, whose values are logically compatible with arbitrary relative frequencies and thus incapable of empirical test. It is an empiricist approach that would appear to have certain advantages over several more familiar accounts, such as those of Richard von Mises and of Reichenbach himself, which Hempel discusses. In his "Intellectual Autobiography," nearly fifty years later, he seems hesitant to commend his own solution to this exceptionally vexing problem, a notable example of his extremely modest and self-effacing disposition.

NOTES

In preparing this introduction, I have benefited from reviewing the memorial remarks of Adolf Grünbaum, James Lennox, Gerald Massey and Barbara Massey, Ilkka Niiniluoto, Wesley C. Salmon, and Paul Benacerraf and Richard C. Jeffrey.

1. Hempel (1934). Aspects of his research were published in Hempel (1935–36) and Hempel (1938). The dissertation, which deserves publication, may be found in the Philosophy of Science Archives of the Univerersity of Pittsburgh.
2. This vita, which must have been prepared to apply for positions in 1939–40, also resides in the the University of Pittsburgh's Philosophy of Science Archives (document 088-35-01), along with another drafted soon thereafter (088-35-03).
3. In some of his later work, Hempel discussed the history of the Vienna Circle and the contributions to logical empiricism of Carnap, Reichenbach, and others. See, for example, Hempel (1973b), Hempel (1991), and especially Hempel (1993).
4. Benacerraf and Putnam (1964), a valuable collection of studies in the philosophy of mathematics, which includes papers by Carnap, Bernays, Godel, and Wittgenstein, among others, reflects the rich and turbulent state of debate at the time.
5. Alternatively, the third element was a methodological commitment to the use of extensional language. The terms "logical positivism" and "logical empiricism" are intended to represent stages in the development of an evolving movement.
6. Indeed, the strongest argument for acceptance as true in scientific contexts arises from the evident consideration that, without acceptance, there would be no covering laws and initial conditions to serve as the premises of explanations.
7. Hempel died in Princeton on November 9, 1997, survived by his wife, Diane, his son, Peter Andrew, and his daughter, Miranda Toby Anne, and hundreds and hundreds—even thousands upon thousands—of students, colleagues, and admirers.

REFERENCES

Benacerraf, P., and R. Jeffrey. 1998. "Memorial Minutes: Carl Gustav Hempel." *Proceedings and Addresses of the American Philosophical Association* 71:147–9.

Benacerraf, P., and H. Putnam, eds. 1964. *Philosophy of Mathematics: Selected Readings.* Englewood Cliffs, N.J.: Prentice-Hall.

Carnap, R. 1928a. *Der Logische Aufbau der Welt.* Berlin. Published in English translation together with Carnap (1928b) as *The Logical Structure of the World/Pseudoproblems in Philosophy.* Berkeley: University of California Press.

———. 1928b. *Scheinprobleme in der Philosophie.* Berlin. Published in English translation together with Carnap (1928a) as *The Logical Structure of the World/Pseudoproblems in Philosophy.* Berkeley: University of California Press.

———. 1936–37. "Testability and Meaning." *Philosophy of Science* 3:419–71 and 4:1–40.

———. 1959. "Basic Sentences, Protocol Sentences." In *Dictionary of Philosophy,* edited by D. Runes. Ames, Ia.: Littlefield, Adams. P. 35.

Church, A. 1959. "Intuitionism (Mathematical)." In *Dictionary of Philosophy,* edited by D. Runes. Ames, Ia.: Littlefield, Adams. Pp. 149–50.

Hempel, C. G. 1934. *Beitraege zur logischen Analyse des Wahrscheinlichkeitsbegriffs.* Ph.D. thesis, Friderich Wilhelm University of Berlin. (Subsequently translated into English by the author as "Contributions to the Logical Analysis of the Concept of Probability.")

———. 1935–36. "Ueber den Gehalt von Wahrscheinlichtkeitsaussagen." *Erkenntnis* 5:228–60. (Translated into English under the title "On the Content of Probability Statements.")

———. 1938. "On the Logical Form of Probability-Statements." *Erkenntnis* 7:154–60.

———. 1942. "The Function of General Laws in History." *Journal of Philosophy* 39:35–48.

———. 1943. "A Purely Syntactical Definition of Confirmation." *Journal of Symbolic Logic* 8:122–43.

———. 1945a. "Geometry and Empirical Science." *American Mathematical Monthly* 52:7–17.

———. 1945b. "On the Nature of Mathematical Truth." *American Mathematical Monthly* 52:543–56.

———. 1945c. "Studies in the Logic of Confirmation." *Mind* 54:1–26 and 97–121.

———. 1950. "Problems and Changes in the Empiricist Criterion of Meaning." *Revue Internationale de Philosophie* 11:41–63.

———. 1951. "The Concept of Cognitive Significance: A Reconsideration." *Proceedings of the Amerian Academy of Arts and Sciences* 80:61–77.

———. 1952. *Fundamentals of Concept Formation in Empirical Science.* Chicago: University of Chicago Press.

———. 1958. "The Theoretician's Dilemma." In *Minnesota Studies in the Philosophy of Science,* edited by H. Feigl, M. Scriven, and G. Maxwell. Vol. 2. Minneapolis: University of Minnesota Press.

———. 1962a. "Deductive-Nomological vs. Statistical Explanation." in *Minnesota Studies in the Philosophy of Science,* edited by H. Feigl and G. Maxwell. Vol. 3. Minneapolis: University of Minnesota Press.

———. 1962b. "Explanation in Science and in History." In *Frontiers of Science and Philosophy,* edited by R. G. Colodny. Pittsburgh: University of Pittsburgh Press.

————. 1962c. "Inductive Inconsistencies." *Synthese* 12:439–69.

————. 1962d. "Rational Action." *Proceedings and Addresses of the American Philosophical Association.* Vol. 35. Yellow Springs, Oh.: Antioch Press.

————. 1965a. "Aspects of Scientific Explanation." In Hempel (1965c).

————. 1965b. "Empiricist Criteria of Cognitive Significance: Problems and Changes." In Hempel (1965c).

————. 1965c. *Aspects of Scientific Explanation.* New York: Free Press.

————. 1966a. *Philosophy of Natural Science.* Englewood Cliffs, N.J.: Prentice-Hall.

————. 1966b. "Recent Problems of Induction." In *Mind and Cosmos,* edited by R. G. Colodny. Pittsburgh: University of Pittsburgh Press.

————. 1968. "Maximal Specificity and Lawlikeness in Probabilistic Explanation." *Philosophy of Science* 35:116–33.

————. 1969a. "On the Structure of Scientific Theories." In *The Isenberg Memorial Lecture Series 1965–1966,* edited by R. Suter. East Lansing: Michigan State University Press.

————. 1969b. "Reduction: Ontological and Linguistic Facets." In *Philosophy, Science and Method: Essays in Honor of Ernest Nagel,* edited by S. Morgenbesser, P. Suppes, and M. White. New York: St. Martin's Press.

————. 1970. "On the 'Standard Conception' of Scientific Theories." In *Minnesota Studies in the Philosophy of Science,* edited by M. Radner and S. Winokur. Vol. 4. Minneapolis: University of Minnesota Press.

————. 1971. "Homage to Rudolf Carnap." In *PSA 1970: In Memory of Rudolf Carnap,* edited by R. Cohen and R. Buck. Dordrecht: Reidel.

————. 1973a. "The Meaning of Theoretical Terms: A Critique of the Standard Empiricist Construal." In *Logic, Methodology and Philosophy of Science 4,* edited by P. Suppes et al. Amsterdam: North Holland.

————. 1973b. "Rudolf Carnap, Logical Empiricist." *Synthese* 25:256–68.

————. 1979. "Scientific Rationality: Normative vs. Descriptive Construals." In *Wittgenstein, the Vienna Circle, and Critical Rationalism,* edited by. H. Berghel, A. Huebner, and E. Koehler. Proceedings of the Third International Wittgenstein Symposium, August 1978. Vienna: Hoelder-Pichler-Tempsky.

————. 1981. "Turns in the Evolution of the Problem of Induction." *Synthese:* 389–404.

————. 1983. "Valuation and Objectivity in Science." In *Physics, Philosophy and Psychoanalysis: Essays in Honor of Adolf Grunbaum,* edited by R. S. Cohen and L. Laudan. Dordrecht: Reidel.

————. 1985. "Wissenschaft, Induktion und Wahrheit." Published as a brochure by Fachbereich Wirtschaftswissenschaft der Freien Universitat Berlin. (Translated into English under the title "Science, Induction and Truth.")

————. 1988a. "Limits of a Deductive Construal of the Function of Scientific Theories." In *Science in Reflection: The Israel Colloquium,* edited by E. Ullmann-Margalit. Vol. 3. Dordrecht: Kluwer.

————. 1988b. "Provisoes: A Problem Concerning the Inferential Function of Scientific Theories", *Erkenntnis* 28:147–64. Reprinted in *The Limitations of Deductivism,* edited by A. Grunbaum and W. C. Salmon. Berkeley: University of California Press, 1988.

————. 1988c. "On the Cognitive Status and the Rationale of Scientific Methodology." *Poetics Today* 9:5–27.

————. 1991. "Hans Reichenbach Remembered." *Erkenntnis* 35:5–10.

————. 1993. "Empiricism in the Vienna Circle and in the Berlin Society for Scientific Philosophy: Recollections and Reflections." In *Scientific Philosophy: Origins and Developments*, edited by Friedrich Stadler. Dordrecht: Kluwer.

Hempel, C. G., and P. Oppenheim. 1945. "A Definition of 'Degree of Confirmation'." *Philosophy of Science* 12:98–115.

————. 1948. "Studies in the Logic of Explanation." *Philosophy of Science* 15:135–75.

Quine, W. V. O. 1951. "Two Dogmas of Empiricism." *Philosophical Review* 50:20–43.

Salmon, W. C. 1989. "Four Decades of Scientific Explanation." In *Scientific Explanation*, edited by P. Kitcher and W. Salmon. Minneapolis: University of Minnesota Press. Reprinted as *Four Decades of Scientific Explanation*, 1990.

Science, Explanation, and Rationality

Prologue

An Intellectual Autobiography: Carl G. Hempel

During his tenure as University Professor at the University of Pittsburgh, Carl G. Hempel was interviewed in Pittsburgh by Richard Nollan to establish a permanent record for the Philosophy of Science Archives located on its campus. The interview was conducted over three sessions, the first two of which were held on 17 and 24 March 1982, the third and final on 1 August 1983. The transcripts, which were tape-recorded, were subsequently transcribed by Richard Nollan and revised by Hempel. A set of notes has been added, the first five authored by Richard Jeffrey (with whom Hempel reviewed the text), the sixth by the editor. Other minor corrections, principally grammatical, have been made by Diane Hempel and the editor.

Interview 1

Nollan: Tell me about your childhood.

Hempel: I was born in 1905 near Berlin. My father was the owner of a large fruit orchard. He gave this up and entered the employ of the city of Berlin. He was a civil servant, and he was in charge of a very large area around the city where fruit was grown. This was his specialty. Before going to Berlin as a small child I went to very small village school. As soon as we went to Berlin we lived in a suburb and there I went to a Realgymnasium. That is a school where I had Latin, French, and English as foreign languages, and where there was a fair amount of emphasis on mathematics and physics.

World War One I do remember. I was nine years old when it started and I remember seeing troop trains. I also remember my father being in the army and being on the Western Front. One day he was very gravely injured by a splinter from a grenade and almost given up for dead. He was taken to a surgeon in the field who extracted this splinter and he survived this.

I also recall the rationing and things of this kind in the First World War; for example, how my mother had to take over. We lived in what was called a district, a farm district which belonged to the city of Berlin. And so my mother was in charge of making allocations when coupons were needed or when meat was needed. In the basement of our house she cut up the weekly portions of meat that were delivered for this district and weighed it out. People could also

3

bid top dollar when they wanted something special for one occasion and that they had to take something less good on another.

In this Realgymnasium I remember that the teaching on the whole was very good. The teachers were highly competent and dedicated—many had Ph.D.s which was pretty customary for teachers. There were a number of highly conservative people, but there were others who were very liberal and who also were quite inspiring and I was certainly influenced by the people who taught science and mathematics. So I thought I would like to study mathematics and physics especially.

In '23 after graduating from this Realgymnasium I went to the University of Göttingen. It was quite customary for students to study at various universities; renting a room and then studying there for a term or a year or several years even. So I started in Göttingen at a time of special glory in mathematics and in physics. I had indeed courses with David Hilbert and with Edmund Landau, the number theoretician, but curiously I had a course with him in the axiomatic foundations of geometry. I had a course with a man who was one of the early workers in the field of symbolic logic and I became very much interested in this field. His name was Heinrich Behmann. He had only three or four students. One of them was a professor from the faculty, another was a Hungarian student whom I thought very old—he was about forty—and then myself. I was immensely impressed by the possibility of handling with certain formalisms certain decision questions in logic and this steered me in a direction where I pursued these matters. In one of Hilbert's courses I heard about Hilbert's program, which he laid out, of proving the consistency of classical mathematics with means which were narrower than classical mathematics, [that is] with a very elementary kind of logic. This too made a deep impression on me. I took some other philosophy courses. I even had another logic course, but at the time it struck me that the mathematical logic was much more interesting and much more rigorous and much more promising than any of the other logic courses that were being offered.

One thing that I might mention is the matter of the accessibility of the faculty. This was very different from what it is here and from what I found it to be when I came to this country. In general, the lecturer, especially if he was a well-known professor, would just walk in and give his lecture. The customary greeting was trampling and then he would start to lecture. In mathematics if there was definite error then there would be shuffling of feet on the floor and he would then ask "What is the matter?" Otherwise you could not interrupt or ask any questions and he went on to the end and there was some more trampling and he left. You could not, especially as a younger student, go and ask him any questions after class. It wasn't that these people were so arrogant; I don't think they were. It was just the standard system. This was done. They had assistants who might answer questions and some who definitely did do that, but to find a professor who was willing to respond to a question was something rare and I remember with great appreciation the people who did in fact during a break in their class respond to a question which I might ask of them. There were a few striking exceptions, among them later on, Reichenbach and Carnap. These two people were very accessible to students, Reichenbach particularly. Other such teachers were the psychologist Wolfgang Koehler and also the psychologist Kurt Lewin. Both of them were interested in the theory of knowledge, both of them were quite accessible. One could discuss with them. But largely one was on one's own and I remember that in choosing courses I sometimes made quite serious mistakes. I chose courses which were much too difficult in mathematics; for example, one with Emmy Noether who was an eminent algebraicist but she wasn't a very good teacher. She tried very hard but it was extremely difficult; I got almost nothing out of the course. But I also couldn't make up my mind to leave because the students dropped out in large numbers and I felt so sorry for her because she was trying hard; so I just didn't have the heart to quit.

Nollan: Perhaps you could say something more general about the atmosphere during that time. There were a lot of discoveries being made in various areas. You've mentioned one by Hilbert, or example, and there were others as well.

Hempel: Yes. Right. In fact I wanted to come back to this point. The atmosphere in Göttingen was very, very stimulating. The two terms there influenced me very strongly and it was an utterly fascinating experience to study with those people, to come across all of these ideas. I was drawn gradually to questions (a) in the foundations of mathematics and (b) in logic. This pull continued later and eventually moved me into philosophy of mathematics and philosophy of science. I remember student fraternities and pressures that were exerted on one, to which I didn't yield, to join drinking or fighting fraternities which were very much *en vogue* at the time. There were also other groups which met just to discuss issues, but I joined none of these groups.

In the fall of the following year, that is, my third semester, I went to Heidelberg for a term. Of it I remember little. In part I have the impression this was my fault. I didn't pick the right people with whom I might have studied. I did mathematics and philosophy, and I think also some physics, but I don't recall very much of this. I know what some of the courses were but that's not worth mentioning.

Then I went to Berlin. I think I must have started there in the winter of '25. I could have just gone on directly towards a doctorate and I might have thought of going into a university career, but this was something which I thought I wouldn't be able to afford, even if I should be intellectually qualified. One would have to be a so-called privatdozent and live on the fees, or a certain fraction of the fees, that the students paid for the course they took. Very frequently the privatdozenten were assigned courses which were highly specialized and the courses which every student in fact had to take if he wanted to go on in a certain field were very often given by the professors. These were not formal requirements but if students had any sense they would take them.

So it was a financially difficult proposition. I didn't see how I could manage this. I therefore prepared myself during my studies to be a high school teacher and that meant taking a special academic examination which was administered by the university and writing a thesis for that. I recall that I wrote a thesis on a certain part of the decision problem in logic. Then I had to take two years of pedagogical training and training in teaching, which was very systematic and very intense. I thought it, in all, very good. My colleagues and I who did this got our training in high schools where there were especially highly equipped teachers who supervised our activities and our training. On the whole I think of them with considerable respect.

After I had passed that examination, I took on some substitute teaching assignments. I taught in some high schools. All of this slowed down my pursuit of a doctorate, but I finally returned to that and I finished my doctorate in '34. I will come back to that in a moment.

While I was doing those things I took a term out to go to Vienna and study in the fall of '29. Why did I do this? There the influence is quite clear. In Berlin I met Reichenbach, who was called there from the Technical University of Stuttgart. He exerted a strong influence on my thinking. I remember, for example, that I was a convinced Kantian and in conversation with Reichenbach this became quite clear. Reichenbach laughed and said, "You seem to have swallowed Kant hook, line, and sinker; but you will get over this." And I did. So Reichenbach and his courses were a very great influence. There was a group in which Reichenbach was the leading figure, *Die Gesellschaft fuer empirische Philosophie* (The Society for Empirical Philosophy). This was, as I remember it, a loosely organized group which was run by Reichenbach. One philosopher very much interested in logic and epistemology at the Technische Hochschule in Berlin was Walter Dubislav. There was also Kurt Grelling, whom I liked and respected very much; he was a high school teacher and didn't want to enter a university career. I don't quite understand why. His name is connected with the discovery of one of the semantics paradoxes, the Grelling paradox or the Nelson-Grelling paradox, after Leonard Nelson who was a teacher of ethics in Göttingen.

These people were the leading figures in this group. During the academic year, the group organized lectures about every month which were held in the great auditorium of the medical school of the university with speakers not just from Berlin but from various other places in Germany; Vienna, for example, Carnap, Neurath, and others. This was the group which later on established rather close links with the Vienna Circle.

Nollan: Do you remember what courses you had with Reichenbach?

Hempel: Yes, I think I do. I remember just after coming back from Vienna I had a course where we were engaged in translating Hilbert's axiomatization of Euclidean geometry to the notion of *Principia Mathematica*. There were some quite serious difficulties about this, especially about the completeness axiom. One very good feeling I have even now about the way the seminar was run was that Reichenbach gave one the sense that one was a member of a team. His seminar was an open forum; he didn't sit there and have the answer, but he said, "What can we do about this?" He had an idea, but he was open to counterproposals and also to criticism. So it was exhilarating. One had a sense of participating in an attack on an important problem. Whereas there were other teachers who would convey the impression that they knew the answers to all the questions and that you had just to sit there and learn this stuff. This was not the case with Reichenbach. Another course I had with him was the Philosophy of Space and Time, another one was Theory of Probability. Perhaps I took some other more general courses from him, but I distinctly remember taking those with Reichenbach. He attracted me further into philosophy and I decided in fact to write my dissertation in philosophy for getting my Ph.D. That was a perfectly good possibility. I was intrigued by some of the questions in the theory of probability, some basic questions to which no satisfactory answer is available even now. Essentially how one can test the statistical probability statement; there is something difficult because they can be neither verified nor falsified and my dissertation dealt with this in a way which is, I think . . . I don't like to look at my dissertation. I have the feeling I would discover something rather disappointing. But I struggled with it.

In Reichenbach's courses we also discussed the writings of some other people, although that was not the predominant thing. There were Carnap's writings and I came across especially Carnap's *Pseudoproblems in Philosophy* and the debate about realism, that was one of them. I don't know the exact English title, *Scheinprobleme in der Philosophie und der Realismusstreit*. The other one was *Der logische Aufbau der Welt*. I was immensely impressed by these books and I thought they contained the solution to all philosophical problems and I must see this man. I went to a meeting in Prague, Erste Tagung für [dic] Erkenntnislehre der exakten Wissenschaften, Prague, 15–17 September 1929 (cf. *Erkenntnis*, vol. 1, 1930–31), to meet Carnap there and ask him whether I could come study with him for a term. He said, "Yes, certainly." So I went to Vienna and had a seminar with him. Also a seminar and a lecture course with Schlick, and a seminar with Friedrich Waismann. Every single one of them was excellent and enormously stimulating and quite influential for my own philosophical thinking. In addition I was permitted to attend the meetings of the Vienna Circle during that term. This group met informally about once a week . . .

Nollan: It might even have been on Thursday nights.

Hempel: Oh, it might be Thursday nights, I'm not sure about that. In the Boltzmanngasse of the Physical Institute. I recall there particularly the leading figure, Schlick, who seemed to preside over the proceeding. Then there was Carnap. At the other end of the spectrum temperamentally and also philosophically was Neurath. Then there were Waismann, the mathematician Hans Hahn, and occasionally, I think, Kurt Goedel, but I am not sure that I saw him at those Circle meetings or perhaps otherwise. I did meet him and talk to him occasionally. Then there was Felix Kaufmann who had phenomenologist leanings, he was much interested in the foundations of mathematics and wrote a book which has just recently been translated into English about the infinite in mathematics and its elimination or its avoidance or something like this. It was a quasi-intuitionist position. There was Olga Hahn-Neurath. I remember that the discussions were intense. I don't think I ever participated in these discussions; I talked about these matters to Carnap informally afterwards, and to Waismann. On some occasions also to Schlick who was somewhat more reserved, he was very friendly but more reserved. There were issues partly raised I think by Wittgenstein on questions of verification and questions about the basis of empirical knowledge, observation sentences, and so on. I cannot really vouch for these topics because some of them may have come up somewhat later. I became quite involved in thinking about them and so I may project these on to what went on in the Vienna Circle at the time.

Then I went back to Berlin and finished my work for my doctorate but at that time the Nazis were coming into the ascendancy. Reichenbach, who was my advisor, left Berlin in 1933 for Turkey. I was on my own. I had to find another advisor, and I did find Wolfgang Koehler with whom I had taken some courses. He was not only interested in psychology, he was a Gestalt psychologist, one of the famous group of Gestalt psychologists there along with Lewin and [Max] Wertheimer. Koehler was very willing to be my sponsor and examiner. But I needed one other examiner. To my very pleasant surprise Nicolai Hartmann, with whose ideas I had no acquaintance really, I had taken one course with him, agreed to do this. He could have, I'm quite sure, failed me in this examination if he had wanted to, but we conducted a very amiable conversation about some broad philosophical questions and so everything went perfectly well in the examination and I must say I appreciate this broad spirit that Hartmann showed and that not all his colleagues would have shown.

It was during all this time, also while I was finishing the dissertation, that I was first in teacher training and then taught as a substitute. This was one area in which I saw the influence of the rising wave of Naziism: increasing and quite explicit discrimination, for example, against Jewish students, expression of extreme nationalist sentiments, flag ceremonies, and so on. Then there were occasions where I worked in the Staatsbibliothek in Berlin, the library of the state of Prussia, where I had spent uncounted hours as a student. Some storm troopers walked in and called out, "All Jews leave the place immediately." This must have been in '33 and I got up immediately also and left. I am not Jewish myself; I have many Jewish friends. There were increasing numbers of these Hitler Youth groups marching around in the streets. It became clear that the intellectuals were gradually getting ready for a change or were actually changing. I recall having worked at writing reviews for the *Deutsche Literaturezeitung*, which was a review published by the Prussian Academy of Sciences. One day there was change in directors and the new young director called me into his office and suggested that it would be a good idea for me to join the party. He pointed to Unter den Linden where his office was. There were as a matter of fact a group of Brown Shirts walking around outside; those of course were boors, but we must reform the party from the inside and therefore it would be good if I joined. Well, I resisted this suggestion. I sometimes ask myself if I could have been able to resist all such suggestions if I had stayed in Germany. But fortunately I had an opportunity to leave and I seized this opportunity.

In about 1930, Reichenbach had introduced me to an acquaintance, Dr. Paul Oppenheim, who was then living in Frankfurt [am Main]. He was by training a chemist and held a high position in a large industrial concern, I. G. Farben. He had an intense interest in philosophical matters and had written a book entitled *The Natural Order of the Sciences*. He felt that the book needed considerable changes and improvements, and he asked me if I would help him effect these changes. I met him a few times in Germany; then, in '33 I think it was, he left Germany for Brussels; his wife was a Belgian citizen. His parents, who were people of wealth, had given strong support to science, had established a chair in theoretical physics (University of Frankfurt), had given a biological research aquarium on the island of Helgoland, and so on. At their insistence, Oppenheim and his wife and sons left Germany for Belgium. His parents were so distressed over developments [in Germany] that they both committed suicide.

Oppenheim asked me whether I would want to come and live in Belgium for a while as his guest and pursue some of my own work as well as some studies with him. I seized this opportunity and he in fact made it possible for me to get into Belgium. One couldn't just leave and go to Belgium because there was the concern that you take somebody else's position away. So he had to vouch for me in this respect. This was therefore an absolutely crucial development for my life. It enabled me to leave Germany. I couldn't just have decided to leave Germany: where could I have gone, how could I have gone on living, what basis for an existence would I have had? At any rate Oppenheim and I worked together on a number of things. There was a book that we wrote on the concept of type in the light of modern logic, it was published in German by a Dutch publisher. We wrote a few more pieces together in Belgium and then later on, when we met again by a very fortunate combination of circumstances, in the United States. Paul Oppenheim had philosophical training but not very intense and not very technical and so he always felt he needed somebody to look after the technical side of things. He referred to himself as a wild horse in these things and proposed ideas some of which were very stimulating. I certainly got started writing my own things under this stimulating kind of influence. Some of this cooperation required changes and critical sifting and so on. Oppenheim also wrote papers alone and with other people. In subsequent years he just pursued his philosophical interests until the end of his life. He died in 1977 in Princeton, where I was then living. We were very close friends.

I have a sense that he saved my life twice, as it were. Once in making it possible for me to leave Germany and, secondly, in another context when in Brussels I had learned how to ride a bike, or supposedly learned. On my first trip I had a very severe accident on the bicycle. I had a double fracture of the skull and was taken to a hospital where my wife was told there was nothing to be done and no point to call a physician. She was to call a priest. It was a Catholic hospital. Well, she called Paul Oppenheim instead who turned up and saw to it that a surgeon was brought in who gave me a spinal tap and after some hours I recovered consciousness and am here to tell the tale. I do not know if I would have survived this if he had not intervened at that moment.

The book on [*Der*] *Typusbegriff* [*im Lichte der neuen Logik*] dealt with the nature of comparative and quantitative concepts and with certain advantages they offer over purely classificatory ones. These ideas were developed by reference especially to the concept of psychological type that played a role at that time largely in German and also American psychological theories arguing that certain physical types were strongly correlated with certain personality types. Oppenheim and I looked at the logic of these arguments and the book is concerned with that.

Also while I was in Brussels I was invited to come over to England by Susan Stebbing for a philosophical conference at Bedford College in London. I read a paper there which was on the logical positivist theory of truth, I think is what I called it. It was the first thing I ever published in English. [*Shuffling through papers looking for the title*]

Nollan: "On the Logical Positivists' Theory of Truth."

Hempel: Ah, yes. The article was published in *Analysis* and that led to some other articles in this area. What I said there about truth was all mistaken in one respect: it should have been said about confirmation, and not truth. This became clear later, when Tarski developed his theory of truth. So I would have to recast this if I were to write it now. At any rate some of my remarks were influenced by Neurath and they irritated Schlick very much. Schlick responded very critically to this, because I wrote there somewhere about the ultimate acceptability of scientific statements depending on the consensus of the scientific community, ideas which are around now again very much with Kuhn and others and which Neurath very explicitly propounded at that time. Schlick didn't like to hear this at all and he wrote "Das Fundament der Erkenntnis" and other pieces in order to rebut this position.

I also met G. E. Moore for the first time at this meeting in England which Stebbing had arranged. I provoked one of his famous outbursts of philosophical indignation which has been described in the literature. I think Keynes has written a memoir about Moore and mentions it there. I had to struggle with my English during the discussion; it was very difficult for me and there were lots of people talking to me. Moore remarked that I didn't seem to observe the difference between a sentence and a proposition. I said I didn't know what the difference was and Moore dropped his jaw, turned purple in his face, shook his head and said, "You don't understand the difference?" He seemed to be so shocked that I had a feeling he might just collapse. It was frightening. It didn't seem to be a fit of rage addressed at me but rather of despair at the fact that the world could be this way, that there could be people who were not aware of this distinction. [Moore and I] got on very nicely and also when I met him again in New York.

Nollan: Did you meet anyone else, like Ayer or Russell?

Hempel: Yes. At the very same meeting there was also Alfred Ayer. In fact he was the one who discussed a lot when I presented that paper and he, in his characteristic way, talked at machine gun speed and that made it very difficult for me to follow what he was saying. I remember that because it was particularly hard, I had to discuss it with him. I have seen him countless times afterward and discussed with him but I also remember this first meeting which was somewhat trying for this reason. Russell I met several times, not on that occasion, but I met him, I think, for the first time in Paris. Yes, at one of the Unity of Science meetings. I met Russell through Paul Oppenheim who knew Russell. Russell stayed at his house. I met him there. We talked a little about philosophical issues and we talked about probability, for example, but the occasions often were social occasions where he held forth about this or that problem or some literary problem, and he seemed always to be extremely witty and sparkling and great fun to listen to. I was greatly impressed by meeting him. I met him also while I was at Yale; he was invited to speak there. However, at that time he acknowledged that he had really lost interest in questions of logic. The graduate students there, for example, were asking him about questions on the theory of types and he said, "Oh, I am not thinking about these issues anymore." He was then concerned more with political and moral issues.

Nollan: While you were in England did you also meet Woodger?

Hempel: Yes. Oh, Woodger, yes, indeed. Known as "Socrates" to his friends. Joseph Woodger, biologist, who was also very much taken by the powers of symbolic denotation and of axiomatization and who therefore advocated very strongly the use of these things in defining certain concepts in biology and hierarchical structures, and so on. I remember while sitting one evening until late in the night at his house and he was introducing me to *Principia Mathematica* notation. In Berlin with Reichenbach we used not exactly that same notation and also not all those details and I remember Woodger telling me about all this. He was a very nice man; I remember him very fondly.

I think now that the faith in the power of axiomatization and the importance of axiomatization was too great. The results were not as fruitful as the people at that time seemed to expect. Perhaps I expected it also myself. I certainly expected more from it than I would now. Now I think there is interest to see a powerful theory axiomatized but I don't know really how illuminating it is for philosophical questions, foundational questions, and so on. Since axiomatization can be achieved for the same theory in many different ways I think some fundamental questions may get short shrift. One may be lulled into a sense of being on top of all these issues thanks to one particular way of axiomatizing these theories. So I am not quite as confident of all this as I used to be.

I should mention a meeting for the Unity of Science, held in Copenhagen in 1936, where the news reached us that Schlick had been shot by one of his students. I think I saw Niels Bohr there for the first time; I didn't talk to him. I met him later also in Princeton personally. He was taciturn and somewhat hard to understand so I didn't have very extensive discussions with him.

Nollan: There were two people that I think of who should be mentioned. The one is Karl Popper.

Hempel: Yes.

Nollan: Had you met him by this time?

Hempel: Yes, as I recall it, I met him in Vienna during that term briefly on a few occasions. I think it was at the Copenhagen Conference where Popper in a discussion or a reply to a paper by Neurath savagely attacked Neurath. I was quite shocked by the way this came out. Popper was and is a man of high principle. When he thinks some fundamental issues are not handled the right way, he gets very excited. But I found Popper interesting and suggestive. I really got a strong impression of him after the book *Logik der Forschung* appeared. I think that was just about the time when he went to New Zealand. I recall that he came through Brussels on the way. Paul Oppenheim was very helpful with some arrangements as I recall. This book, *Logik der Forschung,* for which I wrote a review in the *Deutsche Literaturzeitung,* impressed me very much indeed and I said so in my review. I haven't looked at this review in a long time. I don't know whether at the time I had doubts about the narrowness of his requirement of falsifiability for all scientific statements as I do now. I do know that Popper has said he was very pleased with the review and he has said it somewhere in print. I recently came across the passage maybe in his intellectual biography on the Schillp volume. I did see Popper much later again when he was in London. We had some converations. On the whole I had a sense that it was difficult to discuss with him, that he was too easily hurt and felt this was somehow a personal attack if one took a critical view. So I must confess that I didn't seek out the opportunity very much to discuss with him whereas I was always very much interested in his writings.

Oh, this brings back however one occasion in Brussels when he was there, I don't know in what context. He read a paper the content of which appeared in *The Poverty of Historicism.* He read from this [paper] to a small private group. There was an animated discussion. I think that already there he presented the argument that it was not possible to predict the fate of a civilization at a future time because one would then have to predict what the state of science would be because the development of civilization would depend on that, and if one could predict what the state of scientific knowledge would be fifty years hence or one hundred years hence then one would have that scientific knowledge and so there was an impossibility. This argument sticks very much in my mind. I think it's rather a powerful argument, although one would have to look at it very closely in order to see exactly how far it will carry.

Nollan: There was one incident that I ran across in my research. There was a young man by the name of Willy Strahl who apparently wrote a very strong dissertation that you liked very much. Soon afterward apparently he died. I forget what the reason was.

Hempel: Yes, I have only a faint recollection. I am quite distressed at this. The other day someone asked me about Strahl. I remember that there was such a man studying with Reichenbach and that he was a very bright man but I now have not the slightest recollection of seeing this dissertation. I absolutely cannot remember what it was about and that I should have read it or made comments on it.

Nollan: I think it had something to do with probability. It must have been written around 1933 or soon thereafter because you collaborated with Reichenbach to make an abridged portion of his dissertation suitable for publication in *Erkenntnis*.

Hempel: Oh, it would then have appeared in *Erkenntnis*.

Nollan: I think so. I haven't looked up the reference.

Hempel: I would be interested. I would really have to look this up. I don't have the issues with me. I would like to see it and refresh my memory because I cannot recall. I left Germany in April of 1934 for Brussels. So when would the collaboration have been? Reichenbach went to Turkey. I can't remember that there was an extensive or a substantial exchange of correspondence between us. I think there may have been some. My mind is completely blank on this Strahl except that I remember the name. I remember that there was somebody by that name in the group, whereas I remember these other people, Grelling and Dubislav etcetera, very well. Of course Strahl would have been a student and I wouldn't have seen quite as much of him but he must have been in some of Reichenbach's courses and I can't place him.

Nollan: We have spent a lot of time talking about your student days and the early part of your career. Aside from philosophers and philosophy in general is there anyone in your life that you felt influenced you or helped you tremendously?

Hempel: I really can't say. Except in the senses that I indicated: Paul Oppenheim made it possible for me to get out and this put me in a totally different track from what I had expected to be, because from then on it was quite clear that I could not become a high school teacher. After three years in Brussels I had an invitation to go to Chicago as Carnap's assistant and that had been arranged by Carnap. Then I indeed aimed at an academic position in this country. So Oppenheim was influential and helpful in this respect. But the other people who influenced my thinking or who had something to do with my career were mostly people interested in philosophy.

Interview 2

Nollan: We are going to pick up with some things that we didn't discuss in our last meeting. For example, some discussion of people such as Feigl, Olaf Helmer, and others.

Hempel: Yes. Let me start with people in Berlin and one thing which I remember very vividly. I mentioned people I studied with in Berlin. There were also mathematicians and physicists. I saw Einstein. I took several courses with Max Planck. Berlin was also a very exciting place to study.

I took a course there with von Neumann which dealt with Hilbert's attempt to prove the consistency of classical mathematics with finitary means. I recall that in the middle of the course von Neumann came in one day and announced that he had just received a paper from a young mathematician in Vienna by the name of Kurt Goedel who showed that the objectives which Hilbert had in mind, and on which I had heard Hilbert's course in Göttingen, could not be achieved at all. Von Neumann, therefore, dropped the pursuit of this subject and devoted the rest of the course to the presentation of Goedel's results. The finding evoked an enormous excitement. I recall the mathematicians at the university being really excited about this and some of them wondering whether this really could be true. I was asked this by one of the mathematics professors and I said I was the wrong person to ask. I was just beginning to try to find my way into this material. Reichenbach, who was always very enterprising, in one section of the seminar he gave—I don't know what the seminar was about—said to me, "Hempel, you prepare a lecture on Goedel so that we can all discuss this." I struggled with the Goedel article, I'm not even sure I understood correctly Goedel's argument, but I tried my best. At any rate it shows how fascinated people were with this new development.

This reminds me of another person whom I should have mentioned as belonging to the Reichenbach circle. It was not a formal organization. I've mentioned Dubislav and Grelling, and there was also a fellow student of mine, Olaf Helmer, who was a mathematician and with whom I also took a seminar with Reichenbach in which, as I think I mentioned in the previous interview, the attempt was made to put Hilbert's axiomatization of geometry into the notation of *Principia Mathematica*. I stayed in touch with Helmer. It turned out that when the Nazis came into power Helmer left for England and worked there, studied logic there, [and] got a doctorate with Stebbing after he had earned a doctorate in mathematics in Germany. He became a member of the faculty of the University of Illinois at Urbana and later joined the Rand Corporation. He then went on to another group which I think he cofounded which was concerned with forecasting social, political, and cultural changes. He also taught in the seventy's for some time at the University of Southern California. As it turned out he went to Chicago and I met him there again in Carnap's seminar in 1937 and to that I will come back later.

In Vienna I should mention one person I saw a lot in this country, namely Herbert Feigl. He was the assistant of Schlick, or one of Schlick's assistants, and he was also on good terms with Wittgenstein. Whenever Wittgenstein came to Vienna, Wittgenstein laid down the rules in advance as to who would be allowed to come to these discussions which were held as far as I know in Schlick's apartment. I never attended any of those. Feigl was always allowed to come. His later wife Maria was also on quite friendly terms with Wittgenstein. Feigl had mentioned to me that Wittgenstein's interest in the foundations of mathematics was stimulated by Feigl's insistence that Wittgenstein go and listen to Brouwer, the intuitionist, when he gave a lecture in Vienna. Wittgenstein had been reluctant to do this but then was enthusiastic about it and highly stimulated. Feigl thinks that Wittgenstein's further work on the foundations of mathematics was in part called forth by his attendance at this lecture. Feigl was also the first, or one of the first, of this group to go to the United States. He went to the University of Iowa, then on to the University of Minnesota, and I saw him many times in this country and was in close contact with him.

I have said something about Vienna, I should come back to Berlin briefly to add one more word about the changing political climate there, namely, with the rise of the Nazis. I was at the time, as I mentioned, teaching in the schools, Realgymnasiums, in and around Berlin, partly as a substitute and partly as part of my training. Rising anti-Semitism, discrimination against Jews, students and teachers, became clear; difficulties for my academic teachers who were Jewish rose also. I also remember with particular distress that one of the mathematical teachers whom I had greatly admired, Ludwig Bieberbach, a first-rate mathematician and author of many books, and a splendid teacher whom I had come to know somewhat personally and found him quite congenial, turned overnight as it were Nazi and I seem to recall pretty clearly that he marched into the class one day in a brown shirt and gave the Hitler salute. He also founed a new mathematical journal which was called the *Zeitschrift für Deutsche Mathematik*. If I remember correctly, in the first issue Bieberbach wrote a programmatic article in which he sought to distinguish between Aryan and non-Aryan mathematics. For example, geometry, especially when dealt with in the context of drawn figures, was Aryan; the representation of complex numbers by points in a plane was Aryan; on the other hand, the treatment of complex or hypercomplex numbers as ordered triples of real numbers, or n-tuples of real numbers, was typically Jewish mathematics. There were other cases.

A number of my teachers, among them Reichenbach, left. Reichenbach went to Turkey, and Dubislav, as I think I have said, went to Prague. Helmer, a friend of mine, went to England. Some other people were not in a position to leave. Among the people in the Berlin group there was Kurt Grelling, who was a high school teacher, "professor" as the title was. I am not sure whether he believed things would not turn out as bad as they did in fact. I met him again in Brussels as I will say in a moment. In fact in '34, as I have said before, I had an opportunity to leave just after earning my doctorate; I then went to work with my friend Paul Oppenheim in Brussels for a bit over three years, in part on common projects and in part on things in which I was interested. There were those articles in *Analysis* on the logical positivists' theory of truth and also another article, "Some Remarks on Facts and Propositions," which disturbed Schlick and which were written under the influence of Neurath's thinking. I believe there was a good deal of merit to Neurath's ideas although they were formulated in a way which was not always tenable in that form. Neurath himself left and lived in Holland. I visited him there at least once. Later he then fled when the German armies invaded Holland and escaped to England.

I might perhaps mention at least one other article of that period which was important for my intellectual development and that was a piece which appeared in 1937 in a Scandinavian philosophical journal called *Theoria*. It was called "Le Probleme de la verite" and took the wrong track of confounding truth with confirmation. It was the first place where I presented the raven paradox, which sometimes has been called Hempel's paradox and which eventually led to a good deal of discussion in the literature. It was published in much greater detail in an article in *Mind* called "Studies in the Logic of Confirmation" which appeared in 1945.

A word about the intellectual atmosphere in Brussels. I had access to the lectures which were given at the Institut des Hautes Études. Indeed I was invited to lecture there myself and gave, I think, two lectures which I delivered in French, after having had the text gone over very carefully by a friend of mine. At that time I was fairly fluent in French (and that was a high point in my French-speaking career), but I wasn't exactly received with open arms by all the scholars there. I remember one man who was quite eminent and prominent among the philosophers at the University of Brussels and that was Barzin. His father had been killed by German troops in the First World War as a hostage taken somewhere in Belgium. He had a very bitter resentment against Germans and although we were in the same room, for example, during the meetings of the Institut des Hautes Études, I think I never shook hands with him or rather he never shook hands with me. I remember also that once I had acquired a very severe sunburn on the beach. I saw a physician who was perfectly proper, who advised me on what to do, and said I should have been much more careful. But he never offered me even a seat to sit down. So it was quite clear that there was great deal of animosity against the Germans and I can understand that but at any rate it was quite striking and much in contrast to the reception I found—and which I much appreciated—in this country.

Nollan: Do you remember ever meeting or discussing the works of Hugo Dingler?

Hempel: Hugo Dingler, yes, was discussed in Reichenbach's courses to some extent, and seminars, but Reichenbach took a very critical view of this because Dingler was an extreme conventionalist. I don't believe that anyone in this group was encouraged to, let us say, write a dissertation about this subject. Reichenbach himself was very much interested in the subject of conventions and thought they had a proper role: there was his notion of coordinative definitions by means of which scientific theories are interpreted and also by means of which abstract geometry can be interpreted in order to make it applicable to the world. This has to be done by convention, and Reichenbach spent a good deal of time and effort in making this point in his lectures; pointing out, for example, that in choosing a pendulum in marking units of time, the question whether the units were really equal was meaningless. As long as one didn't have another timepiece to determine this, it was then true by convention. Then we talked about the more complex issues of conventionality in geometry as we did in his philosophy of space and time. As I recall he was quite skeptical as regards Dingler's view.

In Brussels life was quite pleasant for me and for my wife who had accompanied me from Germany but it would have led nowhere. There was absolutely no prospect whatsoever that I would find an academic position or other position in Belgium. So it would have been a dead-end road. Therefore, it was a fortunate turn for me when I received an invitation which Carnap had arranged to come to Chicago for a year.

But I want to mention that in Brussels also Kurt Grelling turned up from time to time at the invitation of Paul Oppenheim, who had left Germany and was living in Brussels, and that we and Oppenheim—the three of us—worked together on some problems. I think I didn't publish jointly with Grelling. We discussed questions about the logic of Gestalt theory and Gestalt qualities in which Oppenheim and Grelling were very much interested. He was a very intelligent, perceptive, and stimulating man to discuss philosophical issues with.

In Brussels, apart from the subjects I have mentioned, some of them explored with Oppenheim, in part logical on types of concepts, comparative versus quantitative or classificatory concepts. I also worked on some matters which were just my interest; in logic, for example, on a generalization of plurivalued systems of logic where it was assumed that statements could be compared only with regard to which was more true and which was less true. I now think this was a formal exercise which was not very profound. It appeared in the *Journal of Symbolic Logic*, but I have my doubts as to whether it has any great significance. It was influenced by Oppenheim's interest in the more general problem of comparative concepts.

In the fall of 1937 I received an invitation to go to the University of Chicago as Carnap's research associate. My first general impressions were that I was overawed by the sight of New York. I was very touched and impressed, as was my wife, by the generosity of the people. There was someone whom we had met at a conference in Eurpoe and who vouched for us, which was essential for getting permission for coming into the country, and who didn't know us all that well. We were also received in a very nice way by the people of Chicago, by the faculty members there. I remember Charles Morris and A. C. Benjamin, for example, and of course Carnap himself. My whole impression of the intellectual and academic atmosphere is that it was very much less stiff and less formal and less rigidly organized than in Europe. The relations between faculty members and between faculty and students was more relaxed and informal, and in fact the students used up a good deal of faculty time; they would come to discuss all sorts of problems, philosophical but also personal. A fair amount of time went into this and they felt rather free to discuss with you whatever questions they had. This would have been unthinkable at a German university, especially when it came to personal problems, but even if one should have failed to grasp some points in the lecture one was on one's own to fill out the gaps. I liked the more relaxed and open and accessible style very much and came to think of the other atmosphere as rather oppressive. By contrast I recall that I once in Berlin wanted to take a seminar and make a report in a seminar which dealt with Kant. I spoke to the lady who was the professor's assistant and she said, "You cannot make a report in this seminar unless have taken it once before." I said, "But I have had other seminars, other work in Kant, and why shouldn't I be able to make a report in this seminar?" "No, you cannot understand the professor's thinking in these matters." It became quite clear to me: what the unfortunate reporter had to do was to just rehash some stuff which had been said in the previous year on the same subject. I think rather with horror on this kind of conducting a seminar. There was so much emphasis on just repeating the words of the teacher.

There were of course personal difficulties that I encountered. There was one [that was] very serious. My wife, who had come with me, had died a few years after our arrival here just shortly after the birth of our first child. Then I was lucky a few years later to marry my present wife. She was quite essential. I think I wouldn't be where I am now without her. She took a very positive attitude to things, also to the changes that occurred in my professional life and to the various travels which we undertook. This was really quite essential to me and I don't know how I would have wound up otherwise. But at any rate about my career as a teacher and my academic work I can say that I have never felt that I wanted any other career than this. I found it extremely satisfying, and still do, and I couldn't have wished for anything better and I think I couldn't have wished for better opportunities to pursue it than I did find in this country.

From Chicago I also remember such things as Neurath turning up there. I remember one or perhaps two visits where the matters of the *Encyclopedia of Unified Science* or *Erkenntnis* were discussed. As far as my work with Carnap was concerned, I attended courses with him and I think one must have been a course in symbolic logic. He issued in 1937 a set of notes which were not published ever, I think, on symbolic logic.

At that time he was extremely interested in semantics. He had come to see that the syntactical approach which he had previously taken in the *Logical Syntax of Language*—the view that philosophy is logical syntax of the language of science—that this conception was too narrow. I recall that when Tarski's semantical theory of truth came out he referred me to it with great eagerness. That was at a meeting at Paris. He himself pursued this approach very energetically and was at the time engaged in this and also in the seminar. He, I think, presented ideas which eventually led to the first of his books in semantics. He wrote two or three.

His seminar style was rather a lecture style with occasional questions put in but it was not a free-for-all discussion. Carnap was an extremely systematic man and he wanted to discuss the points in the most systematic order he possibly could. I think the idea that people might raise questions and anticipate things [that] would come later would have been somewhat disturbing to him. Not that he would have prevented this, but the course did largely take the form oF a lecture with occasional questions.

There were a group of interesting people in this seminar. There were, for example, William Barrett, Marjorie Grene, the writer Paul Goodman, there was Abraham Kaplan, and there was Olaf Helmer, who after earning his degree in England went on to the United States—and there he was in Carnap's seminar. So there was a lot of very intensive discussion; that year in which I had the fellowship was extremely stimulating and enjoyable.

After this it was very difficult to find a position. I tried, at first unsuccessfully, and went back briefly to Brussels to do some more work with Oppenheim in early '38 until the fall of 1939. Then I returned to the United States. I looked around for a job; it looked hopeless, but in the spring term, I believe, I received an invitation to teach during the summer term at the City College of New York at first and then I was taken over into the night school. There I had to do with a very lively group of students at the nighttime who were more mature than the daytime students. Most of them had an eight-hour work day behind them before they came to class. I must say to this day I admired their dedication and their stamina. They were quite critically minded, at least a good number of them were, and raised objections: "What do you mean by this?" and "How do you know that?" So it was challenging and interesting to teach them. I remember one incident. I had a student who was rather quiet in one of these evening courses. There was a break in the middle of the course and I walked around in the hallway, and this man came up to me and said, "I was absent the last two times." I said, "Yes, I noticed that." He said, "I just want you to know that I wasn't just playing hooky, I was on special assignment." I said, "On special assignment?" "Yes, I am with the police force, but I am wearing civilian clothes. But you see here," and he opened his jacket, and there was a belt and a gun strapped to it. He said, "Yeah, I always carry a gun with me." I said, "Fine." Then he walked away, and turned around suddenly and said, "If there should ever be trouble in the class, don't worry—I'll shoot," which made me a little bit nervous given the cantankerous nature of some of these students. But everything went well and I remember once seeing him on his beat near Grand Central Station.

Nollan: How long were you at City College?

Hempel: At City College I was only one year. Then, in the fall of 1940, I went to Queens College which was just a year or a year and a half old and where I stayed until 1948. It was newly founded and there was a pioneering spirit. That was very pleasant. There were also interesting people in the philosophy department. They had a number of people who made quite distinguished careers and made interesting contributions to their fields. There was first my old friend John Goheen who went on to Stanford and who in fact is still teaching there. Then there was Donald Davidson who is one of the top philosophers in the country, known for his work in semantics and the theory of action. Another colleague was Arnold Eisenberg, working in aesthetics, who died years ago at Michigan State University. There was Herbert Bohnert who had been a student of Carnap and also went to Michigan State. At that time a new instructor had to teach fifteen hours a week. I remember how the president called us all together and told us what an honor it was to have been appointed there and we were to be sure to prove ourselves worthy of this honor by publishing a great deal. I belonged at that time to the New York Philosophical Circle. This was an informal group of faculty members of various universities and colleges in New York who met at the house of one or another person and read papers. I recall that as very lively, informal, but quite well focused and useful. There were logicians, John McKinsey among them; Ernest Nagel of Columbia became a close friend; and there were Philip Wiener from City College and a number of other colleagues. We had very lively sessions there. During that time Alfred Tarski, the Polish logician, was in New York and I attended a kind of informal lecture course he gave, I think, at the YMCA, somewhere on the East Side on Lexington Avenue. It wasn't a popular, but a technical course, dealing with logic and perhaps semantics. I learned a great deal from it. I think I still have my notebooks taken during this course where Tarski with immense clarity set out his ideas.

While I was at Queens College I participated in a series of seminars which faculty members attended regularly. I don't remember the details. I was asked at any rate to read a paper, and I wrote a paper on the function of general laws in history. I was later asked to read this paper before the philosophy club at Columbia, then it was published in the *Journal of Philosophy*. It produced a great deal of controversy and debate up to this day which I had absolutely not expected. I had no idea this would be the case nor do I recall what made me choose this particular topic. I have modified my view on that issue; I was a little simplistic, a little bit rash. This article appeared in 1943, but some of the fundamental points I still think right and with some modification I would still stick with them.

One task that concerned me strongly during my years at Queens College and later was that of clarifying the concept of the confirmation of scientific hypotheses by empirical evidence. In the article in *Mind* mentioned earlier, I propounded a definition and theory for a purely qualitative concept of the kind, by means of which one could assert that given evidence e does (or does not) confirm a given hypothesis h, but not how strong the confirmation was. In the 1940s, Oppenheim (who had by that time moved to Princeton), Helmer, and I made a joint effort to define a quantitative degree of confirmation of a given hypothesis by given evidence.

In my work on the qualitative concept of confirmation, which often was quite frustrating, I received encouragement and helpful comments from my friend Nelson Goodman, whom I met in the early forty's. I have had many intensive exchanges of ideas with him over the years and have been much impressed by his highly original ideas. I recall that Carnap in Santa Fe was working on this same subject. He was on vacation in Santa Fe from Chicago. I went to visit him there. I had written Carnap something about our approach to the problem and Carnap had expressed some surprise—alarm is perhaps too strong a word—at the similarity of our approaches. So when I went there I was very curious to find out what he had found. In fact I left with instructions to send a wire back to Oppenheim or to Helmer to stop working if I found that Carnap had already anticipated everything we were doing. I didn't have to send that wire. We had been pursuing somewhat different approaches, but Carnap's without question was the better, the more fruitful one. Articles on both approaches were published in 1945 in *Philosophy of Science*.[1] But Carnap's concept of degree of confirmation, which had the formal properties of a probability, whereas ours didn't, was certainly the superior one.

Nollan: The work that Carnap was doing culminated in the *Logical Foundations of Probability*?

Hempel: That's right, it culminated in that. He published, I believe, an earlier article in 1948, in which he set out the basic ideas in an article in the *Philosophy of Science*.[2] I still think that is a very useful article because the *Logical Foundation of Probability* is such a huge tome that it is hard to get through it. Of course one has to refer to this if one wants to study the details. But that is exactly right. The approach that Carnap took in the big volume was similar to the one he set out in this article in the *Philosophy of Science*.

Nollan: What was the name of the article that you published with Oppenheim and Helmer.[3]

Hempel [looking through papers]: I had one with Oppenheim called "A Definition of 'Degree of Confirmation.'" That appeared in *Philosophy of Science* in 1945. Carnap's must have appeared about the same time Helmer and Oppenheim published an article. I don't have the exact reference here, but they did publish a more technical article on the same subject. Carnap referred to this as "the H_2O definition" of confirmation and it always made me think that it all runs through your fingers and then there isn't anything left.

So in Princeton I kept doing some work with Oppenheim as far as teaching and my own work allowed. Oppenheim during that time also tried very hard to bring Grelling over who was threatened. He had left Germany with his wife. Grelling was Jewish in the sense of the Nazi law and he [and his wife were] not religious. He was in France in a concentration camp and then was taken to the south of France. The German army or the Gestapo was always after that group of people; finally they were caught by them. Grelling would have been able to flee into Switzerland, that was the story, but he was waiting for his wife to come from Berlin. They were caught and they vanished in the gas chambers in Poland as victims of the Nazis. I remember being called as a witness at the State Department for Grelling who had sought admission to the U.S.A.; but the officials there seemed to be clearly dragging their feet. They didn't allow anyone in who was a social democrat and they must have been afraid that he was possibly a communist, but Grelling was nothing like a communist at all. He was in fact a very gentle and not very political person. But nothing—we wrote letters urging the State Department, couldn't they hasten their proceedings?—but nothing happened and both Grelling and his wife were killed.

Nollan: How long were you at Queens College?

Hempel: I was at Queens College until '48. But the last year was a leave year when I had a Guggenheim Fellowship. I began work then on matters of concept formation and this appeared eventually in '52, *Fundamentals of Concept Formation*, a small book that is clearly influenced by earlier ideas of Carnap but develops points in more detail and also has things which are not in Carnap. But clearly the interest and the basic way of categorizing the problems—that was strongly influenced by Carnap.

Nollan: '48 was also the year that you published with Oppenheim "Studies in the Logic of Explanation."

Hempel: That's right. I worked in Princeton on this, and that also I consider a relatively important piece of work for me. "The Studies in the Logic of Explanation" called forth a good deal of discussion, critical and productive, and proposals of alternatives and so I think this was a useful contribution.

In '48 I went on to Yale where I stayed until '55. In the field I was particularly interested in the logician Frederick Fitch, F. Northrop who had written in the philosophy of science, and Henry Margenau whose work embraced both physics and philosophy. There were many good and challenging students. One thing that I remember with pleasure was the fact that in my seminars I had quite a number of very able students from psychology. Several of them have gone on to important positions. They were highly stimulating members of the group. Then there was Adolf Grunbaum who began his graduate studies while I was at Yale and who is now an old friend and colleague in Pittsburgh. Alan Anderson was an undergraduate when I went to Yale: he became a distinguished faculty member of the University of Pittsburgh. He died, unfortunately quite young, several years ago. I don't want to mention all the other students or want to lay claim to their achievements. I am very pleased to have had these and other well-known scholars in my seminars, but what they achieved, they did on their own.

I did more work with concept formation and I published that in 1952. During the penultimate year of my stay at Yale I was a visitor at Harvard ('53 to '54) and there I met Quine, whose writings have increasingly influenced me, and Scheffler. I met C. I. Lewis, I was very impressed by him; a very lively Donald Williams, Burton Dreben. I remember hearing Dreben's fascinating lectures on the development of logic from Frege to the present, the present being 1954.

In 1955 I joined the faculty of Princeton. I am very glad indeed I went there. I found the atmosphere there academically and personally congenial and stimulating. I remember very fondly the chairman, Ledger Wood, who brought me there. There were many others of whom I grew very fond, among them Paul Benacerraf, the present chairman of the department, and Gregory Vlastos, who came from Cornell at the same time that I came from Yale, Richard Jeffrey, Walter Kaufmann, Richard Rorty, and a number of others. I also met physicists and found that highly stimulating: Wigner, Wheeler, and Dickey, for example. I confess that I felt quite awed by these eminent figures, and I now regret that I did not seek them out for more extensive discussions. I had quite a number of exceptionally able students who made these seminars really highly rewarding experiences.

I became interested at that time in questions on the methodology and philosophy of psychology and sociology and historiography and turned also to questions of rational explanation, explanation of human actions by motivating reasons and whether the logic of these explanations is similar to the logic of explanations in the physical sciences. On the whole I argued that that was the case.

In '59 to '60 I was a Senior Fullbright Scholar at Oxford. I met especially Gilbert Ryle and the moral philosopher Richard Hare. Ryle, a very stimulating man, invited me to give a seminar jointly with him, which I was glad to do. I still remember being somewhat taken aback when I asked when we would plan this and just what was going to be discussed and in what order. "Don't worry," he said, "this will all unfold by itself. Why don't I start with a paper and you come back the next time with a reply to this and then there will be somebody who will offer a paper and so on." And indeed it went in this way. I myself like to have my future somewhat more clearly structured than that but it all turned out very nicely. It was lively and there were lots of people in this seminar. They participated eagerly and so it was great fun.

I turned to another aspect of explanation then, namely explanation by probabilistic laws or statistical explanation, which has recently received much attention from philosophers, for example from my colleague Wesley Salmon who joined the faculty here not quite a year ago at the beginning of this academic year. I wrote a longish essay on this subject; it appeared in 1962.

Nollan: Do you remember any of the people you met while you were at Oxford?

Hempel: Besides Ryle, let me mention R. M. Hare, Strawson, Kneale, and Urmson.

Nollan: Popper was there at the same time, wasn't he?

Hempel: No, Popper was not there. He was not in Oxford. Let me see; he would have been at the London School of Economics, but I don't remember now. I certainly must have seen him during the year. My contact with Popper was mostly through his writings. I read his publications with very great interest. I didn't have many discussions with him. I did have a number of conversations with Popper and I can't place these now. There may very well have been one or two during that time but I couldn't vouch for that.

Nollan: How did you find the intellectual atmosphere at Oxford at that time?

Hempel: I found that highly stimulating. One always met some interesting people to talk to. As I said before it seemed to be somewhat informal, the proceedings at the advanced level. For undergraduates there was this extensive tutorial system; there were not so many undergraduate lecture courses.

Nollan: Did you have any student that you remember as especially gifted?

Hempel: No, in fact I didn't teach, I was there as a research fellow. Giving this seminar with Ryle was beyond the call of duty. It was not something called for by my Fulbright Fellowship, it was a research fellowship. So, I sat a good deal of my time in my study and worked on my own ideas. I did discuss with some of the advanced students. Some of them I met again in this country. Then we talked about all sorts of subjects, but I didn't have any students of my own.

Then in '63 to '64 I spent a year at the Center for Advanced Study in the Behavioral Sciences. I found that to be a particularly productive year; the setting there was very helpful. I worked there preparing two things, namely a volume called *Aspects of Scientific Explanation*, a collection of essays enlarged by one very large essay on explanation in which I supplemented and much revised what I had written earlier on explanation, and also an introductory book, *Philosophy of Natural Science*. *Aspects* appeared in '65 and *Natural Science* in '66.

I met Thomas Kuhn at the Center for the first time. He was not a fellow at the Center that year but was teaching at Berkeley. We met several times for discussions and I was very much struck by his ideas. At first I found them strange and I had very great resistence to these ideas, his historicist, pragmatist approach to problems in the methodology of science, but I have changed my mind considerably about this since then. In fact a good deal of the thinking and writing I did subsequently was in one way or another influenced by the problems and issues that have been raised by Kuhn's writings.

Kuhn came to join the faculty at Princeton in the Department of History and he was a member especially in the then existing Program in the History and the Philosophy of Science. There I saw a good deal of him. We even cooperated in giving a course; he volunteered to cooperate with me in my undergraduate course in the philosophy of science. [He is] the most conscientious and stimulating man I have ever had to give a course with, and this helped me to understand what his work was all about. It was a very different way of looking at the problems of methodology. It made me think more about the limitations of the analytic approach, which was the one advocated and developed and modified by the logical empiricists. That was the training I had gone through. I still don't think that a purely pragmatist approach is possible and I have recently written about this subject. But I see considerably more merit in that approach than I had seen before. For example, if one wants to claim that science must conform to certain methodological standards, or if one makes pronouncements about what a proper explanation must be like or what the structure of a theory is or how a theory functions in making predictions and providing explanations—if one wants to do this in the analytic spirit of logical empiricism, it isn't quite clear on what grounds one can justifiy such pronouncements. Analytic empiricists had sharply rejected the naturalistic or pragmatist view that the principles of the methodology of science were basically descriptive of scientific research behavior. Popper has been very explicit on this point. Already in his book *Die Logik der Forschung*, which impressed me very much, he asserted that the principles and standards of his methodology were laid down by convention; they were rules of a game, the game of science. I couldn't help feeling that if there were the rules of a game called "science" why should any philosopher of science be interested in this; there must be some factual side to this. Of course there was and there was also in Popper's position, namely there must be some intention of writing the rules of a game which in its moves at least comes very close to what we find as a matter of fact in the actual research activities of scientists. I have recently written on this subject and have argued that there is, therefore, no fundamental cleavage between the analytic and the pragmatist approach. Both of them have an element of rational analytic reconstructionism and both of them make explicit empirical claims, whether they acknowledge this or not.

Nollan: While you were at the Institute did you have an oportunity to meet and discuss problems with Einstein or any other members of the physics department?

Hempel: Let me just note that the Institute for Advanced Study where Einstein and Bohr and von Neumann were working has always been a research establishment quite separate from Princeton University. But there is a great deal of exchange of ideas and sometimes seminars offered at the Institute and so there is a good deal of intellectual contact.

Yes, I did meet Einstein a number of times. He was a good friend of the Oppenheims and, while Oppenheim was not versed in theoretical physics, Einstein liked to go for Sunday walks with Oppenheim and talk to him about philosophical issues. Perhaps the first time that I actually met Einstein was at Princeton. I had been invited to give a talk before the Philosophy Club there and in the last minute, I was just about ready to start, Einstein appeared in the audience. He didn't say anything during the discussion, but afterward he, Oppenheim, and I walked away together. Einstein raised questions about the soundness of empiricism, but I think these questions were based on misunderstanding. He was very friendly. Einstein was an extremely gentle and considerate person; he always took an interest in what you were doing and did not try to impress you with his ideas. He entertained the idea that logical empiricists believed in somehow inferring scientific theories from experimental data. Actually we entertained no such view at all. Our position was largely in agreement with his own, namely that scientific theories are free creations of the scientific imagination which have to be critically appraised by empirical test.

Nollan: [*changing tape*] Please continue.

Hempel: Well, I met him on some other occasions and I will confess that I felt somewhat awed by the man and didn't really use the opportunity as much as I might to ask questions which were on my mind, which I continue to have on my mind about scientific theorizing and so on. We did talk about these subjects but I largely listened to what Einstein had to say and I didn't engage very much in a discussion. I consider this rather a weakness on my part. I hesitated in these cases to engage people much. Einstein was a very friendly person and I remember he liked to tell little anecdotes in order to illustrate points and he would then chuckle heartily about these stories he told. He liked to go boating and sailing on Lake Carnegie in Princeton, in a very small boat. One summer, while vacationing in Lake Saranac, Einstein went sailing with Oppenheim and Helmer. Einstein's boat capsized. Helmer told me that Einstein first vanished and then popped up again and they held on to the boat. But then Einstein went down once more and he came up triumphantly holding his pipe. He had lost his pipe the first time down and he did not want to lose it.

I met Niels Bohr, too, on some social occasions. He was a taciturn man and at any rate hard to understand, he talked in a sort of mumbling way. Not very explicitly. One had to try to unravel the mystery of what he had in mind. I think that people who had worked with him for a long time were able to do this. I didn't find it easy, so I listened to him. I met him only on social occasions.

Nollan: How would you compare the two men in personality?

Hempel: Einstein seemed to be a much more relaxed person, and on the whole cheerful and friendly and relatively accessible. Of course his secretary, Miss Dukas, watched over him so that not everybody could just walk in. But he was more accessible and not at all intimidating. Bohr seemed to be a somewhat more brooding figure in conversation in dealing with these ideas he wanted to express. [He spoke] in a low voice and I recall struggling to make his ideas clear. There was perhaps a slightly forbidding quality to him. This may be just a difficulty in understanding (a) what he said literally, what words were uttered and (b) what he meant by them. What he was like personally I don't know. I saw him only on a few occasions, among them the meeting in Copenhagen where we got the news about Schlick's assassination. I heard Bohr lecture there, but I didn't have any personal conversation with him. I certainly found him difficult to follow.

On the other hand, John Wheeler, who has since left the physics department at Princeton, one of the eminent members of that department, was by contrast an extraordinarily stimulating and lucid lecturer. I listened to some of his lectures with endless fascination. He has a remarkable gift of presenting his ideas in sequence, as it were, of metaphors, some very precise and explicit statements, and then some other metaphors. He propounded some grand ideas about the structure of space and time and about the identification of elementary particles as worm holes in space-time. He made it all seem as if it was very simple and straightforward and plausible. He was such a polite and outgoing and reasonable person that when one talked with him one almost felt embarassed by his courtesy. He was so courteous and he expressed such admiration for the difficult ideas that philosophers were struggling with, and I couldn't help thinking, "My God, Wheeler's general geometrodynamics is vastly more complicated than the philosophical issues." Anyway, here is a sharp contrast. Wheeler was a very accessible, friendly, and informative person.

In '73 I reached official retirement at Princeton. I went on to teach for two years, to give some seminars. Then I went to teach twice at Berkeley and at the University of California at Irvine, and spent a very pleasant term at Carleton of Minneapolis, which I liked very much. I also taught a term at the Hebrew University of Jerusalem and this was interesting and memorable for many reasons. Teaching these students, all of whom had served in the army—the men at any rate; I don't know whether the women also had—and who were therefore more mature. They had to be ready to be called back into the army on short notice. Some of them would come and say, "Could you give me some assignment because I have been called back in the army." Some would appear in the middle of the term having just been released from the army. This was just after the Yom Kippur War. So it was not an optimum setting for teaching, but nevertheless the students were interested and excited and I found it a very rewarding experience. I also visited other universities there. At the University of Haifa I saw Abraham Kaplan again whom I had first met in Carnap's seminar in Chicago; he was now dean of the social sciences. At the University of the Negev at Bersheba where I read a paper before the departmental faculty, a young faculty member brought me greetings from his mother. I was astonished. He said, "She was a student of yours at Queens College."

In the years after my leaving Princeton I lectured in Australia and then in China.

I came to Pittsburgh in 1976 as a visitor and then accepted an open-ended appointment in the fall of 1977 in the Department of Philosophy. I am very glad I came. I find the colleagues here both in the Department of Philosophy and in the history and philosophy of science very congenial and stimulating. There is a good deal of intellectual exchange, there is a lot going on, in fact there is more than one can avail oneself of: lectures, seminars, colloquia, visitors. My interest here, apart from my teaching undergraduate and graduate courses, has been in the questions of the limitations of analytic empiricism and questions of turning away from a foundationalist to a coherentist view of empiricial knowledge, but it cannot be just simple coherentism, and the question is exactly how to put these ideas. I am struggling with issues of this sort. Also in analytic empiricist accounts of scientific procedure, a great deal of emphasis used to be put, and I think rightly, on deductive procedures, on deducing predictions from theoretical principles and so forth. But there are limits to this deductivist conception, and I am working on some problems concerning the limitations of a deductivist construal of scientific methodology.

Interview 3

Nollan: Would you like to add remarks about others you knew then?

Hempel: Now, what I remember is that I had said nothing about Nelson Goodman and nothing about John Kemeny. About John Kemeny I can't really say very much that would be helpful and am embarrassed by this fact. At that time Kemeny was in Princeton. He had just earned his doctorate with Alonzo Church in logic. This I know for sure. We worked with Oppenheim on some problem, and I am sorry to say I cannot recall what the problem was. I thought it had something to do with the probability of hypotheses, on which we worked a great deal. What I can say from recollection is that Kemeny was an excellent mathematician and logician; a great friend to talk technical problems over with. He struck me always as having a brain that was like a very fast computer. When some problem came up of estimating what would be the value of adopting such and such a probability function in this context, in no time at all he had figured these things out in very elegant way. He also had such original ideas about how to approach the problem, so of course, it was a great intellectual joy to work with him. He then went off to Dartmouth and became a professor of mathematics, then chairman, and later president of Dartmouth College. I think he has now resigned that position and is again teaching in the department of mathematics. That is John Kemeney.

Nollan: Did he get his degree at Princeton?

Hempel: At Princeton with Alonzo Church. I think he was Church's assistant.

Nollan: Was this while you were teaching there?

Hempel: No, that was in fact before I was teaching there. I was still at Yale. But I came over to Princeton from time to time to work with Paul Oppenheim, discuss questions he had on his mind. There I met Kemeny. I moved to Princeton in

1955 and I'm not quite sure whether Kemeny had left by that time or had left early on as I was at Princeton but at any rate, I met him earlier coming from Yale. He had also been an assistant of Einstein. Einstein evidently had appreciated Kemeny's great mathematical facility, and his quick incisive mind, and it was a great joy to discuss with him and work with him.

Nollan: He and Carnap worked together, didn't they, on probability theory?

Hempel: You are quite right. They worked on probability theory. Also, I think there was Carnap's idea of meaning postulates, by means of which Carnap sought to define the notion of analytic truth. If a statement was logically deducible from the meaning postulates of a language, then it was analytic. That was the wider sense of the word, what's sometimes characterized by saying a sentence is analytic if it is true by the virtue of the meanings of the words that occur in it. Carnap had made this somewhat more explicit and precise by saying we assume that these meanings are specified by laying down certain meaning postulates. One of them could be, for example, whatever is green all over is not red all over. Then one could say "If this is green then it is not red" was an analytic sentence because it could be derived from this meaning postulate. There would be other meaning postulates which might be more complicated and sentences which follow from these would then be called "analytic." If one wants to clarify the notion of analyticity and truth by virtue of meaning, one now has to ask, "But how do you know which statements in your language are meaning postulates? And which express perhaps empirical knowledge which is however so well grounded in all your past experience you have never had an exception, that you wouldn't doubt that the next case will conform to it." I heard somewhere the story of an anthropologist—the story may be fictitious—who interviews a native, let us say in Central New Guinea, and asks him, "What do you do when you stand in the clearing and out of the jungle a tiger comes at you?" He says, "I throw my spear at him." "What do you do if two tigers come?" "I turn around and run." "And if three tigers come?" "That cannot happen." Now, "That cannot happen," is this an analytic sentence for this man? That is, is this one of his meaning postulates—if three of a kind can come out of the bushes they can't be tigers, or not only tigers. Or is this an empirical sentence which he now communicates to the anthropologist? Here is one of these cases. One can make much subtler cases. So the clarification by means of meaning postulates isn't very helpful. One could just as well stop and have some definition where one says some sentences are analytic and one gives some sort of list. But if one wants to know by what virtue these sentences are analytic or by virtue of what these meaning postulates are, then the criterion doesn't help much. So that was the difficulty there. I think that the idea of a meaning postulate indeed went back to Kemeny, and Carnap acknowledged this and then made use of it. I believe he wrote an article with Kemeny, an article that was published at the time in a small philosophical periodical by the University of Minnesota Press. I don't know what the name was.[4] So you are quite right, Carnap worked indeed with Kemeny, and was much impressed by his ability. So these are the reminiscences I have of Kemeny.

I have written a few lines, but only a very few lines, where I talk about Nelson

Goodman. [*Looking through his notes*] I say somewhere something about the raven paradox and about the theory of quantitative, qualitative, confirmation. This evidence confirms or does not confirm some hypothesis. In developing these ideas about a sharp definition of confirmation I said, "Here's a piece of information. Does this or does this not support or confirm this hypothesis?" This was very frustrating and difficult a job because I wanted to have a completely general and precise formal criterion for this and I eventually managed to develop such a criterion. Then the theory flowed from this with provable theorems and so on. I discussed this with Goodman, whom I met in the forties, and I have stayed in touch with [him] ever since.[5]

Goodman was very helpful. He was himself interested in problems which had to do with confirmation and induction and so his comments and his questions were very valuable to me in struggling with these problems and eventually coming up with this solution which I proposed. Today I have some doubts about the solution, but all the same it's a very well worked out little theory.

I have great admiration for [Goodman's] general philosophical style. He is an analytic thinker of, I think, great profundity and originality. Especially in his little book, *Fact, Fiction, and Forecast,* he was writing about the question of how one could justify inductive inferences, i.e., inferences from given information to assumptions about as yet unexamined cases whether these be in the past or in the future. This is essentially Hume's problem; how does one justify these beliefs? He had some very interesting ideas about this where he already develops a point of view which much later, I don't know, twenty years later, was systematically advanced and developed in the so-called naturalistic approach to epistemology. Namely, whether a certain kind of inductive inference, and Goodman also said this about deductive inferences, whether a particular inference from this evidence to that hypothesis is valid or not depends on whether it conforms to a rule which we are unwilling to abandon. Here he has a clear reference to human behavior, to dispositions to accept or reject certain claims. Whereas in logical empiricism the idea was "Don't refer to what people do, they make all sorts of mistakes. You must formulate and justify criteria of validity for both inductive and deductive reasoning which are quite independent of what people think and of how people think." That cannot be the justification, and Goodman here says the ultimate justification for a particular inference is that it conforms to a rule which we are unwilling to abandon. Then you say, "What about justifying the rule, on what grounds?" [Goodman] says the rule is justified if it yields inferences which we are unwilling to discard. Since there is a mutual adjustment of the two which is not vicious but celestial and virtuous, and indeed there is something to this, [but] there are some questions left. But what it quite clearly and strongly anticipates is the so-called naturalization of epistemology. The ultimate grounds for knowledge claims and the justification of these claims is found in aspects of human behavior, in this case readiness to accept or reject, or unwillingness or willingness to modify and so on. This he set forth in *Fact, Fiction, and Forecast* in one of the chapters in his characteristic very pithy and persuasive style.

Nollan: Did you ever collaborate with him on anything?

Hempel: No, in fact I think I never collaborated with anyone but Oppenheim on anything. I discussed problems with others who were interested in different pursuits, but I never collaborated, I never published with others. On the whole I would find it a rather difficult enterprise. It is not easy to do this unless you and your collaborators think along much the same lines and have much the same standards. If there are noticable differences in, for example, interests or in a sense of what is important about a question, this can produce quite a tug and tensions which make it more difficult to carry out the collaboration. So on the whole I think it is simpler for me to work by myself. Although with Oppenheim I managed very nicely. At times he insisted on something being very important and we should mention this, and I said, "This is of no real relevance to this issue" and "Why should we bring it up at all?" At times we struck a compromise. But it was never of a kind that I said to myself, "I cannot carry out this collaboration because he is stubborn (and I am stubborn)." It worked out, but on the whole going it alone is simpler than working with someone.

[*Editor's note:* Returning to the subject of his first meeting with Carnap, Hempel remarks:] There is one point when I said I met Carnap first at a meeting in Prague. I have filled in [referring to additions made to the first two interviews] that that was the first meeting for theory of knowledge of *Erkenntnis* in September 1929. I have filled this into the text so that there is a clear reference that, as a student of Reichenbach, I mainly went to Prague to meet Carnap and to ask him if I could come to Vienna for a term to study with him and his colleagues. [*Shuffling through papers*]

Nollan: If you are finished with that [elaboration], I was going to suggest that there was also Richard von Mises.

Hempel: Very good. Among the several mathematicians—very able and stimulating mathematicians, with whom I had studied in Berlin—there was Richard von Mises who, I think, had done very distinguished work in one area of applied mathematics to do with aerodynamics. That became, I believe, important in the development of certain principles for the design for airplane wings, hydrofoils. About this I know absolutely nothing. But his natural, theoretically basic interest was the theory of probability. Here he pursued a statistical approach in which probabilities of occurrences were construed as long-run relative frequencies of those occurrences. So the probability for a miner to develop black lung disease would have to be construed as the long-run percentage if you examine many miners, percentages of those who do develop the disease. For mathematical purposes it isn't good to say "in the long run" because this is no sharp notion. So he sought to make this notion precise by saying we define it as a limit, that is, ideally, we presuppose that there is an experiment which can be repeated indefinitely many times. For example, picking a miner out of the group of the general population and then examining the case as to whether, yes or no, he possesses a certain characteristic, i.e., after twenty years winds up with black lung disease, for example. We assume that this can be done indefinitely and then we write down after each case the percentage of cases so far among the first n cases observed which have this characteristic. It is then assumed in the cases to which probability theory is applicable that this frequency approaches the limit, a number to which it comes closer and closer as you proceed and this limit is then the probability of the occurrence of this event, black lung disease, for example, among miners. He developed this theory in great detail. He wrote, a fascinating book which was addressed to the general but well-trained reader who didn't have to have so much mathematics, but he had to have a keen interest. It is called *Wahrscheinlichkeit, Statistik, und Wahrheit [looking through papers]*. The second of his books. In a rather strict sense, this was a popular presentation of his ideas. I thought it absolutely excellent. There are some classics in mathematics which I admire greatly and one of them was Fraenkel's *Introduction to Set Theory*. Here is this book by von Mises, there is another book in German on infinite series by [Schweisser], and there are a small number of these which are incredibly well-written and immensely lucid without making any compromise of rigor of thought and clarity, and there is no reliance on metaphors and dubious sliding over thin ice. Mises' book is certainly one of those.

Well, I took at least one course with Mises in probability theory and found this quite interesting. By comparison with Reichenbach, the striking thing was that Reichenbach was at the same time developing a theory along similar lines, that is, with the same basic conception of probability, as a statistical relative frequency. Here comes one difference. Mises insisted there was no other use of the word "probability" of which one could make clear sense than the one in which one could translate this into the assertion about "in the long run such and such a percentage of cases will have this characteristic." He argued therefore that if you say "probably it will rain tomorrow" this had no clear meaning at all and similarly about the probability "this patient will survive this illness." All of these could not be treated as serious scientific statements. Reichenbach, on the other hand, tried to give to these also a statistical interpretation very roughly to this effect that if you take a large number of patients, for example, who suffer from the same illness, then the percentage in the long run of those who survive is so and so much. The great problem was then, what do you mean [by] "patients suffering from the same illness"? There could be other features which these patients have and which could be decisive for their survival or nonsurvival and this famous problem of the reference class cropped up. Reichenbach worried a great deal about this. Mises just simply declined to treat cases of this at all as serious cases of probability theory. Similarly he rejected the idea that one should be speaking of the probability, let us say, of the theory of relativity being true. This is just an expression of some intuitive judgement which couldn't be made precise and which was not a possible subject of any rigorous mathematical theory. Reichenbach offered an interpretation for this also, a seemingly precise interpretation which I think is untenable, but at any rate they differed on certain fundamental issues. I had the sense, there was always a certain personal tension between the two which I think was a great pity because here were these two very able, seminal thinkers and they didn't talk to each other nearly as much as I believe, very little in fact, as might have been good for the advancement of the subject. Both were very good lecturers. Mises was an extremely good lecturer, and so was Reichenbach in his way. Of course Mises had very many other mathematical interests and Reichenbach more philosophical interests.

Nollan: You might also say another word about their differences in character; von Mises being from an aristocratic background.

Hempel: Oh, yes. Mises impressed me as an aristocratic figure, tall, erect, aloof, perfectly friendly, and never, never rude, but aloof. You wouldn't, even as an advanced student, even if he knew you, you normally wouldn't just go and raise a question with him even about theoretical matters. Reichenbach was shorter, rounder, he was in the typology of the time "pyknic." He was outgoing, lively, gregarious, and, as I think someone else has said, one of those persons who sing when they take a shower. I cannot imagine Mises singing when he took a shower, he could never do that. Reichenbach always had a group of students, not huge numbers, but a group of students, who would go to a coffeehouse after his seminars, and talk about not only his philosophical concerns, but also about political issues, social issues, questions of education. This was quite rare and, of course, I've never known Mises to do this. It was rare enough that a professor let you ask a question, let us say, in a break between two successive parts of his lecture and when that happened I appreciated it greatly and even that was not a very frequent occurrence.

Mises [was] like many other scholars who were in some way related to, maybe sympathetic with, the efforts of logical positivists. He was not himself a logical positivist, although he wrote a book, and this was an introduction to something like logical positivism; it was his version of this and I think strongly based on the ideas of verification. So Mises was sympathetic to the general concerns of logical positivism. I think perhaps that this antagonism which I suspect existed between Reichenbach and Mises had more to do with a kind of rivalry in efforts to advance this particular subject of a statistical probability theory and in determining how far this theory could in fact be developed and whether one could speak of the probability of hypotheses and theories and so on.

He also left Germany, and he came to Harvard, just as Reichenbach left and went to Turkey, and then went, I think, directly to UCLA. Carnap left from Vienna to go to Prague, and then left from there to go to Chicago, later to UCLA. There was also, Mises reminds me of this, a theoretical physicist, who had been the successor of Einstein in the chair of theoretical physics in Prague, and that was Philipp Frank. I met him I think at the Prague meeting, and I came to know him somewhat better in Prague, where he would visit Carnap, with whom I stayed at least once for several weeks as a visitor. He, too, later came to the United States and was at Harvard. He was a broadly knowledgeable man, in mathematical method of physics and in theoretical physics. He had a very strong interest in the questions of epistemology, particulary concerning physics. He took a somewhat narrow operationalist and verificationist stand on these issues, but then this was a very long time ago. But he had some very sharp insights and he would always understate these things, in literally a throwaway remark. He would mumble, and suddenly one took notice and saw that he had said something quite interesting and important. [One] said, "Now tell me more about this" and there it was. He wrote a very interesting philosophical book on the principle of causality in physics and that would be an excellent work to introduce serious students into the field and it developed also his philosophical views on the foundations of physics [and] perhaps of science in general. I don't know whether it was ever translated into English. I doubt it.[6] The German edition was practically totally destroyed in the warehouse of the publisher named Springer who published it in the series which was edited by Schlick and maybe Frank himself—the series in which Popper's book *Logik der Forschung* had appeared. Frank went on to teach, I think on the one hand some theoretical physics and on the other hand these broader issues in the philosophy of physics also when he came to Harvard. A very nice dry sense of humor; a very engaging person.

There will always be some other people who occur to me. I have mentioned Ernest Nagel only briefly in connection with a philosophical discussion group. Nagel was a student of Morris Cohen. Nagel taught most of his life at Columbia. We met early on after my arrival in this country and became close friends. I have very high regard for him. I thought of him also as a modern kind of Aristotle. He was enormously widely read; I could not touch him in this respect. He had a very lucid way of presenting his ideas. He was lucidly critical in discussions in two groups to which I belonged. There was one which I mentioned earlier, where every month, I think it was a group of members from the philosophy departments of Columbia, NYU, City College, and perhaps some other places met at the house of one of the members to discuss. That was a younger group, very lively and very stimulating. Ernest Nagel was a regular member of that group. Then there was another one which was called the New York Philosophy Club. It met during the academic year in the men's faculty club at Columbia University. Among the members were a number of philosophers from Columbia and also people from other places; in fact some came in from Yale. I don't know whether there was also somebody from Harvard or from the University of Pennsylvania. Ernest Nagel was a member and always had interesting and helpful things to say. There was one very curious system in these meetings at Columbia, namely after the paper had been presented there was a discussion. But the discussion was not your usual free form, i.e., whoever has something to say raising his hand. Rather the discussion went around the table and everybody was expected to say something no matter whether he knew anything about this subject, or even if he knew about it and had anything to say that was worth mentioning. So I remember the horror I sometimes felt as I saw how this came around. Like a sort of chicken hypnotized by a snake I sat there and thought, "My God, what will I say? Now, I don't know what to say about this paper." Ernest Nagel always had interesting and thoughtful things to say. I remember one case where Abraham Kaplan, then I think at the University of

Michigan, read a paper and there were objections, and they were totally diverse, and that was characteristic and was to be expected. You had maybe fifteen or so people raising points of objections and no one could sit there and write down quickly what one could catch of these, and the standard order of reply was to say that Mr. A had said such and such. But Kaplan, as soon as his turn came to reply, had organized the entire thing into a group of topics and then discussed concerning these topics, these colleagues had said something and such and so. . . . It was an astonishing bravura performance which I haven't forgotten to this day. I could never match this. I must say, I do not really think it is a good idea to have a discussion with this peculiar style. It isn't productive and a good deal of time is wasted, and indeed I do remember quite clearly that on several occasions some of the members who did not know what to say would then say what an enriching experience it had been to listen to this lecture, and how many fascinating ideas had been expressed and all the time they were looking nervously at their watch to see whether they had now used up their allotted three minutes. Everybody was allowed the same amount of time, I mean whatever time was left until dinner was served, divided by the number of participants. So you might have to talk for five minutes on something about which you knew nothing or had nothing in this context to say. I thought it was a very unfortunate, not a very good idea.

Nollan: Nothing philosophically interesting.

Hempel: No, very frequently not. On the other hand, there were other people who had lots to say on this and they had to be cut off because their three minutes were up. It was an otherwise interesting and enjoyable thing. We all sat around for a jolly dinner afterwards, but this important part of the transactions I think was not optimum.

NOTES

1. That is, Carnap (1945a) and Hempel and Oppenheim (1945). In the same year a more technical version of this article appeared, by a different H & O: Helmer and Oppenheim (1945). What Carnap dubbed "the H_2O definition" appears in both of these H & O articles.
2. No publication of Carnap's quite fits the description. But see Carnap (1945a, 1945b, 1947).
3. Actually, there was no such name, and no one such H_2O article—just the two H & O articles (see note 1).
4. The Carnap-Kemeny article was really two separate articles, both of which appeared in the same issue of *Philosophical Studies*: Kemeny (1952) and Carnap (1952).
5. On the topic of qualitative confirmation, see references to Nelson Goodman in Hempel (1965, pp. 3–51).
6. The work to which Hempel refers is Philipp Frank, *Das Kausalgestz und Seine Grenzen* (*The Law of Causality and Its Limits*) (Vienna: Julius Springer, 1932), to which several citations may be found in Philipp Frank, *Philosophy of Science: The Link Between Science and Philosophy* (Englewood Cliffs, NJ: Prentice-Hall, Inc., 1957).

REFERENCES

Carnap, R. 1945a. "On Inductive Logic." *Philosophy of Science* 12:72–96.

———. 1945b. "The Two Concepts of Probability." *Philosophy and Phenomenological Research* 5:513–32.

———. 1947. "Ou the Application of Inductive Logic." *Philosophy and Phenomenological Research* 8:133–48.

———. 1952. "Meaning Postulates." *Philosophical Studies* 3:65–73.

Helmer, O., and P. Oppenheim. 1945. "A Syntactical Definition of Probability and of Degree of Confirmation." *Journal of Symbolic Logic* 10:25–60.

Hempel, C. G. 1965. *Aspects of Scientific Explanation*. New York: Free Press.

Hempel, C. G.. and P. Oppenheim. 1945. "A Definition of 'Degree of Confirmation.'" *Philosophy of Science* 12:98–115.

Kemeny. J. 1952. "Extension of the Methods of Inductive Logic." *Philosophical Studies* 3:38–42.

I

SCIENTIFIC REASONING

1

Hempel and the Vienna Circle

MICHAEL FRIEDMAN

I first met Hempel when I was an undergraduate at Queens College. Hempel had taught there in the years 1940–48, as his first regular position at an American University, and he had now returned (I believe it was in the academic year 1967–68) for a period of two weeks as a Distinguished Visitor. I had just become seriously interested in the philosophy of science, and I vividly remember the sense of profound excitement I felt while attending the variety of talks, seminars, and discussions Hempel held during this visit. His clarity and acuity of mind, wide-ranging knowledge and interests, and singular kindness and enthusiasm were exhilarating, and I resolved then and there to apply for graduate study at Princeton, where Hempel taught from 1955 until 1975. I attended Princeton in the years 1969–72 and took several inspiring seminars from Hempel. I remember one, in particular, when Hempel was working out his ideas on the problem of "provisoes," where we in attendance were simply enthralled by the experience of witnessing a major philosopher fundamentally change his mind, and in the most open and relaxed way imaginable, about a central question of philosophical methodology that had essentially shaped much of his previous work. This experience left an indelible stamp on my own attitudes toward the subject.

I had initially intended, largely because of Hempel's influence, to write a dissertation on scientific explanation. I wanted to extend a basically deductive-nomological approach from the explanation of singular events to the explanation of laws of nature, and this work eventually resulted in one of my first publications in the field. During my years at Princeton, however, I also encountered the philosophy of physics, and I ended up instead writing a dissertation on space, time, and relativity under the direction of Clark Glymour. Already in this dissertation work I began looking at the logical empiricist movement from a historical point of view, an interest that was stimulated and encouraged by both Glymour and Hempel. And this area later became a major preoccupation of mine, as I delved more deeply into the background and evolution of the thought of Rudolf Carnap in particular, who, in turn, had been perhaps the most important influence on Hempel himself. In this essay I would like to take the opportunity to come full circle, as it were, by exploring the intellectual roots of

Hempel's thought in his own encounter with the Vienna Circle. We will see, perhaps somewhat surprisingly, that virtually all the seeds of his later development can be found there, including his later turn away from what has come to be identified as the characteristic mode of philosophizing of logical empiricism to what he himself calls a more pragmatic and naturalistic approach.

Hempel received the bulk of his philosophical education at the University of Berlin, which he attended from 1925 to 1934, when he completed a doctoral dissertation on the logical analysis of the concept of probability directed principally by Hans Reichenbach. Hempel had become acquainted with Reichenbach when the latter arrived at the university in 1926, whereupon he became one of Hempel's most important influences and teachers at Berlin, along with the methodologically oriented psychologists Wolfgang Köhler and Kurt Lewin. Hempel was a member of Reichenbach's Society for Empirical Philosophy, which included the philosopher-logicians Walter Dubislav and Kurt Grelling and often attracted a number of other distinguished visitors, such as, in particular, the logician Paul Bernays, with whom Hempel had earlier studied in Göttingen. In 1928 Hempel read Carnap's *Der logische Aufbau der Welt* and *Scheinprobleme in der Philosophie* and immediately decided to study in Vienna for a term—a decision that was reinforced, so he reports, by meeting Carnap in person at the first *Tagung für die Erkenntnislehre der exakten Wissenschaften* at Prague in September 1929. Hempel visited the University of Vienna in the winter term of 1929–30, where he attended lectures and seminars given by Moritz Schlick, Carnap, and Friedrich Waismann. Most important, with a letter of introduction from Reichenbach, he was invited to attend the discussions of Schlick's Philosophical Circle, which included, besides Carnap, Schlick, and Waismann, Otto Neurath, Hans Hahn, Herbert Feigl, Kurt Gödel, and Karl Menger. When he arrived in Vienna Hempel was quite a young man, not yet twenty-five years old. (For his own recollections of these events, see Hempel [1973, 1981, 1991, 1993].)

Unfortunately, we do not have a record of the discussions in the Circle that Hempel attended. We do know, however, that the period 1928–30 represents the very beginnings of the so-called protocol-sentence debate within the Circle, wherein a quite fundamental split developed between Schlick and Waismann, on the one side, and Neurath, followed quickly by Carnap, on the other. The two sides can be seen as adopting opposing stances toward the *Aufbau*, with the Schlick-Waismann camp (often referred to as the right wing of the Circle) pushing in a foundationalist-subjectivist direction and the Neurath-Carnap camp (often referred to as the left wing of the Circle) pushing in a "physicalist" or intersubjectivist direction. In 1928–30 Neurath began criticizing the *Aufbau* for its reliance on "methodological solipsism," whereas Schlick can be read as objecting to the *Aufbau* from the opposite direction, on behalf of the need, in the end, for purely ostensive reference to individual subjective experience.[1] We also know that Hempel's very first publications, appearing in *Analysis* in 1935–36, are central contributions to this debate, in which Hempel weighs in clearly and explicitly, at a more public and developed stage of the debate, on the side of the "radical physicalism" of the Neurath-Carnap camp. It seems very likely, then, that one of the central topics of discussion during Hempel's stay in Vienna in 1929–30 was precisely (the beginnings of) the protocol-sentence debate.[2] In any case, it is clear from his own reports of this stay that the Circle philosophers Hempel was most impressed by, and felt most attracted to, were Neurath and Carnap (see especially Hempel [1981, sec. 2]).

The heart of the protocol-sentence debate, in its public phase, consists of a series of papers involving first Neurath and Carnap, and then a later sharp protest from Schlick, published in *Erkenntnis*, the official organ of the Circle, in 1932–34. The exchange begins with Neurath (1932a) and Carnap (1932a), published immediately following one another in *Erkenntnis* (vol. 2); continues with Neurath (1932b) and Carnap (1932b), again immediately following one another in *Erkenntnis* (vol. 3); and concludes with Schlick (1934) and Neurath (1934) (*Erkenntnis*, vol. 4). This last pair of papers then constitutes the starting point for Hempel's first *Analysis* paper, which, as Hempel (1935a, p. 49) explains, was "suggested by a recent discussion between Prof. Schlick and Dr. Neurath, made public in two articles which appeared in volume 4 of *Erkenntnis*." Hempel's language here again strongly suggests that he had earlier been privy to a less public phase of the debate.

Section 1 of Neurath (1932a), entitled "Physicalism Free of Metaphysics," argues that metaphysics is best definitively overcome by rejecting any point of view outside the language of unified science—including, according to Neurath (1932a, pp. 395–7), that of *Tractarian* "elucidations" purporting to relate language to "experience as a whole," "the world," or "the given" from some "not yet linguistic" standpoint, "as Wittgenstein and certain representatives of the 'Vienna Circle' seek to do." On the contrary, metaphysics can only be finally overcome by resolutely remaining entirely within the linguistic world of unified science itself:

> Unified science formulates statements, corrects them, makes predictions; but it cannot itself anticipate its future state. There is not a *"true" system of statements* over and above the present system of statements. It is meaningless to speak of such a thing, even as a limiting concept. *We can only ascertain that we are operating today with the space-time system to which that of physics corresponds*, and thereby achieve successful predictions. This system of statements is that of unified science—this is the standpoint which may be designated as *physicalism* (cf. [Neurath (1931)], p. 2). . . .
>
> The one unified science peculiar to a definite historical period, as physicalism, proceeds, remote from all meaningless sentences, from statement to statement, which are combined together in a self-consistent system as a tool for successful predictions, and thus life. (1932a, pp. 397–8)

Neurath thus emphasizes in the strongest possible terms that "physicalism," for him, means precisely this essentially interlinguistic standpoint.

Moreover, within this standpoint, as Neurath explains in section 2, "Unified Language of Physicalism," the concept of "successful prediction" also involves no reference whatsoever to an extralinguistic "given." On the contrary, it entails only that we compare the statements of unified science with other such statements—those which express the percipient state of an observer and are themselves expressible in neurophysiological and/or behavioristic terms within the very same physicalistic language. And it is in precisely this connection, moreover, that Carnap's *Aufbau* stands in need of correction:

> Since the views presented here stand closest, above all, to the works of Carnap, let it be emphasized that the special *"phenomenal language,"* from which Carnap seeks to derive the physical language, is eliminated. The exclusion of the "phenomenal language," which does not even seem to be usable for "prediction," i.e., for what is essentially scientific, in the form it has taken so far, will surely necessitate much modification in the constitutional system. In this way we also eliminate "methodological solipsism" (Carnap, Driesch), which may be conceived as an attenuated residue of idealistic metaphysics, a position from which Carnap constantly attempts to distance himself. One cannot scientifically formulate this thesis of "methodological solipsism"—as even Carnap would likely concede—but [also] one cannot even use it any longer to indicate a definite standpoint, which is an alternative to some other standpoint, because there exists only *one* physicalism. Everything scientifically formulable is contained within it. (1932a, pp. 401–2)

Carnap, in the *Aufbau*, had suggested a variety of forms for a unified "constitutional system" for the totality of concepts of empirical science. A phenomenal or "auto-psychological [*eigenpsychisch*]" system corresponding to the demands of "methodological solipsism" best represents the standpoint of epistemology, whereas a system with "physical basis" in the fundamental concepts of physics best represents the "univocal lawlikeness" sought by empirical science (see Carnap [1928, secs. 54–60]). Carnap's antimetaphysical standpoint of the time demands that both systems be equally possible and legitimate. For Neurath, by contrast, a truly antimetaphysical attitude requires that *only* the physicalistic system be admitted.

Carnap (1932a) considers two languages: the "protocol-language" (sec. 3) and the "physical language" (secs. 4–7). The former language, according to Carnap (1932a, pp. 437–8), represents the process of "empirical testing" by formulating "simplest possible sentences" or "protocol-sentences," which "do not themselves require a confirmation, but which serve as the basis for all the remaining sentences of science." Carnap (1932a, pp. 438–9) then mentions three possible forms for such sentences: a sense-datum form of the type "here now blue," a Gestalt form as in the *Aufbau* recording holistic sensory fields, and a form expressing common-sense observations of the type "a red cube lies on the table." The important point, however, is that all three possibilities express the epistemological point of view of a single subject. The physical language, by contrast, is essentially intersubjective (sec. 4). Further, it can serve as a *universal* language for science (sec. 5), in that all empirical statements—including those of the protocol-language itself (sec. 6)—can be expressed within it. In particular, as Neurath has shown, all statements of both psychology and sociology are expressible within the single universal physical language.

Here Carnap adds a footnote referring to Neurath (1932a), and also Neurath (1931):

> Neurath decisively required, as the first in the discussions of the Vienna Circle and then in the cited paper, that one should no longer speak of "contents of experience" and a comparison between sentences and "reality," but only of sentences. Further, he established the thesis of physicalism in its most radical form. I am grateful to his indications for much valuable stimulation. In that I now introduce the distinction between "formal" and "material" modes of speech, point out the pseudo-problems to which the material mode leads, indicate the possibility of rigorously carrying though the formal mode by means of the construction of a metalogic (here only suggested), and demonstrate the universality of the physical language, I have arrived at results that fully justify Neurath's standpoint. Further, through the demonstration that even the protocol-language, too, can be embedded in the physical language (§ 6), our earlier difference of opinion on this point ("phenomenal language"), which Neurath still mentions in his paper, is now set aside. Neurath's indications, which are often met with by opposition, have thus proved themselves to be fruitful in all essential points. (1932a, p. 452)

From Carnap's point of view, then, there are no longer any reasons for dispute.

From Neurath's point of view, however, Carnap has still not understood his point. For Carnap still speaks of two possible languages here, a protocol-language and a physical language, whereas Neurath's point is that traditional metaphysical influences (especially of an idealist or subjectivist variety) can be avoided only by staying entirely within the one single language of unified science, that is, the physical language. Neurath (1932b) therefore launches a full-scale attack on Carnap's characterization of the protocol-language and, in particular, on Carnap's characterization of protocol-sentences as those which "do not themselves require a confirmation, but which serve as the basis for all the remaining sentences of science." For Neurath protocol-sentences are simply those in which the proper name of a particular scientist occurs, as the latter reports particular observations or perceptions at a particular time, and such sentences, like all other sentences of unified science, are certainly revisable in the progress of scientific knowledge. Moreover, over and above protocol-sentences in this sense there are no sentences expressing a peculiarly first-personal epistemological point of view, for it is precisely here that we slide into idealistic metaphysics:

> Even in Carnap's case we here encounter the emphasis on an "I" that is familiar to us from idealistic philosophy. In the universal-slang one can no more meaningfully speak of one's "own" protocol than of "now" or "here." In the

physical language the personal names are replaced precisely by coordinates and state-magnitudes. One can only distinguish an "Otto-protocol" from a "Karl-protocol" but not, in universal-slang, one's "own protocol [*eigenes Protokoll*]" from an "other's protocol [*fremden Protokoll*]." The entire problematic of the "auto-psychological [*Eigenpsychischen*]" and the "hetero-psychological [*Fremdpsychischen*]" disappears.

"Methodological" solipsism and "methodological" positivism (cf. [Carnap (1932a)], p. 461) do not become thereby more useful by adding the word "methodological" (cf. [Neurath (1932a)], p. 401). (1932b, pp. 211–2)

We can thus only overcome such metaphysics once and for all by rigorously confining ourselves within the single universal language of physicalism.

Carnap (1932b) responds by again considering two possible forms for the total language of science. In the first alternative there is a separate language of protocol-sentences distinct from the "system-language" or physical language. In this case, in order to test sentences in the system-language, there must be rules of translation of the latter into the protocol-language. In the second alternative, however, protocol-sentences belong to the system-language—either in Neurath's special linguistic form involving personal names or, following a suggestion by Karl Popper, having any linguistic form whatsoever. And, particularly if we follow Popper's suggestion, it is then entirely clear that protocol-sentences are in no way epistemologically privileged. For this reason, above all, the Neurath-Popper form of language is actually preferable, for, according to Carnap (1932b, p. 228), it is indeed most effective in overcoming the "residue of idealistic absolutism . . . in the logical positivism of our Circle"—the residue of "an absolutism of the 'given', of 'experience', of the 'immediate phenomena'"— and Neurath, in particular, deserves full credit for this antimetaphysical move, since, within the Vienna Circle, "Neurath was the first to turn decisively against this absolutism, in that he rejected the unrevisability of protocol-sentences."

So far, except for a new emphasis on universal revisability within the physical language, Carnap (1932b) appears quite similar to Carnap (1932a). Nevertheless, there are two significant differences. In the first place, when considering the first alternative (protocol-language separate from the system-language), Carnap drops all references to a first-person epistemological point of view. Instead, he proceeds entirely behavioristically, by imagining a "machine" (or a human being) which responds with various "signals" to various stimuli; rules of translation are then stated for interpreting these signals in terms of the system-language. And it is precisely this purely behavioristic understanding of the first alternative that leads Carnap (1932b, p. 228) to state that "[idealistic] absolutism can be excluded . . . also with the first of the two language forms here treated." In the second place, however, Carnap explicitly appeals to his own antimetaphysical standpoint of "tolerance," a standpoint he is simultaneously developing in his more general theory of logical syntax or metalogic:

Not only the question whether protocol-sentences occur outside or inside the system-language, but also the further question of their more exact characterization, is to be answered, it seems to me, not by an assertion, but rather by a convention [*Festsetzung*]. Although I earlier ([Carnap, (1932a)], p. 438) left this question open and only indicated a few possible answers, I now think that the different answers do not contradict one another. They are to be understood as suggestions for conventions; the task consists in investigating these various possible conventions with regard to their consequences and in testing their practical utility. (1932b, p. 216)[3]

It is here that the fundamental difference between Carnap's antimetaphysical standpoint and Neurath's first becomes fully explicit. For Carnap metaphysics is overcome by adopting the metalogical standpoint of logical syntax, the discipline he soon comes to call *Wissenschaftslogik*, relative to which a plurality of alternative forms for the total language of science is possible and legitimate. For Neurath, as I have repeatedly observed, metaphysics can only be overcome by deliberately confining ourselves to a single language—the "universal-slang" of physicalism.

And it is here, too, that we see the full force of Neurath's naturalism. There is only the language of unified empirical science. So the discipline Carnap calls *Wissenschaftslogik* must itself belong to empirical science, that is, to the psychological-sociological study of the actual linguistic behavior of empirically and historically given scientists as they continuously fashion and refashion the "ship" of knowledge (that is, the totality of currently accepted statements) without ever being in a position, in the famous words of Neurath (1932b, p. 206), "to build it anew out of the best constituents"—so that there is also a limit to the logical precision we can require or attain, since "imprecise, unanalyzed terms ('*Ballungen*') . . . are always in some way constituents of the ship." For Carnap, by contrast, *Wissenschaftslogik* is a fully precise and rigorous subdiscipline of mathematical logic, where our task is not to describe actual linguistic behavior (which of course always remains less than fully precise) but rather to investigate in a fully precise way the consequences of adopting one or another *proposal* for the logical form of the total language of science. Carnap thus hopes to overcome traditional metaphysics by reinterpreting its "theses" as logico-linguistic proposals. Neurath, by contrast, will have none of this reinterpretive project but aims rather at a complete dismissal of the metaphysical tradition on behalf of empirical science.

We know that the fundamental contrast between Neurath's naturalism and Carnap's conception of *Wissenschaftslogik* is central to understanding Hempel's own later turn from the latter point of view to a version of the former one. (I was privileged to have heard two of Hempel's last public statements of this contrast: the first at a conference in honor of Thomas Kuhn at the Massachusetts Institute of Technology in May 1990; the second at the first biannual Pittsburg-Konstanz Colloquium in the Philosophy of Science, on the occasion of Hempel's receipt of an honorary degree from the University of Konstanz, in May 1991. On both occasions Hempel joyfully described his own conversion from the point of view of Carnapian "explication" or "rational reconstruction" to the point of view of Kuhnian historical and sociocultural naturalism as a return to Neurath's original conception of the ineliminable necessity of "*Ballungen*.")[4] In order fully to understand the roots of Hempel's later development, however, it is first necessary to consider the remainder of the protocol-sentence debate, beginning with the exchange between Neurath and Schlick that precipitated Hempel's first official involvement in the pages of *Analysis*.

Schlick (1934) is a response to Neurath (1932b) and Carnap (1932b). Schlick's main complaint, as is well known, is that the holistic conception represented by the latter two papers, according to which all sentences of science are revisable through confrontation with other such sentences, leads to a version of the "coherence theory of truth." Any logically consistent system of sentences, on this conception, is thus an equally good candidate for the "true" system of sentences. But what empiricism rather requires, according to Schlick, is that some particular class of statements, those reporting the "raw facts" of immediate experience, be absolutely fixed in the process of empirical testing.

> The absurdity [of the coherence theory] is only avoided if one does not permit the rejection or correction of arbitrary assertions, but rather indicates those which are to be held fast and in accordance with which the remainder have to be judged. (1934, p. 87)

And Schlick finds such fixed assertions, as is also well known, in his "*Konstatierungen*," assertions that, according to Schlick (1934, p. 89), "express a *present* fact of one's own 'perception' or 'experience' [*einen in der Gegenwart liegenden Tatbestand der eigenen 'Wahrnehmung' oder des 'Erlebens'*]." For my understanding of such an assertion, according to Schlick (1934, p. 97), consists precisely in the circumstance that "I [ostensively] compare it with the facts"—the very facts that make it true—so that "together with its sense I simultaneously grasp its truth." In this way, *Konstatierungen*, in a manner closely analogous to analytic statements, are necessarily absolutely certain.

Neurath (1934) is a point-by-point rebuttal of Schlick. Neurath of course rejects the demand for fixed and absolutely certain assertions against which all others are to be tested. And, in accordance with his (and Carnap's) earlier papers, he rejects all talk of a comparison between sentences, on the one side, and "reality" or "experience," on the other: what takes place in unified science, by contrast, is simply a comparison, and consequent mutual adjustment, involving sentences with one another. But what is of perhaps most interest is the way in which Neurath responds to Schlick's problematic of the "coherence theory of truth" and the possibility, in particular, that any logically consistent system of sentences may count as "true." Neurath (1934, p. 356) argues that "[t]he terms 'sentence', 'language', etc. must be historically-sociologically defined." Moreover, when one takes such a historical-sociological perspective on science, one sees, according to Neurath (1934, p. 352), that "[t]he practice of life reduces all the ambiguity [arising from alternative mutually consistent systems of hypotheses] very quickly," so that in real life "the individual scarcely has the power properly to carry out *one* system, to speak nothing of several systems." In science as an actual historically given social system, in other words, as opposed to any mere logical collection of propositions imagined by philosophers, Schlick's problem posed by the threat of mere logical coherence as our "criterion of truth" simply does not arise.

Schlick, for his part, had already implicitly rejected such a historical-sociological perspective on science. In particular, Schlick (1934, p. 90) considers the "theoretical" possibility that "the assertions made by all other people about the word would in no way be confirmed by my own observations," where in such a case, according to the Neurath-Carnap view, "I would simply have to sacrifice my own 'protocol-sentences', since the overwhelming mass of the others, all in harmony with one another, would stand opposed to them." This, however, could never happen.

> I would under no circumstances whatsoever give up my own observation-sentences. Rather, I find that I can only assume a cognitive system into which they fit without mutilation. And I could always construct such a system. I need only view the other people as dreaming fools, in whose madness lies a remarkable method, or—to express the same thing more objectively—I would say that the others live in another world than I, which has only so much in common with mine that communication in the same language is possible. In any case, no matter which world-view I construct, I would always test its truth only against my own experience. I would never allow this resting place to be stolen from me; my own observation-sentences would always be the ultimate criterion. I would, so to speak, cry out: "What I see, I see!" (1934, pp. 90–1)

And it is in this essentially individualistic conception of science, according to which all demands of intersubjectivity can, at least in principle, be sacrificed on behalf of one's "own" subjective experience, that Schlick's version of "empiricism" fundamentally diverges from both Neurath's sociological naturalism and Carnap's logico-linguistic pluralism.

In January 1935 Hempel was invited by Susan Stebbing to present a lecture in London on the latest developments within the Vienna Circle and, in particular, on the exchange between Neurath and Schlick that had just appeared in the pages of *Erkenntnis*. Hempel (1935a) is a "hurriedly condensed" version of this lecture[5]—prepared, as is indicated at the end of the published version, in December 1934. Hempel (1935a, p. 49) accepts Schlick's characterization of "the logical positivists' theory of truth" (that is, the theory of Neurath and Carnap) as a "coherence-theory," although of a "restrained" kind. Hempel then sets out to describe the historical evolution of this theory from the ideas of Wittgenstein's *Tractatus*, understood as a "correspondence-theory." A decisive step in this evolution, and one that finally enables us to clear up the confusions surrounding the notion of a correspondence or comparison between sentences and "facts," is Carnap's introduction of the distinction between the formal and the material modes of speech:

> As Carnap has shown, each non-metaphysical consideration of philosophy belongs to the domain of Logic of Science, unless it concerns an empirical ques-

tion and is proper to empirical science. And it is possible to formulate each statement of Logic of Science as an assertion concerning certain properties and relations of scientific propositions only. So also the concept of truth may be characterized in this formal mode of speech, namely, in a crude formulation, as a sufficient agreement between the system of acknowledged protocol-statements and the logical consequences which may be deduced from the statement and other statements which are already adopted. (1935a, p. 54)

Hempel thus appeals to Carnap's conception of *Wissenschaftslogik* ("Logic of Science"), in particular, in formulating an explicit statement—admittedly "crude"—of the coherence theory of truth.

It is precisely this characterization of the concept of truth, however, that allows us to respond to Schlick's main objection—the specter of alternative, internally consistent but mutually incompatible, "true" systems of sentences:

As Carnap and Neurath emphasize, there is indeed no formal, no logical difference between the two compared systems, but an *empirical* one. The system of protocol statements which we call true, and to which we refer in every day life and science, may only be characterized by the historical fact, that it is the system which is actually adopted by mankind, and especially by the scientists of our cultural circle; and the "true" statements in general may be characterized as those which are sufficiently supported by that system of actually adopted protocol statements. (1935a, p. 57)

It is theoretically possible, Hempel (1935a, p. 57) continues, that "the protocol statements produced by different men would not admit the construction of one unique system of scientific statements," but fortunately this abstract possibility is not realized in fact, since "by far the greater part of scientists will sooner or later come to an agreement, and so, as an empirical fact, a perpetually increasing and expanding system of coherent statements and theories results from their protocol statements." In this way, by synthesizing Carnap's conception of *Wissenschaftslogik* with Neurath's historical-sociological naturalism, Hempel hopes to provide a definitive clarification of the Neurath-Schlick debate.

We can here leave aside a more detailed discussion of Schlick (1935), which is a gently mocking rejoinder to Hempel (1935a), as well as the ensuing Hempel (1935b) and Hempel (1936). Although the last two papers emphatically underscore Hempel's commitment to the "radical physicalism" represented by the Neurath-Carnap camp, none of these adds anything essentially new to my consideration here of the protocol-sentence debate. By contrast, a striking new twist to this debate is added by further discussion of the concept of truth among the participants, stimulated, above all, by Alfred Tarski's work.

Carnap, when first articulating his ideas on logical syntax and *Wissenschaftslogik* in 1934, initially denied that the concept of truth, as applied to empirical propositions, is a meaningful component of *Wissenschaftslogik*:

[T]*ruth and falsehood are not genuine syntactic properties;* whether a sentence is true or false cannot generally be seen by its design, that is, by the kinds and serial order of its symbols. (This fact has usually been overlooked, because one has normally been dealing not with descriptive, but only with logical languages, and in relation to these 'true' and 'false' in fact coincide with 'analytic' and 'contradictory', respectively, and are thus syntactic concepts.) (1934a, 268–9)[6]

Indeed, on precisely this basis, Carnap objected, in a letter of 23 January 1935, against Hempel's attempt to formulate a coherence theory of truth within *Wissenschaftslogik*:

I am not entirely sure whether it is appropriate to designate our conception as coherence-theory. I would like to characterize in this way only a conception that uses the agreement of sentences among one another *as sole criterion of truth.*

. . .

But "true" is not a syntactic concept, [and] cannot be formally characterized! Better so: there is no theoretical criterion of truth in the domain of synthetic sentences. (ASPRC 102-14-42)

With this last remark, explicitly directed against Hempel's attempt, already cited, to synthesize Carnapian *Wissenschaftslogik* with the sociological conception of truth due to Neurath, Carnap has in fact decisively undercut that synthesis.

By September of that same year, at an International Congress for Scientific Philosophy held in Paris, the Neurath-Carnap synthesis has become fully and explicitly unraveled. Carnap (1963, p. 61) describes how he had in the meantime become acquainted with Tarski's semantic definition of truth, and had urged Tarski to present a paper, published as Tarski (1936), in which the new conception was first made publicly accessible to the wider community of scientific philosophers. At the same Congress, and with explicit reference to Tarski's paper, Carnap himself presented a paper, published as Carnap (1936b), which cast an entirely new light on the protocol-sentence debate. Carnap (1936b, p. 18) introduces a sharp distinction between the concepts "true," on the one side, and "confirmed" or "scientifically accepted," on the other. The former is a timeless, logical concept, whose unobjectionable formal definition within metalogic has just been achieved by Tarski. The latter, by contrast, is a temporally relative, nonlogical concept, whose adequate articulation, according to Carnap (1936b, p. 19) requires "not a logical, but rather a (psychological-sociological) presentation belonging to empirical science." From this point of view, the Neurath-Hempel characterization of "true," as applying to those sentences currently accepted by the community of scientists, is thus seen to rest on a fundamental confusion.

Carnap does not explicitly draw this last moral himself, but he does proceed to apply his new distinction to the protocol-sentence debate. Although it is true that no sentences of science are ever definitively established, with no possibility of revision, in the actual process of confirmation, it is still important, according to Carnap (1936b, pp. 19–20), to distinguish between two different types of sentences (which, however, form a continuum): the "directly testable" and those which are "only indirectly testable." The former are sufficiently testable by "one or few observations" to be accepted (at least for the moment). In the case of the latter sentences, such as universal laws, for example, no such "direct" process of acceptance is possible, but only a gradual increase of confirmation in terms of already accepted singular sentences of the first kind. There are thus two essentially different operations constituting the process of confirmation: "confrontation of a sentence with observation" (sec. 1) and "confrontation of a sentence with already previously accepted sentences" (sec. 2). In the case of the first operation, moreover, we can easily state simple rules in accordance with which such direct acceptance takes place, for example, "[w]hen one sees a key, one may accept the sentence, 'here lies a key'," and "[a]t this point," Carnap (1936b, p. 21) continues, "the definition of the concept of truth enters into the problem of confirmation; the rules in question follow from this definition."

The lesson Carnap here draws from Tarski, therefore, is not only that the Neurath-Hempel characterization of "true" is inadequate, but also that there are importantly correct elements in Schlick's opposing conception. Thus, Carnap immediately points out that Tarski's definition, in general, and his own description of the operation of "confrontation of a sentence with observation," in particular, entails that there is a perfectly good sense in speaking of a comparison between facts and propositions after all:

> If one understands by "comparison of a sentence with a fact" that procedure we have earlier called the first operation, then it is to be granted that this procedure is not only possible, but necessary for scientific confirmation. (1936b, p. 21)

Indeed, Carnap strongly warns against neglecting such "confrontation" in terms quite congenial to Schlick:

> One must also be careful, if one denies the formulation in question ["comparison of a sentence with a fact"], that one does not reject the procedure likely meant by it, namely, confrontation with observation, and does not overlook its significance and necessity by placing only the second operation ["confrontation of a sentence with already previously accepted sentences"] in the foreground. . . . If someone were really to deny the first operation—and I do not believe that anyone from our Circle wants to do this—then his conception would no longer be empiricist. (1936b, p. 23)

Although Carnap here continues to diverge from Schlick in rejecting any absolute fixity and unrevisability for observation-sentences, he has nonetheless arrived at a conception of both truth and confirmation which is much closer to Schlick's insistent "empiricism" than to the "coherentism" of Neurath and Hempel. Tarski's theory of truth has enabled him to have his cake and eat it.

Carnap's deviation from the Neurath-Hempel position, and the Tarskian conception of truth on which this deviation was based, did not of course pass unnoticed. On the contrary, Carnap's and Tarski's papers at the Paris Congress provoked, according to Carnap (1963, p. 61), "vehement opposition" and "long and heated debates." As Carnap himself reports on these debates (p. 61), Neurath, in particular, "believed that the semantical concept of truth could not be reconciled with a strictly empiricist and anti-metaphysical point of view"— on account, presumably, of the "timeless" and "absolute" character of this concept that sharply separates the "true" sentences of science from those accepted at any particular time (including the present). For, as we have seen, Neurath had branded any such separation as meaningless and metaphysical in his very first contribution to the protocol-sentence debate. Within a couple of months, however, things had cooled off considerably. In particular, in notes on Carnap's Paris presentation sent to Hempel on 15 November 1935 (ASPRC 110-02-01), Neurath admits that the concept Tarski has defined is in fact legitimate. It is not obvious, however, that this captures the unambiguous meaning of the traditional conception of truth. In particular, the characterization Neurath has defended, according to which the "true" sentences are indeed those agreeing with the scientific "encyclopedia" we have currently picked out, is also a perfectly acceptable clarification of the traditional conception—which, moreover, has perhaps even better claims to historical continuity. In any case, because there is thus more than one permissible clarification of the traditional conception, Carnap should frame his own defense of the semantic concept rather as a *suggestion*.[7]

Hempel, in comments sent along to Carnap together with Neurath's notes on 17 November, emphatically endorses this last idea:

> Here it seems to me that N[eurath']s first remark is very important. It also seems to me that, e.g., the interpretation chosen by N[eurath] of "true" as "belonging to the accepted encyclopedia" is entirely defensible, even in the sense of historical continuity. Therefore, perhaps better [set up] the first section as suggestion. (ASPRC 110-02-03)

Moreover, Hempel continues to identify the "problem of truth" with the problem of verification or confirmation in his own writings, and proposes, in Hempel (1937, p. 206), a method "to establish the criteria for truth" that "will consist in a logical and methodological analysis of the procedures which are employed, in science, to verify a proposition." The main result of Hempel (1937, p. 216) is then that "it is logically impossible ever to arrive at a complete proof of the truth [of any empirical proposition]," so that "[f]or this reason it is preferable not to speak of empirical truth or falsity." Toward the end of his reflections, to be sure, Hempel does admit that Tarski has recently defined a concept of truth that is not to be equated with confirmation or verification in this way. Indeed, prodded especially by Kokoszynska (1936), Hempel admits that Tarski's concept is in fact "absolute" in being (timelessly) independent of any historically given state of knowledge. Nevertheless, in perfect harmony with his and Neurath's point of view in November 1935, Hempel (1937, p. 227) concludes that "each of the two concepts ('truth' and 'confirmation') clarifies and makes precise a certain facet of the ordinary and rather vague notion of truth."

Carnap, however, by no means accepts this point of view. Entirely ignoring the pleas from Neurath and Hempel in November 1935 to frame his own discussion of truth as merely one possible "suggestion," he persists, in the published version, Carnap (1936b), in insisting on the necessity for sharply distinguishing between "true" and "confirmed." Why does Carnap, the thoroughgoing advocate of "tolerance," staunchly resist such an attitude here?

Light is shed on this question by a second paper Carnap delivered in Paris, published as Carnap (1936a). Carnap (1936b) characterizes truth as a logical concept, whereas confirmation, by contrast, is counted as a nonlogical, "psychological-sociological" concept. The main point of Carnap (1936a) is that such a sharp distinction between logical and psychological considerations is absolutely central to fully clarifying the nature of properly scientific philosophy, especially as it has been practiced within the Vienna Circle:

> It seems to me that *epistemology*, in the form it has taken until now, is an *unclear mixture out of psychological and logical constituents*. That holds also for the works of our Circle, not excepting my own earlier works. Many unclarities and misunderstandings result from this. Thus, a short time ago, for example, an article in *Erkenntnis* called forth a great variety of hesitations and objections and lively discussions through its apparently logical theses, until the author finally explained that his statements are not meant as logical, but rather as psychological analysis. From this we see how important it is, in the case of every so-called epistemological discussion, to make clear and explicit whether logical or psychological questions are meant. (1936a, pp. 36–7)

There can be very little doubt, moreover, that the article in question is precisely Schlick (1934). For the conclusion of Schlick (1935) contains the following words:

> It is one thing to ask how the system of science has been built up and why it is generally believed to be true, and another thing to ask why I myself (the individual observer) accept it as true. You may regard my article on "Das Fundament der Erkenntnis" as an attempt to answer the last question. It is a psychological question. (1935, p. 69)

Carnap (1936b) has then evidently translated the distinction Schlick makes here into Carnap's own distinction between the "second operation" ("confrontation of a sentence with already previously accepted sentences") and the "first operation" ("confrontation of a sentence with observation"). Carnap's present point of view, therefore, is that the entire Schlick-Neurath-Hempel debate rests on a fundamental unclarity about the distinction between logical and psychological questions—an unclarity which is fully resolved, in Carnap's mind, by Carnap (1936b). It is no wonder, then, that Carnap resolutely insists on the central importance of this distinction, together with the closely related distinction between truth and confirmation.

Carnap's first major publication in English was Carnap (1936–37). This famous paper further develops and applies the basic point of view of Carnap (1936a) and Carnap (1936b). Carnap repeatedly insists, in particular, on the importance of distinguishing psychological and logical investigations. Indeed, this distinction determines the very structure of the paper, the heart of which consists of section 2, "Logical Analysis of Confirmation and Testing," section 3, "Empirical Analysis of Confirmation and Testing." In describing this two-part structure in the introductory section (1), Carnap (1936–37, p. 421) remarks that "[t]he difficulties in discussions of epistemological and methodological problems are, it seems, often due to a mixing up of logical and empirical questions; therefore it seems desirable to separate the two analyses as clearly as possible." And later in section 1 Carnap repeats the warning from Carnap (1936a) almost word for word:

> In fact, however, epistemology in the form it usually takes—including many of the publications of the Vienna Circle—is an unclear mixture of psychological and logical components. We must separate it into its two kinds of components if we wish to come to clear, unambiguous concepts and questions. (1936–37, p. 429)

Carnap (1936b) is equally important, however, for the primary "empirical" or "psychological" element introduced in section 3 is precisely the notorious explanation of "observable":

> *Explanation 1.* A predicate "P" of a language L is called *observable* for an organism (e.g., a person) N, if, for suitable arguments, e.g., "b," N is able under suitable circumstances to come to a decision with the help of few observations about a full sentence, say "P(b)," . . . of such a high degree that he will either accept or reject "P(b)." (1936–37, 454–5)

This explanation, which, according to Carnap (1936–37, p. 454), belongs "strictly speaking, to a biological or psychological theory of language as a kind of human behavior," again repeats, almost word for word, the explanation of "directly testable" sentence from Carnap (1936b).[8]

Just as in Carnap (1936b), therefore, Carnap is here envisioning a two-step procedure of testing or confirmation: confrontation of a sentence with observations, on the one hand, and confrontation of a sentence with other previously accepted sentences, on the other. The latter procedure, moreover, is an essentially logical one. Once certain initial sentences are accepted on the basis of observations, all remaining operations and comparisons involve purely logical relationships among sentences—just the sort of relationships that are described in section 2. Carnap himself emphasizes this point at the very beginning of section 3:

> We shall take two descriptive, i.e., non-logical, terms of this field as *basic terms* for our following considerations, namely, "*observable*" and "*realizable.*" All other terms, and above all the terms "confirmable" and "testable," which are the chief terms of our theory, will be defined on the basis of the two basic terms mentioned; in the definitions we shall make use of the logical terms defined in the foregoing chapter [sec. 2]. (1936–37, p. 454)

Thus even Carnap's "empirical analysis of confirmation and testing," the heart of which consists in a number of "definitions" and "theorems," takes place largely within the purely formal discipline of "logical syntax."

Here the fundamental tension between Carnap's conception of *Wissenschafts-logik* and Neurath's has become intolerable. According to Neurath's naturalistic understanding of this discipline, there is only the single unified language of empirical science. There is no room, therefore, for a metalanguage or syntax language describing the process of empirical testing from some idealized point of view outside the language of empirical science itself. Neurath's conception of *Wissenschaftslogik* is thus a historical-sociological one, wherein we describe how science, considered as an actual social system, operates with empirically and factually given real sentences and utterances (as opposed to mere "serial-structures" belonging to "pure syntax").[9] From this historical-sociological point of view, as we have seen, the actual comparison of sentences and utterances among one another is indeed placed in the foreground (although it is also important, to be sure, that some of these are what we call protocol-sentences). Moreover, as we have also seen, it results from this point of view, in addition, that there is a limit to the precision that can be required or attained in the actual historical-social process. We can certainly introduce logical precision into our actual scientific methods, by axiomatization, for example, but it makes no sense either to represent or to replace our actual procedures by a fully precise logical version. An ineliminable residue of "imprecise, unanalyzed terms ('*Ballungen*') . . . are always in some way constituents of the ship."

In a letter to Carnap of 27 October 1935, sent along with his own comments on the manuscript version of Carnap (1936–37), which "are mostly of a purely technical nature," Hempel replies to a question Carnap posed to him concerning whether he should attempt to rewrite the manuscript in response to some fundamental objections from Neurath.

Although I understand N[eurarath']s tendencies in this connection, and would go along with them to a certain extent, I still have certain hesitations about recommending this radical procedure in the present situation: first, it would likely be very tedious to modify the entire article from this point of view, and second, it seems to me difficult to carry through the formal consideration concerning the testability of sentences with operators [i.e., quantifiers] and the like with reference to such vague initial concepts. N[eurath] of course rages when he hears such arguments, but I say to him on the other side: if one presupposes that all concepts and sentences of the language about which one undertakes logical investigations are as vague and smeary [*schmierig*] as N[eurath] would like, then there is properly speaking no longer a point of entry for the least amount of logical analysis. (The language admitted by N[eurath] would be syntactically characterized thus: the sentences of the language are *schmierige Ballungen*, and no transformation rule [is] without exception.) (In this connection it seems to me that N[eurath] is entirely correct in his remark that one may shut oneself off from many insights by taking unsuitable models as one's basis. The question now is: Is logic in the form you presuppose an unsuitable model, and what can such an assertion, strictly taken, mean?) (ASPRC 102-14-40)

Hempel thus appears to be clearly torn here between Neurath's naturalism, on the one side, and Carnap's conception of *Wissenschaftslogik*, on the other.

In an excited letter to Neurath of 22 September 1938, by contrast, Hempel seems quite strongly inclined in Neurath's direction—stimulated, this time, by a surprising source. Since this letter sheds considerable light, I believe, on Hempel's later development, I here quote a substantial piece of it.

> Your remarks about discussion with Tarski interest me very much. On the whole I had a very pleasing impression, not only because T[arski] is in general very sharp and stimulating, but also more specifically in reference to the questions of empiricism. Among others, a conversation with him about the logic of testing empirical hypotheses made a very great impression on me. T[arski] thought, of course, that the Wittgensteinian idea of complete verifiability for empirical hypotheses is entirely naive; but also that, in his opinion, Carnap's logical theory in Test[ability] and Meaning, based on much more liberal principles, did *not* achieve what was desired: in fact he is acquainted with no single example of a reduction-sentence that actually reduces a concept, say of physical theory, to concepts of the observation-language in materially correct fashion (i.e., so that the empirical investigator would agree). All examples known to him, e.g., C[arnap']s example "soluble," are schematizations, which the empirical [investigator] must view as inappropriate: in fact it can happen that a material is put in water, does not disappear, and yet is soluble. And no matter how many additional conditions and clauses one may add, "exceptions" are still always thinkable. . . . In his opinion we so far have no theory that erects in materially adequate fashion a logical connection between theory, on the one side, and the realm of observations, on the other. . . . Tarski's hesitations are shared (and are perhaps in part stimulated) by Wundheiler and Poznanski. However, whereas the latter, as T[arski] indicated, are still hopeful about the search for a logical bridge (as Carnap and, e.g., myself, in his opinion, still take one to be constructible), it appears to him that it is at the very least not excluded that no such bridge can be forged in an adequate manner, and that the judgement of theories by means of observations perhaps follows instinctively, as it were, without being able to deduce theoretically the first predictions in the form of observation-sentences with the help of reduction-sentences, etc. (ASPRC 102-46-17)

Tarski is suggesting, then, that logic, in the form Carnap presupposes, is indeed an "unsuitable model." Whereas Carnap had appealed to Tarski's semantical conception in opposing, among other things, the sociological naturalism represented by Neurath's and Hempel's account of truth as community-wide agreement, a different, more skeptical side of Tarski can now be enlisted on behalf of precisely the "*schmierige Ballungen*" favored by Neurath.

What I find most remarkable here is that it is essentially Tarski's argument, although in a clearer and more explicit form, that constitutes the centerpiece of Hempel (1988). And this article, published, appropriately enough, in *Erkenntnis*, is in turn the centerpiece of Hempel's later conversion, noted several times already, from the Carnapian program of logical "explication" or "logical reconstruction" to a more naturalistic emphasis on historical, sociological, and other broadly "pragmatic" factors.[10]

Hempel (1988, p. 148) raises the question of the logical relationship between two sentences: "*b* is a metal bar to which iron filings are clinging," and "*b* is a magnet." According to what Hempel calls the problem of "theoretical or inductive assent" (sec. 3), there is no deductive route from the first sentence to the second, even in the context of the whole of the theory of magnetism—for, according to Hempel (1988, p. 149), "the theory of magnetism surely contains no general principle to the effect that when iron filings cling to a metal bar, then the bar is a magnet." This problem is of course well known and often discussed. What is not so well understood, however, is the problem of "provisoes" (sec. 4), according to which there is not even a deductive route from the second sentence to the first, again even in the context of the whole of the theory of magnetism. For the theory of magnetism does not rule out the presence of disturbing factors (perhaps other counteracting magnetic forces, for example) which prevent the iron filings clinging to the magnet in this case. We can arrive at the result that the iron filings will in fact cling only by adding a *ceteris paribus* clause, which, according to Hempel (1988, p. 156), remains necessarily "vague and elusive." In particular, we cannot use such a *ceteris paribus* clause even to generate a determinate *probability* that the filings will cling—for, according to Hempel,

> surely, the theory of magnetism contains no sentences of this kind [probabilistic laws connecting our two sentences]; it is a matter quite beyond its scope to state how frequently air currents, disturbing further magnetic fields, or other factors will interfere with the effect in question. (1988, p. 153)

And, more generally, according to Hempel (1988, p. 158), since "[a] scientific theory propounds an account of certain kinds of empirical phenomena, but it does not pronounce on what other kinds there are," there is no way precisely to formulate the proviso ruling out *all* disturbing factors within any particular such theory.

This "problem of provisoes" is of course identical to the problem Tarski had raised for Carnap's account of theoretical terms in Carnap (1936–37). Here "magnetic" plays the role of "soluble," and "iron filings cling" is the observational counterpart of "dissolves in water." Just as Tarski had pointed out that a material may be soluble without dissolving in water and that "no matter how many additional conditions and clauses one may add, 'exceptions' are still always thinkable," Hempel here points out that the very same situation holds with respect to the logical relationship between his two sentences. Accordingly, Hempel makes perfectly clear how his problem bears on Carnap's account of reduction-sentences in section 5, which begins, in fact, with an explicit criticism of Carnap's theory:

> The foregoing considerations show in particular that when a theory contains interpretive sentences in the form of explicit definitions or of Carnapian reduction chains based on the antecedent vocabulary, the applicability of these sentences is usually subject to the fulfillment of provisoes; they cannot be regarded as unequivocal complete or partial criteria of applicability for theoretical expressions. (1988, p. 151)

Hempel's rejection of the Carnapian program of "Testability and Meaning" in 1988 is therefore entirely of a piece with the Tarskian rejection of the same program that Hempel had reported to Neurath some fifty years before.

It is by no means surprising, then, that the conclusion of Hempel (1988) points in the same naturalistic direction that had been most strongly defended, in the context of the earlier discussions, by Neurath:

> There is a distinct affinity, I think, between the perplexing questions concerning the appraisal of provisoes in the application of scientific theories and the recently much discussed problems of theory choice in science.
>
> As Kuhn in particular has argued in detail, the choice between competing theories is influenced by considerations concerning the strength and the relative importance of various desirable features exhibited by the rival theories; but these considerations resist adequate expression in the form of precise explicit criteria. The choice between theories in the light of those considerations, which are broadly shared within the scientific community, is not subject to, nor learned by means of, unambiguous rules. Scientists acquire the ability to make such choices in the course of their professional training and careers, somewhat in the matter in which we acquire the use of our language largely without benefit of explicit rules, by interaction with competent speakers.
>
> Just as, in the context of theory choice, the relevant idea of superiority of one theory to another has no precise explication and yet its use is strongly affected by considerations shared by scientific investigators, so in the inferential application of theories to empirical contexts, the idea of the relevant provisoes has no precise explication, yet it is by no means arbitrary and its use appears to be significantly affected by considerations akin to those affecting theory choice. (1988, p. 162)

That Hempel's later turn in a strongly Kuhnian direction may at the same time be viewed as a return to the conception earlier represented within the Vienna Circle by Neurath is thus perhaps even more true than Hempel himself ever realized.

The episodes I have been reviewing form a set of brackets, as it were, around the most productive and influential phase of Hempel's career, which consists, as is well known, of a series of papers on confirmation and explanation—beginning with Hempel (1943), Hempel (1945), Hempel and Oppenheim (1945), and Hempel and Oppenheim (1948)—which dominated discussion in the discipline now known as philosophy of science for the better part of two decades.

These papers show Hempel as the master of Carnapian "explication," dedicated, above all, to finding a precise and explicit characterization in purely formal-logical terms of the crucial relationship between scientific theory, on the one side, and observational statements, on the other. Whether we look at this relationship in terms of confirmation (of theory by observational evidence) or explanation (of observational statements by theory), the central ambition is that it be reconstructed as perfectly precise and explicit, and, therefore, as "objective." This point stands out most clearly, perhaps, in the conclusion of section 2 of Hempel (1945):

> Perhaps there are no objective criteria of confirmation; perhaps the decision as to whether a given hypothesis is acceptable in the light of a given body of evidence is no more subject to rational, objective rules than is the process of inventing a scientific hypothesis or theory; perhaps, in the last analysis, it is a "sense of evidence," or a feeling of plausibility in view of the relevant data, which ultimately decides whether a hypothesis is scientifically acceptable. This view is comparable to the opinion that the validity of a mathematical proof or of a logical argument has to be judged ultimately by reference to a feeling of soundness or convincingness; and both theses have to be rejected on analogous grounds: they involve a confusion of logical and psychological considerations. . . . A rational reconstruction of the standards of scientific validation cannot, therefore, involve reference to a sense of evidence; it has to be based on objective criteria. In fact, it seems reasonable to require that the criteria of empirical confirmation, besides being objective in character, should contain no reference to the specific subject matter of the hypothesis or of the evidence in question; it ought to be possible, one feels, to set up purely formal criteria of confirmation in a manner similar to that in which deductive logic provides purely formal criteria for the validity of deductive inference. (1945, pp. 8–9)

A more explicit argument in favor of Carnapian "explication," phrased in just the terms that had most sharply divided Carnap from Neurath (and also, at least in part, from Hempel himself) in the mid- to late 1930s, could hardly be constructed or imagined.

What is the explanation for this striking turn of events? Why does Hempel now find himself firmly in the Carnapian camp, without even a memory, it seems, of the fiery opposition such a purely logical perspective on science had once provoked within the Vienna Circle (and for which he himself had once expressed considerable sympathy)? We are here faced, I believe, with one of the many consequences of the full-scale intellectual migration that moved the majority of "scientific philosophers" from Europe to the United States in the mid- to late 1930s. This cataclysmic political and geographical shift had, as recent scholarship is just beginning to reveal, the most fundamental intellectual consequences as well. In the case of the logical empiricist movement, in particular, it entailed a process of thoroughgoing adjustment and accommodation to a new cultural and political climate, a new language, and a dramatically different intellectual environment.

The Vienna Circle was founded in the midst of the cultural, political, and intellectual turmoil of the Weimar period. Neurath, in fact, viewed the Vienna Circle as the counterpart, within philosophy, of the movement for a *neue Sachlichkeit* typified by the Bauhaus—and, indeed, as providing the philosophical underpinnings for a radical form of Marxian socialism. In this perspective he was quickly joined by Carnap, although the latter, to be sure, had a much less explicitly politicized conception of philosophy than the former. In opposition to the more genteel and individualistic liberalism championed by Schlick, however, both Neurath and Carnap viewed their enterprise as part of a revolutionary intellectual movement, deeply intertwined with the other mass movements of the time. And it is in this context that both Neurath and Carnap proposed radical transformations of the discipline of philosophy itself—the former in the direction of an historical-sociological naturalism with fundamentally Marxist revolutionary ambitions, the latter in the direction of a logico-linguistic pluralism with deep affinities to the currently popular movements for an international language. In this sense, the opposition between a "right wing" and a "left wing" of the Vienna Circle that surfaced during the protocol-sentence debate had quite explicit cultural and political significance.[11]

The fall of Weimar in 1933 set off a massive intellectual migration to the New World. But the complex cultural struggles dominating the intellectual life of central Europe during the Weimar period could not be easily transplanted onto American soil. In the case of the logical empiricists, in particular, the revolutionary context and rhetoric of radical philosophical transformation, especially in light of its explicitly Marxist overtones, had to be quickly forgotten, as the erstwhile "scientific philosophers" from central Europe were embraced by the more down-to-earth and pragmatically minded American logicians and philosophers of science Charles Morris, W. V. Quine, Nelson Goodman, and Ernest Nagel. Moreover, key contributors to the old "scientific philosophy" were left behind, as neither Schlick nor Neurath made it to the New World; the former was murdered by a deranged student at the University of Vienna in 1936, and the latter died in exile in England in 1945.

Carnap, with Morris's help, settled at the University of Chicago in 1936. There, in a philosophical environment that was generally hostile to him, he began to work out his ideas on semantics, the logic of modalities, and the logical foundations of probability in the late 1930s and early 1940s. And it was at this time that he first developed the idea of philosophy as "explication," the process of reconstructing initially vague and imprecise concepts in terms of fully exact logically analyzed ones. This idea, to be sure, was certainly implicit in much of Carnap's earlier work—in the "logical reconstructions" of the *Aufbau*, for example, and in the construction of various types of formal languages (each intended to represent one or another philosophical position) characteristic of the *Syntax* period. In the 1940s, however, the idea was extracted, as it were, from the radical programmatic setting of the earlier period, and this allowed Carnap, among other things, to forge deliberate links with the much less threatening and politically loaded notion of "analysis" deriving from British philosophy. As Giere (1996, p. 340) points out, when Carnap introduces the idea of "explication" in section 2 of Carnap (1947), for example, he adds a footnote to C. H. Langford's article on "analysis" in the G. E. Moore volume of the Library of Living Philosophers, published in 1942.

With financial help from the Rockefeller Foundation, Carnap brought Hempel and his close friend Olaf Helmer to the University of Chicago for the academic year 1937–38. As Carnap (1963, p. 35) explains, "[t]he three of us talked often about logical problems, mainly those of semantics, which I was trying to develop systematically." Another close friend of Hempel, Paul Oppenheim, with whom Hempel had worked intensively in Brussels in 1935–37, emigrated to Princeton, New Jersey, in 1939. And it was in close cooperation with both Helmer and Oppenheim, as we know, that Hempel worked out the central ideas of his fundamental papers of the 1940s.

Hempel's thoroughgoing immersion in the practice of Carnapian "explication" during this period is thus easily explained. Of all the leading members of the logical empiricist movement, Hempel had always been on closest terms, from a personal point of view, with Carnap. Now, in a new country, and a new cultural and intellectual environment, he owed his very presence there to Carnap. Being himself particularly gifted in logical analysis, moreover, Hempel found himself surrounded with close friends and colleagues interested in this philosophical methodology above all. It is no wonder, then, that Hempel's major contributions of the time closely parallel Carnap's, and, more specifically, Carnap's developing work on the logical foundations of probability. Thus, for example, the argument for the "objective" and fundamentally logical character of the concept of confirmation earlier, cited from Hempel (1945), based, as it is, on Carnap's old sharp distinction between psychological and logical questions, closely parallels the discussion in Carnap (1950, secs. 11–2).[12]

The Carnap-Hempel ideal of "explication" remained the standard in philosophy of science until approximately 1960. At that time, as we know, new winds of change began to blow over the discipline from a decidedly naturalistic direction. For Hempel personally the work of Quine and Kuhn was particularly important. Quine (1960) propounded epistemological holism and attacked the sharp distinction, fundamental to Carnap's thought, between logical and empirical truth, and Quine there used a motto from Neurath (1932b) as his emblem for such a holistic and naturalistic point of view. Kuhn (1962) developed a historical and sociological perspective on scientific change, which, especially in Hempel's own eyes, could be seen as applying such a fundamentally Neurathian perspective to the detailed study of science. The tension between a Carnapian and a Neurathian conception of philosophy of science, which had fundamentally shaped his earliest work but had long since lain dormant, was stimulated, and came to life, once again. With the work that eventuated in Hempel (1988)—which, as we have seen, recapitulates a defining moment from the earlier period—Hempel awoke from what he himself soon came to regard as a dogmatic slumber. This awakening is perhaps better described, therefore, as a reawakening.

I last saw Hempel in the spring of 1992, when I delivered some lectures at Princeton on Carnap's *Aufbau* and the development of logical empiricism. Hempel was extraordinarily gracious and kind, as always, but I still remember the gently bemused look on his face when I explained my revisionary reading of the *Aufbau* as owing less to traditional empiricism and more to contemporary strains of thought of a Kantian and neo-Kantian character. I remember one moment especially when Hempel irrepressibly exclaimed that I was now becoming more Carnapian than Carnap himself ever was. Soon after I returned home I received a paper in the mail. It was a duplicate of Hempel's own copy, signed to him by the author, of Neurath (1928).

NOTES

1. For an extremely careful and detailed analysis of the protocol-sentence debate, including the early hesitations about the *Aufbau* program expressed by Neurath and Schlick, see Uebel (1992). Neurath (1928) implicitly objects to "methodological solipsism" but also, and more explicitly, to Carnap's reliance on perfectly precise logical methods. Hempel's stay in Vienna comes at the end of what Uebel characterizes as "stage one" of the debate.

2. Hempel (1982, p. 1) describes his stay as follows: "In Fall 1929 I attended Schlick's seminar in Vienna and his lectures on natural philosophy with great interest, and I heard him and Neurath debate in the lively sessions of the Vienna Circle."

3. The more general theory of logical syntax, and the conception of philosophy as *Wissenschaftslogik*, is developed at length in Carnap (1934b). In section 17 Carnap states "the *principle of tolerance*" as: "*we do not aim to set up prohibitions, but rather to stipulate conventions* [*wir wollen nicht Verbote aufstellen, sondern Festsetzungen treffen*]."

4. Section 4 of Hempel (1993), entitled "Methodology of Science: Normative or Descriptive?" explains how "Neurath rejected Carnap's idea of a rational reconstruction, or explication, of science in terms of sentences all of which had precisely specified meanings," and held that "[r]*eliance on a universal slang with its fuzzy Ballungen is inevitable in the formulation of our ideas at any stage of scientific inquiry.*" This should be compared with Hempel's prefatory remarks in Horwich (1993), which collects together the papers that were presented at the earlier occasion.

5. This characterization is given in an extremely polite letter to Schlick of 27 May 1935 (ASPRC 102-46-25), which also carefully explains the invitation from Stebbing, written on receipt of Schlick (1935).

6. This passage, which was left out of the German original of Carnap (1934b) due to lack of space, appears in section 60b of the English translation, published in 1937. Hempel, when referring to Carnap's notion of *Wissenschaftslogik* in Hempel (1935a), cites Carnap (1934b) but not (1934a).

7. Neurath prepared a report on the Congress that appeared in *Erkenntnis* (1936). He here reports the discussion in considerably milder terms than does Carnap. Indeed, according to Neurath's report (p. 399), "the presentations of Tarski and Lutman-Kokoszynskas [who had defended Tarski's theory as a reconstruction of 'the absolute concept of truth'] found a large measure of agreement," although he also reports that "[i]n the debate it was pointed out that it is not very obvious why one

would choose these terms 'absolute truth' and 'actual world', in a meaning unsuitable for every-day language, especially since through the use of these terms views of an obviously metaphysical kind may take themselves to be supported." He reports, in addition (pp. 400–1), that "Hempel warned against such consequences, since one very easily arrives at the formulation: one is confronted with *one* reality, and now has the task of describing this reality through 'the' system of true propositions."

8. This explanation, in Carnap (1936b, pp. 19–20), reads in full: "By a directly testable sentence we will mean one for which circumstances are thinkable in which we would already feel confident on the basis of one or few observations in viewing it either as so strongly confirmed that we accept it or as so strongly disconfirmed that we deny it."

9. For the distinction between "pure" and "descriptive" syntax see Carnap (1934b, sec. 2): "[*Pure syntax*] is nothing but *combinatoric* or, if you prefer, *geometry* of finite discrete serial-structures of a certain kind. *Descriptive syntax* is to pure [syntax] as physical is to mathematical geometry; it treats of the syntactic properties and relations of empirically occurring expressions (e.g., of the sentences in a certain book)." See also Carnap (1963, p. 29) for the contrast between his and Neurath's ways of approaching the syntax of language.

10. A note at the end of Hempel (1988, pp. 162–3) explains that it "has grown out of a paper read in November 1980 at a workshop held under the auspices of the Center for Philosophy of Science at the University of Pittsburgh." As I have indicated, Hempel was already discussing the problem in seminars in the early 1970s.

11. For discussion of the cultural and political context of the Vienna Circle, including remarks, in particular, on the intellectual consequences of the American immigration, see Feigl (1969), Galison (1990), and Giere (1996). For Carnap's own recollections of his and Neurath's political attitudes, see Carnap (1963, pp. 22–4, 51–2); for "language planning" and international languages, see Carnap (1963, pp. 67–71).

12. In 1945 Carnap presented (1945a; 1945b) his new conception of inductive logic for the first time. He explains (1945a, p. 95) that a "rational reconstruction" is "a theory . . . offered as a more exact formulation . . . of a body of generally accepted but more or less vague beliefs." And he begins (1945b, p. 513): "we have here an instance of that kind of problem—often important in the development of science and mathematics—where a concept already in use is to be made more exact or, rather, is to be replaced by a more exact new concept. Let us call these problems (in an adaptation of the terminology of Kant and Husserl) problems of *explication*." To the best of my knowledge, this is the first time Carnap introduces the notion of "explication" in print. (Thus it is not true, as Giere [1996, p. 340] suggests, that Carnap first publicly introduces the notion in Carnap [1947].) Moreover, although the discussion is not as developed as in Carnap (1950, secs. 11–2), Carnap also warns (1945b, pp. 524–5) against the dangers of psychologism in both deductive and inductive logic.

REFERENCES

Archives for Scientific Philosophy (ASP). University of Pittsburgh Libraries. References are to file folder number. All rights reserved.

Ayer, A. J., ed. 1959. *Logical Positivism.* New York: Free Press.

Carnap, R. 1928. *Der logische Aufbau der Welt.* Berlin: Weltkreis. Translated as *The Logical Structure of the World.* Berkeley: University of California Press, 1967.

————. 1932a. "Die physikalische Sprache als Universalsprache der Wissenschaft." *Erkenntnis* 2:432–65. Translated as *The Unity of Science*. London: Kegan Paul, 1934.

————. (1932b), "Über Protokollsätze." *Erkenntnis* 3:215–28. Translated as "On Protocol Sentences," *Nous* 21 (1987):457–70.

————. (1934a). "Die Antinomien und die Unvollständigkeit der Mathematik." *Monatshefte für Mathematik und Physik* 41:263–84.

————. (1934b). *Logische Syntax der Sprache*. Vienna: Springer. Translated as *The Logical Syntax of Language*. London: Kegan Paul, 1937.

————. 1936–37. "Testability and Meaning," *Philosophy of Science* 3:419–71, 4:1–40.

————. 1936a. "Von der Erkenntnistheorie zur Wissenschaftslogik." In *Actes du Congrès international de philosophie scientifique*. Vol. 1. Paris: Hermann.

————. 1936b. "Wahrheit und Bewährung." In *Actes du Congrès international de philosophie scientifique*. Vol. 4. Paris: Hermann, 1936. Translated (in part, together with other material) as "Truth and Confirmation" in *Readings in Philosophical Analysis*, edited by H. Feigl and W. Sellars. New York: Appleton-Century, 1949.

————. 1945a. "On Inductive Logic," *Philosophy of Science* 12:72–97.

————. 1945b. "The Two Concepts of Probability," *Philosophy and Phenomenological Research* 5:513–32.

————. 1947. *Meaning and Necessity*. Chicago: University of Chicago Press.

————. 1950. *Logical Foundations of Probability*. (Chicago: University of Chicago Press.

————. 1963, "Intellectual Autobiography." In *The Philosophy of Rudolf Carnap*, edited by P. Schilpp. La Salle, Ill.: Open Court.

Feigl, H. 1969. "The Wiener Kreis in America." In *Intellectual Migration: Europe and America, 1930–1960*, edited by D. Fleming and B. Bailyn. Cambridge: Harvard University Press.

Galison, P. 1990. "Aufbau/Bauhaus: Logical Positivism and Architectural Modernism." *Critical Inquiry* 16:709–52.

Giere, R. 1996. "From *Wissenschaftliche Philosophie* to Philosophy of Science," In *Origins of Logical Empiricism*, edited by R. Giere and A. Richardson. Minneapolis: University of Minnesota Press.

Hempel, C. G. 1935a. "On the Logical Positivists' Theory of Truth," *Analysis* 2:49–59. Also in Hempel (2000).

————. 1935b. "Some Remarks on 'Facts' and Propositions." *Analysis* 2:93–6. Also in Hempel (2000).

————. 1936. "Some Remarks on Empiricism." *Analysis* 3:33–40. Also in Hempel (2000).

————. 1937. "Le problème de la vérité." *Theoria* 3:206–46. Translated as "The Problem of Truth," in Hempel (2000).

————. 1943. "A Purely Syntactical Definition of Confirmation." *Journal of Symbolic Logic* 8:122–43.

————. 1945. "Studies in the Logic of Confirmation." *Mind* 54:1–26, 97–121. Also in Hempel (1965).

————. 1965. *Aspects of Scientific Explanation*. New York: Free Press.

————. 1973. "Rudolf Carnap, Logical Empiricist." *Synthese* 25:256–68. Also in Hempel (2000).

————. 1981. "Der Wiener Kreis und die Metamorphosen seines Empirismus." In *Das geistige Leben Wiens in der Zwischenkriegszeit*, edited by N. Leser. Vienna: Österreichischer. Translated as "The Vienna Circle and the Metamorphoses of its Empiricism," in Hempel (2000).

————. 1982. "Schlick und Neurath: Fundierung *vs.* Kohärenz in der wissenschaftlichen Erkenntnis." *Grazer philosophische Studien* 16/17:1–18. Translated as "Schlick and Neurath: Foundations vs. Coherence in Scientific Knowledge," in Hempel (2000).

————. 1988. "Provisoes: A Problem Concerning the Inferential Function of Scientific Theories." *Erkenntnis* 28:147–64. Also in Hempel (2000).

————. 1991. "Hans Reichenbach Remembered." *Erkenntnis* 35:5–10. Also in Hempel (2000).

————. 1993. "Empiricism in the Vienna Circle and in the Berlin Society for Scientific Philosophy." In *Scientific Philosophy: Origins and Developments,* edited by F. Stadler. Dordrecht: Kluwer. Also in Hempel (2000).

————. 2000. *Selected Philosophical Essays.* Edited by R. Jeffrey. Cambridge: Cambridge University Press.

Hempel, C. G., and P. Oppenheim. 1945. "A Definition of 'Degree of Confirmation'." *Philosophy of Science* 12:98–115. Also in Hempel (2000).

————. 1948. "Studies in the Logic of Explanation." *Philosophy of Science* 15:135–75. Also in Hempel (1965).

Horwich, P., ed. 1993. *World Changes: Thomas Kuhn and the Nature of Science.* Cambridge, Mass.: MIT Press.

Kokoszynska, M. 1936. "Über den absoluten Wahrheitsbegriff und einige andere semantische Begriffe." *Erkenntnis* 6:143–65.

Kuhn, T. 1962. *The Structure of Scientific Revolutions.* Chicago: University of Chicago Press.

Neurath, O. 1928. "Rezension: R. Carnap, *Der logische Aufbau der Welt* und *Scheinprobleme der Philosophie.*" *Der Kampf* 21:624–6.

————. 1931. *Empirische Soziologie. Der wissenschaftliche Gehalt der Geschichte und Nationalökonomie.* Vienna: Springer.

————. 1932b. "Soziologie im Physikalismus." *Erkenntnis* 2:393–431. Translated as "Sociology and Physicalism," in Ayer (1959), and as "Sociology in the Context of Physicalism," in Neurath (1983).

————. 1932a. "Protokollsätze." *Erkenntnis* 3:204–14. Translated as "Protocol Sentences," in Ayer (1959), and as "Protocol Statements" in Neurath (1983).

————. 1934. "Radikaler Physikalismus und 'Wirklicher Welt'." *Erkenntnis* 4:346–62. Translated as "Radical Physicalism and the Real World," in Neurath (1983).

————. 1983. *Philosophical Papers:1913–1946.* Edited by R. Cohen and M. Neurath. Dordrecht: Reidel.

Quine, W. V. 1960. *Word and Object.* Cambridge, Mass.: MIT Press.

Schlick, M. 1934. "Über das Fundament der Erkenntnis." *Erkenntnis* 4:79–99. Translated as "The Foundation of Knowledge," in Ayer (1959), and as "On the Foundation of Knowledge," in Schlick (1979).

————. 1935. "Facts and Propositions." *Analysis* 2:65–70. Also in Schlick (1979).

————. 1979. *Philosophical Papers. Vol. 2. 1925–1936.* Edited by H. Mulder and B. van de Velde-Schlick. Dordrecht: Reidel.

Tarski, A. 1936. "Grundlegung der wissenschaftlichen Semantik." In *Actes du Congrès international de philosophie scientifique.* Vol. 3. Paris: Hermann.

Uebel, T. E. 1992. *Overcoming Logical Positivism from Within: The Emergence of Neurath's Naturalism in the Vienna Circle's Protocol Sentence Debate.* Amsterdam: Rodopi.

2

Hempel's Logicist Philosophy of Mathematics

Background and Sequel

JAAKKO HINTIKKA

The main tenets of Hempel's philosophy of mathematics are easily described. This philosophy is a paradigmatic form of what is known as the logicist approach to mathematics. Its main theses are (a) that mathematical truths are analytic a priori and (b) that mathematics is a branch of logic. The second thesis can be looked upon as a way of helping to establish the former. In other words, (a) mathematical propositions cannot be disproved by any conceivable empirical evidence, but they do so only at a price: they do not convey any factual information. The second thesis (b) concerning the status of mathematics as a branch of logic is taken by Hempel to mean that

a. All the concepts of mathematics, i.e., of arithmetic, algebra, and analysis, can be defined in terms of four concepts of pure logic.
b. All the theorems of mathematics can be deduced from those definitions by means of the principles of logic (including the axioms of infinity and choice). (Hempel 1945b, p. 233)

A discussion of Hempel's philosophy of mathematics will hence be essentially a discussion of the logicist philosophy of mathematics in general. The incarnation of logicism in Hempel's thought nevertheless offers a natural occasion to contextualize it, which in turn makes it easier to appreciate its strengths and weaknesses.

By and large, the logicist approach to the foundations of mathematics has fallen into disrepute since the days of Hempel's classic exposition (1945b). It is not clear, however, who has the last word on the subject of logicism. New results have in fact been reached recently that put the entire matter in a new light. The weaknesses of Hempel's position seem to be largely due to his background. It is hence in order to see how Hempel came to hold his logicist views and how subsequent developments have affected the grounds for a logicist philosophy of mathematics.

The first observation that can be made here is that if the second thesis (b) is true, the first thesis (a) can be proved by showing that (c) logic is analytic a priori. How did Hempel and other logical positivists come to hold such a view about logic? The received answer to this question is to attribute it to the influence of Wittgenstein's *Tractatus* where it was held that logical truths are empty of any empirical content, being mere tautologies. This is a historical misperception, however. The uninformativeness of logical truths (whether they were labeled "tautologies" or "analytic" or not) had been maintained by a long tradition of philosophers on the continent, most recently before the Vienna Circle by Mach (1905, p. 300) and the early Schlick (1918, p. 96). If Wittgenstein had merely maintained the uninformativeness of logical truths, he would not have taken a single step beyond these sometime Viennese philosophers. What was new in the *Tractatus* was the striking defense of the tautological character of logical truths. He thought that he had reduced the logic we need in a true *Begriffsschrift* to truth-functional logic. And in truth-functional logic logical truths are indeed empty in that they allow (are true in) all possible circumstances, corresponding to all the different distributions of truth-values to elementary sentences. Just because they allow all these possibilities, they cannot fail to be true. But, by the same token, they are empty, for they do not exclude any possibilities and thereby convey any information.

Why did this Wittgensteinian idea of tautology fail to satisfy logical positivists like Hempel? Perhaps the question is otiose, for the Tractarian view did not satisfy Wittgenstein for long, either. The weak link in the *Tractatus* argument is the dependence of Wittgenstein's tautologicity doctrine (as applied to our actual discourse) on a crucial assumption. This assumption is the mutual independence of elementary propositions. If they are not independent of each other, some distributions of truth-values or elementary propositions are excluded for logical reasons. Then there will be logically true sentences (viz. those not admitting the excluded combinations of truth-values) that are not tautologies.

The independence assumption was given up by Wittgenstein in 1928–29. (See Hintikka 1988.) He might seem to have acted too rashly, for his own test case of color incompatibility can be accommodated by an appropriate notation. (One only needs to construe the concept of color as a mapping (function) from space-points into color-space, as was pointed out in Hintikka and Hintikka (1986, pp. 120–4).) Yet Wittgenstein's insight was fundamentally correct; in the long run the independence assumptions cannot realistically be maintained. This failure of independence (in a slightly generalized sense) can take two forms. There can be interdependencies between the nonlogical concepts expressed in our language. Furthermore, in those areas of logic that go beyond propositional logic the best approximation to elementary sentences are sometimes interdependent for logical reasons.

I will discuss the second question first. It is in effect answered by the work I did in the sixties and early seventies. (See here Hintikka 1970; 1973, chap. 10; 1989.) It suffices here to consider the situation in first-order logic. Very briefly expressed, in propositional logic each truth-function is a disjunction of conjunctions specifying a truth-distribution to elementary propositions. (In the case of two elementary propositions A, B they are $(A \ \& \ B)$, $(A \ \& \ {\sim}B)$, $({\sim}A \ \& \ B)$, $({\sim}A \ \& \ {\sim}B)$.) In a similar way, in a first-order language there are at each level of quantificational depth, certain sentences called constituents playing the same role as these con-junctions. Each sentence of that depth (or of a lower depth) can be expressed as a disjunction of some (or all) of these constituents. This disjunction is its disjunc-tive normal form. If that disjunction comprises all constituents (of that depth), it is logically true. Then it does not say anything, just because it does not exclude any possibilities. But a sentence can be logically true even if it does not admit all possibilities described by the different constituents, the reason being that some of the constituents missing from its normal form are inconsistent for logical rea-sons. That inconsistency cannot usually be seen directly, but involves more or less complicated arguments. All purely deductive argumentation can be thought of as elimination of some such merely apparent possibilities.

Now it can be seen how we can eat our tautological cake and keep it, too. The more constituents a sentence (in its disjunctive normal form) omits, the more informative it obviously is. But we can—and must—distinguish two different kinds of information. If we assign zero weight to all inconsistent constituents, we obtain a sense of information (I have called it depth information, but per-haps it would be better to call it factual information) in which all and only logi-cal truths are uninformative. But if we somehow assign nonzero weights also to the inconsistent constituents (merely apparent possibilities) we obtain an-other sense of information which might be called logical (or perhaps deductive or computational) information. (I used to call it surface information.) In this sense, a purely logical argument can produce new information. In fact, one can in principle use the surface information yielded by a logical argument as a measure of its power or nontriviality.

These developments vindicate in a sense Hempel's and other logical positiv-ists' thesis (c) of the uninformativeness of logical truths. A logical argument cannot increase the information one has available to oneself about reality, namely, its factual information. A logical truth does not convey any informa-tion about reality, because it does not rule out any prima facie possibilities that could be realized. It can rule out only apparent ones. In an important sense, Hempel was right in thinking of all logical truths as being uninformative (analytic).

At the same time, logical positivists like Hempel were mistaken in assuming in effect that factual information is the only objective sense of information. This led them into difficulties in explaining how valid logical inference can be useful and can make us aware of truths we were not previously cognizant of. Hempel was driven to maintain that the only sense in which new knowledge logical inference can yield is purely psychological. According to him,

[m]athematical as well as logical reasoning is a conceptual technique of making explicit what is implicitly contained in a set of premises. The conclusions to which this technique leads assert nothing that is *theoretically new* in the sense of not being contained in the content of the premises. But the results obtained may well by *psychologically new*: we may not have been aware, before using the techniques of logic and mathematics, what we committed ourselves to in accepting a certain set of assumptions or assertions. (Hempel 1945b, p. 235)

The possibility of defining objective measures of deductive information shows that Hempel is wrong here. He does not use the term "information," but the notions of "new" and "contains" are subject to the same ambiguity as "information." The information that the conclusion of a logical inference gives one may be "new" in the sense of increasing my deductive information, even if it does not enhance my factual information. What is crucial here is that this additional deductive information is not a purely psychological matter.

Hempel would have been right if he had made the distinction and focused on specifically the information that our sentences convey, at least potentially, about reality, in other words, on factual information. Ironically, the same criticism of missing the important distinction between the two kinds of information can be leveled at much recent discussion, but in the reverse direction. In that discussion, factual information has been largely forgotten in favor of computational (deductive, logical) information. A recognition of the ambiguity of the notion of information and an acknowledgement of the true element in Hempel's position could have a most salutary effect at the present time.

This leaves open the other question, namely, the question of how possible interdependencies between our nonlogical primitives affect the philosophical status of logical (conceptual, analytical) truth. For the sake of argument, we can think of them as being captured by explicit "meaning postulates," as they used to be called. Hempel in effect maintained that the need to resort to meaning postulates does not violate the analytic (uninformative) character of a priori truths. For the status of the meaning postulates as delineating the meanings of the terms involved made it possible to maintain that they "are true simply by virtue of definitions or of similar stipulations which determine the meaning of the key terms involved" (Hempel 1945a, p. 224). This was in fact the main defense of the noninformative (analytical) character of logical truths mounted by the logical positivists after they lost their faith in Wittgenstein's notion of tautology.

But unfortunately for the logical positivists, this idea of a priori truth as being grounded on the meanings of our expressions did not square very well with their other doctrines. Among them there was—for at least for a brief period in the early thirties—the avoidance of semantical concepts and preference of syntactical theorizing. An extreme version of this preference maintained the inexpressibility of semantical concepts of a language in the same language. Applied to our actual working language (Tarski's "colloquial language") it implied that its semantics is literally ineffable.

The syntactical viewpoint exercised in fact a stronger control of Hempel's ideas than is appropriate, at least in the light of hindsight. One indication of this is that Hempel meant by an uninterpreted axiom system a system in which even symbols for logical constants were uninterpreted. This is out of step with the intentions of such theorists (and practitioners) of the axiomatic method as Hilbert. Hilbert may have said that in his geometry you could speak, instead of points, lines, and circles, equally well of tables, chairs, and beer mugs. In other words, for Hilbert the nonlogical concepts of an axiomatic system were uninterpreted.

In contrast, the basic logical constants had to be taken to have their normal meaning, for the whole point of a Hilbertian axiom system was to see what could be proved from it by logical principles. And by that he meant interpreted logical principles.

But if we consider meaning postulates merely on the syntactical level, there is nothing to distinguish them from general empirical assumptions. Nor does it seem possible to drive a wedge between allegedly meaning-based (conventional) assumptions like meaning postulates and general factual truths in terms of speaker's linguistic behavior (including my own behavior). This is in a nutshell the basis of Quine's criticism of the analytic-synthetic distinction and by implication of Hempel's thesis of a priori truths as characterized by their being analytical.

I have argued elsewhere (Hintikka 1997) that Quine's position is based on several highly restrictive presuppositions, among them the ineffability of semantics. Hence we cannot take Quine's criticisms to imply anything like a final judgment on Hempel's views. The constructive reaction to the situation is to note that the thesis of the ineffability of semantics simply cannot be maintained. In certain interesting paradigm cases one can in fact build languages in which one can express part of its own semantics in that language itself, for instance define a truth predicate for that very language. (See Hintikka [1996a], especially "Defining truth, the whole truth and nothing but the truth.") Thus Quine's criticisms will lose much of their cutting edge in the light of such new results.

Even though I cannot undertake a full-dress rehearsal of the requisite arguments here, I can say that in the light of such results there can scarcely be any major problem about treating basic arithmetical laws as being true in virtue of the meaning of the basic mathematical terms.

In any case, this question is largely irrelevant to the evaluation of Hempel's thought. The reason is that, as far as mathematical (in the sense of arithmetical) truth is concerned, Hempel avoids the problem of the status of meaning postulates by suggesting that the basic arithmetical concepts can be explicitly defined. This means a reduction of mathematics to logic, that is, thesis (b) rather than thesis (c) or (a).

After the status of logical truths has thus been clarified, the question of the reducibility of mathematics to logic still remains open. It is because of the difficulty (many philosophers would say, impossibility) of this reduction that Hempelian logicism has been generally abandoned.

Hempel illustrates the reduction by first considering Peano arithmetic as an uninterpreted formal theory. Then he envisages an interpretation of this formal theory by means of purely logical definitions of its apparently nonlogical primitives, including "integer" and "successor." What he does not emphasize is that the crucial mathematical concepts cannot all be defined in the received core area of logic, that is, in ordinary first-order logic. These concepts apparently need for their definitions quantification over higher-order entities, such as classes and functions. Hempel considers the concepts "x is an element of class C" and "the class of all things x such that" purely logical. Even if we accept this, the fact remains that we need quantification over classes in order to define the primitives of Peano arithmetic. For instance, the principle of induction pre-supposes quantification over classes. Likewise, the definitions of successor and number presuppose the notion of equicardinality or two classes of β. And this concept apparently cannot be defined except by quantifying over higher-order objects, for instance classes or functions. For instance, we can say that α and β are equicardinal if and only if

(1) $(\exists f)(\exists g)(\forall x)(\forall y)\,(((x \in \alpha) \;\rightarrow\; (f(x) \in \beta))\;\&\;((y \in \beta) \;\rightarrow\; (g(y) \in \alpha))$
       $\&\;(y = f(x)) \leftrightarrow (x = g(y))))$

Here the functions g and f are obviously inverses of each other.

There exists nevertheless a strong suspicion of higher-order entities among philosophers just because they involve speaking about the existence of higher-order entities. They want to restrict logic to first-order quantification. Any higher-order logic involving quantification over entities other than individuals is a taboo for such critics. In Quine's words, higher-order logic is "set theory in sheep's clothing." The only viable way we have, according to this view, of deal-ing with higher-order entities, such as sets, is to construct a first-order theory about them. This is the role in which set theory has been cast. Hence math-ematics apparently cannot be reduced to logic, only to set theory. And set theory is nearly universally thought of as a mathematical rather than purely logical theory. Admittedly, in set theory, sets are dealt with on the first-order level as if they were individuals. But then mere logic does not suffice. We need there assumptions that do not seem purely logical, including the axiom of choice.

But mathematical truth cannot be characterized fully by purely logical (first-order) means even when the axioms of set theory are taken for granted. For one thing, when set theory is formulated explicitly as a first-order axiomatic theory, it cannot force its models to be of the desired kind. For instance, by the Löwenheim-Skolem theorem, it cannot force its models to be nondenumerable. The simplest general characterization of the "desired" (intended) models is that at least suitable fragments of theirs should be standard in Henkin's sense, that is, every (extensionally possible) class of entities of a certain type should have an existing representative at the next higher type level. Typically, standardness implies that all the subsets of some given set must exist. For instance, all classes of natural numbers should exist in the model. But such requirements just can-not be implemented on the first-order level—or so it seems.

It has turned out, however, that all these animadversions are predicated on too narrow a concept of logic. Ordinary first-order logic is supposed to be the logic of quantifiers. Yet it excludes many perfectly possible patterns of depen-dence and independence between quantifiers (and between quantifiers and connectives). They can be restored by a notation exemplified by $(\exists x/\forall y)$ which exempts $(\exists x)$ for the scope of $(\forall y)$. The result is a stronger first-order logic which I have proposed to call independence-friendly (IF) first-order logic.

The possibility of IF first-order logic changes radically the prospects of Hempel-type logicism. For many of the notions that could not be defined in ordinary first-order logic and were therefore exiled from the realm of pure logic turn out to be definable in IF first-order logic. For instance, the equicardinality of α and β can now be defined as follows:

(2) $(\forall a)(\forall y)(\exists z/\forall y)(\exists u/\forall x)(((x \in \alpha) \to (z \in \beta))$ & $((y \in \beta) \to (u \in \alpha))$ & $((y = z) \leftrightarrow (x = u)))$

This may be compared with (1).

Furthermore, IF first-order logic (suitably extended) not only enables the range of mathematical concepts that can be defined on the first-order level. It enables us to capture important ways of mathematical inference in purely logical terms. For instance, the principle of induction can be expressed as the contradictory negation of an IF first-order sentence. Hence all we have to do in order to accommodate such modes of reasoning in IF first-order logic is to extend it by admitting to it contradictory negation. This is necessary, for the usual negation characterized by its usual laws turns out not to satisfy *tertium non datur* in IF first-order logic, with the sole exception of the ordinary first-order fragment of IF logic. It turns out also that contradictory negation can occur only sentence-initially, never prefaced to open formulas. Now whatever complications there may be about such negations, one thing is clear. Such a formulation of the principle of induction is a completely first-order proposition. It does not involve quantification over entities other than individuals (members of the domain of a model).

In a sense, all that we need in mathematics can be done on the first-order level by means of IF logic. (See Hintikka [1996b, chap. 9].) It was seen that the crucial requirement is that all subsets of a given set must exist. This requirement can be captured on the first-order level by means of IF logic amplified by a sentence-initial contradictory negation. (The normal negation does not satisfy *tertium non datur* in IF logic.) Hence in principle all mathematics can be expressed in (extended) IF first-order logic.

In general terms, (unextended) an IF first-order language is equivalent (intertranslatable) with the Σ_1^1-fragment of the corresponding second-order language. Now instances of one of the formulations of the axiom of choice, namely, of the schema

(3) $(\forall x)(\exists y)\, S[x,y] \supset (\exists f)(\forall x)\, S[x, f(x)]$

belong to this fragment. Hence they have a translation to an IF first-order language. They are easily seen to be logically true there. In this sense, it can be seen that the axiom of choice is a purely logical principle, just as Hilbert (1922, p. 157) thought it could be shown to be.

Hempel discusses also branches of mathematics such as topology and group theory which are not based on the concept of number (1994a, pp. 235–6) and geometry (1944b). As far as they are concerned, the same two questions come up as were seen to arise in arithmetic. On the one hand, there is the question whether the axioms of such a theory can be formulated adequately by purely logical means, plus of course suitable nonlogical primitives. For instance, in Hilbert's axiomatization of elementary geometry (1903), the two axioms that apparently cannot be formulated on the first-order level are the Archimedean axiom and the so-called Axiom of Completeness.

On the other hand, it can be asked whether the defined concepts of such a mathematical discipline and our ways of arguing about them can be captured in logical terms. For instance, it may be asked whether the topological concept of continuity can be captured on the first-order level.

It would take me too far afield to attempt an exhaustive analysis here. Suffice it to say that practically all the best known axioms, concepts, and modes of reasoning can without much difficulty be formulated by means of IF first-order logic. The main exception is offered by axioms that prescribe the maximality of the domain of the intended model or models. They present a problem which goes beyond the purview of this essay.

Apart from such residual problems, Hempel's logicist thesis (b) can be vindicated to a considerable extent, not unlike the thesis (a) of the uninformative character of logical and mathematical truths. In the light of hindsight, Hempel's philosophy of mathematics is thus on the right track much more than most of its later critics have acknowledged.

Certain corrections are nevertheless in order in what Hempel says. For instance, the second clause (b) of his reducibility claim quoted earlier loses its literal sense when we realize that our basic logic, IF logic, is not axiomatizable. What is arguably true is that all the theorems of the relevant parts of mathematics are logical consequences of the appropriate definitions. However, this consequence relation cannot be exhausted by any set of rules of step-by-step deduction.

REFERENCES

Dreben, Burton S., and Juliet Floyd. 1991. "Tautology: How Not to Use the Word." *Synthese* 87:23–49.
Hempel, Carl G. 1934–35. "On the Logical Positivists' Theory of Truth." *Analysis* 2:49–59.
———. 1945a. "Geometry and Empirical Science." *American Mathematical Monthly* 52:7–17. Reprinted in *Readings in Philosophical Analysis,* edited by Herbert Feigl and Wilfred Sellars. New York: Appleton-Century-Crofts, 1949. (Page references are to the reprint.)
———. 1945b. "On the Nature of Mathematical Truth." *American Mathematical Monthly* 52:543–56. Reprinted in *Readings in Philosophical Analysis,* edited by Herbert Feigl and Wilfred Sellars. New York: Appleton-Century-Crofts, 1949. (Page references are to the reprint.)
Hilbert, David. 1903. *Grundlagen der Geometrie.* 2nd ed. Leipzig: Teubner. (This was the first edition of Hilbert's book to include the axiom of completeness.)
———. 1922. "Neubegründung der Mathematik (Erste Mitteilung)." *Abhandlungen aus dem mathematischen Seminar der Hambergischen Universität* 1:157–77.
Hintikka, Jaakko. 1970. "Surface Information and Depth Information." In *Information and Inference,* edited by Jaakko Hintikka and Patrick Suppes. Dordrecht: Reidel.
———. 1973. *Logic, Language-Games and Information.* Oxford: Clarendon Press.
———. 1988. "'Die Wende der Philosophie': Wittgenstein's New Logic of 1928." In

Ludwig Wittgenstein: Half-Truths and One-and-a-Half-Truths. Dordrecht: Kluwer. Originally published in 1988.

————. 1989. "G. H. von Wright on Logical Truth and Distributive Normal Forms." In *The Philosophy of G. H. von Wright,* edited by P. A. Schilpp. Library of Living Philosophers. La Salle, Ill.: Open Court.

————. 1996a. *Lingua Universalis vs. Calculus Ratiocinator.* Dordrecht: Kluwer Academic.

————. 1996b. *The Principles of Mathematics Revisited.* Cambridge, England: Cambridge University Press.

————. 1997. "Three Dogmas of Quine's Empiricism." *Revue Internationale de Philosophie* 51:457–77.

Hintikka, Merrill B., and Jaakko Hintikka. 1986. *Investigating Wittgenstein.* Oxford: Blackwell.

Mach, Ernst. 1905. *Erkenntnis und Irrtum.* Leipzig: Johann Ambrosius Barth.

Schlick, Moritz. 1918. *Allgemeine Erkenntnislehre.* Berlin: Springer.

II

PROBABILITY AND INDUCTION

3

Probable Inferences versus Probable Conclusions

HENRY E. KYBURG, JR.

A Distinction

In "Aspects of Scientific Explanation" and "Deductive Nomological vs. Statistical Explanation," (Hempel 1961, 1965), Hempel drew attention to a distinction that even now, nearly forty years later, is insufficiently appreciated. This is the distinction between uncertain inference, and inference about uncertainty. Hempel even introduced a useful notation to embody the distinction.

The statistical probability of recovery, given a streptococcal infection and treatment by penicillin is close to 1: $P(R/S \wedge P) = 1 - \epsilon$; John Jones had a streptococcal infection, and was treated by penicillin, $S(j) \wedge P(j)$; therefore (uncertain inference) John Jones will recover, $R(j)$. Or (inference concerning uncertainty) John Jones is almost certain to recover. The latter is represented by a traditional scheme:

$$P(R/S \wedge P) = 1 - \epsilon$$
$$\frac{S(j) \wedge P(j)}{}$$

It is practically certain that $R(j)$.

The former is represented by a variant:

$$P(R/S \wedge P) = 1 - \epsilon$$
$$S(j) \wedge P(j)$$

makes it practically certain that $R(j)$.

In its purest form, the form discussed by Hempel (1965), we have premises that include a statistical law or generalization SL and some particular empirical data (boundary conditions, application conditions) ED, and we perform an act of inference. For example, the statistical law might be one that asserts that the probability that a gambling casino will make a profit in a twenty-four-hour period that it is open is very large. The empirical data may be that Edward's is a gambling casino, and that it is open between 12:00 noon on Tuesday and 12:00 noon on Wednesday.

We conclude . . . what? As Hempel pointed out, it isn't clear. One possibility, represented by the first schema, is that we conclude that the probability is very high (in virtue of the statistical law) that Edward's will make a profit between 12:00 noon Tuesday and 12:00 noon Wednesday. On some views of probability this is a straightforward deductive consequence of the premises. What we are explaining is the fact that a certain event was highly probable. The explanation itself can be made to fit the standard deductive pattern.

Another possibility is that we conclude, not that the probability is high that Edward's will make a profit, but that Edward's *will* (or did) make a profit in the period at issue. The conclusion is categorical, unqualified. The qualification that characterizes an inference based on a statistical law concerns *the inference itself* rather than the conclusion. This is represented by the second schema.

This is an easy distinction to lose sight of (and no doubt some ordinary language philosophers would suggest that we *ought* to lose sight of it!): the distinction between arriving via truth-preserving inference at a *qualified* conclusion (*probably* the casino will make a profit) and arriving via *uncertain, probable* inference at the categorical conclusion that the casino *will* make a profit, is one that may be taken to be a red herring. Some writers (Morgan 1998) deny that the latter inference *is* a rational inference at all.[1]

Hempel (1965) seems to come down firmly in support of the second view. He says (p. 383) that the argument, construed in the first way, is "misrepresented." But the reason he gives is that it is *relative to the evidence* that the explanandum $R(j)$ is practically certain. This provides an opportunity for the interlocutor of Bayesian persuasion to say, "Right! Our conclusion is not that Jones will probably recover, but that *relative to the evidence provided by the statistics and the other data* the conditional probability that Jones will recover is high." In short, *of course* the high probability of the conclusion is relative to the premises.

But if the conclusion is that the conditional probability of $R(j)$ given $S(j) \wedge P(j)$ and $\mathcal{P}(R/S \wedge P) = 1 - \epsilon$ is high, it hardly makes sense to cite the premises as if we were constructing an argument. The conclusion represents a logical or psychological fact which stands on its own.

Again the Bayesian can reply, "Right!" He could claim that the only point of the display of the argument (in the first form) is to draw attention to important features of the evidence on which the probability is conditioned.

Hempel agrees that it is often exactly the conditional probability that characterizes the double line—the inference itself—in the second form of argument. He speaks of "inductive support of h relative to e" (1965, p. 385).

Some authors, for example Morgan (1998), have argued that there is no nonmonotonic logic—no form of inference that leads to conclusions that may need to be withdrawn in the light of further evidence. Many philosophers have defended this view with regard to the possibility of inductive logic. Thus they would argue that the second form of the inference is incoherent: we can conclude only that the probability is high that the casino will make a profit, regardless of how high that probabilty may be. Other authors—those who defend inductive logic or some form of nonmonotonic logic—argue that uncertain inference in the sense that leads from premises to categorical (but tentative) conclusions is both a crucial feature of human cognition, and an essential logical feature of scientific inference. Hypothesis testing in statistics, in which hypotheses are rejected in response to the observation of samples in the "rejection region" of the test, also appears to conform to this pattern.

It is interesting to note that this is an issue on which Rudolf Carnap and Karl Popper agreed, despite their fierce disagreements concerning induction. Both Popper and Carnap agreed that one should never "accept" an inductive conclusion: the result of successfully testing a hypothesis, for Popper, is to be motivated to look for more *severe* tests. For Carnap, it is to assign the appropriate degree of confirmation to the hypothesis, relative to the evidence bearing on it (Carnap 1968; Popper 1968). For a view supporting acceptance, see Salmon's contribution to the same discussion (1968).

Our object here is not to resolve this question, but to explore its connections to a number of other concerns in the philosophy of science, many of which have been addressed by Hempel. Indeed, to resolve this question would be a major result in the philosophy of science. Some arguments will be offered in the final section, but it is not to be expected that they will convince everybody.

The Paradoxes

Hempel's early work on induction included his extended and meticulous discussion of a number of inductive "paradoxes." What is interesting about them in the present context is the fact that they only make sense as *paradoxes* if induction is construed as uncertain inference—that is, on the model of insecure inference to a categorical conclusion.

Take, for example, the paradox of the ravens. This is the "paradoxical" fact that the generalization

(1) $(\forall x)(Rx \supset Bx)$

is confirmed not only by $Ra \wedge Ba$ (a is a raven and a is black) but also by b is a shoe and b is white, and c is a poker and c is black, in virtue of the *equivalence condition*, the requirement that anything that confirms a statement S will confirm any logically equivalent statement T.

A number of writers (Hosiasson-Lindenbaum 1995; Alexander 1958; Good 1960; Suppes 1966), as well as Hempel himself (1945) have pointed out that if we construe confirmation quantitatively, there is no paradox: the odd "confirming instances" are only oddly called "confirming" because they contribute very little to the *increase* in confirmation of the generalization. That is, in terms of the first schema, where we write E for general background knowledge, W for "is white," and S for "is a shoe."

$$\frac{\mathcal{P}\left[(\forall x)(Rx \supset Bx)/E \wedge Sa \wedge Wa)\right] = r}{E \wedge Sa \wedge Wa}$$

The probability of (1), relative to the evidence, is r.

It is intuitively reasonable that the observation of a white shoe will confirm the generalization about black ravens less than the observation of (another) black raven. But if we are talking about acceptance, once we have accepted (1), the observation of a white shoe will not increase its probability, which is now 1. But of course, neither will the observation of a black crow increase its probability. On the other hand the observation of a lot of white shoes will not lead to the acceptance of (1), while the observation of a lot of black crows (at least under the right additional conditions) *may* lead to its acceptance by means of some inductive rule.

"Confirms"

Carnap, in *The Logical Foundations of Probability* (1950) makes use of the idea of a "development" of concepts from the qualitative (hot, not hot; confirmed by *e*, not confirmed by *e*) to the comparative (*x* is hotter than *y*; *x* is more confirmed by *e* than *y* is confirmed by *f*, to the truly *scientific* quantitative (the temperature of *x* is 37°; *x* is confirmed by *e* to degree *p*). In the first edition (1950) the relata *e* and *f* got left out, and this allowed Popper (1954) to attack Carnap's story. In the introduction to the second edition (1952), Carnap answered Popper by referring to this construction.

What makes this relevant here is that Hempel, in his discussion of measurement (1952), adopts exactly the same stance. The image one gets is that of the Neanderthal discovering that some berries are good, while others are not good. Along comes the more intellectual and more careful Cro-Magnon, who notes that we can establish a finer classification of berries: some berries are *better than* others. The Homo sapiens advertising executive achieves true science by devising a scale of the goodness of berries: the goodness of berry *A* is 0.347.

Applied to berries, this construction is silly. Applied to length, it is often assumed to make sense. Applied to degree of confirmation or degree of belief, combined with little else, it leads (for example, in Cox [1961]) to the probability axioms. One may take this as illustrating how to get something from nothing, or one may take it as reflecting the weighty hidden content of a few rather inoccuous-sounding assumptions.

I would argue that, on the contrary, the fundamental notion that gives rise to quantitative properties is always a comparative one. In the case of length, what is fundamental is that some objects are judged to be longer than others, and that these judgments are "objective" in that there is immediate and extensive interpersonal agreement about them. Everybody agrees that whale *W* is longer than dolphin *D*. Almost as immediate is the agreement that "seems longer than" is a transitive relation. This is not true, note, of the complementary relation: "does not seem longer than."

Starting with the comparative notion, the absolute or classificatory notion is given by context: "this ant is big" and "this whale is small" are perfectly clear, and may well be true. The natural interpretation is that this ant is bigger than most run-of-the-mill ants, and that this whale is smaller than we expect a whale to be. There are no surprises here. "Huge" and "tiny" are possibly learned very early in life by English speakers, and so have a better claim to absolute status than large and small. Even here, however, a case could be made that the basic sense of the terms is comparative: in this case "huge" or "tiny" relative to the language learner itself.

It is traditional to use the comparative notion as the starting point for a quantitative notion: to provide axioms for "longer than" and then define a quantitative measure of length in terms of a standard unit. There is one difficulty in this standard treatment: it requires that we take the relation we start with to be precise enough to generate equivalence classes; this in turn requires that the complement of the relation also be transitive. Specifically, in the case at hand it requires: If h is not confirmed by e as much as g is confirmed by b, and f is not confirmed by c as much as g is confirmed by b, then h is not confirmed by a as much as f is confirmed by c. It is easier symbolically. Writing $(h, a) > (g, b)$ for h is confirmed by a more than g is confirmed by b, transitivity is:

$$(h, a) > (g, b) \land (g, b) > (f, c) \rightarrow (h, a) > (f, c).$$

What is more problematic is what is also required for the generation of equivalence classes:[2]

$$(h, a) \not> (g, b) \land (g, b) \not> (f, c) \rightarrow (h, a) \not> (f, c).$$

The upshot is that it is not at all clear that our intuitions about confirmation support a real-valued measure. But without such a measure, the quantitative assessment of scientific inference—the use of Hempel's first schema, according to which we assign each hypothesis its appropriate degree of confirmation—becomes highly problematic.

The Dilemma

Acceptance of scientific theory leads straight to the theoretician's dilemma. Hempel saw very clearly that inference to *theoretical* conclusions was problematic. Craig's lemma and Ramsey's theorem show that from a deductivist point of view, "theories" are logically unnecessary in getting from observations to predictions.

The inductive dilemma is that on the one hand, Craig's lemma and Ramsey's theorem show that the theory that yields observational consequences can be rewritten without theoretical terms, and can only be more "acceptable" in that form, so long as we are construing acceptability in terms of probability. Whatever the language L we are speaking, whatever evidence we have, whatever probability measure we assign to the sentences of L, the probability of the

Craigification (or Ramsification) of a theory *T must* have a higher probability than *T* itself, unless the probabilities of both purely theoretical and mixed sentences are all 0. The theoretical terms constitute excess baggage, and drag down the probability, and hence acceptability, of the theory.

This, of course, is just what Popper has taken to be the most important feature of scientific inference: that a "better" hypothesis is a stronger one, one that says *more*, one that, in consequence, is *less* probable, and is certainly not "acceptable."

So one is tempted to think that the acceptance schema is wrong, and, ignoring Popper, to side with Carnap: we assign probabilities to hypotheses, rather than accepting them. Popper, too, is willing to talk of a measure of the impact a piece of evidence has on a hypothesis: the *corroboration* of a hypothesis by a piece of evidence, or the corroboration of a hypothesis by a piece of evidence *given* background knowledge. If the Bayesian view were to resolve the "theoretician's dilemma" one might be tempted to decide that scientists and other ordinary people were just confused when they spoke of "acceptance."

This is wrong. A less familiar form of the dilemma applies directly to the Bayesian reconstruction of scientific inference (Earman 1992; Kyburg 1978; Niiniluoto 1978). Suppose evidence *e* renders theory *t* probable, and the probability of the prediction *o*, given the theory *t*, is high. Then it is easy to see that the probability of the prediction *o*, given the evidence *e*, is even higher. The theory has content beyond that of the prediction, and so the probability of the theory plus the prediction must be less than that of the prediction. It is claimed (Niiniluoto 1978) that the theory can add "systematization" and thus increase the probability of the observational consequences of the theory. It is not hard to see that this must be false.

Let *SDT* be the set of state descriptions in which the theory holds, *SDTO* the set of state descriptions in which the theory and a set of observational consequences of the theory hold, and *SDO* the set of state descriptions in which the observational consequences hold. (All this can be relativized to evidence, and to boundary conditions, without significant change.) The ratio of the measure of *SDO* to *SDE*, the set of state descriptions in which the evidence holds, has to be at least as large as the ratio of the measure of *SDTO* to the measure of *SDE*, unless the theory is regarded a priori as vacuous. If that is the case, it clearly fulfils no function in supporting the observational consequence.

We have not gained anything by introducing the theoretical terms. What is true of deduction is true of probability assessments.

Probability Shifts

Two extreme positions have suggested themselves. Acccording to one position —which, for want of a better label, I will call Bayesian—what happens in human experience and what happens in science are much the same thing. Given a language (always an essential), the human agent or the scientific community "begins" with an a priori distribution of probability over the sentences of that language. As experience impinges on the agent, or data accumulates for the scientist, the probabilities assigned to the sentences of the language shift.

The task of the scientific epistemologist is to characterize that shift; from a normative point of view, it is to provide standards of rationality for probability shifts.

One very simple form of shift is that in which certain statements come to have the probability value 1.0, and other statements change their probabilities in accord with Bayes' theorem: that is, by Bayesian conditionalization.[3] If the initial probability of $S \wedge E$ is $\mathcal{P}(S \wedge E)$ and E is an "observable" sentence, then, when E is observed, and so obtains the status of certainty $\mathcal{P}(E) = 1$, the probability of S becomes $\mathcal{P}(S \wedge E) / \mathcal{P}(E)$.

This presupposes that "evidence" can be construed as incorrigible: that once a statment enters the scientific corpus as evidence, it is inexpungeable. No new evidence—not even the evidence that the lab assistant forgot to plug in the plasma detector—can rationally lead to the rejection of an evidence statement. ("No plasma was present.") This seems bizarrely unrealistic. We could say that what the citizen and the scientist *call* evidence was not really evidence, but low-level hypothesis. What is *really* evidence is something like "The screen of the plasma detector was blank."

But this opens a slippery slope whose lower end is shrouded in darkness. For perhaps the screen of the plasma detector was not really blank, but just seemed to be; perhaps the piece of equipment wasn't really the plasma detector; perhaps we weren't looking at the screen; perhaps what you thought you saw and what I thought I saw were different; perhaps the whole episode was a result of indigestion . . . One is led toward purely phenomenological evidence; but phenomenological evidence itself carries heavy theoretical baggage from psychology and from the commitments of ordinary language.

Very well, perhaps it would be better to follow Jeffrey (1965) and take the initial impact of evidence to be a *shift* in probability measure confined to a part of the language. Rationality consists in propagating that shift in accord with the probability calculus, so that one moves from one *coherent* asssignment of probabilitiy to another *coherent* assignment of probability. The job of the scientific epistemologist is to characterize the rational constraints on such shifts. (Or, in conformity to the politically correct doctrine of intellectual relativity, to characterize the shifts that people actually perform.)

Levels of Acceptance

One striking advantage of the view that allows for the acceptance of inductive conclusions, aside from its conformity to prima facie practice, is that it allows us to base probabilities on statistical knowledge: the probability of heads is about a half because we *accept* the hypothesis that about half of coin tosses yield heads. This allows our probabilities to be *objective* in the sense that they depend on statements that in turn are supported by objective evidence. There are problems with this view that must be overcome—for example, the problem of choosing the right reference class—but these are fairly straightforward problems at which we can work.

The looming shadow of an approach to inductive inference that treats it as *inference* is that paralleling the problem of evidential acceptance on the Bayesian view. Once we accept a theory (special relativity, the laws of statics, the hypothesis that a fraction of about 0.51 of human births are the births of males), how can we ever learn better? How can we account for the obvious nonmonotonicity of scientific inference?

The first step is to make a distinction between the set of statements that are accepted and the set of evidence statements *on the basis of which* those statements are accepted. When the set of evidence statements expands, a previously acceptable statement may no longer be acceptable. In Hempel's notation:

$$\frac{\mathcal{P}(R/S \wedge P) = 1 - \epsilon}{S(j) \wedge P(j)} \text{makes it practically certain that}$$

$R(j)$.

But

$$\frac{\mathcal{P}(R/S \wedge P \wedge Q) < 1 - \epsilon}{S(j) \wedge P(j) \wedge Q(j)} \text{doesn't make it practically certain that}$$

$R(j)$.

In short, when we add $Q(j)$ to our evidence, we no longer accept $R(j)$. If we were to simply have added $R(j)$ to the same body of evidence that holds $S(j) \wedge P(j) \wedge Q(j)$ it is hard to see how $R(j)$ can cease to be accepted because its probability is locked to 1.0.

Now of course we want *evidence* to be acceptable in the same sense: we want it to be corrigible, to be accepted subject to further evidence. The proposal that was advanced in Kyburg (1974) and elsewhere is to take two sets of statements to reflect our epistemic state in a given context, where these two sets of statements are characterized by distinct parameters. Specifically, *evidential certainty* is characterized by the parameter $1 - \epsilon/2$ when *practical certainty* is characterized by the parameter $1 - \epsilon$.

The idea is that in accepting S as evidence, we are taking its (maximum) probability of error to be less than $\epsilon/2$. It is relative to a collection of such statements that we judge the acceptability of the conclusion C, and C is acceptable (practically certain) when its (minimum) probability is greater than $1 - \epsilon$.[4]

Put in these terms, the import of Hempel's first schema may be put as follows. If the premises listed are in the *evidential corpus*, then the conclusion may be included in the practical corpus. Put this way, it is wrong, as Hempel went on to show. We require not only that the premises be in the evidential corpus, but that there be no further evidence in the evidential corpus that undermines the assignment of probability at least $1 - \epsilon$ to $R(j)$; in short that $S \wedge P$ consitutes the *right reference class* for $R(j)$. We may take this to be implicit in the characterization "makes it practically certain that" that attaches to the inference.

Given that the schema, thus construed, makes sense and captures something important in scientific inference, two questions immediately arise. What of the potential infinite regress? If $R(j)$ is acceptable as a practical certainty of level $1 - \epsilon$ relative to a corpus of evidential certainties of level $1 - \epsilon/2$, what do we say about those evidential statements? Don't we want to say that they are acceptable only relative to a corpus of hyperevidential statements of level $1 - \epsilon/4$? And so on, in a dizzying regress? And what of *theoretical* statements that do not seem to fit this picture of being the instantiation of a statistical law or generealization? How could one compute the probability of the laws of statistical mechanics according to the pattern of the first schema?

One answer to the first question is that we should raise only one question at a time. If we are concerned about the justification of $R(j)$ at the level $1 - \epsilon$, then the body of evidence we may cite in providing that justification is comprised by statements that are justifi*able* at the level $1 - \epsilon/2$. To ask for a justification of one of *those* statements is to change the subject. We are no longer asking for a justification of $R(j)$ at the level $1 - \epsilon$, but for a justification of a statistical law or geneeralization—say, $\mathcal{P}(R/S \wedge P) = 1 - \epsilon$— at the level $1 - \epsilon/2$. We have an answer to this new question, if we can show that relative to a set of evidentially acceptable statements the probability of $P(R/S \wedge P) = 1 - \epsilon$ is at least $1 - \epsilon/2$. These new statements must themselves have a level of acceptance of $1 - \epsilon/4$ in order to be used to justify the statistical law in question. Of course, in principle, some of the premises for this inference may be questioned in turn.

Must this process come to a halt? No end to the process can be specified in advance, but no interlocutor can keep raising questions forever. It need not be the case that there exists an *incorrigible* set of evidence statements on the basis of which all justification must ultimately rest. It suffices that every acceptable statement can be justified by reference to statements that are acceptable at a higher (more demanding) level.

The answer to the second question is not as clear. One possible answer is that sometimes it is possible to find a statistical basis for assigning a probability to a theory. For example consider the theoretical claim that the molecular weight of carbon monoxide is 44.01. One source of this claim is that a mol of the gas weighs 44.01. But of course we can't weigh a sample of gas and obtain the result that it weighs 44.01 grams. However we do the weighing, we encounter both uncertainty in measuring the *amount* of gas, and in measuring its *weight*. What we can infer is that the weight of a mol of gas is (say) in the interval [44.00,44.02]. From this we can infer that the molecular weight of carbon monoxide lies in the same interval. (The level of practical certainty at which this inference can be defended is dictated by the distribution of errors of measurement characteristic of the process we used in making the measurement.) This is certainly a theoretical claim, relative to a body of background information, relative to a distribution of errors of measurement, and relative to the measurement observations we actually made. So at least in some cases quite abstract and theoretical claims can be defended in terms of acceptance on the basis of high probability.

It seems unlikely that this can *always* be done, however. Part of the body of background information we took for granted in the last inference is, no doubt, Dalton's atomic theory, or something very like it. It is not at all clear how such general and pervasive theories can be reduced to a form in which they are equivalent to something that admits of statistical testing. It seems that there are at least some fragments of scientific theory that cannot be accounted for this way.

One way of treating large questions is to adopt a kind of conventionalism (Kyburg 1977, 1990). This can be supposed to operate on a small scale with regard to measurement. I already noted this with regard to the transitivity of the relational complement of a comparative relation such as "longer than." We do not have adequate observational grounds for the empirical generalization:

$$(\forall x,y)(\neg L(x,y) \wedge \neg L(y,z) \supset \neg L(x,z)).$$

Nevertheless, we adopt it as a useful feature of our comparative judgements: with it we can develop a quantitative theory of length; without it we can't. This metaphysical assumption more than earns its keep. (It might be argued that the same cannot be said for the corresponding relation for comparative conditional probability.)

We might characterize this approach as taking certain very general scientific hypotheses to be *features of our scientific language*, to be functionally a priori. By "functionally a priori" I mean to emphasize that we do not arrive at these very general hypotheses by the exercise of pure reason from the comfort of our armchairs, but only by considering the way they *organize* a large body of acceptable empirical knowledge.

While it seems possible to make a good case for doing this in the case of measurement, it remains obscure how far we would have to go in treating general scientific principles as "features of the language." Furthermore, if we want to argue that this attenuated conventionalism can provide whatever else, beyond probability, we need in the way of accounting for scientific inference, we take on a new problem: that of providing an account of when it is rational to prefer one scientific language to another. This is a question that has been little addressed.

Pragmatism?

Hempel's schemata have suggested two visions of scientific inference. One vision involves shifting the fabric of probability measures in response to the pushes and pulls of experience. The other involves the nonmonotonic or inductive acceptance of empirical conclusions, that may, in the light of additional evidence, need to be withdrawn.

The structure of inference, according to the first version, is simple and clear. All *inference* is truth preserving and deductive. In its simplest form, it involves no more than applying Bayes's theorem to sentences of a given language, on which a classical probability function is defined. There are two parameters of this vision: the specification of the language, and the specification of the probability function. Faced with the modification of the language—the introduction of new terms (*oxygen*), the deletion of old terms (*phlogiston*)—we have no normative constraints on our response: we accept the modification, or we don't. Not quite so clearly, the probability function may be taken as purely logical (but no purely logical function has yet been proposed that most people find satisfactory) or as purely subjective (but the specification of a purely subjective probability function is already problematic, as Harman [1989] has argued), or as some combination of logical and subjective factors. Alternatively, we may take the Bayesian view as being essentially local—as requiring initial agreement as to both language and probability within a limited domain.

According to the second vision, as Hempel already showed (1965, 1945), the structure of inference must be taken as quite complex. Deductive closure becomes questionable; some form of the principle of total evidence is required. Some principles going beyond the acceptance principle are required for evaluating proposed shifts in the structure of the language of science. The possibility of an infinite chain of justifications must be faced. On the other hand, this way of looking at things allows the assignment of probabilities to be *objective:* grounded in relative frequencies in the world. The possibility that choice between languages may be grounded in objective fact is at least open.

On what basis do we choose between these two visions?

It could be argued that, as a matter of reason and rationality, only the acceptance view is acceptable. This would not be to say that inferences whose conclusions have the form of probabilities are never valid or called for: on the contrary, the inference from the premises that heads are distributed binomially with a parameter equal to a half, to the conclusion that the probability is 0.995 that of a thousand tosses, between four hundred and six hundred will yield tails is a perfectly good inference. It would be to say, however, that many of the most important arguments encountered in science, as well as in public and private life, call for the acceptance of conclusions that are categorical in nature, even though they are uncertain and might have to be withdrawn in the face of new evidence. Finally, this position reflects what goes on in science: science aims at results; it is results that are published in journals, propagated in courses, and occasionally withdrawn, when new data indicates that they are in error.

The alternative position is that first-order logic (or perhaps some extension of first-order logic) captures all there is of reason and rationality, and that therefore no inference is rational whose conclusion is not *entailed* by its premises— that is, no so-called inductive or nonmonotonic inference is reasonable or rational, and therefore there cannot be any "logic" of such inference. This is the view of Charles Morgan (1998), who takes as a *condition of adequacy* for a logic that it never lead us astray. What is reasonable and rational is the adjustment of probabilities in the light of evidence (better: in the light of initial shifts of probability). Furthermore, this is all we *need* for decision-making and the conduct of life in general. Not only is the "acceptance" of statements on the basis of inadequate evidence irrational, but it is gratuitous and unnecessary! What we need for making decisions and choosing among alternatives are probabilities: the probabilities of particular events.

The negative side of this position is that there seems to be no rational way for the modifications of the web of probability to be initiated, and that the propagation of these modifications, despite Jeffrey's formula, is also highly problematic.

These two alternatives appear to represent two coherent epistemic stances that one can take with regard to empirical knowledge and scientific inference. What I think can be said is that there are pragmatic reasons for adopting the first position. The Bayesian position seems, as Gil Harman (1989) has pointed out, completely intractable if we are thinking of assigning the prior probabilities on the basis of our actual degrees of belief. Life is too short to have a degree of belief about everything. Furthermore, it is not clear that it would even be possible to assign a degree of belief to each sentence of a countable language except by means of some systematic procedure.

Conclusion

Hempel (1965) gives us two visions of scientific inference, the acceptance view and the probabilistic view. Although he seems to find the acceptance view intuitively appealing, he is accutely aware of the difficulties it entails. On the other hand, the probabilistic view is not without its own implausibilites. In any event, Hempel has set us a compelling problem. It is one that has not yet been seriously taken up (or even acknowledged) by many philosophers of science. Yet it seems to me that it represents a critical issue. It is one up to which we should begin to face.

NOTES

1. Richard Jeffrey (1995, p. 5) does not note the distinction at all.
2. We can get suitable equivalence classes in other ways—for example, by taking the *real* relation in question to be an abstract and theoretical one: A is really longer than B just in case everything that is judged to be longer than A is also judged to be longer than B.
3. Other possibilities have been suggested: imaging (Lewis 1976) and a generalization of imaging (Gardenfors 1988).
4. Although it is not directly germane to our purposes here, an explanation of the relation of these two parameters may be of interest. It may be the case that P and Q are among our evidential certainties, yet that their conjunction is not. Surely (we may think) their conjunction is *practically* certain. It can be shown that if the lower

probabilities of *P* and of *Q* are greater than $1 - \epsilon/2$ then the probability of their conjunction is greater than $1 - \epsilon$; but that in general this is the most we can say about the probability of their conjunction.

REFERENCES

Alexander, H. Gavin. 1958. "The Paradoxes of Confirmation." *British Journal for the Philosophy of Science* 9:227–33.

Carnap, Rudolf. 1950. *The Logical Foundations of Probability*. Chicago: University of Chicago Press.

———. 1952. *The Continuum of Inductive Methods*. Chicago: University of Chicago Press.

———. 1968. "On Rules of Acceptance." In *The Problem of Inductive Logic*, edited by Imre Lakatos. Amsterdam: North Holland.

Cox, Richard T. 1961. *The Algebra of Probable Inference*. Baltimore: Johns Hopkins University Press.

Earman, John. 1992. *Bayes or Bust?* Cambridge, England: Cambridge University Press.

Gardenfors, Peter. 1988. *Knowledge in Flux: Modeling the Dynamics of Epistemic States*. Cambridge, Mass.: MIT Press.

Good, I. J. 1960. "The Paradox of Confirmation." *British Journal for the Philosophy of Science* 11:145–9.

Harman, Gilbert. 1989. Change in View. Cambridge, Mass.: Bradford Books.

Hempel, Carl G. 1945. "Studies in the Logic of Confirmation." *Mind* 54:1–26, 97–121.

———. 1952. *Fundamentals of Concept Formation in Empirical Science*. Chicago: University of Chicago Press.

———. 1961. "Deductive-Nomological vs. Statistical Explanation." In *Minnesota Studies in the Philosophy of Science 3*, edited by Herbert Feigl. Minneapolis: University of Minnesota Press.

———. 1965. *Aspects of Scientific Explanation*. New York: Free Press.

Hosiasson-Lindenbaum, Janina. 1995. "On Confirmation." *Journal of Symbolic Logic* 5:133–48.

Jeffrey, Richard C. 1965. *The Logic of Decision*. New York: McGraw-Hill.

———. 1995. "A Brief Guide to the Work of Carl Gustav Hempel." *Erkenntnis* 42:3–14.

Kyburg, Henry E., Jr. 1974. *The Logical Foundations of Statistical Inference*. Dordrecht: Reidel.

———. 1977. "All Acceptable Generalizations Are Analytic." *American Philosophical Quarterly* 14:201–10.

———. 1978. "An Interpolation Theorem for Inductive Relations." *Journal of Philosophy* 75:93–98.

———. 1990. "Theories as Mere Conventions." In *Scientific Theories*, edited by Wade Savage. Vol. 14. Minneapolis: University of Minnesota Press.

Lewis, David. 1976. "Probabilities of Conditionals and Conditional Probability." *Philosophical Review* 85:297–315.

Morgan, Charles. 1998. "Non-monotonic Logic Is Impossible." *Canadian Journal of Artificial Intelligence* 42:19–25.

Niiniluoto, Illkka. 1978. "High Probability and Inductive Systematization." *Journal of Philosophy* 75:737–739.

Popper, Karl R. 1954. "Degree of Confirmation." *British Journal for the Philosophy of Science* 5:143–9.

———. 1968. "On Rules of Detachment and So-called Inductive Logic." In *The Problem of Inductive Logic,* edited by Imre Lakatos. Amsterdam: North Holland.

Salmon, Wesley C. 1968. "Who Needs Inductive Acceptance Rules?" In *The Problem of Inductive Logic,* edited by Imre Lakatos. Amsterdam: North Holland.

Suppes, Patrick. 1966. "A Bayesian Approach to the Paradoxes of Confirmation." In *Aspects of Inductive Logic,* edited by Patrick Suppes and Jaakko Hintikka. Amsterdam: North-Holland.

4

Hempel on the Problem of Induction

RISTO HILPINEN

In his paper "Inductive Inconsistencies" (1960/1965, p. 53) Carl G. Hempel observes:

> In the philosophical study of induction, no task is of greater importance than that of giving a clear characterization of inductive procedures: only when this has been done can the problem of justification significantly be raised.

Hempel divides "the problem of induction" into two subproblems,

(Q1) the characterization problem; the characterization of inductive procedures; and

(Q2) the justification problem; the problem of justifying inductive reasoning. (See Hempel 1981, pp. 389–90; 1984.)

Usually "the problem of induction" has been understood as the latter problem. Hempel (1981, p. 389) describes the problem of induction as follows.

> In everyday pursuits as well as in scientific research we constantly rely on what I will call the method of inductive acceptance, or MIA for short: we adopt beliefs, or expectations, about empirical matters on logically incomplete evidence, and we even base our actions on such beliefs—to the point of staking our lives on some of them.
>
> The *problem of induction* is usually understood as the question of what can be said in justification of this procedure.

According to this account, the characterization problem is the problem of characterizing "the method of inductive acceptance." It is clear that the nature and the proper formulation of the justification problem depends on an answer to (Q1). Hempel has done significant work on both problems: his discussions of inductive inconsistencies and the apparent paradoxes of induction have clarified and articulated the characterization problem and improved our understanding of it, and his work on cognitive decision theory and the concept of epistemic utility has suggested a new way of approaching the justification problem.

The word 'induction' (Lat. *inductio*) as an expression for nondeductive inference is a translation of the Greek work *epagôgê* (Cicero *Topica* x.42), used by
Aristotle to refer to an argument type which is "the opposite of deduction"
and proceeds "from particulars to universals" (*An. Pr.* B 23.68b32–33; *Topica*
1.7.105a14–15). Aristotle's characterization of induction appears to correspond
to inductive generalization, and the word has often been used in this sense, to
mean the inference to a general proposition from its instances. Inductive inference has also been understood in a wider sense, that is, as nondemonstrative
(or nondeductive) reasoning in general, as in the paragraph just quoted from
Hempel (1981). However, it is clear that not every case of the acceptance of a
proposition without conclusive grounds can be called an induction; for example,
if someone learns that there are black swans in Australia and concludes from
this that God exists, we would not call this "inference" an induction. To qualify
as an induction, an inference must conform to some meaningful and prima
facie reasonable pattern of nondemonstrative reasoning which people tend to
follow in the formation and justification of beliefs. The identification of such
patterns is part of the characterization problem of induction. The reasonableness of a pattern of inference means that it is regarded as justified; thus the
characterization problem and the justification problem are dependent on each
other.

The word 'induction' has sometimes been understood in a more restricted
sense (but not necessarily in the sense of inductive generalization), and induction
has been contrasted with other forms of nondemonstrative reasoning. In his
Prior Analytics, Aristotle distinguished two forms of nondeductive argument:
epagôgê, or induction, an inference to the major premise of a syllogism, and
an inference called *apagôgê*, which leads to the minor premise of a syllogism
(*An. Pr.* B. 25.69a20–30). Charles Peirce transformed this Aristotelian distinction into a distinction between two main types of nondemonstrative (or
nonnecessary) reasoning, *abduction* and *induction*: Peirce meant by 'abduction' a tentative acceptance of an explanatory hypothesis, and used 'induction' to refer to the evaluation of the trustworthiness of a hypothesis in the
light of its testable consequences (that is, consequences that can be derived
from it together with the relevant background beliefs). He regarded induction as "the process of *verification*," and called the logic of induction "the logic
of the verification of theories" (Peirce 1964, MS 475, p. 24). Peirce's distinction between abduction and induction has become generally accepted in the
recent philosophy of science (Josephson and Josephson 1994), even though
these two forms of nondemonstrative reasoning are occasionally confused, for
example, when induction is characterized as "inference to the best explanation" (Harman 1968).

Hempel did not use the expression 'abduction', but he and other logical empiricists adopted a distinction which corresponds to Peirce's distinction between
abductive and inductive inference, namely, the distinction between the context
of the discovery of a hypothesis and the context of its justification by empirical

data. Thus, according to Hempel (1966, p. 118), the rules of induction cannot be regarded as rules for the discovery of a hypothesis (or explanation):

> [the] rules of inductive inference . . . have to be conceived, not as canons of discovery, but as criteria of validation for proposed inductive arguments; far from generating a hypothesis from given evidence, they will *presuppose* that, in addition to a body of evidence, a hypothesis has been put forward, and they will then serve to appraise the soundness of the hypothesis on the basis of the evidence.

This view of induction (and the rules of induction) is essentially the same as that put forward by Peirce. Even though Hempel and other logical empiricists were apparently unwilling to discuss or recognize the existence of a logic of discovery (or the logic of abductive *inference*), Hempel's "logical conditions of adequacy" for explanations (Hempel and Oppenheim 1948/1965, pp. 247–8) can be regarded as principles of the logic of abduction. The logical empiricists had a tendency to view questions about discovery as psychological questions, but in their actual work they were concerned with the *logic* of discovery (as distinguished from the logic of confirmation or justification), as Hempel's work on the logic of explanation shows.

In the light of the passage just cited, inductive inference can be characterized as follows. Let us assume that a hypothesis H has been "put forward." Induction consists in the appraisal of (the soundness of) the hypothesis on the basis of some body of available evidence E. Why (for what purpose) has the hypothesis H been "put forward"? Presumably because it is a potential answer to some problem or question, for example, an explanation-seeking question (why-question) (Hempel 1966, p. 115). A question is a request for information; thus H has been put forward because it may provide the information an inquirer is looking for. But the informativeness of the hypothesis does not suffice to make it worthy of belief (acceptable as true): the appraisal of the "soundness" of H on the basis of the evidence E means the appraisal of H as an object of belief (the appraisal of the credibility of H), not merely the appraisal of the informativeness of H with respect to a given question. Thus the function of induction is to change the cognitive modality of a proposition (i.e., the way or sense in which the proposition is accepted) from a mere hypothesis into a confirmed (or disconfirmed) statement. Peirce called inductive logic "the logic of verification," but Hempel's expression "logic of confirmation" (Hempel 1945/1965) is better and less misleading.

Hempel (1981) observed that induction can be characterized in two ways: it can be regarded as a process which prescribes or recommends the acceptance new beliefs and expectations on the basis of logically inconclusive evidence, or induction can be regarded as a method of assigning probabilities or degrees of credibility to statements and hypotheses relative to evidential propositions, without assuming that the hypotheses in question should be "accepted" on the basis of the evidence. In the latter approach, the characterization problem is the problem of assigning probabilities (degrees of credibility) to hypotheses; this was Rudolf Carnap's (1950) approach to inductive logic. The former approach operates with rules of acceptance or "rules of induction" in the conventional sense. Hempel called this approach "the accepted information model of scientific knowledge" (1962, p. 150) or "the method of inductive acceptance." In the accepted information model, the problem of justification is the problem of justifying acceptance rules; in the quantitative approach it is that of justifying probability assignments. The two approaches can of course be combined: one could try to justify acceptance in probabilistic terms, and then give a separate justification to the assignment of probabilities.

Much of Hempel's work on the characterization problem was related to the accepted information model. He attempted to develop and articulate a reasonable and consistent version of the model, but the results were largely negative. In the course of this work he discovered that many conventional "rules of induction" are apt to lead to inconsistencies (to the acceptance of mutually inconsistent hypotheses) or are incompatible with intuitively plausible criteria of confirmation.

In his early papers on the logic of confirmation, Hempel (1937, 1943, 1945/1965) studied the general formal properties of the concept of confirmation and the representation of certain familiar patterns of nondemonstrative reasoning. His investigation of the formal properties of the concept of confirmation led to the discovery of the paradox of confirmation, often called the raven paradox, which led to a great deal of discussion about the concept of a *positive instance* or a *confirming* instance of a generalization: the paradox and the subsequent discussion showed that the concept of confirming instance was not as well understood as had been thought.

The raven paradox arises from the conflict between the following seemingly plausible assumptions about the concept of confirmation:

(CC1)   Hypotheses of the form 'All *A* are *C*' are confirmed by
         A-objects which are *C* (for example, the hypothesis that all
         ravens are black is confirmed by black ravens), and disconfirmed
         by *A*-objects which are not *C* , and only these kinds of
         evidential data are directly relevant to the hypothesis.

(CC2)   Logically equivalent hypotheses have the same confirmation
         conditions.

The first condition was explicitly formulated by the philosopher Jean Nicod, and it is therefore usually called Nicod's criterion of confirmation (Hempel 1945/1965, p.10). The second assumption is called the equivalence condition. Both assumptions seem plausible. To determine whether all ravens are black one should presumably make observations of ravens: only the observation of a raven is capable of refuting the generalization, and therefore, it might be argued, only such observations can count as confirmatory instances. The equivalence condition seems at least as plausible as Nicod's criterion. But if universal generalizations are understood (and formalized) as universal material conditionals of the form

(1)   (x)(Ax → Cx),

then Nicod's criterion and the equivalence condition are obviously inconsistent, because (1) is logically equivalent to

(2)   (x)(¬Cx → ¬Ax),

but according to Nicod's criterion, this is confirmed only by observations of objects which are neither *A* nor *C*. This paradox (or the conflict between Nicod's criterion and the equivalence condition) depends on the assumption

(CC3)   The content of 'All A are C' is expressed by
        (x)(Ax → Cx).

Nicod expressed universal laws by the schema '*A entails C*', and it is not clear that a material conditional (1) is a good translation of Nicod's schema. For example, subjunctive conditionals do not satisfy the principle of contraposition, and if the connection between *A* and *C* is expressed as a subjunctive conditional (of a suitable kind), then the hypothesis that *A* entails *C* need not be equivalent to the hypothesis that not-*C* entails not-*A*. But if the hypotheses under consideration are universal generalizations of form (1), then the defense of Nicod's criterion suggested earlier fails: as was stated, only the observation of an *A*-object can refute (1), but it is equally true that only the observation of an object which is not *C* can refute (1), hence, if the generalization that all ravens are black is confirmed by observations of black ravens, it should also be confirmed by observations of nonblack nonravens, for example, white shoes. According to the interpretation expressed by (1), 'All *A* are *C*' says simply that there are no *A*s which are not *C*, that is,

(3)   ¬(Ex)(Ax & ¬Cx),

and is completely symmetrical with respect to *A*-objects (e.g., ravens) and non-*C*-objects (e.g., nonblack objects).

If (CC3) and the equivalence condition are accepted, how should the appearance of a paradox be explained? One of the earliest solutions was proposed by Janina Hosiasson-Lindenbaum (1940). If it is assumed that the qualitative concept of confirmation is based on a comparative or quantitative concept of confirmation (degree of confirmation), for example, the increase of the probability of a hypothesis (i.e., positive relevance of *E* with respect to *H*), it may be argued that if the number of *A*-objects (e.g., ravens) in the universe is smaller than the number of not-*C*-objects (e.g., nonblack objects), then it should be easier to find a counterexample to the hypothesis among the *A*-objects than among the non-*C*-objects, and therefore observations of *A*-objects, if they do not disconfirm the hypothesis, should also confirm it to a higher degree than observations of non-*C*-objects. Relative to the background knowledge that the number of *A*C-objects is very small in comparison with non-*A*-non-*C*-objects, the evidence provided by objects of the former kind increases the probability of (1) much more than evidence of objects of the latter kind—provided, of course, that (1) has a positive prior probability.

This observation is the basis of many Bayesian accounts of the raven paradox (Suppes 1966; Horwich 1982, pp. 56–7; Howson and Urbach 1989, p. 90). If the qualitative concept of confirmation is now defined as a *sufficiently high* degree of confirmation (sufficient positive relevance) and not merely as *some* positive degree of confirmation, then, by choosing the required degree in a suitable way, we can obtain the result that *A*C-objects "confirm" the generalization (1), but non-*A*-objects do not. Since the number of ravens is very small in comparison with the number of nonblack objects (and nonravens), this result holds in the case of the raven example. If mere positive relevance (and not significant or sufficient relevance) is regarded as sufficient for qualitative confirmation, the apparently paradoxical instances must, according to this solution, be regarded as confirming instances (Hempel 1964/1965, pp. 47–8). During the past fifty years Hempel's raven paradox has generated an enormous literature on the conditions of confirmation, and continues to be discussed in the contemporary philosophy of science. (See Maher 1999.)

In his "Inductive Inconsistencies" (1960/1965) Hempel considered some familiar patters of nondemonstrative reasoning, the so-called statistical syllogisms, and simple rules of inductive generalization, and observed that the usual formulations of these inference schemata lead to inconsistencies.

The following formulation of a statistical syllogism is a case in point.

(SS1)   a is G.

$\dfrac{\text{Prob}_{st}(F/G) \text{ is close to 1.}}{\text{So, it is almost certain that a is F.}}$

'Prob$_{st}$' here represents the concept of statistical probability. This rule can obviously lead to the acceptance of logically incompatible conclusions on the basis of previously accepted information. Hempel concluded that the qualifier 'almost certain' in (SS1) cannot be regarded as part of the conclusion detached from the premises, but should be understood as qualifying the relationship between the premises and the conclusion; thus the following representation is preferable to (SS1):

(SS2)   a is G.

Prob$_{st}$(F/G) is close to 1.

=================================== Almost certainly

a is F.

Here the expression 'almost certain' should be regarded as an expression for inductive support. But even if statistical syllogisms are understood in this way, they are apt to lead to inconsistent conclusions from true premises, just like any other purely probabilistic rules of acceptance. According to Hempel, statistical syllogisms do not give us "rules of induction" in the sense required by the accepted information model, because their conclusions cannot be "detached" from their premises.

In the same article (1960/1965), Hempel observed that many conventional induction rules, for example, the rule of inductive generalization which authorizes the inference of 'All *As* are *C*' from 'All examined instances of *As* have been *C*' cannot be construed as rules of acceptance (detachment), because such rules allow the possibility of accepting mutually inconsistent generalizations; Hempel took for granted that the body of accepted information ought to be logically consistent.

Hempel's answer to the problem of the apparent inconsistencies generated by statistical syllogisms was an appeal to *the principle of total evidence*: the support which the premises of a statistical argument give to a hypothesis can be used to determine the credence of the hypothesis at a given time only if the premises constitute all the relevant evidence available at that time (Hempel 1960/ 1965, p. 64). An analogous problem arises for inductive-statistical explanations; here Hempel's answer is *the requirement of maximal specificity* of the explanatory premises, which can be regarded as a special case of the principle of total evidence (Hempel 1965, pp. 399–400; Salmon 1984, p. 28).

Hempel's discussion of "inductive inconsistencies" concerns the defeasible and nonmonotonic character of inductive and probabilistic reasoning. New premises can undermine previously accepted inductive conclusions; this is one of basic differences between nondemonstrative and demonstrative reasoning. In recent years the study of defeasible and nonmonotonic reasoning has grown into a substantial research area in logic and computer science. (See Brewka et al, 1997.)

The negative results just discussed led Hempel to consider other ways to understand and systematize the concept of inductive acceptance. In his "Deductive-Nomological vs. Statistical Explanation" (1962) and "Inductive Inconsistencies" (1960/1965) he considered the acceptance of a hypothesis as a form of cognitive decisionmaking, and applied the tools of utility theory and decision theory to the analysis of inductive reasoning.

According to Hempel (1962, 1960/1965), an inductive acceptance rule can be regarded as a rule which authorizes the addition of a sufficiently supported new hypothesis to a body of previously accepted information. The accepted information model represents scientific information (for example, the beliefs of investigators) by a set B_t (briefly B) whose elements are all accepted as presumably true by the scientists at time t. The system of accepted statements can be revised in two basic ways: by adding new statements to the system or by eliminating previously accepted statements from it. In the recent literature on belief revision the former type of change is called an expansion, the latter change a contraction (Levi 1975/1984, pp. 115–6; Gärdenfors 1988, pp. 15–6). Hempel did not consider cognitive decision problems involving the contraction of a system; according to him, inductive acceptance is always a matter of expanding a consistent system of statements into a larger consistent system. The accepted information model, also called the *belief set* model, is one of the standard tools of the recent and contemporary work on the logic of belief revision and theory change. (See Gärdenfors 1988; Hansson 1997.)

New statements can be accepted into B in two ways: *directly*, on the basis of suitable experiences and observations, or *inferentially*, on the basis of inference from previously accepted statements. Inferential acceptance can be deductive or inductive, depending on whether the hypothesis under consideration is a logical consequence of or merely more or less confirmed (supported) by the previously accepted statements. Isaac Levi (1979/1984, pp. 90–1) has characterized inferential acceptance as a *deliberate* expansion of the system B, as opposed to a *routine* (noninferential or direct) expansion of B.

If the inferential acceptance of a statement *h* is regarded as analogous to a decision—as a cognitive or epistemic decision—the cognitive options available to an investigator in a given situation are the following:

(4) (i) *Ah*: the acceptance of *h*, that is, the addition of *h* to B.
(ii) *Rh*: the rejection of *h*, which means the acceptance of ¬*h* into B.
(iii) *Sh*: the suspension of judgment with respect to *h*; leaving B unchanged.

In this context the "rejection" of *h* does not mean the elimination of *h* from B (i.e., a contraction), but the acceptance of the negation of *h*.

What are the values or utilities which determine the desirability of the options (4.i–iii)? At this point Hempel introduced the term "epistemic utility" for the purely cognitive or scientific values which determine the desirability of the actions of a cognitive decisionmaker: epistemic utilities determine the value of an investigator's choices from the point of view of pure research.

Perhaps the most obvious (and traditionally recognized) epistemic utilities are truth and information. Assume that *b* is a statement which expresses the content of an investigator's belief system B (the content of the current corpus of knowledge). According to Hempel, the epistemic utility of accepting *h* depends on how much information *h* adds to the system codified by *b*, that is, the excess content of *h* relative to *b*. The content of a statement is determined by what it excludes; thus the common content of *h* and *b* is determined by their disjunction *h* v *b*. Statement *h* is equivalent to ((*h* v *b*) & (*h* v ¬*b*)), and the conjuncts *h* v *b* and *h* v ¬*b* have no content in common since their disjunction is a logical truth; consequently the content the hypothesis *h* adds to *b* is expressed by *h* v ¬*b*.

In this argument Hempel assumes that the content of a proposition *s* can be measured by a content measure *Cont* such that

(5) (i) $0 \leq Cont(s) \leq 1$,
(ii) $Cont(s) = 0$ if *s* is a logical truth, and
(iii) $Cont(s_1 \& s_2) = Cont(s_1) + Cont(s_2)$ if s_1 and s_2 are content-exclusive, that is, if s_1 v s_2 is a logical truth (or $Cont(s_1$ v $s_2) = 0$).

If the content measure is defined by

(6) $Cont(h) = 1 - m(h),$

where m satisfies the probability axioms, it will have properties (5.i–iii). The value of accepting a hypothesis should also depend on whether it is true, not merely on its informativeness. Let $u(Ah,t,b)$ be the epistemic utility of adding h to b if it is true, and let $u(Ah,f,b)$ be the corresponding utility if h is false. According to Hempel, the utility of accepting a true hypothesis should be a monotonically increasing function of the excess content of h over b (what h adds to b). Hempel chooses the measure

(7) $u(Ah,t,b) = k \cdot Cont(h \lor \neg b)/Cont(b),$

where k is a positive constant, and takes the utility of accepting a false h to be

(8) $u(Ah,f,b) = -k \cdot Cont(h \lor \neg b)/Cont(b).$

Suspension of judgment (Sh) can be regarded as equivalent to adding nothing but the logical consequences of b to it; thus we get, according to (5.i–ii),

(9) $u(Sh,t,b) = 0.$

(In this case no false content can become added to b.)

Hempel adopts the rule of maximizing expected utility as the basic rule of cognitive decisionmaking. According to (7)–(9), the expected epistemic utility of accepting h on the basis of the background knowledge b, $E(Ah,b)$, has the following properties:

(10) If $Prob(h/b) > .5$, $E(Ah,b) > E(Sh,b)$;
      if $Prob(h/b) = .5$, $E(Ah,b) = E(Sh,b)$;
                    and
      if $Prob(h/b) < .5$, $E(Ah,b) < E(Sh,b)$.

In other words, Hempel's measure of epistemic utility leads to a purely probabilistic acceptance rule:

(RAcH) (a) Accept h if $Prob(h/b) > .5$.
        (b) If $Prob(h/b) = .5$, h may be accepted or held in suspense.
        (c) If $Prob(h/b) < .5$, h ought to be rejected.

As Hempel observed, this rule is obviously unsatisfactory. For example, like any purely probabilistic acceptance rule, it leads immediately to the so-called lottery paradox, in other words, it leads to the same kinds of inconsistencies as the rules based on statistical syllogisms and the simple rules of induction criticized by Hempel.

The lottery paradox can be avoided if the rule is applied only the sets of mutually exclusive hypotheses; Hempel (1960/1965, p. 77) suggested such a formulation of the rule—but it is clear that it is unsatisfactory even in such a restricted version. It allows the acceptance of statements which clearly do not deserve to be regarded as part of the corpus of scientific knowledge.

In his "Turns in the Evolution of the Problem of Induction" Hempel observed that the rule based on his measure of epistemic utility was obviously quite unsatisfactory, but added (1981, p. 399):

> Yet, I believe there is something fundamentally right about the idea of epistemic value, and that the failure of the utility measure just considered may be attributable to a too narrow construal of the objectives of basic research. Science is interested not only in questions of truth and informational content, but also in the simplicity of the total system of accepted hypotheses, in its explanatory and predictive powers, and other factors, all of which a theory of inductive acceptance ought to take into account.

All the factors mentioned by Hempel are obviously important, but the discussion which followed Hempel's pioneering works (1960/1965, 1962), in which he introduced the idea of epistemic utility, showed that even if epistemic utilities are defined only in terms of truth and information, it is possible to obtain reasonable acceptance rules by making suitable adjustments in Hempel's utility measure. In Hempel's analysis, the informativeness of a hypothesis turns out to be irrelevant to its acceptability: thus his definition of epistemic utility leads to a purely probabilistic rule. This result is due to his assumption that $u(Sh,t,b) = 0$ and

(11) $u(Ah,f,b) = -u(Ah,t,b)$.

More generally, if $u(Sh,t,b) = s$, the objectionable rule is obtained if

(12) $u(Ah,t,b) - s = s - u(Ah,f,b)$.

(See Hilpinen 1972, p. 155.) This result is avoided if epistemic utilities satisfy the following condition (Levi 1967/1984, p. 60):

(13) $u(Ah,x,b)$ is an increasing function of $Cont(h)$ regardless of whether $x = t$ or $x = f$.

Hempel's measure does not satisfy (13): according to it, $u(Ah,f,b)$ is inversely related to $Cont(h)$. This means that according to Hempel's measure, an investigator who is interested in true and informative hypotheses, but who is constrained to choose among hypotheses which are false, would minimize the informativeness of the hypothesis he chooses; Levi regarded this as a counterintuitive result (Levi 1967/1984, p. 63). Moreover, Jaakko Hintikka and Juhani Pietarinen (1966) pointed out that it seems counterintuitive to take the disutility of the false guess that h to be the (incremental) content of h, for if $\neg h$ is the case, the only relevant available utility is the information content of $\neg h$; thus the utility of accepting a false hypothesis h should be a function of the content of $\neg h$ rather than h.

Insofar as truth is preferred to error (or, at least, error is never preferred to truth), epistemic utilities should also satisfy the condition

(14) $u(Ah,t,b) \geq u(Ag,f,b)$ for any hypotheses h and g.

It is clear that Hempel's measure satisfies (14). In fact, (14) seems a somewhat unrealistic requirement if closeness to truth or verisimilitude is regarded as a significant feature of a hypothesis: informative falsehoods which are close to the truth may well be preferred to uninformative truths. Condition (14) seems reasonable if considerations of verisimilitude are excluded. I present hereafter a short outline of how Hempel's ideas about epistemic utility and cognitive decision theory were developed in the 1960s and 1970s by Isaac Levi (1967, 1967/ 1984) and other philosophers.

Hempel's conception of induction as a process of testing and evaluating a hypothesis which has been put forward (possibly as an answer to some question) suggests a distinction between the background information or background knowledge to which the hypothesis is added, and the evidence used for testing the hypothesis; let *e* be a statement which describes such evidence. In his analysis of the epistemic utility of a hypothesis Hempel does not make this distinction: according to him, the proposition *b* which represents the body of knowledge to which the hypothesis is added includes both the background information and the evidence used for assessing the acceptability of the hypothesis.

It is clear that the informativeness and the epistemic utility of a hypothesis should depend on what it adds to the background knowledge (which gives rise to the question to which the hypothesis is proposed as an answer), but the utility of *h* should not depend on what it adds to the evidence *e* used for testing it; on the contrary, if we take the concept of inductive support seriously, we should assume that the test results, to confirm a hypothesis, ought to "cover" its content as well as possible. Thus we should let the content of *h* (and the epistemic utility of accepting *h*) be relative only to the background information, for example,

(15) $Cont_b(h) = 1 - Prob_b(h),$

where $Prob_b(h)$ is the probability of *h* relative to the background knowledge *b*. In the following I omit the explicit reference to the background information *b*, and express the content (measure) of *h* simply by $Cont(h)$ ($= 1 - Prob(h)$); thus the utility of accepting *h* will be expressed simply as $u(Ah,x)$, where $x = t$ or $x = f$. As suggested by Hintikka and Pietarinen (1966), the epistemic utility of accepting *h* when it is false, that is, when ¬*h* is true, should be inversely related to $Cont(¬h)$ so that condition (13) will hold. Let *c* be some contradictory statement (e.g., *h* & ¬*h*), and let

(16) $u(Ac,f) = 0$

and

(17) $u(Sh,t) = s,$

in other words, we take the value of accepting a contradiction as the zero point of the epistemic utility function, and let *s* be the epistemic value of the suspension of judgment (which amounts to accepting nothing but logical truths or statements entailed by the background knowledge). According to (16) and condition (14), $s \geq 0$. In accordance with Isaac Levi's condition (13), let

(18) $u(Ah,x) - u(Ag,x) = q(Cont(h) - Cont(g))$

where q is nonnegative. If (following Levi 1967, pp. 79–81) the unit of the utility function is taken as

(19) $q + s = 1,$

(16)–(18) entail

(20)   (a) $u(Ah,t) = q{\cdot}Cont(h) + 1 - q,$
         (b) $u(Ah,f) = -q(1 - Cont(h));$

thus, by definition (15),

(21)   (a) $u(Ah,t) = 1 - q{\cdot}Prob(h)$
         (b) $u(Ah,f) = -q{\cdot}Prob(h).$

According to (21), the expected utility of accepting h on the basis of evidence e is

(22) $E(Ah,e) = Prob(h/e) - q{\cdot}Prob(h)$

Condition (22) gives us an acceptance rule which makes the acceptability of a hypothesis on the basis of given evidence e depend on the positive relevance of e with respect to h, which seems an intuitively reasonable criterion: the concept of confirmation or support has usually been defined as positive relevance. According to (19), $0 \leq q \leq 1$; q has a plausible interpretation as an "index of caution" (Levi 1967): the smaller q is, the more the evidence e has to decrease the probability of a hypothesis to justify its rejection. To avoid difficulties analogous to the lottery paradox, we should assume that the hypotheses under consideration are regarded as disjunctions of certain "ultimate partitions" of basic alternatives which are the most informative potential answers to a given question (Levi 1967, pp. 32–6); the rule selects the disjunction which maximizes (22) as the strongest hypothesis h^* accepted by induction (Levi 1967, p. 86; Hilpinen 1972, p. 158). The cognitive decision problem is regarded as the problem of choosing h^*. (The logical consequences of h^* and the background knowledge may be accepted on the basis of deductive rules.) Thus a suitable choice of the measure of epistemic utility can lead to an intuitively reasonable acceptance rule even in a simplified situation in which only the truth and the informativeness of the hypothesis are taken into account. It is clear that this is a highly simplified and idealized account: as Hempel has pointed out, the desiderata (desirable characteristics) of scientific hypotheses (for example, theories) are complex and varied. (In fact, in one of his last papers on the goals of science Hempel [1990] deemphasized the significance of truth as an epistemic utility.) Hempel's pioneering work on cognitive decision theory and the concept of epistemic utility provided the original impetus to a great deal of interesting research in this area. (For a recent example, see Maher [1993].)

Hempel and other logical empiricists did not think there is a special nondemonstrative form of reasoning which leads to the formulation of new hypotheses; that process was regarded as belonging to the context of discovery—and discovery was not thought to be subject to logical rules. Logic, it was thought, was only concerned with the justification and evaluation of hypotheses which had been put forward. In other words, logical empiricists did not try to develop a "logic of abduction."

However, Hempel did formulate principles which can be regarded as rules of abduction (in the sense intended by Peirce); he did this in his theory of scientific explanation. He divided the "conditions of adequacy" for deductive explanations into logical conditions and an empirical condition; the latter is simply the condition that the explanans should be true. The logical conditions are the following (Hempel and Oppenheim 1948/1965, pp. 247–8):

(CE-1) The explanandum must be a logical consequence of the explanans.

In Hempel's account of inductive-statistical explanations, this condition assumes the form:

(CE-1') The explanans should make the explanandum highly probable (expected).

In addition,

(CE-2) The explanans must contain general laws,

and

(CE-3) The explanans must have empirical content, that is, the explanans must be, at least in principle, testable by experience and observation.

It is interesting to compare Hempel's conditions with C. S. Peirce's rules of abduction. According to Peirce, the goal of abduction is to find an explanation for some surprising phenomenon. Peirce's general schema for abduction looks as follows (Peirce 1997, p. 245):

(23) The surprising fact, *c*, has been observed. But if *h* were true, *c* would be a matter of course. Hence, there is reason to suspect that *h* is true.

Peirce's "first rule of abduction" is

(RA1) The hypothesis *h* (the "conclusion" of an abduction) must be capable of being subjected to empirical testing,

which is the same as Hempel's condition (CE-3). Peirce's second rule of abduction,

(RA2) The hypothesis must explain the surprising facts,

corresponds to Hempel's conditions (CE-1)–(CE-2). Peirce observes that the explanation may be a deductive explanation which renders the facts "necessary" or it may make the facts "natural chance results, as the kinetic theory of gases does." (Peirce 1958, par. 7.220).

Peirce's logic of abduction contains a third rule which has no counterpart in Hempel's theory:

> (RA3)   In the third place, and quite as necessary a consideration as those I have mentioned, in view of the fact that the hypothesis is one of innumerable possibly false ones, in view, too, of the enormous expensiveness of experimentation in money, time, energy, and thought, is the consideration of economy. Now economy, in general, depends upon three kinds of factors: cost, the value of the thing proposed, in itself, and its effect upon other projects. Under the head of cost, if a hypothesis can be put to the test of experiment with very little expense of any kind, that should be regarded as giving it precedence in the inductive procedure. (Peirce 1958, par. 7.220, n.18)

This rule may be termed the principle of economy. (RA3) is quite different in character from (RA1) and (RA2) and from Hempel's logical conditions of adequacy for explanations. It is not a logical rule in the same sense as the latter, but rather a *strategic* or *pragmatic* rule for selecting explanatory hypotheses for testing, that is, for targets of inductive reasoning (or "the inductive procedure"). Rule (RA3) is not dependent on (CE-1)–(CE-3), but is related to Hempel's "empirical condition of adequacy," the requirement that:

(CE-4)   The sentences constituting the explanans must be true.

Without (CE-4), no experimental testing of a hypothesis (and thus no induction) would be necessary.

If abduction is distinguished from induction in the way just suggested, the problem of the justification of nondemonstrative reasoning (and the justification of induction) assumes a new form. In the preceding discussion of epistemic utilities, the distinction between induction and abduction was taken into account by making the informational value of a hypothesis relative to the background knowledge, but not to the evidence which forms the basis of induction. Assume that the rules of abduction — for example, Hempel's criteria for a good explanation and the strategic rules suggested by Peirce — have provided us with a hypothesis to be tested. The choice of the hypothesis to be tested is justified by the rules and principles of abduction — for example, by Hempel's conditions of adequacy for scientific explanations. At this stage, the informational virtues of the hypothesis justify its tentative acceptance (for the purpose of testing): information is the main desideratum of "abductive" acceptance. (The relevant information need not be the total content of a hypothesis; it may be, for example, its informativeness about the phenomenon to be explained.) Let us assume that the test results agree with predictions made on the basis of the hypothesis in question. Why should we now have more confidence in the hypothesis than before the tests? This is a question about the justification of induction. The answer is, of course, that positive results do not always increase the credibility of a hypothesis: the effects of induction depend on how the test results have been obtained. (The view that confirmation is a context-independent logical relation between a hypothesis and an evidential proposition contradicts this fact.) The purpose of experimental design or the design of observation procedures is to insure that the test results distinguish the hypothesis to be tested from its alternatives and competitors: good experimental design is an essential feature of good inductions. The "standards for observational and experimental procedures," which Hempel took to be relevant to direct (noninferential) acceptance of new statements (1962, p. 150), function as standards for inductive acceptance as well. If the results of an experiment are what may be expected on the basis of a hypothesis, it would be irrational to give up the hypothesis — in such a case the experiment might as well not have been performed at all. The acceptance of the hypothesis depends on the (possibly defeasible) belief that the experiment has been well designed.

According to Hempel's decision-theoretic approach to inductive acceptance, inductive procedures are justified in the same way as other choices, that is, deliberate actions: on the basis of the goals (the epistemic utilities) and the background beliefs of the investigator or decisionmaker. Such justification is always local and contextual, but local justification may well be all we can expect (Levi 1967, pp. 3–6). In his discussion of theory choice in science, Hempel expressed this view as follows.

> The imposition of desiderata (desirable characteristics of scientific hypotheses and theories) may be regarded, at least schematically, as the use of the set of means aimed at the improvement of scientific knowledge. But instead of viewing such improvement as a research goal that must be characterizable independently of the desiderata, we might plausibly conceive the goal of scientific inquiry to *be* the development of theories that ever better satisfy the desiderata. On this construal, desiderata are different constituents of the goal of science rather than conceptually independent means for its attainment. (1981, p. 404)

It might be said that this way of looking at the justification problem does not address the traditional problem of the justification of induction. However, Hempel has shown that there is no single "problem of induction," but a host of interrelated questions about the characterization and the justification of various inductive procedures (see Hempel 1981, p. 402).

NOTE

An earlier version of this paper was presented in March 1999 in a Colloquium of the Committee on the History and Philosophy of Science at the University of Colorado at Boulder. I am grateful to the participants of the colloquium for fruitful discussion and comments.

REFERENCES

Aristotle. 1983. *The Categories. On Interpretation. Prior Analytics.* Translated by H. P. Cooke and H. Tredennick. Loeb Classical Library 325. Cambridge: Harvard University Press.
———. 1984. *Posterior Analytics. Topica.* Translated by H. Tredennick and E. S. Forster. Loeb Classical Library 391. Cambridge: Harvard University Press.
Brewka, Gerhard, Jürgen Dix, and Kurt Konolige. 1997. *Nonmonotonic Reasoning: An Overview.* Stanford: CSLI.
Cicero. 1949. *De Inventione. De Optimo Genere Oratorium. Topica.* Translated by H. M. Hubbell. Loeb Classical Library 386. Cambridge: Harvard University Press.
Carnap, Rudolf. 1950. *Logical Foundations of Probability.* Chicago: University of Chicago Press.
Gärdenfors, Peter. 1988. *Knowledge in Flux: Modeling the Dynamics of Epistemic States.* Cambridge, Mass.: MIT Press.
Hansson, Sven Ove. 1997. "What's New Isn't Always Best." Editor's introduction to *Theoria: A Swedish Journal of Philosophy* 63 (special issue on Non-Prioritized Belief Revision, edited by S.-O. Hansson):1–13.
Harman, Gilbert. 1968. "Enumerative Induction as Inference to the Best Explanation." *Journal of Philosophy* 65:529–33.
Hempel, Carl G. 1937. "Le problème de la vérité." *Theoria* (Göteborg) 3:206–46.
Hempel, Carl G. 1943. "A Purely Syntactical Definition of Confirmation." *Journal of Symbolic Logic* 8:122–43.
———. 1945/1965. "Studies in the Logic of Confirmation." In Hempel (1965). Reprinted (with some changes) from *Mind* 54:1–26, 97–121.
———. 1946. "A Note on the Paradoxes of Confirmation." *Mind* 55:79–82.
———. 1960/1965. "Inductive Inconsistencies." In Hempel (1965). Reprinted (with some changes) from *Synthese* 12:439–69.
———. 1962. "Deductive-Nomological vs. Statistical Explanation." In *Minnesota Studies in the Philosophy of Science,* edited by H. Feigl and G. Maxwell. Vol. 3. Minneapolis: University of Minnesota Press.
———. 1964/1965. "Postscript (1964) on Confirmation." In Hempel (1965).
———. 1965. *Aspects of Scientific Explanation and Other Essays in the Philosophy of Science.* New York: Free Press.
———. 1966. "Recent Problems of Induction." In *Mind and Cosmos,* edited by R. G. Colodny. Pittsburgh: University of Pittsburgh Press.
———. 1981. "Turns in the Evolution of the Problem of Induction." *Synthese* 46:389–404.
———. 1984. "Science, Induction and Truth." A lecture delivered in celebration of receiving an honorary doctorate in economics, University of Berlin, 12 December 1984.
———. 1990. "The Significance of the Concept of Truth for the Critical Appraisal of Scientific Theories." *Nuova Civiltà delle Macchine* 8(32):109–13.
Hempel, Carl G., and P. Oppenheim. 1945. "A Definition of 'Degree of Confirmation'." *Philosophy of Science* 12:98–115.
———. 1948/1965. "Studies in the Logic of Explanation." In Hempel (1965). Reprinted from *Philosophy of Science* 15:135–75.

Hilpinen, Risto. 1972. "Decision-Theoretic Approaches to Rules of Acceptance." In *Contemporary Philosophy in Scandinavia*, edited by R. E. Olson and A. M. Paul. Baltimore: Johns Hopkins Press.

Hintikka, Jaakko, and Juhani Pietarinen. 1966. "Semantic Information and Inductive Logic." In *Aspects of Inductive Logic*, edited by J. Hintikka and P. Suppes. Amsterdam: North-Holland.

Horwich, Paul. 1982. *Probability and Evidence*. Cambridge, England: Cambridge University Press.

Hosiasson-Lindenbaum, Janina. 1940. "On Confirmation." *Journal of Symbolic Logic* 5:133–68.

Howson, Colin, and Peter Urbach. 1989. *Scientific Reasoning: The Bayesian Approach*. La Salle, Ill.: Open Court.

Josephson, John R., and Susan G. Josephson. 1994. *Abductive Inference: Computation, Philosophy, Technology*. Cambridge, England: Cambridge University Press.

Levi, Isaac. 1967. *Gambling with Truth*. New York: Knopf.

———. 1967/1984. "Information and Inference." In Levi (1984). Reprinted from *Synthese* 17:369–91.

———. 1975/1984. "Truth, Fallibility and the Growth of Knowledge." In Levi (1984). Reprinted from *Language, Logic and Method*, edited by R. S. Cohen et al. Dordrecht: Reidel.

———. 1979/1984. "Abduction and the Demands for Information." In Levi (1984). Reprinted from *The Logic and Epistemology of Scientific Change*, edited by I. Niiniluoto and R. Tuomela. Amsterdam: North-Holland.

———. 1980. *The Enterprise of Knowledge*. Cambridge, Mass.: MIT Press.

———. 1984. *Decisions and Revisions: Philosophical Essays on Knowledge and Value*. Cambridge, England: Cambridge University Press.

Maher, Patrick. 1993. *Betting on Theories*. Cambridge, England: Cambridge University Press.

———. 1999. "Inductive Logic and the Ravens Paradox." *Philosophy of Science* 66:50–70.

Peirce, Charles S. 1958. *Collected Papers of Charles Sanders Peirce*. Vol. 7. Edited by Arthur Burks. Cambridge: Harvard University Press.

———. 1964. *The Charles S. Peirce Papers*. Cambridge: Harvard University Library. Microfilm.

———. 1997. *Pragmatism as a Principle and Method of Right Thinking. The 1903 Harvard Lectures on Pragmatism*. Edited by Patricia Ann Turrisi. Albany: State University of New York Press.

Salmon, Wesley C. 1984. *Scientific Explanation and the Causal Structure of the World*. Princeton: Princeton University Press.

Suppes, Patrick. 1966. "A Bayesian Approach to the Paradoxes of Confirmation." In *Aspects of Inductive Logic*, edited by K. J. Hintikka and P. Suppes. Amsterdam: North-Holland.

III

THE COVERING-LAW MODELS

5

The Paradoxes of Hempelian Explanation

JAMES H. FETZER

Among Carl G. Hempel's most admired achievements were his contributions to the theory of induction, including the paradoxes of confirmation, and his contributions to the theory of explanation, especially the covering-law model (Hempel 1965). The purpose of this presentation is to suggest that Hempel's work on the theory of induction can shed light on his theory of explanation, where there appear to be explanatory counterparts to the paradoxes of confirmation that illuminate certain inadequacies in the covering-law model. I shall propose that these "paradoxes of explanation" clarify connections between causation and explanation and also indicate the direction a more adequate theory may be found.

Hempel's approach to explanation has always been motivated by the assumption that *explanations* explain the occurrence of events by deriving their descriptions from premises that include at least one lawlike sentence, where a *lawlike sentence* is a sentence that would be a law if it were true, which thereby display their nomic expectability. In the simplest cases, explanations have the form (1.1),

$$(1.1) \quad \text{Premises} \quad \begin{array}{c} C1, C2, \ldots, Ck \\ L1, L2, \ldots, Lr \\ \hline \end{array} \Bigg] \quad \text{Deduction} \\ \text{Conclusion} \qquad E$$

where $C1, C2, \ldots, Ck$ describe specific conditions and $L1, L2, \ldots, Lr$ general laws, E describes the event to be explained, and E follows deductively from its premises.

In the introduction to his classic work "The Theoretician's Dilemma," Hempel extends this thesis—which I am going to call *the core conception*—to encompass predictions and postdictions as well as explanations, where their differences are supposed to be pragmatic: relative to the time at which the argument is advanced, *tn*, an argument of form (1.1) qualifies as a *prediction* only if E describes an event that occurs later than *tn* and qualifies as a *postdiction* only if E occurs earlier than *tn* (Hempel 1958, p. 174). Hempel remarks that their differences "require no fuller study here," since the purpose of his discussion is just to note the role of general laws in arguments of these kinds. As will become evident, however, these remarks may tend to conceal fundamental differences between "scientific inference" and "scientific explanation."

Hempel on Induction

The paradoxes of confirmation arise from the adoption of three individually plausible assumptions that jointly yield highly counterintuitive results, namely: (1) *extensionality*: the assumption that at least some lawlike sentences can be represented by completely general material conditionals in predicate calculus; (2) *Nicod's criterion*: the assumption that these conditionals are confirmed by instances of their antecedents that instantiate their consequents, disconfirmed by instances of their antecedents that do not instantiate their consequents, and neither confirmed nor disconfirmed by noninstances of their antecedents; and, (3) *equivalence condition*: the assumption that evidence that confirms a lawlike sentence confirms any logically equivalent sentences (Hempel 1945, pp. 14–5).

Thus, if the material conditional under consideration happens to be that all ravens are black, then, using the "$\ldots \rightarrow \_\_\_$" as the material conditional, it may be represented, "$(x)(t)(Rxt \rightarrow Bxt)$" by assumption (1).[1] Such a sentence should therefore be confirmed by instances of its antecedent that instantiate its consequent (ravens that are black), disconfirmed by instances of its antecedent that do not instantiate its consequent (ravens that are not black), and neither confirmed nor disconfirmed by noninstances of its antecedent (nonravens) by assumption (2). This sentence is logically equivalent to "$(x)(t)(-Bxt \rightarrow -Rxt)$," however, which may be confirmed by instances of nonblack nonravens, which implies that white shoes, for example, confirm the hypothesis "All ravens are black," by assumption (3), which is an odd result.

In spite of enormous resistance to his analysis, Hempel remained steadfast in defense of these paradoxes as psychological rather than logical in kind (Hempel 1965, pp. 47–51). Another consideration that motivated his belief is that these sentences are logically equivalent to "$(x)(t)(-Rxt \vee Bxt)$." (In most systems of truth-functional logic, the material conditional '$\ldots \rightarrow \_\_\_$' is *defined* as an abbreviation for '$-\ldots \vee \_\_\_$'.) Sentences of this form, presumably, are confirmed by instances of their left-hand conjuncts ("$-Rxt$") or their right-hand conjuncts ("Bxt") or both, which would accommodate white shoes as well as black ravens. The only disconfirming cases would be those that instantiate neither conjunct, which suggests why there can be no corresponding "paradoxes of falsification."

Hempel on Explanation

The core of the Hempelian theory of explanation is the conception that explanations explain the occurrence of events by deriving descriptions of those events from premises that include at least one lawlike sentence. This account was implemented semiformally by means of the classic conditions of adequacy, (CA-1) derivability, (CA-2) lawlikeness, (CA-3) empirical content, and (CA-4) truth, where Hempel acknowledged that (CA-3) was a redundant condition, insofar as the satisfaction of the others implies its satisfaction (Hempel and Oppenheim 1948, pp. 247–9). The derivation of that description (*the explanandum*) from its premises (*the explanans*) was taken to insure the adequacy of an explanation.

In order to demonstrate the existence of paradoxes of explanation that parallel those of confirmation, the following three assumptions should be adopted: (1') *extensionality*: the assumption that at least some lawlike sentences can be represented by completely general material conditionals in predicate calculus; (2') *the core conception*: the assumption that explanations explain the occurrence of events by deriving their descriptions from premises that include at least one lawlike sentence, which is actually needed for such derivations; and (3') *equivalence condition*: the assumption that logically equivalent premises have equal entitlement to function as covering-laws in adequate explanations, even though the explanans and the explanandum may differ from case to case.

The rationale for these assumptions may or may not be completely obvious, but there appear no reasonable grounds to reject them. Assumption (1') is actually identical with assumption (1). Assumption (2') might be tentatively disputed on the grounds that the Hempelian desideratum motivating (what I am calling) *the core conception* is that explanations explain by displaying the nomic expectability of their explanandum outcomes, which is a matter that I shall address hereafter. Assumption (3') appears to be justified on the basis of the conjunction of (1') with Hempel's defense of the paradoxes of confirmation as psychological rather than logical, where we need to broaden our intuitions to encompass multiple formulations of lawlike sentences and the consequences that attend them.

Classical Preconceptions

As Richard Jeffrey (1969) has observed, Hempel's conception harmonizes well with the classical Aristotelian conception of *scientific knowledge*. Thus, Aristotle proposed that "demonstrative arguments" are productive of scientific knowledge,

> [where] the premises of demonstrated knowledge must be true, primary, immediate, better known than and prior to the conclusion, which is further related to them as cause to effect. . . . Syllogisms there may indeed be without these conditions, but such syllogism, not being productive of scientific knowledge, will not be demonstration. (*Posterior Analytics* 1.71–2)

Thus, Jeffrey remarks, Hempel's conception bears comparison with Aristotle's insofar as Hempel's conditions appear to capture counterparts to Aristotle's conditions. Both are characterizing plausible conditions of adequacy for scientific explanations. That Aristotle's conditions are stronger than Hempel's, of course, warrants notice.

Indeed, the comparison with Aristotle emerges even more strikingly from the perspective of Aristotle's theory of *the four causes*, the discovery of which is the aim of scientific inquiries about specific things: the material cause (that of which it is made), the efficient cause (that by which it comes into being), the formal cause (its essential pattern), and the final cause (that for which it exists). For, in relation to a causal explanation relating conditions $C1, C2, \ldots, Cn$ to some effect E, parallel distinctions may be drawn, which might be roughly schematized along these lines:

(3.1)   The Material Cause: $(C1, C2, \ldots, Cn) \rightarrow E$
        The Efficient Cause: $C1, C2, \ldots, Cn$

$$\underline{\hspace{6cm}} \Bigg] \text{The Formal Cause}$$

        The Final Cause: E

where the law itself describes the material cause, the initial conditions the efficient cause, the explanandum the final cause, and the deductive relationship between the explanans and the explanandum the formal cause, satisfying Aristotle's conception.[2]

Jeffrey, of course, was not proposing a return to "good old-fashioned Aristotelianism," and neither am I. Jeffrey's interest, in particular, is with statistical arguments. Jeffrey believes that there are some perfectly adequate *statistical explanations* that do not qualify as *statistical inferences*, a matter to which I shall return. Aristotle, indeed, also separates merely universal from commensurately universal properties of things, just as Hempel distinguishes between accidental generalizations and bona fide general laws. It should come as no surprise if arguments that appeal to accidental generalizations might support inferences that fail to qualify as adequate explanations. It may turn out that we can *know that* something is the case without *knowing why*. Hempel's conditions of adequacy are intended to specify *when we know why*.

The Paradox of Transposition

Various anomalies follow from the adoption of Hempel's assumptions, however, and thereby yield paradoxes of explanation parallel to those of confirmation. Consider, for example, the following explanation of why bird *c* is black, namely, that it is black because it is a raven and *all ravens are black*, which might be formalized using the letters "R" and "B" for raven and black and other symbols used before:

(4.1)   Covering-Law: $(x)(t)(Rxt \rightarrow Bxt)$ Explanans
        Initial Conditions: $\underline{Rct'}$

        Event Description: Bct' Explanandum

where it appears to be difficult to deny that this explanation would readily satisfy Hempel's conditions of adequacy and thereby qualify as "adequate." No doubt, it satisfies the four conditions of adequacy (CA-1) to (CA-4), specified earlier.

Consider the following premises, however, which include a sentence that is logically equivalent to the extensional generalization that occurs in schema (4.1). The following explanation of why thing d is not a raven appeals to the premises that thing d is not black and that *nonblack things are nonravens*.

(4.2) Covering Law: $(x)(t)(-Bxt \rightarrow -Rxt)$ Explanans
       Initial Conditions: $-Bdt'$
       Event Description: $-Rdt'$ Explanandum

But surely the adequacy of such an "explanation" would be in serious doubt. Suppose, for example, that thing d happens to be a white shoe. Then, while it certainly follows from these premises *that* thing d cannot be a raven, it by no means offers any explanation for *why* thing d is a nonraven.

This anomaly, which might be called *the paradox of transposition*, occurs as a consequence of the three assumptions that have been embraced. If laws are appropriately represented by completely general material conditionals as the assumption of extensionality maintains; if explanations explain the occurrence of events by deriving their descriptions from premises that include at least one lawlike sentence, which is actually needed for such derivations, as the core conception requires; and if logically equivalent premises have equal entitlement to function as covering laws in adequate explanations, then there appears to be no way to avoid them. For intuitively unacceptable explanations such as this to be excluded, at least one of these assumptions must be wrong.

The Assumption of Extensionality

One diagnosis of the nature of the paradox of transposition focuses on (1'), the *assumption of extensionality*, which maintains that at least some lawlike sentences can be adequately represented as material generalizations. If this assumption should turn out to be false, then that might also pave the way for a solution to the paradoxes of confirmation, which might themselves be rooted in attempts to represent intensional relations between properties by means of extensional connectives (Fetzer 1981, chap. 7). Indeed, if lawlike sentences cannot be adequately represented as material generalizations, then they may not have logically equivalent formulations of the kinds that generate the paradox.[3]

Suppose, for example, that lawlike sentences are only properly represented as subjunctive conditionals concerning what would be the case were something else the case. Then their formalization would require the use of a *subjunctive conditional*, '. . . $\Rightarrow$ ___', say, in lieu of a material conditional, where assertions of subjunctives predicate the hypothetical (possibly counterfactual) satisfaction of their antecedents. Unlike material conditionals, whose truth depends upon the history of the actual world, the truth of subjunctive conditionals appears to depend on the history of any possible world that was like this world in certain specific respects, such as those worlds in which the same laws of nature obtain.

Such distinctions must be drawn with care, however, where worlds are *logically possible* when descriptions of their history do not violate the laws of logic, *physically possible* when descriptions of their history do not violate the laws of nature, and *historically possible* (relative to time *tn*) when their descriptions do not violate the history of the actual world (to time *tn*)—assuming, of course, that historically possible worlds are physically possible and that physically possible worlds are logically possible (Fetzer 1981, pp. 54–6). Some subjunctives may be true on syntactical or semantical grounds alone, but their properties seem to be well understood. The hard problem concerns subjunctives that are logically contingent. What determines the truth values of these contingent subjunctives?

Permanent Properties

One solution to this problem introduces a distinction between two kinds of logically contingent relations between properties, namely, those that are permanent and those that are transient, in relation to a presupposed reference property. Then an attribute is a *permanent property* of any instance of a reference property when there is no process or procedure, natural or contrived, by means of which some thing could lose that attribute without also losing that reference property, even though the possession of that attribute does not follow from the possession of that reference property on logical grounds alone (Fetzer 1981, chap. 2). Other logically contingent properties that are not permanent are *transient*.

The color of ravens (the malleability of gold, the mass of neutrinos, and the combustibility of paper) are among their permanent properties, while the age, weight, and location of ravens (the size, shape, and selling price of things that are gold, and so on) are among their transient properties. These are attributes that ravens (things that are gold, and so forth) could lose without losing their reference property (of being a raven, of being made of gold, and so on). Thus, *accidental generalizations* may arise when every member of a reference class possesses the same attribute, even though it happens to be a transient rather than a permanent property. The difference between them warrants the use of subjunctives for permanent properties and material conditionals for transient.

Thus, if every Ferrari, say, happened to be painted red, even though that is not part of what it takes to be a Ferrari on definitional grounds alone, then the completely unrestricted material generalization that *all Ferraris are red* would be true. It could be formalized in the obvious way and an argument fashioned:

(6.1) Covering-Law: $(x)(t)(Fxt \rightarrow R'xt)$ Explanans
       Initial Conditions: Fet'

       Event Description: $R'et'$ Explanandum

Yet it would be a mistake to suppose that this argument explains *why* thing *e* happens to be red, because there are processes and procedures, such as repainting, for example, by virtue of which *e* could lose its color and remain a Ferrari. Such an inference might support a prediction but cannot supply an explanation.[4]

Subjunctive Conditionals

The existence of a permanent property relation between an attribute *A* and a reference property *R* transcends representation by means of truth-functional connectives because these relations are not merely truth-functional. As in the case of other kinds of conditionals, including causal conditionals, it would be a blunder to represent them by transposable connectives. When cause *c brings about* an effect *e*, ordinarily, there is no corresponding connection by virtue of which *the absence of e* brings about *the absence of c*. When *A* is a *permanent property* of *R*, it does not mean that *the absence of R* is a permanent property of *the absence of A*, which would conflate logical and nomological necessities and thus contradict the assumption of contingency (Fetzer 1981, pp. 193–4).

Logically contingent subjunctive conditionals can serve as lawlike premises, where why thing *f* happens to be black, for example, may be appropriately explained when *f* is a raven and blackness is among their permanent properties:

(7.1)   Covering-Law: $(x)(t)(Rxt \Rightarrow Bxt)$

 Initial Conditions: $\underline{Rft'}$ Explanans

 Event Description: Bft' Explanandum

The truth of the subjunctive implies the truth of counterpart extensional conditionals, but their truth does not imply the truth of transposed subjunctives, which means that covering laws are not logically equivalent to their material conditional counterparts, contrary to Hempel's assumption of extensionality.

Once this assumption has been rejected, the equivalence condition does no harm. And a distinction can be drawn between *direct tests* of covering laws, which require instantiations of their antecedents, and *indirect tests* of those hypotheses, which do not require instantiations of their antecedents. And it should come as no surprise if the evidential weight of the results of indirect tests might vary greatly in relation to the evidential weight of the results of direct tests, which appears to be both intuitive and in harmony with Nicod's criterion. This consequence is rooted in logic and not merely in psychology, moreover, suggesting that the paradoxes of confirmation are logical consequences of Hempel's mistaken adoption of purely extensional methodology.

The Ontic versus the Epistemic

The conception of lawfulness that is required, as the preceeding discussion implies, must be understood as an ontic notion that is not reducible to merely epistemic considerations. This is in striking contrast to the approach of many contemporary thinkers. David Lewis (1973), for example, elaborates a theory in the tradition of F. P. Ramsey according to which *natural laws* are the fewest and most general assumptions that bring order to the universe or the fewest general propositions from which every uniformity found in nature might be deductively inferred. Since mere uniformities are not invariable reflections of nomic necessity, Lewis' codifications, even were they successful, could not be guaranteed to systematize natural laws (van Fraassen 1989; Fetzer 1991a).

The underlying conception is that of bringing order to our *knowledge* of the universe. Yet there are at least three reasons why even complete knowledge of every empirical regularity that obtains during the course of the world's history might not afford an adequate inferential foundation for discovering the world's laws. First, some laws might remain uninstantiated and therefore not be displayed by any regularity. Second, some regularities may be accidental and therefore not display any law of nature. And, third, in the case of probabilistic laws, some frequencies might deviate from their generating nomic probabilities "by chance" and therefore display natural laws in ways that are unrepresentative or biased.[5]

A world whose composition includes some probabilistic properties may therefore be historically indistinguishable from a world whose composition includes no probabilistic properties—either because there are no appropriate trials, or too few appropriate trials, or enough appropriate trials which, by chance, happen to yield unrepresentative frequencies. Even if a world were *indeterministic* by instantiating probabilistic as well as nonprobabilistic properties, the history of that world could be indistinguishable from the history of a *deterministic* world insofar as they might both display identical relative frequencies and constant conjunctions, where their differences were concealed "by chance." It follows that, if some of the world's properties are probabilistic, not only may the same laws generate different world histories, but the same world histories may be generated by different laws—under the very same initial conditions (Fetzer 1983b, p. 31)!

Intensional Methodology

The resolution of the paradoxes of confirmation and of the paradox of transposition thus appears to require resources that far transcend those permitted by merely extensional methodology. Unraveling the connection between syntax, semantics, and ontology has proven to be a daunting task that has challenged the most sophisticated thinkers. The work of Lewis (1973), Robert Stalnaker (1968), or perhaps John Pollock (1974, 1976), for example, might be thought to hold the key to resolving these outstanding problems, especially since they have exerted considerable efforts to understand the nature of subjunctive and counterfactual conditionals. The application of their research to understanding the nature of natural laws, however, may not be quite so straightforward as it may initially appear.

Thus, although they have advanced a number of logical calculi that are intended to capture the logical properties of subjunctive and counterfactual discourse, these systems seem unsuitable for the purpose of reflecting the use of such conditionals within *scientific language*. Lewis's *VC*, Stalnaker's *C2*, and Pollock's *SS*, for example, all contain as theorems the principle that "If '*p* & *q*' is true, then 'if *p* were the case, then *q* would be the case' is true," which might or might not be objectionable within the context of *ordinary language* but would hopelessly obscure the basic difference between lawlike and accidental generalizations in scientific discourse and could not possibly be satisfied in an indeterministic universe, where one or another outcome, *q* or -*q*, might occur under precisely the same conditions *p* (Fetzer 1981, pp. 34–5).[6]

For reasons such as these, it appears to be overly optimistic to assume that their results could be directly transferred, in principle, to the resolution of the problems that confront the theory of science. A suitable solution appears to depend upon the distinction between "permanent" and "transient" properties discussed earlier, where permanent properties are contingent dispositions which something cannot lose without losing a corresponding reference property. Dispositions are viewed, in turn, as single-case causal tendencies that may be of universal or of probabilistic strength. These conceptions supply an ontological foundation for fixing the truth conditions of scientific conditionals and support a formal semantics based upon selection functions for permanent and dispositional properties (Fetzer and Nute 1979, 1980).

The Modus Tollens Paradox

It may come as some surprise, therefore, that other paradoxes of explanation remain even after the paradoxes of confirmation and of transposition have been dissolved by embracing an intensional methodology, which suggests that, in the case of explanation, their roots may be even deeper yet. Consider the following:

(10.1)   Covering-Law: $(x)(t)(Rxt \Rightarrow Bxt)$
        Initial Conditions: $-Bgt'$ Explanans
        Event Description: $-Rgt'$ Explanandum

which purports to explain why thing *g* is not a raven by inference from a covering-law asserting that, for all *x*, if *x* were a raven, then *x* would be black, and initial conditions asserting that g is not black. While it does indeed follow from these premises that *g* is not a raven, such an "explanation" hardly explains why.

Argument (10.1), of course, is simply the *modus tollens* counterpart of the *modus ponens* argument (7.1). Certainly, derivations from premises to conclusions by *modus tollens* are no less valid than derviations from premises to conclusions by *modus ponens*. Therefore, both (7.1) and (10.1) satisfy the core conception that explanations explain the occurrence of events by deriving their descriptions from premises that include at least one lawlike sentence, which is actually needed for such derivations. No doubt, without the initial premise, which is the same in both cases, their conclusions would not follow from their premises. Its counterintuitive character justifies calling this the *modus tollens* paradox.

Thus, even arguments that satisfy the core conception, including the four conditions of derivability, lawlikeness, empirical content, and truth, may be inadequate—seemingly, by virtue of their logical form, even though they are valid! Perhaps even more strikingly, even when the assumption of extensionality, which was the source of the paradoxes of confirmation, has been rejected, the paradoxes of explanation remain, a result that indicates that something is seriously wrong with the core conception, which may include some conditions that are unneeded or exclude a requirement essential to explanatory adequacy, a problem that can no longer be attributed to the assumption of extensionality.

Nomic Expectability

No doubt, it would be worthwhile to consider the alternative to the core conception that was mentioned before, namely, that explanations explain by showing that their explanandum outcomes are nomically expectable. That this is indeed a fundamental desideratum within the Hempelian scheme is beyond serious doubt. Yet it appears equally clear that—with the exception of peculiar problems encountered in the case of probabilistic explanations—Hempel sought to implement this desideratum by means of the core conception, namely, that explanations explain the occurrence of events by deriving their descriptions from premises including at least one lawlike sentence that is actually needed.[7]

Hempel drew distinctions between "explanation", "prediction", and "postdiction" in relation to arguments satisfying conditions (CA-1) to (CA-4), namely:

> While explanations, predictions, and postdictions are alike in their logical structure, they differ in certain other respects. For example, an argument [satisfying those conditions] will qualify as a *prediction* only if [the explanandum event] refers to an occurrence at a time later than that at which the argument is offered; in the case of a *postdiction*, the event must occur before the presentation of the argument. (Hempel 1958, p. 174)

Thus, Hempel tended to minimize the differences between them, which were supposed to be *pragmatic differences* that depended upon the circumstances under which explanations are advanced, including considerations of the time at which the argument is fashioned and the available background knowledge.[8]

Arguments of *modus tollens* form not only display the insufficiency of the four conditions of adequacy, however, but also reveal the limitations of Hempel's nomic expectability desideratum. Explanations such as (10.1) not only fail to explain why their explanandum events occur but also do so in spite of the derivation of their explanandum sentence from premises including a law that is actually required for that purpose. Since these outcomes are clearly "nomically expectable" in the sense that their occurrence was to be expected, given the initial conditions and the covering laws included in their premises, it appears inescapable that neither the core conception nor the nomic expectability desideratum—nor both together—is sufficient for explanatory adequacy.

The Causal Paradoxes

There are causal as well as noncausal explanations of the kind that have been under investigation to this point. Some students of explanation may be inclined to believe that the problems discussed here are "special cases" that can easily be accommodated when causal considerations are given their due. This is harmonious with the slogan "Let's put the 'cause' back into 'because',", which has been associated with the work of Wesley C. Salmon, among others, as an invitation to reconsider the role of causal relations as components of—perhaps even fundamental constitutents of—adequate explanations. This is not an implausible suggestion, moreover, insofar as causal relations involve temporal sequence and brings-about connections that appear relevant here.

Thus, a minimal conception of causal relations appears to imply that one event, called the cause, occurs temporally prior to another, called its effect, where the cause "brings about" its effect. Within theories that distinguish deterministic from indeterministic causation, there may be differences in the stength of causal tendencies. On the single-case propensity conception, for example, *deterministic causal relations* obtain when the occurrence of an event of kind c invariably (or, with universal strength) brings about an event of kind e, while *indeterministic causal relations* obtain when the occurrence of of an event of kind c probably (or, with probabilistic strength) brings about an event of kind e. The difference is the strength of the tendency (Fetzer 1981).

Even these considerations appear to make no difference. Consider, for example, any sufficient conditions for bringing about a person's death, such as being run over by a steamroller, being stepped on by an elephant, and so on. A causal law asserting that anyone run over by a steamroller at time t will be dead by time t^* (where $t^* = t + d$, a fixed temporal interval) could be fashioned by employing "$\ldots =u\Rightarrow \_\_\_$" as the universal strength causal conditional here:

(12.1)
Covering Law:	$(x)(t)(SRxt =u\Rightarrow Dxt^*)$	Explanans
Initial Conditions:	$-Dht'^*$	
Event Description:	$-SRht'$	Explanandum

which supports the inference that person h was not run over by a steamroller at time t' because he is not dead at time t'^*. For those who are still alive, therefore, we can infer *that* they have never been run over by a steamroller, stepped on by an elephant, and so on. Yet these arguments fail to explain *why* they have not been run over by a steamroller, stepped on by an elephant, and so on (Fetzer 1983a).

Maximal Specificity

In fact, being run over by a steamroller is insufficient to bring about death, since in marshy wetlands and other circumstances, it may cause injury but not death, as exemplified by a recent case near London (Jepson 1998). This reflects the crucial consideration that a necessary condition for the truth of a lawlike sentence requires that its antecedent include the presence or absence of every property whose presence or absence makes a difference to (the strength of the occurrence for) its outcome consequent. In other words, if "p" is the antecedent and "q" the consequent of a lawlike sentence that is true, then for every predicate "F" describing a property that is nomically relevant to "q", "p" implies either "F" or "$-F$" (Fetzer 1981, pp. 50–1). This is called *the requirement of maximal specificity*.

Unlike Hempel's conditions of the same name, especially Hempel (1968), this condition is relative to a language L but not to an epistemic context K.[9] It is thus an objective condition based upon an intensional analysis of nomic relevance for which a predicate "F" is *nomically relevant* to an outcome predicate "O," relative to a language L and reference predicate "R," if and only if the strength of the tendency for "O" given "R & F" differs from the strength of the tendency for "O" given "R & $-F$" (Fetzer 1981, p. 50). This formulation thus encompasses both noncausal and causal tendencies, which may be deterministic or indeterministic, within its scope, where nomically relevant properties are logically contingent, necessarily.

This intensional conception must be differentiated from its extensional counterpart, where a predicate "F" is *statistically relevant* to an outcome predicate "O", relative to a language L and reference predicate "R", if and only if the relative frequency for "O" given "R & F" differs from the relative frequency for "O" given "R & $-F$" (Fetzer 1981, pp. 88–9). When subjected to appropriate tests, repetitions of fixed sets of nomically relevant conditions tend to produce sequences of outcomes with characteristic relative frequencies, which provide an empirical basis for evaluating hypotheses about their strength, more or less as Salmon (1984) has proposed, but contrary to the statistical relevance account of explanation Salmon previously endorsed (1971), which does not sufficiently differentiate laws from correlations

Predictions and Postdictions

Even the adoption of intensional conceptions of nomic relevance does not resolve these causal paradoxes. An alternative response might be to observe that Hempel's relativization of predictions and of postdictions to the times tn at which *those arguments were advanced* in relation to the times of occurrence of their explanandum events—where predictions are offered prior to the occurrence of the explanandum, but postdictions subsequent to the occurrence—should instead be advanced in relation to the times tm of occurrence of *their initial con-*

ditions! It would then be possible to maintain that arguments are explanatory only when their initial conditions occur prior to the events that they are invoked to explain.

This would have the import of strengthening Hempel's conditions in a fashion that implements Aristotle's requirement that the premises should stand to the conclusion as cause to effect, where Aristotle urged his stronger conception—in particular, that the premises of a demonstration must be better known than and prior to the conclusion, which is further related to them as cause to effect—on these grounds:

> The premises must be the causes of the conclusion, better known than it, and prior to it; its causes, since we possess scientific knowledge of a thing only when we know its causes; prior, in order to be causes; antecedently known, this antecedent knowledge being not our mere undersanding of the meaning, but knowledge of the fact as well. (*Posterior Analytics* 1.71–2)

Although it may not have been Aristotle's intent, these conditions might be taken to imply that "initial conditions" must be *temporally prior* to explanandum events.

The adoption of this requirement in lieu of the redundant condition (CA-3), no doubt, would have the beneficial consequence of precluding the causal paradoxes and the *modus tollens* paradoxes, at least for any cases in which the initial conditions were not temporally prior to the explanandum event, such as (10.1) and (12.1). Hempel's original conditions then appear to capture requirements for *scientific inference* generally rather than those for *scientific explanation* specifically. But this approach, although appealing, does not take into account noncausal cases in which initial conditions and explananda-events are temporally simultaneous. An important class of these explanations, such as (7.1), would also be excluded, which suggests that the incorporation of this specific condition appears to be too strong.

Probabilistic Paradoxes

It seems most unlikely that the substitution of causal in lieu of noncausal law-like premises in arguments of this kind could possibly be enough to overcome the underlying problems. Neither considerations of nomic expectability nor considerations of causation appear to make a difference when confronted with arguments having *modus tollens* form. Indeed, considerations of nomic expectability and of causation came together in Hempel's studies of probabilistic explanation, where other explanatory paradoxes emerged as a result of the high probability requirement, which was motivated by Hempel's desire to retain the nomic expectability desideratum even when outcomes are merely probable and not invariable effects of the conditions that bring them about.

Consider, for example, a coin that is slightly bent to favor one side as the outcome of each toss. Suppose that, when it is given a flip, the probability of heads is .6 and of tails .4. Then employing the probabilistic causal conditional "... $=n\Rightarrow$ ___", it would be possible to formalize a probabilistic argument that would explain why the outcome of a flip of a coin i at t resulted in heads at t^*:

(15.1)   Covering Law: $(x)(t)(Fxt =.6 \Rightarrow Hxt^*)$ Explanans
         Initial Conditions: Fit'
         ————————————————————$[.6]$
         Event Description: Hit'^* Explanandum

where the bracketed numeral represents "the degree of nomic expectability" with which that explanandum ought to be expected, where Hempel insisted the value of this variable must be equal to or greater than .5 (Hempel 1968).

This condition has the paradoxical effect that probabilistic explanations of results that occur only with low probability are logically impossible, in principle.[10] If the outcome of an ace given a toss of a die occurs with a probability of only ⅙, for example, then such an outcome was not to be expected and therefore cannot be explained. Unfortunately, it might be the case that each of the possible outcomes only occurs with a probability that is less than ½, as with tosses of dice, in general, where neither the outcome of an ace nor a deuce nor a trey could be explained, while the occurrence of a nonace or a nondeuce or a nontrey could be explained, consistent with this account.

Inference versus Explanation

Jeffrey (1969) pursues these issues, suggesting that some statistical inferences are not, even potentially, statistical explanations. Thus, for example, he remarks that, for ten successive tosses with a fair coin for which the probability of heads equals ½, the probability of having at least one head equals 1023/1024:

> The number 1023/1024 is a good measure of the proper strength of our expectation of that fact; but I deny that it is a good measure of the strength of the explanation which the inference gives us. Indeed, I think it is misleading to think of the statistical inference as being an explanation at all.

He supplements his position by observing that if, for two successive tosses, the improbable were to occur and two tails occurred, which had only ¼ probability, we would have as complete an understanding of the why and the how as if it had high probability.

In his response to Jeffrey, Hempel acknowledges the suggestion that results of this kind "happen by chance" as the result of the operation of a probabilistic (or "stochastic") process, where the specific degree of nomic expectability does not affect our understanding of the processes involved. He agrees with Jeffrey:

> the understanding that statistical laws give us regarding particular events is not the deeper or more complete, the greater is the probability which the laws attribute to the event. The explanation consists of the characterization of the

stochastic process that produced the event and of what the statistical law specifies for the probabilities of the various results of this process. (Hempel 1977)

He concludes that corresponding explanans for probabilistic explanations explain the occurrence of improbable outcomes "no less well" than they explain the occurrence of probable outcomes. He thus abandons the high probability requirement.

It should be observed, however, that abandoning the high probability requirement does not necessitate abandoning the conception of explanations as arguments that display the nomic expectability of their explananda events. When *inferences* are identified with arguments that confer measures of support upon their conclusions of strength .5 or greater, then abandoning the high probability requirement entails abandoning the conception of explanations as *inferences*. But there may be alternative conceptions.[11] So long as degrees of nomic expectability do not have to have values that are $\geq$ .5, revised covering-law *explanations* could still display the degrees of nomic expectability of their explanandum events, but when they confer expectabilities that are < .5, then they could not also qualify as *predictions*.

Objective Probabilities

Hempel persists in relativizing statistical explanations to a knowledge context K, however, given his despair over the development of an objective conception of probability. And, in fact, even the most sophisticated thinkers have encountered difficulties of the kinds troubling Hempel in developing formal semantics for objective probabilities. Lewis (1980), for example, has offered a semantic conception of the *objective probability* for an outcome O in relation to world w and time t, with respect to sentences of the form "$Ptw(O) = r$", intended to capture the notion of the "propensity" or "the chance" for outcome O in world w at time t, which depends on the proximity of world w to the actual world W. The values of objective probabilities hinge on complete states of worlds w and W at t, which appears to be an indefensible position. Most properties of worlds are nomically irrelevant to the occurrence of specific outcomes, suggesting that Lewis may have committed a blunder.

Indeed, at least three kinds of considerations militate against relativizing the values of propensities or chances to complete states of the world at times. One is the *logical* consideration that complete states of the world are unique and irrepeatable, suggesting that, since O either occurs or fails to occur under those conditions, its value must equal 1 or 0, a problem that plagues statistical relevance accounts (Fetzer 1981, chap. 4). Another is the *physical* consideration that, given the truth of the theory of relativity, events that are simultaneous with or subsequent to O cannot be nomically relevant to its occurrence, which is restricted to events that occur within its backward light cone. Only such events are causally connectible to the occurrence of O, as Minkowski space/time diagrams display (cf. Salmon 1984, chap. 5).

The third is *historical* since, even within that backward light cone, only events that are causally connected to the occurrence of *O* can make a difference to its propensity or chance. That a fellow is run over by a steamroller in a marshy wetland might make a difference to his life expectancy, but not the color of his hair or the name of his wife. There are infinitely many properties whose presence or absence makes no difference at all to the strength of the tendency for an outcome *O* to occur or not and therefore make no difference to its propensity or chance. Encompassing infinitely many nomically irrelevant properties in determinations of the values of *r* drastically misrepresents the ontology of objective probabilities, not to mention the epistemic problems that it generates for ascertaining values of *r* for unique events.[12]

A Semantics for Propensities

Indeed, the maximal specificity requirement holds the key to unraveling the semantics of propensities. Assume that a world is a *p*-world when it satisfies some set of conditions described in language *L*. Every *p*-world might also be a *q*-world, where "*q*" describes some specific outcome, when either (i) *q* is *logically necessary* given *p* given the syntax and semantics of *L*, (ii) *q* is *physically necessary* given *p* because *q* is a permanent property of everything that is *p*, or (iii) *q* is *causally necessary* given *p* because *p* brings about *q* with universal strength. When *p*-worlds bring about *q*-worlds with *probabilistic strength* or *q* is merely a *transient property* of *p*, however, not all *p*-worlds can be *q*-worlds. When specific probabilistic or nonprobabilistic subjunctive or causal conditionals relating *p* and *q* are true-in-*L*, then *selection functions* across *p*-worlds that preserve appropriate permanent and dispositional properties of things obtaining in this world *W* yield the right results.[13]

While the truth of a logical implication requires that every *p*-world be a *q*-world in relation to language *L*, a permanent property relation between "*p*" and "*q*" entails that every *p*-world that is "close enough" to the actual world is a *q*-world. A simple subjunctive of the form, "$p \Rightarrow q$" is therefore ambiguous, since logical necessity, "$\Box(p \rightarrow q)$", implies "$p \Rightarrow q$", but a permanent property implies "$-\Box(p \rightarrow q)$". The truth of a causal conditional of universal strength *u* of the form "$p = u \Rightarrow q$" likewise entails that every *p*-world that is "close enough" to *W* is a *q*-world, but, unlike permanent properties, where "*p*" is temporally prior to "*q*". The problematical case is that of causal conditionals of strength *n* of the form "$p = n \Rightarrow q$", which are true when *p*-worlds that are "close enough" bring about *q-worlds* with *x probabilistic strength n*.

Since these probabilistic causal conditionals bring about one or another outcome within a fixed set of possible outcomes, some *p*-worlds are −*q*-worlds. The truth of "$p = n \Rightarrow q$" thus entails that both "$p = u \Rightarrow q$" and "$p \Rightarrow q$" must be false. Replicating exactly the same conditions from *p*-world to *p*-world with constant probability *n* qualifies sequences of *p*-worlds as sequences of independent random variables to which the central limit theorem applies. Thus, the vast majority of sequences of p-worlds will be sequences in which q-worlds occur with relative frequencies close to those of their generating probabilities. And across infinite sequences of infinite sesequences of p-worlds, those sequences collectively will have a normal distribution of sequences in which their relative frequencies equal their generating probabilities.[14]

Paradoxes of Irrelevance

The probabilistic anomalies described here—according to which an event can be explainable if it occurs with high probability, while an alternative that occurs under the same conditions but with low probability cannot—may appropriately be envisioned as *probabilistic paradoxes*, since it seems highly counterintuitive that the adequacy of an explanation should depend solely upon the degree of nomic expectability that it confers upon its explanandum. All of these problems—the paradox of transposition, the *modus tollens* paradox, the nomic expectability and causal anomalies, and the probabilistic paradoxes—are distinct in kind from other counterexamples that have been widely discussed in the work of Wesley Salmon and Henry Kyburg, which exemplify *paradoxes of irrelevance* as explanations that are not satisfactory because they include conditions irrelevant to their outcomes.

Kyburg, for example, advanced the hexed table salt example, in particular:

(19.1)   This sample of table salt dissolves in water, for it has had a dissolving spell cast upon it, and all samples of table salt that have had dissolving spells cast upon them dissolve in water. (Kyburg 1965)

And Salmon demonstrated that it was not difficult produce other examples:

(19.2)   John Jones avoided becoming pregnant during the past year, for he has taken his wife's birth control pills regularly, and every man who regulary takes birth control pills avoids pregnancy. (Salmon 1971)

These cases are paradoxical, because they provide "explanations" that explain their explananda by citing factors in addition to those that make a difference to the outcome to be explained, where men do not become pregnant whether or not they take birth control pills and table salt dissolves even without a hex.

Diagnosing the Problem

Apart from the peculiar problems posed by probabilistic explanations, all of these problematic examples have the following features. They all satisfy the core conception, and yet none of them explains its explanandum outcome. All of them satisfy Hempel's four conditions of adequacy, (CA-1) to (CA-4), yet not one of them is adequate. Each of them satisfies Hempel's desideratum of nomic expectability, yet none of them fulfills our intuitive expectations. Each of them seems to fulfill the Hempelian standard (with respect to his semiformal explication), yet none of them satisfies Hempelian expectations (with respect to their capacity to explain their explananda). Each of them provides an inference that something is the case, yet none of them successfully explains why it is the case.

If there were no more to explanations than inferences from premises including laws, then the core conception would be sufficient. These counterexamples make it manifest that the core conception is insufficient, because there is more to explanations than inferences from premises including laws. Causal relations suggest the direction in which an appropriate solution to these difficulties may be found, because events that bring about other events are causally responsible for their occurrence. The desideratum of *nomic expectability* must be replaced by the desideratum of *nomic responsibility* (Fetzer 1992). Explanations explain by citing all and only those properties whose presence made a difference to the occurrence of their explanandum events. And properties whose presence made no difference to their occurrence must be excluded as explanatorily irrelevant.

Arguments that satisfy the desideratum of nomic responsibility by citing all and only those factors, causal or noncausal, as the case may be, that were responsible for their explanandum events also display the—high or low—nomic expectability of those very occurrences, but the converse is not the case. Being nonblack may be sufficient to warrant the inference that something is a nonraven, but that property is surely not nomically responsible for that being the case. Being alive may be enough to warrant the inference that someone has not been run over by a steamroller, but it does not establish the conditions that are nomically responsible for that being the case. The solution requires imposing a new condition to exclude properties not nomically relevant to the explanandum.

Solving the Problem

In the paradoxical examples involving *modus tollens*, for example, the explanans include lawlike premises and initial conditions, where those conditions are not nomically responsible for their explanandum-events. Even though sentences describing those conditions are related logically by their argument form to sentences describing those outcomes, they are not nomically related in a way which insures that they are permanent attributes of reference properties or as cause to effect. The crucial consideration thus appears to be fixing the relationship between the antecedents of the lawlike premises in relation to the explanandum events to insure that an appropriate explanatory connection obtains between the initial conditions and the explanandum event when they are related by law.

The problem cannot be solved merely by restricting the antecedents of lawlike premises to conditions that are nomically relevant to their consequents. In fact, even the examples of paradoxes of irrelevance have *modus tollens* variants, which suggest that the problems involved here are deeper in kind. Consider the lawlike generalization that all men who regularly take birth control pills do not become pregnant relative to Mary Smith, who happens to be pregnant, namely:

(21.1)   Mary Smith is not a man who regularly takes birth control pills, because all men who regularly take birth control pills do not become pregnant, and Mary Smith is pregnant.

No one should want to claim such an argument "explains why" its explanandum—that Mary Smith is not a man who regularly takes birth control pills—is true.

Since men do not become pregnant, whether or not they take birth control pills, it may be tempting to suppose that the problem could be solved merely by restricting the antecents of lawlike premises to conditions that are nomically relevant to their consequents. The result, however, assumes a familiar form:

(21.2)   Mary Smith is not a man, because men do not become pregnant, and Mary Smith is pregnant.

Once again, although this argument may be sound, it does not explain why its explanandum event—that Mary Smith is not a man—is the case, a consequence that can be overcome by imposing the stronger requirement that the antecedents of the lawlike premises of explanations must be restricted to properties that are nomically relevant to their explananda, known as *the requirement of strict maximal specificity* (Fetzer 1981, pp. 125–6; cf. Salmon 1984, p. 31).

A Better Covering-Law Account

Hempel contributed greatly to clarifying the difference between various kinds of questions, such the difference between knowing *that* something is the case and knowing *why* something is the case. The core conception provides an answer to the first of these questions, because we can know that something is the case when we can derive its description from premises that include laws. But adequate answers to the first are not necessarily adequate answers to the second. In order to implement the desideratum of nomic responsibility, therefore, a condition that excludes nomically irrelevant factors from the laws that appear in the explanans of adequate explanations *relative to the explanandum* must be added to his conditions as a substitute for redundant condition (CA-3).

Thus, an improved covering-law account emerges from this discussion, one that incorporates conditions of (CA-1) derivability, (CA-2) lawlikeness, (CA-3') strict maximal specificity, and (CA-4) truth (Fetzer 1981, pp. 124–36; Salmon 1984, p. 31). An unexpected benefit of this model, moreover, is that it places the nomic expectability desideratum into perspective relative to probabilistic and nonprobabilistic explanations alike. While it might be appropriate to preserve the high probability requirement in relation to *predictions*, there appears to be no justification for its retention in relation to *explanations*. The adequacy of an explanation does not hinge on the strength of its nomic expectability. When complete sets of relevant factors that bring an event about have been taken into account, the specific strength of nomic expectability, high or low, does not matter.

Ultimately, therefore, distinctions must be drawn between two conceptions of explanation between which Hempel did not sufficently differentiate, namely:

Explanation1 =df an argument that displays the nomic expectability of the occurrence of its explanandum-event based on general laws and other conditions; and

Explanation2 =df an argument that displays the general laws and other conditions nomically responsible for the occurrence of the explanandum-event (Fetzer 1992, p. 259).

An adequate *explanation2* entails an adequate *explanation1*, but not conversely. This distinction appears to supply the foundation for an improved covering-law account that supplies a better theory of explanation in the Hempelian tradition.

Explanation versus Inference

It would not be mistaken to suppose that this revised covering-law theory of explanation incorporates stronger conditions than those Hempel proposed and in that sense represents a shift in the direction of a more Aristotelian conception. The requirements that the premises of demonstrations must be "true, primary, immediate, better known than and prior to the conclusion, which is further related to them as cause to effect" appear to be calculated to insure that the premises describe conditions that are nomically responsible for their explananda events. Even arguments of form (6.1), for example, seem to exemplify predictions that are not also potential explanations because they are based on *accidental generalizations*, which are merely universal rather than commensurately universal regularities in Aristotelian language.

Employing the conception of predictions and postdictions as inferences to events that are later than or earlier than their initial conditions, arguments of form (12.1) display *postdictions* that are not also explanations, while arguments of form (15.1) involving low probabilities display *explanations* that are not also predictions. If we call inferences to simultaneous events retrodictions, then arguments of form (10.1) are *retrodictions* that are not also explanations. The postdictions and retrodictions are further illuminated from the perspective of Aristotle's theory of the four causes, since it ought to be obvious that the absence of efficient causation does not serve as a suitable basis for *explaining* the absence of effects it would otherwise bring about, where their premises do not stand as causes in relation to their conclusions as effects.

Hempel's classic conditions—of extensionality, the core conception, and the equivalence condition—thus appear to define a broad class of arguments that qualify as instances of *scientific reasoning* that are nonexplanatory. Hempel's commitment to extensional methodology, which was robust but Spartan, precluded the development of adequate conceptions of probabilistic or of nonprobabilistic laws, which are essential to the theory of explanation. Yet even the revised Hempelian account incorporates the core conception for a logical display of the nomic expectability of explanandum events. Hempel also acknowledged other patterns that do not require lawlike premises, which implied that his constraints were not necessary conditions for reasoning to be scientific, but they surely are patterns of inference of great practical and theoretical importance.

Inference to the Best Explanation

A subtle point remains for consideration, however, since the abandonment of the high-probability requirement implies that scientific *explanations* are not invariably scientific *inferences*, when "inferences" are understood as arguments that confer high probabilities on their conclusions. As Hempel would emphasize (Hempel 1965, 1968), the point of an explanation is not to establish the truth of the explanandum sentence, because explanations are characteristically advanced to account for events whose occurrence has already been established on independent grounds. This has encouraged several students of explanation, including Salmon (1971), to suppose that degrees of nomic expectability are not required even for probabilistic explanations, for which they propose alternative accounts that dispense with them.[15] It turns out, however, that "inferences" are better understood as arguments that provide *strong support* for their conclusions, which may or may not require establishing their high probability.

Abandoning nomic expectabilities appears to be a blunder, because these logical probabilities forge the linkage between explanation, prediction, and inference. Such bracketed values not only represent estimates of the truth frequencies with which explanandum sentences of that form may be expected to be true over extended sequences of trials, given the truth of premises with the form of those explanans sentences, but also function as a designation of the degree of nomic expectability for such outcomes to occur on each individual trial with the force of logical necessity, a benefit derived from the propensity account of probability that in turn provides an ingredient essential for *inference to the best explanation* (Fetzer 1981, 1993).

When the likelihood L of hypothesis h, given evidence e, is defined as equal to the probability P of e, given h, this relationship may be formalized as follows:

(24.1) $L(h/e) = P(e/h)$

which might be applied to probability hypotheses generally. A special version is required to apply for inference to laws in relation to the nomic expectability of evidence describing the initial conditions and the explanandum, specifically:

(24.2) $NL(L/IC \ \& \ E) = NE(E/L \ \& \ IC)$

which asserts that the nomic likelihood *NL* that law *L* obtains, given the initial conditions *IC* and the explanandum *E*, equals the nomic expectability *NE* of the explanandum *E*, given an explanans of *IC* and the law *L* (Fetzer 1981, p. 223).

This conception permits the application of Hacking's *law of likelihood* as the fundamental principle of reasoning for inference to the best explanation, where (1) evidence *e* supports hypothesis *h1* better than it does hypothesis *h2* when the likelihood of *h1*, given *e*, exceeds that of *h2*, given *e*, and (2) evidence *e* supports *h1* better than it supports *h2* when the likelihood ratio of *h1* to *h2* exceeds 1 (Hacking 1965, pp. 70–1). While satisfying these relations may make *h1* preferable to *h2*, however, that does not mean that *h1* is therefore acceptable as well, which depends upon the quantity and quality of the available evidence *e*.

Nomic Likelihoods

The conception of nomic likelihoods appears to apply to inferences to laws as explanations of relative frequencies as well as to explanations that use laws to draw inferences to explanations for singular events. Consider, to begin with, an explanation for the occurrence of decay by an atom of polonium[218], namely:

$$(25.1) \quad (x)[P^{218} xt \Rightarrow (Txt = 3.05 \text{ min} =.5 \Rightarrow Dxt + 3.05 \text{ min})]$$
$$P^{218}jt' \ \& \ Tjt' = 3.05 \text{ min}$$
$$\overline{\rule{8cm}{0pt}}=[.5]$$
$$Djt' + 3.05 \text{ min}$$

whose lawlike premise asserts that, if *x* were an atom of polonium[218], subjecting *x* to a time trial of 3.05 minutes duration would bring about its decay with propensity .5, where the nomic expectability for such an outcome is [.5].

That the halflife of polonium[218] is 3.05 minutes not only means that a single atom *j* has a propensity of .5 to decay during a 3.05 minute interval but also imples that that same atom has a propensity of .5 to not undergo decay during that same interval. It also implies that, for large numbers of atoms of polonium[218] given at a specific time, very close to one-half will still exist 3.05 minutes later, the remainder having disintegrated by decay (Hempel 1966, p. 66). And if the halflife of polonium[218] were not known, repeated observations of decay on this order would support such an inference as the hypothesis that provides the best explanation for the frequency data.

Alternative hypotheses that might deserve consideration would include those that cluster around the observed relative frequency of decay in large samples, which would have values close to 3.05 minutes. Those hypotheses would have high likelihoods by virtue of making those outcomes highly probable, which indicates that more than one hypothesis can have high likelihood within the framework of this nonprobabilistic account (Fetzer 1981, p. 276). When repeated sequences of random trials are conducted under suitable test conditions and yield stable relative frequencies for decay, the hypothesis with the highest likelihood would deserve to be accepted (Fetzer 1981, chap. 9).

Induction and Explanation

Thus, measures which are internal to the evidence can provide a standard for determining that sufficient evidence has become available, namely: when the relative frequencies for possible outcomes have "settled down" and display stable values that have resisted our best efforts to change them, then we have appropriate evidence for the acceptance of the most likely hypothesis. While the severity of the tests that should be employed for this purpose tends to depend upon the seriousness of the consequences of making mistakes, objective criteria for acceptance have been advanced that make the sufficiency of evidence a function of the distribution of the data (Fetzer 1981, especially pp. 244–54).

One such approach proposes the degree of divergence of the observed data from a normal distribution as a suitable measure of epistemic caution, where no hypothesis may be accepted from the set of alternatives unless its likelihood is greater than this degree of divergence, which might be measured by the Levy distance (Gnedenko and Kolmogoroff 1954, p. 33). Hypotheses with high likelihood on the data may be acceptable *even* when our measure of confidence happens to be low, while hypotheses with low likelihood on the data will be acceptable *only* when our measure of confidence happens to be high (Fetzer 1981).[16]

If these considerations are well founded, then degrees of nomic expectability are not only fundamental to the theory of explanation but also indispensable for the theory of induction. The purpose of this inquiry was to suggest that Hempel's work on the theory of induction could shed light on his theory of explanation by exposing various paradoxes of explanation. By embracing an intensional methodology, I have discovered solutions to these problems that relate explanation to prediction and to inference. Degrees of nomic expectability appear to be fundamental to scientific reasoning, including the pattern known as inference to the best explanation. It is testimony to Hempel's enduring genius that his theory of explanation appears to clarify and illuminate the nature of induction at least as much as his theory of induction clarifies and illuminates the nature of explanation.

NOTES

I am indebted to Donald E. Nute and to Ellery Eells for comments and criticism.

1. While Hempel initially allowed "general analytic sentences" to count as lawlike, where the adequacy of an explanation does not depend on the logical contingency of each of its individual premises but upon the empirical content of the totality of those premises collectively (Hempel and Oppenheim 1948, p. 265), he would later emphasize that lawlike sentences must be empirical and not merely logical truths (Hempel 1968, p. 125). In this context, I assume that the logical requirements for lawlike sentences entail both logical contingency and unrestricted generality. He proposed that "fundamental" as opposed to "derivative" laws be formulated by means of purely qualitative predicates and endorsed the desideratum elaborated by Nelson Goodman

(1947, 1955) that lawlike sentences should have the capacity to support subjunctive and counterfactual conditionals, which Goodman analyzed as a pragmatical phenomenon (Fetzer 1993, pp. 26–33).

2. During my junior year as a Princeton undergraduate in 1960–61, I submitted a paper to G. Dennis O'Brien, then an instructor but later president of the University of Rochester, making the same observations. He marked my paper "Fantastic!" and called me in to ask whether I had made this up myself or had obtained it from another source. I reassured him. I had thought it was obvious.

3. With respect to unrestrictedly general material conditionals that are not lawlike, the paradoxes no longer appear paradoxical, since it appears unsurprising that whatever confirms them in one formulation should confirm every other.

4. Although Hempel originally assumed that explanations and predictions must satisfy the same conditions and are therefore symmetrical (Hempel and Oppenheim 1948, p. 249), he subsequently accepted criticism from Israel Scheffler and conceded that some forms of scientific prediction, such as inferences from finite samples to finite samples, do not qualify as explanatory, while persisting in maintaining that every adequate explanation is potentially predictive, had its explanans been taken into account at some suitable earlier time (Hempel 1963, pp. 119–20).

5. Van Fraassen remarks that Lewis's account is the most empirical of the theories of lawfulness he considers (van Fraassen 1989, p. 40). The counterexamples that I offer here do not depend upon whether or not Lewis's approach is epistemic in a strict sense, since they apply to any account of the general kind that he endorses in specifying reasons why empirical uniformities are not therefore lawful in kind.

6. Thus, for example, the sentences "Caesar is assassinated" and "*Crest* fights cavities" may be timeless truths, but it is absurd to infer from their conjunction (or its commutation) to corresponding subjunctives "If it were the case that Caesar is assassinated, then it would be the case that *Crest* fights cavities" or "If it were the case that *Crest* fights cavities, then it would be the case that Caesar is assassinated." And it requires of specific coin flips (or specific time trials of atoms of polonium^{218}) that if that coin is flipped and comes up heads (or that atom undergoes decay) then it must be true that any replication of that same coin flipping on that same occasion would have come up heads (or that same time trial of that polonium^{218} atom would have undergone decay), which contradicts the assumption that these processes are indeterministic, where two or more outcomes are possible under those conditions. These features are not incidental to these accounts, moreover, but result from the adoption of inherently inadequate possible-world similarity conditions. For more discussion, see Nute (1975), Fetzer and Nute (1979 and 1980), and Fetzer (1981).

7. Thus, deductive (or "deductive-nomological") explanations show that their outcome events are nomically expectable because they are *the only possible outcomes*, given the truth of their explanans-premises. In this case, the desiderata of nomic expectability and of predictability coincide. In the case of probabilistic (or "inductive-statistical") explanations, however, *other outcomes are possible*, even given the truth of their explanans-premises. In imposing the requirement of high probability, Hempel identified *expectability* with *predictability*, which dictated that expectable outcomes must have logical probabilities ≥ 0.5. For futher discussion, see the section "Inference versus Explanation" hereafter.

8. In a study of Adolf Grünbaum's defense of the symmetry thesis (Grünbaum 19–63), I suggested that he "may have been inspired in part by somewhat vague and

ambiguous passages" introducing "The Theoretician's Dilemma," which are those under consideration here (Fetzer 1974, p. 186). It appears evident in retrospect that Hempel was simply stating a consequence of "the core conception." He had already conceded that some predictions are not potential explanations (n. 3).

9. The importance of language relativity for philosophical inquiries, in Hempel's conception, was brought home to me by his response after I sent him a copy of Fetzer (1977), which I considered my most important paper. He told me that he could not evaluate its significance, because the claims that I made therein were not relative to a language L, an objection I sought to overcome in Fetzer (1981).

10. During my senior year, 1961–62, I participated in Hempel's senior seminar. When he advanced his original account of statistical explanation, Burleigh Taylor Wilkins leaned over to me and remarked, "Doesn't this mean that explanations of events with low probability are logically impossible?", with which I agreed. At his urging, I asked Hempel the same question, which he acknowleged was indeed the case, while apologizing for having no better solution for the problem at hand.

11. Probabilistic explanations with low probabilities, such as those that explain the occurrrence of two tails as the outcome of two tosses with a fair coin, do not have "detachable conclusions," which is why their adequacy requires the truth of their explananda-sentences as well as the truth of their explanans-premises. Jeffreys's example not only appears to qualify as an adequate explanation that cannot qualify as a potential prediction but also as a classic example of "statistical inference."

12. Indeed, propensities satisfy the Markov condition that renders most of the world's history nomically and therefore explanatorily irrelevant (Fetzer 1983a). Lewis compounds the problem by embracing a form of possible worlds' realism that makes other possible worlds "just as real" as the actual world (Lewis 1986). Stalnaker avoids this difficulty, at least, viewing possible worlds as "abstractions from the dispositions of rational agents" for representing and relating meanings (Stalnaker 1984, p. 166). Pollock appears to fare least well, not only committing himself to the thesis that "p & q" implies "$p \Rightarrow q$" but also to the conception that the values of objective probabilities are relative to "the entire state of the universe" that is earlier than or simultaneous with O (Pollock 1990, pp. 269, 272).

13. What is fundamental is the truth of these conditionals in relation to the actual world W, which is determined by its permanent and dispositional properties, not by classes of possible worlds. The world's ontological structure thus determines the distribution of possible worlds, not vice versa, as Lewis and others presume.

14. These relationships are reflected by the probabilistic causal calculus C, which Nute and I developed (Nute 1975; Fetzer and Nute 1979, 1980; Fetzer 1981). The criticism advanced by Ellery Eells (1983)—namely, that there is no way to order sequences of sequences of possible worlds to insure the right result—is therefore mistaken at least to the extent to which it is predicated upon the assumption that it is the possible-world distributions that determine the truth conditions of these conditionals, when it is the ontology that dictates the syntax and the semantics. For further discussion, see Harper et al. (1981), Eells (1983), and Fetzer (1984).

15. In his most recent work on causal-mechanistic conceptions of explanation, Salmon acknowledges the role of degrees of nomic expectability in partitioning references classes (Salmon 1984). Railton (1978, 1981) and Humphreys (1981, 1983, 1985), however, eschew them entirely. For discussion of other problems that these accounts may encounter, see Fetzer (1983a, 1987, 1991b, 1992).

16. Since the relative frequencies displayed during the history of the world maybe unrepresentative "by chance," inferences drawn in accordance with Hacking's law of likelihood are *fallible*, which reflects their character as outcomes of inductive reasoning. Science progresses on the assumption that the segment of world history to which we have access through experience represents a *random* sample, which is testable relative to new hypotheses, new technology, and new evidence. This consideration is closely related to the justification of induction (Fetzer 1981, chap. 7).

REFERENCES

Eells, E. 1983. "Objective Probability Theory Theory." *Synthese* 57:387–442.

Fetzer, J. H. 1974. "Grunbaum's 'Defense' of the Symmetry Thesis." *Philosophical Studies* 25:173–87.

———. 1977. "A World of Dispositions." *Synthese* 34:397–421.

———. 1981. *Scientific Knowledge*. Dordrecht: Reidel.

———. 1983a. "Probabilistic Explanations." In *PSA 1982*. edited by P. Asquith and T. Nickles. Vol. 2. East Lansing, Mich.: Philosophy of Science Association.

———. 1983b. "Transcendent Laws and Empirical Procedures." In *The Limits of Lawfulness*, edited by N. Rescher. Lanham, Md.: University Press of America.

———. 1984. "Probabilistic Metaphysics." In *Probability and Causality*, edited by J. Fetzer. Dordrecht: Reidel.

———. 1987. "Critical Notice: Wesley Salmon's *Scientific Explanation and the Causal Structure of the World*." *Philosophy of Science* 54:597–610.

———. 1991a. "Are There Laws of Nature? Discussion Review of Bas van Fraassen, *Laws and Symmetry*." *Philosophical Books* 32:65–75.

———. 1991b. "Critical Notice: Philip Kitcher and Wesley C. Salmon, eds., *Scientific Explanation*; and Wesley C. Salmon, *Four Decades of Scientific Explanation*." *Philosophy of Science* 58:288–306.

———. 1992. "What's Wrong with Salmon's History: The Third Decade." *Philosophy of Science* 59:246–62.

———. 1993. *Philosophy of Science*. New York: Paragon House.

Fetzer, J. H., and D. Nute. 1979. "Syntax, Semantics, and Ontology: A Probabilistic Causal Calculus." *Synthese* 40:453–95.

———. 1980. "A Probabilistic Causal Calculus: Conflicting Conceptions." *Synthese* 44:241–6. Errata, *Synthese* 48:493.

Gnedenko, B. V., and A. N. Kolmogorov. 1954. *Limits Distributions for Sums of Independent Random Variables*. Reading, Mass.: Addison-Wesley.

Goodman, N. 1947. "The Problem of Counterfactual Conditionals." *Journal of Philosophy* 44:113–28.

———. 1955. *Fact, Fiction,and Forecast*. Cambridge, Mass.: Harvard University Press.

Grunbaum, A. 1963. *Philosophical Problems of Space and Time*. New York: Knopf.

Hacking, I. 1965. *Logic of Statistical Inference*. Cambridge, England: Cambridge University Press.

Harper, W., et al., eds. 1981. *Ifs*. Dordrecht: Reidel.

Hempel, C. G. 1945. "Studies in the Logic of Confirmation." *Mind* 54:1–26, 97–121. (Page references in the text are to the article as reprinted in Hempel [1965].)

———. 1958. "The Theoretician's Dilemma." In *Minnesota Studies in the Philosophy of Science*, edited by H. Feigl, M. Scriven, and G. Maxwell. Vol. 2. Minneapolis: University of Minnesota Press. (Page references in the text are to the article as reprinted in Hempel [1965].)

————. 1963. "Explanation and Prediction by Covering Laws." In *Philosophy of Science: The Delaware Seminar*, edited by B. Baumrin. Vol. 1, 1961–62. New York: Interscience.

————. 1965. *Aspects of Scientific Explanation*. New York: Free Press.

————. 1966. *Philosophy of Natural Science*. Englewood Cliffs, N.J.: Prentice-Hall.

————. 1968. "Lawlikeness and Maximal Specificity in Probabilistic Explanation." *Philosophy of Science* 35:116–33.

————. 1977. "Postscript 1976: More Recent Ideas on the Problem of Statistical Explanation." In *Aspekete Wissenschaftlicher Erkldrung*. Berlin: de Gruyter. (An English translation by Hazel Maxian appears in *The Philosophy of Carl G. Hempel*, edited by J. H. Fetzer. New York: Oxford University Press, 2001.)

Hempel, C. G., and P. Oppenheim. 1948. "Studies in the Logic of Explanation." *Philosophy of Science* 15:135–75. (Page references in the text are to the article as reprinted in Hempel [1965].)

Humphreys, P. 1981. "Aleatory Explanations." *Synthese* 48:225–32.

————. 1983. "Aleatory Explanations Expanded." In *PSA 1982*, edited by P. Asquith and T. Nickles. East Lansing, Mich.: Philosophy of Science Association.

————. 1985. *The Chances of Explanation*. Princeton: Princeton University Press.

Jeffrey, R. C. 1969. "Statistical Explanation vs. Statistical Inference." In *Essays in Honor of Carl G. Hempel*, edited by N. Rescher. Dordrecht: Reidel.

Jepson, A. 1998. "I Was Squished by a Steamroller." *National Enquirer*, 19 May, p. 10.

Kyburg, H. 1965. "Comments." *Philosophy of Science* 32:147–51.

Lewis, D. 1973. *Counterfactuals*. Cambridge: Harvard University Press.

————. 1980. "A Subjectivist's Guide to Objective Chance," in W. Harper et al., *Ifs* (Dordrecht: Reidel, 1980), pp. 267–297.

————. 1986. *On the Plurality of Worlds*. New York: Blackwell.

Nute, D. 1975. "Counterfactuals and the Similarity of Worlds." *Journal of Philosophy* 72:773–8.

Pollock, J. 1974. "Subjunctive Generalizations." *Synthese* 28:199–214.

————. 1976. *Subjunctive Reasoning*. Dordrecht: Reidel.

————. 1990. *Nomic Probability and the Foundations of Induction*. New York: Oxford University Press.

Railton, P. 1978. "A Deductive-Nomological Model of Probabilistic Explanation." *Philosophy of Science* 45:206–26.

————. 1981. "Probability, Explanation, and Information." *Synthese* 48:233–56.

Salmon, W. C. 1971. *Statistical Explanation and Statistical Relevance*. Pittsburgh: University of Pittsburgh Press.

————. 1984. *Scientific Explanation and the Causal Structure of the World*. Princeton: Princeton University Press.

Stalnaker, R. 1968. "A Theory of Conditionals." *American Philosophical Quarterly*, supplementary monograph no. 2 Oxford: Blackwell.

————. 1984. *Inquiry*. Cambridge, Mass.: MIT Press.

van Fraassen, B. 1989. *Laws and Symmetry*. Oxford: Clarendon Press.

6

Hempel's Theory of Statistical Explanation

ILKKA NIINILUOTO

Deductive-Nomological Explanation

Carl G. Hempel's seminal papers "The Function of General Laws in History" (1942) and "Studies in the Logic of Explanation" (1948, with Paul Oppenheim) opened a new research area in the philosophy of science. The logical empiricists in Berlin and Vienna had initiated in the 1920s the application of exact conceptual tools from logic to the analysis of the language of science and the structure of scientific theories, and this program was continued after the war in the English-speaking analytic philosophy of science. One of the main items in the new philosophical agenda resulted from Hempel's proposal to make precise, or to "explicate" in Rudolf Carnap's sense, the notion of scientific explanation. Hempel's most extensive account of his own view, with replies to critics, was given in the essay "Aspects of Scientific Explanation" (1965).

According to Hempel's *deductive-nomological (D-N) model*, scientific explanations are arguments which answer why-questions about particular events or general regularities by "subsuming" them under general laws and particular antecedent conditions. The *explanandum* is a statement E about a fact, an event, or a regularity which is already known (or believed) to be true. Therefore, Hempel distinguished "explanation-seeking why-questions" from "reason-giving why-questions" which seek epistemic grounds or justification for believing or asserting that E is the case (Hempel 1965, p. 334). Still, he required that rationally acceptable answers to the question 'Why did E occur?' must offer information which shows that E was to be expected (p. 367). Hence, according to Hempel's symmetry thesis, every adequate explanation is a potential prediction, and every prediction is a potential explanation.

The "subsumption theory" of explanation has also been called the covering-law model, since it requires that the *explanans* contains at least one law. The D-N model can be summarized as follows.

$L_1, L_2, \ldots, L_r$	General laws	
$C_1, C_2, \ldots, C_k$	Statements of antecedent conditions	Explanans

Logical deduction

$$E$$ | Description of the event or regularity to be explained | Explanandum.

A D-N explanation is *true,* if its explanans is true. This was initially one of the Hempel-Oppenheim adequacy conditions, but later Hempel found it appropriate to relax this requirement and introduce the notions of *well-confirmed* and *potential* explanation (1965, pp. 249, 338). Even though the truth value of the premises of a potential D-N explanation may be unknown, the explanans should in any case include *nomic* or *lawlike* premises.

According to the Humean "regularity" view, laws of nature are simply extensional "constant conjunctions" between properties or types of events. Thus, the logical form of the *universal* or *deterministic law* 'All Fs are G' is simply $(x)(Fx \rightarrow Gx)$.[1] Hempel supplemented this view with the requirement that a lawlike generalization has to be "essentially generalized," that is, not logically equivalent to a conjunction of singular sentences (1965, p. 340). In other words, the predicates 'F' and 'G' should be "nomic" in the sense that they are not restricted to a finite number of instances on purely logical grounds (Hempel 1968). Richard Braithwaite (1953) and Ernest Nagel (1961) defended sophisticated forms of the regularity view by linking lawlikeness with the methodological functions of universal generalizations, especially their systematic connections with other laws in scientific theories. Another methodological criterion, advocated by Nelson Goodman (1955), is the ability of laws to receive inductive support or confirmation from their instances (see Hempel 1965, p. 342).

However, the task of distinguishing genuine laws from merely accidentally true generalizations turned out to be a hard problem. As the hallmark of lawlikeness is the ability to sustain counterfactual and subjunctive conditionals (see Hempel 1965, p. 339), non-Humean or "realistic" analyses take laws to involve "nomic," "physical," or "causal" necessities (see Lewis 1973; Fetzer 1981) or second-order relations between Aristotelian universals (see Armstrong 1983; Tooley 1987).

If the logical form of lawlike statements is expressed by (or at least entails) universal generalizations, paradigmatic simple examples of D-N explanations are represented by

(1) $(x)(Fx \rightarrow Gx)$
          Fa
          ─────────
          Ga

(2) $(x)(Fx \rightarrow Gx)$
$(x)(Hx \rightarrow Fx)$
$(x)(Hx \rightarrow Gx).$

But the general task of giving sufficient and necessary conditions for adequate deductive scientific explanations proved to be surprisingly difficult, and several attempts led to no definitive conclusions (see the surveys in Tuomela 1977; Stegmüller 1983; compare Schurz 1995–96).

In the late 1950s, Hempel's D-N model was criticized for its restriction to a syntactic-semantic approach which excludes pragmatic aspects of explanation (e.g., the epistemic state and interests of the person raising the explanatory question). However, it seems more correct to say that Hempel was always concerned with understanding provided by *scientific* explanations (see Hempel 1965, p. 333), so that his treatment of explanation presupposes as given a particular pragmatic context, namely, inquiry within the scientific community. Recent interrogative approaches to explanation suggest that Hempel's treatment is by no means incompatible with the pragmatics of explanation (see Sintonen 1989), and the D-N model in a sense even gets support from the logic of why-questions (see Hintikka and Halonen 1995).

Historical Remarks on the Subsumption Theory

Hempel's articles on explanation have had a decisive impact on the later analytic philosophy of science. But to understand and appreciate his achievement, it is important to consider also his precursors. This is a topic which is largely neglected in Wesley Salmon's in many other ways illuminating historical survey (1989) of the "four decades of scientific explanation." According to Salmon, "the 1948 Hempel-Oppenheim article marks the division between the prehistory and the history of modern discussions of scientific explanation" (p. 10). His historical account jumps directly from Aristotle to Hempel, mentioning only John Stuart Mill and Karl Popper in a footnote (p. 187).

After Hempel's (1942) paper about the deductive-nomological pattern of historical explanation, Karl Popper complained that Hempel had only reproduced *his* theory of causal explanation, originally presented in *Logik der Forschung* (1935; see Popper 1945, chap. 25, n. 7; Popper 1957, p. 144). With his charming politeness, Hempel pointed out that his account of D-N explanation is "by no means novel" but "merely summarizes and states explicitly some fundamental points which have been recognized by many scientists and methodologicists." Hempel went on to quote definitions of explanation as subsumption under laws from the 1858 edition of John Stuart Mill's *A System of Logic* (first edition 1843), from Stanley Jevons's *Principles of Science* (first edition 1873), and from the books of Ducasse (in 1925), Cohen and Nagel (in 1934), and Popper (in 1935) (see Hempel 1965, p. 251). Later he added N. R. Campbell (in 1920) to this list (Hempel 1965, p. 337).

In the same spirit, with sarcasm directed at Popper, von Wright has remarked that "in point of fact the 'Popper-Hempel' theory of explanation had been something of a philosophic commonplace ever since the days of Mill and Jevons" (von Wright 1971, p. 175).

In an often quoted passage, Mill says that "an individual fact is said to be explained by pointing out its cause, that is, by stating the law or laws of causation of which its production is an instance," and "in a similar manner, a law of uniformity in nature is said to be explained when another law or laws are pointed out, of which that law itself is but a case, and from which it could be deduced" (1906, p. 305). This is an elaboration of Auguste Comte's assertion in 1830 that science endeavors to discover the "actual laws of phenomena," or "their invariable relations of succession and likeness," so that "the explanation of facts . . . consists henceforth only in the connection established between different particular phenomena and some general facts" (Comte 1970, p. 2).

Comte and Mill defended the subsumption theory of explanation in a strict empiricist form where laws express verifiable general connections between observable phenomena. Many later positivists and instrumentalists excluded explanations from science, since they thought that science should drop *why*-questions in favour of descriptive *how*-questions. Pierre Duhem in 1907 explicitly expressed the fear that the aim of explanation would "subordinate" science to metaphysics (Duhem 1954, p. 10). Carnap has given the testimony that Ernst Mach in the late nineteenth century, as well the Vienna Circle of his own youth in the 1920s, reacted against "the philosophical climate of German idealism," but in the postwar United States such a caution is no longer necessary—and the idea of explanation by laws can be defended (Carnap 1966, p. 12).

The subsumption theory of explanation is a natural ally of the *hypothetico-deductive method*, as developed by René Descartes, Robert Boyle, and Isaac Newton in the seventeenth century, and John Herschel and William Whewell in the nineteenth century. They demanded that a good hypothesis or theory should "explicate," "explain," "prove," "demonstrate," or "account for" known facts. In this view, a theoretical hypothesis, even if it is not directly verifiable, receives inductive support or confirmation from those observed facts that it successfully explains. The hypothetico-deductive method was also defended by Hempel against the "narrowly inductivist view" which claims that hypotheses can be inductively inferred from evidence (see Hempel 1965, p. 75). Inductivism in this sense tends to restrict the methodological function of theories to the prediction of new observable phenomena.

The origin of the theory of deductive explanation goes even further back in early history—to the Aristotelian ideal of demonstrative science. Aristotle distinguished four types of "causes" or "explanatory factors" (Greek *aitia*) and argued that inquiry proceeds from knowing *that* to knowing *why*. "We cannot claim to know a subject matter until we have grasped the 'why' of it, that is, its fundamental explanation." (Aristotle 1961, p. 28.) First we know by observation that there is a fact; then the answer to a why-question is provided by a *scientific syllogism* which demonstrates the fact as an effect of its cause. This explanatory stage of science was called *compositio* (synthesis) by medieval and Renaissance Aristotelians. The paradigmatic examples (1) and (2) of Hempelian D-N explanations are arguments which can be formulated in the mode of Aristotle's *Barbara* syllogism. Aristotle's *Posterior Analytics* can thus be viewed as the first systematic attempt to disclose the deductive structure of scientific explanation.

Aristotle's historical position in the logical theory of deductive explanation does not diminish our appreciation of Hempel's achievement. While the Aristotelian conception of science overemphasized the role of explanatory demonstrations, whereas the inductivist view overemphasizes predictions, Hempel maintained a healthy balance between explanation and prediction as the two main types of "scientific systematization." Hempel did not rely on Aristotelian essentialism—and thereby activated philosophical debates about lawlikeness. As he did not restrict the D-N model to the simple forms of Aristotle's syllogisms, he reopened the study of the general logical structure of explanatory arguments. One of the outcomes of this liberalized treatment was Hempel's pioneering work on statistical explanation.

Inductive-Statistical Explanation

Already in 1942, Hempel hinted that some explanatory arguments may replace the universal or "deterministic" laws of the D-N model with "probability hypotheses" which (together with the antecedent conditions) make the explanandum event "highly probable" (1965, p. 237). His example is Tommy's coming down with the measles two weeks after his brother; here the law asserts that contagion occurs "only with high probability." Hempel referred to a 1941 article by Edgar Zilsel, where Zilsel suggested that historical laws are of a statistical character like some macrolaws of physics. Hempel also considered the explanation of why the Dust Bowl farmers migrated to California and noted that it would be difficult to state accurately in the form of a general law the hypothesis that "populations will tend to migrate to regions which offer better living conditions."

In 1948, Hempel mentioned examples from economics (supply and demand) and linguistics (phonologic decay), and added—again with reference to Zilsel—that the involved laws may be statistical (1965, pp. 252-3). He remarked that the subsumption under "statistical laws" has "a peculiar logical structure" which "involves difficult special problems" (p. 251).

One of the "difficulties" in this context is the problem of giving an adequate formulation of *statistical laws*. The simplest statistical counterparts of Humean universal generalizations are obviously statements about the *relative frequency* $rf(G/F)$ of an attribute G in a class F; this relative frequency is one if all Fs are G. As a student of the famous frequentist Hans Reichenbach in Berlin, Hempel had himself, already in the early 1930s, written about the logical form of probability statements. In Hempel (1935), he attempted to defend a "finitistic" version of the frequency interpretation where probability statements are applied only to finite reference classes, but Reichenbach immediately rejected that account in his comment in *Erkenntnis*.[2] In Hempel (1937–38), the finitistic standpoint was not mentioned any more, and probability statements were defined as limits of relative frequencies of properties in infinite sequences. Hempel emphasized the relativity of probability statements to such infinite sequences, criticizing Reichenbach's incomplete notation for his probability implications, and suggested that "absolute" probability statements could be obtained only by quantifying over kinds of sequences. The long-run frequency interpretation is again briefly mentioned in the Hempel-Oppenheim article (Hempel 1965, p. 250).

In Hempel (1962), statistical laws were characterized as probability statements of the form $P(G/F) = r$, where 'r' takes values between zero and one. By this time Hempel had already struggled with the distinction between nomic and accidentally true universal generalizations, and he wished to make a similar distinction between genuine statistical laws and statements of relative frequencies in some finite set. In the former case, the reference class F is not assumed to be finite, but the probability r "refers" to the class of all the potential instances of F (1962, p. 123). One way of making sense of this requirement is to treat statistical probability as a disposition, as in Popper's propensity interpretation. The dispositional interpretation was mentioned again in 1965 (see Hempel 1965, p. 178). In Hempel (1968) probability is again a long-run frequency, but the relevant predicates in a lawlike probability statement are required to be "nomic."

Another line leading Hempel to nondeductive explanations starts from the concept of "explanatory power." Hempel and Oppenheim (1948) defined a measure of the *systematic power* of a theory. The underlying idea is deductivist: count how many sentences a theory is able to entail in a given finite class of data. But the germs of this idea are related to Hempel's earlier work with the Reichenbachian method of defining the "probability of a theory" (as the relative frequency with which the theory entails true consequences from true initial conditions) (see Nagel 1939, p. 63). Further, a probabilistic version of the obtained measure can be given by

(3) $syst(T,S) = P(\sim T/\sim S)$,

that is, the systematic power of theory T with respect to data S equals the inductive probability of $\sim T$ given $\sim S$ (Hempel 1965, p. 287). This measure has its maximum value one, if T entails S, but it may receive high values also in cases where only a nondeductive or inductive relation obtains between T and S. Hempel and Oppenheim hinted that the theory of scientific explanation should be extended to cover such cases as well (p. 278).

It may seem surprising that, after the suggestive remarks in 1948, the formulation of Hempel's model of statistical explanation was delayed for fourteen years—and no one else picked up the topic for study in the meantime. The only exception seems to be Ernest Nagel, who argued by examples that the explanation of individual actions in history is probabilistic (see Nagel 1961, pp. 550–63). Finally in 1962 Hempel published his article "Deductive-Nomological vs.

Statistical Explanation," and soon in the same year Nicholas Rescher's (1962) paper on the possibility of statistical explanation in discrete state systems appeared.

What was the real cause of this delay? Later Hempel reported that he discovered already in 1945 the problem of the "ambiguity of statistical syllogisms" (Hempel 1962, p. 138). This problem was not noted by D. C. Williams (1947) in his extensive treatment of predictive statistical syllogisms, but it was discussed in detail by Stephen Barker (1957). The problem arises, because the statistical probability $P(G/F)$ of outcome G in the class F depends on the reference class F. Then two arguments of the form

(4) $P(G/F)$ is nearly 1
      Fa
      So, it is almost certain that a is G

(5) $P(\sim G/H)$ is nearly 1
      Ha
      So, it is almost certain that a is not G

may both have true premises, even if their conclusions are inconsistent with each other.

Rudolf Carnap, who started to develop his logical theory of induction in the 1940s (see Carnap 1950/1962), assured Hempel that this ambiguity is "but one of several apparent paradoxes of inductive logic which result from violations of the requirement of total evidence" (Hempel 1962, p. 138; 1965, p. 397). In "Inductive Inconsistencies" (1960), Hempel offered the solution that, in a statistical syllogism, probability should not be understood as a *modal qualifier* of the conclusion but rather as a *relation* between the premises and the conclusion. This relation involves logical or inductive probability, or a degree of confirmation in the sense of Keynes and Carnap. Thus, instead of (4), we should say that 'Ga' is highly probable relative to the statements '$P(G/F) \approx 1$' and 'Fa' (Hempel 1965, p. 60). Schema (4) can now be written in the form

(6) $P(G/F)$ is nearly 1
      Fa
      ================   [makes almost certain]
      Ga

where the double line indicates that (6) is an inductive rather than a deductive argument. It is not inconsistent with (6) that 'Ga' may be very improbable relative to some other premises.

With this reasoning, Hempel was finally ready to formulate his model of *inductive-statistical* (*I-S*) *explanation* in 1962. This model can be expressed by the schema

(7) $P(G/F) = r$
      Fa
      ========== $[r]$
      Ga

where 'r' in the lawlike premise '$P(G/F) = r$' is a *statistical probability*, and 'r' in the brackets indicates the *inductive probability* of the explanandum 'Ga' given the explanans. Further, Hempel required that r should be close to one.

Hempel's I-S model still allows that there may be inductive arguments of the form (7) with true premises but with incompatible conclusions 'Ga' and '$\sim Ga$'. For the purpose of prediction this is clearly a problem, as then it is not yet known whether 'Ga' is true or not. But in the contect of explanation the choice of the correct explanation between such alternatives is already determined by the assumption that the explanandum sentence is known to be true (see Coffa 1974; Salmon 1989, p. 69). Hempel knew this, but he insisted that it is unnatural to admit that, in giving an I-S explanation of a fact, we could have "just as readily" explained its opposite from true premises (see Hempel 1968, p. 119).

To handle this problem of *ambiguity*, Hempel (1962, p. 146), formulated a "rough criterion of evidential adequacy for simple statistical systematizations": the rule (7) should be "based on the statistical probability of G within the narrowest class, if there is one, for which the total evidence available provides the requisite statistical probability." This is a counterpart for explanation of Hans Reichenbach's (1938) advice in the context of prediction: use the statistical probability statement with the narrowest available reference class for determining the "weights" of single cases. But, as Hempel was careful to note, one must distinguish the content of a statement and evidence for it: while his own condition requires that the statistical probability of G in the narrowest class F is known, for Reichenbach the total evidence provides a statistical report on a finite sample from the class F.

A precise formulation of the *Requirement of Maximal Specificity* was given by Hempel (1965, pp. 397–400). The total evidence is now represented by the set K of "all statements accepted at the given time." K is assumed to be deductively closed and to contain the axioms of probability theory. If K contained the explanandum 'Ga', then trivially the logical probability of this statement relative to K would be equal to one. Therefore, K is assumed not to contain the explanandum (but see Hempel 1968). In a situation where the premises of the argument (7) are known, the relevant knowledge situation K should satisfy the following.

(RMS)   For any class F_1 for which K implies that F_1 is a subclass of F and that F_1a, K also contains a law to the effect that $P(G/F_1) = r_1$, where $r_1 = r$, unless that law is a theorem of probability theory.

The unless-clause excludes the use of classes like $F \cap G$ and $F \cap -G$ for the choice of F_1. RMS thus attempts to specify what information of our knowledge situation K is of potential explanatory relevance to the explanandum.

In Hempel (1968), the principle RMS concerning explanation was sharply distinguished from the principle of total evidence which is valid in prediction or in reason-giving argumentation. The inductive probability r associated with explanation (7) is the probability of 'Ga' relative to its two premises, not relative to the whole *K*. (Therefore, the explanandum may be assumed to belong to *K*.) When RMS is satisfied, this probability *r* expresses the *nomic expectability* of *Ga* on the basis of the explanans. Hempel (1968) reformulated RMS so that it applies to predicates rather than classes, and is less demanding on the existence of known statistical laws.

(RMS*)   If *K* contains statements 'F_1a' and '$(x)(F_1x \rightarrow Fx)$' and the lawlike statement '$P(G/F_1) = r_1$', then $r_1 = r$, unless r_1 is one or zero.

Suppose that the knowledge situation *K* allows us to place individual *a* in two different reference classes F_1 and F_2 with different probabilities for *G*. If *K* does not contain information about the probability of *G* in $F_1 \cap F_2$, then the original RMS is not satisfied. The modified RMS* holds, but in this situation both F_1 and F_2 are maximally specific for *G* in *K*, and the model gives no recommendation for the choice between them. Hempel (1968) added to RMS* a further requirement that *K* should contain '$P(G/M) = r$' for all maximally specific predicates '*M*' related to '*Ga*' in *K*; relative to this strong condition, there is no acceptable inductive explanation in the given situation (see also Tan 1997).[3]

Both RMS and RMS* are relativized to *K*. Hempel claimed that this is unavoidable, so that the notion of potential I-S explanation (unlike D-N explanation) makes sense only if relativized to a knowledge situation. This is Hempel's thesis of the *epistemic relativity* of statistical explanation (1965, p. 402).

Later in his "Nachwort 1976" to the German edition of his *Aspects of Scientific Explanation*, Hempel (1977) reformulated RMS* by dropping the condition 'F_1a' from its antecedent. In this form, it requires that we do not know of any subclass F_1 of *F* such that the probability of *G* in F_1 differs from the probability of *G* in *F*. In other words, the reference class *F* should be *epistemically homogeneous* for *G* in the sense of Salmon (1971, 1984). At the same time, Hempel dropped the requirement that the probability *r* is high. Further, he stated that it would be "very desirable" to find an objective, not epistemically relativized formulation of maximal specificity, but left it open whether such a definition can be found (1977, p. 123). These modifications were responses to lively debates about Hempel's I-S model.

Discussion of Hempel's I-S model

In the debates following the appearance of Hempel's I-S model in the 1960s, some philosophers still denied altogether the idea that probabilistic arguments could serve as explanations. In particular, G. H. von Wright (1971) and Wolfgang Stegmüller (1973, 1983) argued that Hempel's I-S model does not answer explanatory why-necessary questions but is valid only for inductive predictions and other reason-giving arguments.

Another kind of criticism was presented by Isaac Levi (1969, 1977): I-S explanation is not covering-law explanation, since there are no extensional statements that could serve as true and lawlike premises in "direct inference" of the type (7). Levi also rejects the possibility that the appropriate intensional probabilistic laws would have truth values, and suggests that they are replaced by rules of inference.[4] Related work on direct inference, with frequency statements as surrogates for probabilistic laws, has been done by Henry Kyburg (see Bogdan 1982).

One of the early objections to Hempel's I-S model is that high probability is not necessary for statistical explanation. This question was raised by Rescher (1962) and Salmon (1965). Also Carnap (1966, p. 8), while endorsing the covering-law model, pointed out that a statistical medical law may state that 5 percent of the people who eat a certain food will develop a certain symptom, but "even when a statistical law provides only an extremely weak explanation, it is still an explanation." A forceful statement against the high probability requirement—and, more generally, against the view that statistical explanation are arguments—was presented by Richard Jeffrey (1969; see also Salmon 1970). Some philosophers still demanded that the probability of the explanadum has to be at least 1/2; this was called the "Leibniz condition" by Stegmüller (1973) (see Tuomela 1977). Hempel's (1977) response was that eventually he dropped the high probability requirement.

Another issue is that the idea of inductive support or confirmation could be explicated, instead of high conditional probability, by the *positive relevance* criterion (see Carnap 1950/1962; Hempel 1965, p. 50). Thus, we might require that the explanans increases the probability of the explanandum. This proposal was made by Wesley Salmon (1965), who developed his *statistical relevance (S-R) model* of explanation as a rival to Hempel's I-S model (Salmon 1970, 1984). Positive relevance is also the key of the theory of probabilistic causality by Patrick Suppes (1970).

With Jeffrey (1969), Salmon rejects Hempel's high probability requirement. He also replaces the epistemic principle RMS with a requirement that the reference class F should be *objectively homogeneous* for attribute G, that is, no property H (independent of G) divides F in a "statistically relevant" way to a subclass $F \cap H$ such that $P(G/F) \neq P(G/F \cap H)$. According to Salmon's S-R model, an answer to a question 'Why does this member a of B have the property G?' is obtained by partitioning B into subclasses $B \cap F_i$, $i = 1, \ldots, n$, such that each $B \cap F_i$ is objectively homogeneous for G, and $P(G/B \cap F_i) \neq P(G/B \cap F_j)$ if $i \neq j$. The answer $a \in B \cap F_k$ thus locates the place of individual a in this classification, and assigns it to a *maximal* homogeneous reference class.

One difference between the S-R and I-S models is Salmon's requirement that the reference class should be maximal. This relevance condition leads to unintuitive results already in the deductive case, since in some cases we may be unwilling to combine two separate causes into one broader class (e.g., to explain why a piece of white substance melted in water by the disjunctive fact that it was salt *or* sugar)—and the same holds for probabilistic causes that produce the same effect with the same statistical probability (see Hempel 1977, p. 109; Fetzer 1981, p. 91; Niiniluoto 1982). Hempel (1968) himself argued that one should not generally demand the choice of a *minimal* maximally specific reference class, so that his RMS leaves some freedom in the choice of the reference class. Fetzer (1981, p. 99), instead suggests that RMS should be strengthened so that it yields "a unique description solution as well as a unique value solution."

In Salmon's model, in contrast to his original 1965 proposal, it may happen that $P(G/B \cap F_k)$ is higher, smaller, or equal to the initial probability $P(G/B)$ (positive relevance, negative relevance, irrelevance, respectively). It is an interesting question whether this move could be justified by a suitable "global" conception of explanatory power (see Salmon et al. 1971; Niiniluoto and Tuomela 1973; Tuomela 1977; Niiniluoto 1981, 1982). Stegmüller (1973) argued that Salmon's S-R model is not an explication of statistical explanation but instead of "statistical depth analysis." Salmon (1984) defends his model as exemplifying the *ontic* conception of explanation: the explanandum event should be fitted into the nexus of causal or lawlike regularities, and the epistemic idea of expectation is irrelevant to the aim of explanation (see also Salmon 1989, pp. 117–22).[5]

The crucial question about the ontic conception is the possibility of giving a reasonable explication of the notion of "objectively homogeneous" reference class. An obvious difficulty is that, taken extensionally, a class F will always contain subclasses F_1 such that the relative frequency of attribute G in F differs from the corresponding value in F_1 until it equals zero or one. This is the reason why Fetzer claims against Salmon that an adequate ontic solution of the problem of probabilistic explanation cannot be given within the frequentist theory of statistical probability (see Fetzer 1981, p. 101; 1993, p. 71). To find such a solution, one may try to find some restriction concerning the choice of the permitted subclasses. Richard von Mises employed the idea of "place selection rules" in defining random sequences (see von Plato 1994). Hempel did this by restricting his RMS to a knowledge situation K. J. Alberto Coffa (1974) proposed to transform Hempel's epistemic RSM to an ontic version by replacing K with the class T of all true sentences, but this is not sufficient without some ontological and semantical assumptions about the relevant ideal scientific language where T is expressible. For example, one might appeal to "nomic predicates" which define physical properties, and deny that all mathematically existing subclasses correspond to ontologically existing properties. (This amounts to the idea that one adopts a nonstandard interpretation of second-order quantification; see Niiniluoto [1976].)

Hempel's doubts about objective or nonepistemic formulations of RMS led him to announce the epistemic relativity of I-S explanation, but—as he acknowledged later (Hempel 1977)—this argument was not conclusive. On the other hand, Coffa's (1974) and Salmon's claim that the epistemic relativity thesis commits Hempel to determinism was not conclusive, either: it is conceivable that for every probabilistic law $P(G/F) = r$ there are nomic predicates defining subclasses $F_1, F_2, \ldots$ of F such that the probabilities $P(G/F_i) = r_i$ differ from each other, so that an objective formulation of RMS is violated, but nevertheless these probabilities r_i do not reduce (or converge) to one or zero (see Niiniluoto 1976).

Salmon's strategy in developing the ontic conception has been to rely on a long-run frequency interpretation of statistical probability, together with a theory of causal processes.[6] Another approach is to base the analysis of statistical laws on the *single-case propensity* interpretation of probability, defended in the early 1970s by Hugh Mellor, Ron Giere, and James Fetzer. Instead of viewing physical probabilities as sure-fire dispositions to produce long-run frequencies, as Peirce and Popper suggested, the single-case interpretation takes propensities to be degrees of possibility that are displayed by a chance setup in each single trial of a certain kind. Probabilities are thus tendencies that generate, via laws of large numbers, relative frequencies within sequences of trials. According to this view, a lawlike probability statement $(x)[Hx \rightarrow P_x(G/F) = r]$ asserts that every chance setup x of type H has a dispositional tendency of strength r to produce a result of type G on each single trial of kind F. (A more complete notation would assign such dispositions to pairs (x,u), where x is a system and u is a trial on x, and quantify also over trials.) In the special case $r = 1$ this analysis reduces to a non-Humean intensional analysis equating lawlikeness either with "physical necessity" (i.e., truth in all physically possible worlds) or counterfactual conditionality. Probability in physical laws $P(G/F) = r$ (where $r < 1$) is then a modal operator which is weaker than physical necessity. If $0 < r < 1$, such a law implies that setups of type H are *indeterministic* systems.[7]

A clear formulation of a *propensity model* of probabilistic explanation was given by James H. Fetzer (1974). A typical explanation with such single-case propensity laws is as follows:

(8) $(x)[Hx \rightarrow P_x(G/F) = r]$
       Ha & Fa
       $=\!=\!=\!=\!=\!=\!=\!=\!=\!=\!=\!=\!=\!=\!=$ [r]
       Ga

where r in brackets is again the degree of nomic expectability of outcome G on the relevant trial with chance setup a. Alternatively, r is the degree of "nomic responsibility" of the causally relevant conditions to produce Ga in the given situation (see Fetzer 1992, p. 258). Here it is natural that the two values of 'r' are equal, as the law is a generalization over single cases, and there is no step from long-run characteristics to single cases. A separate RMS condition for this model is unnecessary (relative to H and F), since already the law in (8) presupposes that *each* setup of kind H in *each* trial of kind F has the same propensity to produce G, that is, H and F together are objectively homogeneous for G.[8] However, in contrasting his causal-relevance model to Salmon's statistical-relevance model, Fetzer (1993, pp. 76–7), gives a requirement of "strict maximal specificity" to the effect that the predicate 'F' in (8) should make a difference to the single-case propensity, that is, $P_x(G/F) \neq P_x(G/\sim F)$. A problem with this formulation is that the latter probability does not always strictly speaking make sense in the single-case interpretation, since the tendency of x to produce G may have different strengths within trials in the class defined by $\sim F$.[9]

Joseph Hanna (1981) argues against the propensity model by proposing a continuity principle: the conditional probability of a state of a chance setup can be made arbitrarily close to one by considering intermediate states close to the final state. However, there does not seem to be any reason to believe that this principle is valid for genuinely indeterministic systems, such as radioactive decay (see Fetzer 1983).

It is characteristic to the model (8) that it allows genuine probabilistic explanations only in the case of indeterministic systems. For example, if coin tossing can be described by a deterministic model, as the theories of ergodic and chaotic systems suggest (see Ford 1983; von Plato 1994), then single tosses do not involve propensities, and probabilistic accounts of their results are not objectively homogeneous. Still, Hempel's I-P model with an epistemic RMS condition may be applicable to such examples (see Niiniluoto 1981).

Paul Humphreys (1989) argues that the propensity model is too strict, when it requires that all and only nomically relevant factors are included in the explanans. He argues that this is "a hopelessly unrealistic ideal" (p. 111), as "even absurdly small probabilistically relevant factors" may not be omitted. Instead, Humphreys proposes a model of "aleatory explanations" of the form '*A* because *Q*, despite *S*', where *Q* is a set of contributing causes and *S* a (possibly empty) set of counteracting causes. In this model, the explanatory value of probabilities is rejected (p. 114).

However, an alternative way of construing partial explanations, giving a more flexible generalization of the Hempelian I-S model than (8), uses true lawlike statements of the form $(x)[Hx \rightarrow P_x(G/F) \geq r]$ to replace the strict law in (8); then the degree of nomic expectability is likewise replaced by '$\geq r$' (see Niiniluoto 1982, p. 177). Here 'H' and 'F' need not be maximally specific for 'G', but still the relevant probabilities in the subclasses of systems and trials vary so little that a lower bound for the propensity values is guaranteed. It might be the case as well that all the propensities are approximately (or in the average) equal to a definite value r. This idea can be viewed as an ontic or objective counterpart to the epistemic condition of *resiliency* (invariance) introduced by Brian Skyrms (1980). It may be applicable to explanations involving risks and tendencies both in the natural and social sciences, where the strict law of (8) is not true (see Niiniluoto 1976).

In his later work, Hempel (1988) discussed the role of "provisoes" which are "essential, but generally unstated, presuppositions of theoretical inferences," but he did not explicitly state any conclusions for his account of deductive or probabilistic explanation. Interesting related work has been done in the 1980s in the study of inferences with incomplete information within artificial intelligence (AI). Counterparts to statistical reasoning, without numerical probability values, are investigated within nonmonotonic logics. In default logic, statements like 'Usually, birds fly' are formulated by means of "default rules." Yao-Hua Tan (1997) argues in detail that the principles of extending default theories are analogous to Hempel's I-S model. In particular, default logic needs rules of "specificity" to resolve conflicting ways of making such extensions, in the same manner as the rule of maximal specificity RMS is needed for I-S inferences. Even though the main problem in the AI contexts seems to be prediction rather than explanation, it is interesting to see how AI research has independently been led to constructions similar to Hempel's model two decades earlier.

Explanation of Statistical Facts

Most philosophers have concentrated their efforts on analyzing explanations of singular facts and events. However, as Hempel noted, the D-N model can be applied also to the explanation of deterministic laws.[10] Similarly, the explanandum could be taken to be a probabilistic law (Hempel 1962, p. 147). Thus, while schema (7) is a statistical counterpart to the singular D-N inference (1), Hempel's concept of *deductive-statistical (D-S) explanation* corresponds to the universal syllogism (2). A D-S explanation is an argument where a statistical probability statement is derived from other such statements by means of the theory of probability (Hempel 1965, pp. 380-1).

D-S explanations have received very little attention in the philosophical literature. Nagel (1961, pp. 509–20), suggested that the formal structure of explanations of statistical generalizations in the social sciences is always deductive. As he had in mind probabilistic laws, his examples may be taken to be instances of Hempel's D-S explanation. Hempel himself stated that "ultimately, however, statistical laws are meant to be applied to particular occurrences and to establish explanatory and predictive connections among them" (1965, p. 381).

Hempel (1962, p. 166), concluded his major essay on statistical explanation by stressing the need of a "statistical-probabilistic concept of 'because'." His example of such probabilistic causality quotes Richard von Mises: "[i]t is because the die was loaded that the 'six' shows more frequently." Earlier in the paper, he gave examples from Mendelian genetics, where the argument explains "the approximate percentages of red- and white-flowered plants in the sample" (p. 142) and the theory of radioactivity, where the statistical law about radon's half-life explains the behavior of a large sample of such atoms (p. 142). In these examples, it is clear that the explanandum is not a statistical or probabilistic *law*, but rather a *statistical generalization* or *fact* about a particular *finite* class. The explanation of such statistical generalizations does not follow the structure of I-S and D-S models (see Niiniluoto 1976, pp. 357–8); yet, it may be the most typical of the applications of statistical ideas in science.

Three different models for the explanation of statistical facts are distinguished in Niiniluoto (1981, pp. 440–2). First, a universal law may be combined with a statistical fact to give a deductive explanation of another statistical fact. For example, assume that a disease G is deterministically caused by a gene F, and that the relative frequency of genes F in a given population H is r. Then the relative frequency of disease G in H is at least r; if F is also a necessary condition for G, the latter relative frequency equals r.[11] This inference follows the pattern

(9) $(x)(Fx \rightarrow Gx)$
       $rf(F/H) = r$
       ——————————
       $rf(G/H) \geq r.$

Second, statistical facts can also be inductively explained by probabilistic laws and universal generalizations. For example, if a radon atom decays within 3.82 days with probability ½, if it is not subjected to environmental radiation, and the decays are probabilistically independent, then by Bernoulli's theorem it is highly probable that in a large sample of radon atoms the number of decays within 3.82 days is approximately ½. This inference, which is a straightforward generalization of Hempel's I-S model for singular explanation, has the form

(10) $P(G/F) = r$
        H_n is a large finite sample of Fs
        =====================$[p_n]$
        $rf(G/H_n) \geq r.$

The degree of nomic expectability p_n, which depends on r and n, can be calculated by the probability theory.

Third, as a generalization of (9) and (10), a probabilistic law may be combined with a statistical fact to give an inductive explanation of another statistical fact:

(11) $P(G/F) = r$
        $rf(F/H) = s$
        ============ $[p]$
        $rf(G/H) \geq rs.$

For example, if gene F produces disease G with probability r, then it is highly probable that the relative frequency of G in a large subclass $F \cap H$ of a given finite population H is approximately r. If now the relative frequency of gene F in population H is s, then the relative frequency of G in H is at least rs.

Peirce on Probabilistic Explanation

Having surveyed recent discussions of statistical explanation, I now return to the "prehistory" of scientific explanation which I discussed in the second section. Hempel's *Aspects of Scientific Explanation* (1965) does not mention at all the name of the American pragmatist Charles S. Peirce. Others who have listed nineteenth-century advocates of D-N explanation have also failed to refer to Peirce's contribution. Even though Peirce's reputation grew only slowly in our century, and some of the important additional evidence comes from his early *Writings* published in the 1980s, this silence is quite surprising in view of the fact that Peirce's paper "Deduction, Induction, and Hypothesis" (1878), which gives very clear examples of deductive explanations, was available in the collection *Chance, Love, and Logic* in 1923. Further, Peirce's *Collected Papers* (1931–35) contains a reprint of the article "A Theory of Probable Inference"

(1883), which formulates a theory of probabilistic explanation, with deductive explanation as a special case.

Peirce's writings on probability and induction were of course well known to many philosophers before 1950: they were discussed, among others, by Keynes, Ramsey, Braithwaite, Nagel, von Wright, Carnap, and Williams.[12] While it was recognized that Peirce was interested both in inductive inference from a sample to a population and in "probable deduction" from a population to a sample or to single cases, it was almost always thought that the latter type of inference— variously called "the use of *a priori* probabilities for the prediction of statistical frequency" (Keynes 1921), "the problem of the single case" (Reichenbach 1938), "statistical syllogism" (Williams 1947), or "direct inference" (Carnap 1950/ 1962)—was concerned with *prediction* rather than *explanation*.[13] Peirce himself never made such a restriction, however.

I have pointed out (Niiniluoto 1982, p. 160) that "strangely enough, it seems that the modern literature on statistical explanation does not contain even a single reference to Peirce's theory of explanatory statistical syllogisms." In another article, I have ventured to suggest that "Peirce should be regarded as the true founder of the theory of inductive-probabilistic explanation" (Niiniluoto 1981, p. 444).

Salmon, who takes 1962 to be "the year in which the philosophical theory of scientific [statistical] explanation first entered the twentieth century" (1983, p. 179), has expressed disagreement with my judgment, since "one isolated and unelaborated statement" about explanatory statistical syllogisms "can hardly be considered even the beginnings of any genuine theory" (Salmon 1984, p. 24). In Salmon's survey article some years later (1989), Peirce is not mentioned at all, nor is he listed in the bibliography.

However, it can be argued against Salmon that Peirce had a serious and systematic concern for scientific explanation ever since 1865, and that his 1883 account of "probable" and "statistical deduction" gives a rich and detailed model for the structure of statistical explanation. Indeed, it seems to me that the relation of Peirce's work to the I-S model parallels the relation of Aristotle to the D-N model (see Niiniluoto 1993).

Peirce's interest in the structure of scientific explanation arose from his early studies in Aristotle's logic. In his Harvard Lectures during the spring of 1865, the young Peirce observed that there is a type of reasoning that is neither deductive nor inductive (*W* 1:180).[14] This reasoning, which Peirce called hypothesis (and later abduction), can be represented as the inference of the minor premise of a syllogism, or inference of a cause from its effect. The classification of inferences into deduction, induction, and hypothesis was elaborated in Peirce's Lowell Lectures in the fall of 1866 and published in the next year. Ten years later, this distinction was presented in the article "Deduction, Induction, and Hypothesis."

Already in the Harvard Lectures 1865, Peirce made it perfectly clear that hypothesis is an inference *to an explanation* (*W* 1:267). In the Lowell Lectures 1866, Peirce said that hypothesis—which alone "enables us to see the *why* of things"—is the inversion of the corresponding *explaining syllogism*. For example, from the fact that light is polarizable we may abductively infer that light is ether waves, since the following syllogism is explanatory:

Ether waves are polarizable.
Light is ether waves.
∴ Light is polarizable.

In the spirit of Mill, Peirce states generally that "to explain a fact is to bring forward another from which it follows syllogistically," that is, "we say that a fact is *explained* when a proposition—possibly true—is brought forward, from which that fact follows syllogistically" (*W* 1:428, 425, 440, 452).

Another important influence came from Peirce's fascination with probability theory. In his 1867 review of *The Logic of Chance* by John Venn (1866), the first systematic treatment of the frequency interpretation of probability, Peirce discussed inferences of the form:

(12)   *A* is taken at random from among the *B*s.
Two-thirds of the *B*s are *C*.
∴ *A* is *C*.

Peirce's justification for schema (12) is in terms of *truth-frequencies*: in the long run an argument of form (12) would yield a true conclusion from true premises two-thirds of the time (*CP* 8.2).

Peirce formulated induction, hypothesis, and analogy as probable arguments in 1867, where probability is measured by the proportion of cases in which an argument "carries truth with it." In 1878, he formulated probabilistic versions of the *Barbara* syllogism and its inversions by replacing the universal law with a statistical generalization of the form "Most of the beans in this bag are white" (*CP* 2.508–16, 2.627).

The article "A Theory of Probable Inference" (1883) gives several models of probable inference, where the term "deduction" is used for reasoning from a statistical premise about a population to a sample from that population. *Simple Probable Deduction* is a statistical version of singular syllogism in *Barbara* (compare [1]):

(13)   The proportion r of the *F*s are *G*s;
a is an *F*;
it follows, with probability r, that a is a *G*.

As Peirce noted, the conclusion here can be taken to be '*a* is a *G*', and probability indicates (see *CP*. 2.695.) "the modality with which this conclusion is drawn and held to be true." Here Peirce anticipated Hempel's discussion of "inductive inconsistencies," that is, the patterns (4)–(6). Further, it is required as "a maxim of conduct" that the instance a "should be an instance drawn *at random* from among the *F*'s".

> The volition of the reasoner (using what machinery it may) has to choose a so that it shall be an F; but he ought to restrain himself from all further preference, and not allow his will to act in any way that might tend to settle what

particular F is taken, but should leave that to the operation of chance. . . . [T]he act of choice should be such that if it were repeated many enough times with the same intention, the result would be that among the totality of selections the different sorts of F's would occur with the same relative frequencies as in experiencies in which volition does not intermeddle at all. In cases in which it is found difficult thus to restrain the will by a direct effort, the apparatus of games of chance—a lottery-wheel, a roulette, cards, or dice—may be called to our aid. (CP 2.696)

Peirce observed that, in this kind of random sampling (with replacement) from a finite population, "what is really sampled is not the finite collection of things, but the unlimited number of possible drawings" (CP 2.731). His randomness condition thus guarantees that the result G is obtained with the long-run frequency within the unlimited population of possible drawings from the class of Fs. Hence, the inference schema (13), that is,

(14) $rf(G/F) = r;$
      a is a random member of F;
      ∴ a is a G,

with a relative frequency statement as a premise, can be formulated as a probabilistic argument with a lawlike statistical premise

(15) $P(G/F) = r$
      Fa
      $$\frac{\qquad\qquad}{Ga,} \quad [r]$$

where r in the brackets is a long-run truth-frequency.

Nagel's idea of probabilistic explanation, which he applies to the historical explanation of human action, is based on the Peircean schema (8), where the statistical law is treated as a rule of inference with a characteristic truth-frequency (see Nagel 1961, p. 563). Salmon (1989, p. 34), mentions Nagel's examples in his history, but states that Nagel does not provide "an analysis" of probabilistic explanation.

The schema (15) corresponds to Hempel's model (7) of I-S explanation—with the difference that [r] indicates an objective probability or truth-frequency rather than an epistemic or inductive probability. The difference with Hempel is not very great here, since Peirce added—by appealing to Fechner's law—that there is a relation between objective probabilities and degrees of belief: as a matter of fact we do have "a stronger feeling of confidence about a sort of inference which will oftener lead us to the truth than about an inference that will less often prove right" (CP 2.697).

If probability is understood as a long-run propensity, as Peirce suggested in 1910 (CP 2.664), pattern (15) comes close to the propensity model (8) of probabilistic explanation. However, Peirce did not propose single-case propensities.

Besides simple probable deduction (13), Peirce formulated a schema for *statistical deduction* which proceeds from a population to a finite sample:

(16)   The proportion r of the Fs are Gs,
      a',a'',a''', etc., are a *numerous set,* taken at random from among
      the Fs;
      Hence, *probably* and *approximately* the proportion r of the *a*s are
      Gs.

(See *CP* 2.700.) This inference can be formalized in the following way:

(17) $rf(G/F) = r$;
      $\{a',a'',a''', \ldots\}$ is a random sample of *Fs*
      $\therefore rf(G/\{a',a'',a''', \ldots\}) \approx r,$

where, as Peirce showed by the binomial formula, r is the most probable value of the relative frequency in the conclusion. Further, by Bernoulli's theorem, the probability of the conclusion given the premises approaches one when the size of the sample a',a'',a''', . . . increases without bound (*CP* 2.698–700). Again the condition for randomness allows us to reformulate (17) by

(18) $P(G/F) = r$
      $\underline{\underline{Fa' \ \& \ Fa'' \ \& \ Fa''' \ \& \ldots}}$
      $rf(G/\{a',a,a'''\, \ldots\}) \approx r.$

This schema is the same as the often neglected pattern (10) of statistical explanation (see the preceding section, "Explanation of Statistical Facts").

It is philosophically interesting to note how Peirce's discussion of probable reasoning was anticipated by Mill and Venn. Mill's *System of Logic* contained a brief discussion of the application of an approximate generalization (like 'Most *A* are *B*' or 'Nine out of ten *A* are *B*') to its individual instances. Mill required that we should know nothing about such instances "except that they fall within the class A" (Mill 1906, p. 391; Niiniluoto 1981, p. 444). In a rough form, this guarantees that Hempel's RMS is satisfied relative to the given instance—without yet implying the stronger condition that the class *A* itself is objectively or epistemically homogeneous.

Similarly, Venn's *Logic of Chance* formulated the rule that statistical inferences about an individual case should refer it to the narrowest series or class that still secures "the requisite degree of stability and uniformity" (Venn 1888, p.220; see Reichenbach 1938).

However, Mill and Venn never said that such a statistical inference could be applicable for the purpose of *explanation.* For Mill approximate generalizations were important primarily "in the practice of life," but in science they are valuable as "steps towards universal truths." Moreover, Venn explicitly restricted his attention to attempts "to make real inferences about things as yet unknown," that is, to *prediction* (Venn 1888, p. 213). Peirce, on the other hand, reasserted his earlier view that "Inductions and Hypotheses are inferences from the conclusion and one premise of a statistical syllogism to the other premise. In the case of hypothesis, this syllogism is called the *explanation.*" Indeed, Peirce repeated, "we commonly say that the hypothesis is adopted *for the sake of* the explanation." A statistical syllogism "may be conveniently termed the explanatory syllogism" (*CP* 2.716–7).

Peirce's treatment illustrates vividly one reason for the difficulty of accepting the idea of probabilistic explanation. He was aware that in explanation it is usually impossible to choose the individual under consideration by a random selection. Hence, one might argue that the schema (14) is not applicable to explanation, since in explaining why a is a G we already know the individual a, and therefore we cannot draw it randomly from the class F. Here is Peirce's reply.

> Usually, however, in making a simple probable deduction, we take that instance in which we happen at the time to be interested. In such a case, it is our interest that fulfills the function of an apparatus for random selection; and no better need be desired, so long as we have reason to deem the premiss 'the proportion r of the F's are G's' to be equally true in regard to that part of the F's which are alone likely ever to excite our interest. (*CP* 2.696)

The intuition seems to be that the "interesting" subclasses of F should preserve the probability of G, that is, the schema (14) can be used for explanation as long as the reference class F is epistemically homogeneous for G relative to our typical knowledge situation.

We may conclude that Peirce gave a clear account of the structure of inductive-statistical explanation and of some of its generalizations. He had an intuitive idea about the need of a condition of randomness or homogeneity, but never proposed any explication of that condition that would be comparable in precision to Hempel's RMS.

Peirce's views of the nature of probability and of the role of "real chance" in nature went through changes that deepened his insight into the indispensability of statistical explanation. Evidence from science suggested that some of the best theories have a statistical character: in "The Fixation of Belief" (1877), Peirce referred to the 1851 theory of gases by Clausius and Maxwell and the 1859 theory of evolution by Darwin (*CP* 5.364, 1.104, 6.47, 6.613). In his 1892 papers for the *Monist*, Peirce formulated his evolutionary metaphysics, with its principles of absolute chance (*tychism*) and continuity (*synechism*) in nature (*CP* 6.13). His argument is directed against the "necessitarians" or determinists: variety and diversity cannot explained by mechanical uniformities, but by evolving probabilistic laws, that is, by "chance in the form of spontaneity which is to some degree regular" (*CP* 6.62).

In the first years of the twentieth century, Peirce radicalized his criticism of Hume's "Ockhamist" views of the laws of nature, adopted a realist view of dispositional and modal conceptions, and proposed a long-run propensity interpretation of probability as a "would-be" of a physical chance setup (see Niiniluoto 1988).[15]

After reading my paper for the 1989 Peirce Congress (Niiniluoto 1993), Hempel told me "with a strong sense of embarrassment" that he had been "un-

aware of Peirce's writings on probabilistic theorizing and statistical explanation."[16] The orientation of philosophical inquiry in the Berlin group and the
Vienna Circle was "basically a-historical." Hempel acknowledged that Peirce's
ideas on statistical explanation "constitute important pioneering contributions
to the field," even though "they are not as precisely formulated and as theoretically integrated and comprehensive as are more recent accounts, of which
Salmon's theory is a fine example."

After his conclusion in the letter, Hempel added one remark: "I have never
thought of myself as the founder of the theory of statistical explanation, but
only as the proponent of one explicatory approach to that important problem
complex." With all respect, this is a remarkably modest statement. At least we
should give to Hempel the great glory of being the first philosopher who was
able to give definitions and arguments that convinced his contemporaries of the
existence of statistical explanations.

NOTES

1. This analysis is most directly applicable to qualitative laws of coexistence (such as
   'All ravens are black'), but it covers also quantitative laws: for example, Newton's
   law of gravitation says that, for all x and y, if x and y are physical bodies, they attract each other with a force $F(x,y)$ which is proportional to the masses of x and y
   and inversely proportional to the square of their distance. Further, when applied to
   events or systems with transitory states, it covers also laws of succession (such as
   causal laws and dynamic laws). For Hempel, causal explanation is a special case of
   D-N explanation, but not all laws and explanations are causal (see Hempel 1965,
   p. 352).
2. Hempel's finitistic theory was partly based upon the coherence theory of truth that
   he (following Otto Neurath) still advocated in 1934. After learning about Alfred
   Tarski's theory of truth in 1935, Hempel accepted with Carnap a sharp distinction
   between truth (as a semantic notion) and confirmation (as an epistemic notion) (see
   Hempel 1937–38; 1965, p. 42). However, traces of Hempel's earlier fascination with
   the coherence theory can be found in his later work, especially in his treatment of
   confirmation as a relation between sentences (1965, p. 21). In a late article, he seems
   to come close to his youthful views by arguing that "the empiricist desideratum of
   evidential support for scientific claims has no bearing at all on the question of their
   truth" (1992, p. 49).
3. This requirement was motivated by an example of Richard Grandy, but it was later
   observed that the example could be ruled out without such an extra condition (see
   Stegmüller 1973, pp. 320–1; Niiniluoto 1982, p. 165).
4. See also Fetzer (1974). Compare Niiniluoto (1981), where probabilistic laws are not
   used as premises but rather as rules for calculating degrees of nomic expectability.
   Hempel discussed, in the context of deductive explanation, the conception of laws as
   inference rules (see Hempel 1965, pp. 354–8). He attributed this view to Moritz
   Schlick, Gilbert Ryle, and Wilfrid Sellars.
5. In a monograph, which was not widely known, von Wright (1945, pp. 35–6), advocated the principle that scientific prediction should be based on a minimal epistemically
   homogenenous reference class.

6. For a recent critical review, see Hitchcock (1995). Salmon (1988) accepts propensities as causes of frequencies. The criticism of the propensity interpretation by Salmon (and Paul Humphreys) is discussed by Niiniluoto (1988): the point is that the inverse probability of a potential cause given an effect is an epistemic probability, so that it need not be assumed to be a propensity. A more general defense of the propensity interpretation is given by McCurdy (1996).

7. See Fetzer (1974, 1981, 1993), Niiniluoto (1976, 1981, 1988), Tuomela (1977). As Fetzer points out, in a continuous probability space there are possible outcomes with the measure zero, so that it may be appropriate to distinguish propensity one from necessity. For an attempt to give a precise semantics for probabilistic conditionals, see Fetzer and Nute (1979) and Fetzer (1981).

8. Fetzer (1992) has protested that Salmon's (1989) history gives an inaccurate picture of the early history of the propensity model, especially concerning Coffa's 1973 doctoral dissertation. Fetzer argues that Coffa had a short-run (rather than single-case) conception of propensities, and that his account of explanations is not an ontic generalization of Hempel's D-N schema (as [8] is). Peter Railton's (1978) model derives from a general propensity law the singular consequence "a has probability r to be G at time t_o" and adds that a became G at t_o. But it would be misleading to take the relevant explanandum to be '$P(Ga) = r$' rather than 'Ga'.

9. The recent treatment of laws as second-order relations between universals has been extended to probabilistic laws as well, but no new account of statistical explanation has emerged. Armstrong, who assumes a strong principle of instantiation for universals, is forced to conclude that probabilistic statements satisfy a kind of the principle of plenitude (see Niiniluoto, 1988): if a law states that with a probability Fs are Gs, then there must at some time exist an F which is a G instantiating the law (Armstrong 1983, p. 129). Tooley (1987) avoids this difficulty by allowing noninstantiated universals, but his account of probabilistic laws appeals to logical probabilities (p. 153). Tooley takes it to be an advantage that his account is "free from any reference to possible worlds." For a propensity theorist, on the other hand, who regards probabilities as degrees of physical possibility, such a reference to modal notions cannot be avoided (see Niiniluoto 1988).

10. Inductive-deterministic explanations are discussed in Niiniluoto and Tuomela (1973, pp. 88–117).

11. It can be proved that for some deterministic dynamical systems the frequencies of outcomes are largely independent of the mechanism which chooses the initial conditions. More precisely, any continuous distribution of initial conditions gives the same long-run frequencies of outcomes. This approach, which was called the method of arbitrary functions by Henri Poincaré, was applied to classical chance devices, such as coins and roulettes, already at the turn of the nineteenth century (see von Plato, 1994, p. 170).

12. Reichenbach mentioned Peirce in his work in the late 1930s, but G. H. von Wright (1941/1957, p. 243), noted that Reichenbach "does not seem to be aware of the intimate relatedness between his solution of the inductive problem and the ideas of Peirce," even though "actually almost everything that is true and essential in the views of Reichenbach on the justification of induction has already been explicitly stated by Peirce."

13. Williams (1947, p. 57), who relied heavily on Peirce, mentioned that statistical syllogism could be used for explanation, but did not develop this idea further. Nagel

does not mention Peirce's ideas on statistical explanation, but his own sketch of probabilistic explanation of human action refers to Peirce's conception of probability as a truth-frequency (see Nagel 1961, pp. 563–4).

14. Using the standard notation, *W* refers to the Chronological Edition of Peirce's *Writings*, and *CP* to his *Collected Papers*.

15. For an account of the "erosion of determinism" and the introduction of probabilistic ideas in the latter part of the nineteenth century, see Hacking (1990). See also von Plato (1994).

16. A private letter dated 20 December 1989. Quoted with permission of Professor Hempel.

REFERENCES

Aristotle 1961. *Physics*. Lincoln: University of Nebraska Press.

Armstrong, D.M. 1983. *What Is a Law of Nature?* Cambridge, England: Cambridge University Press.

Barker, S. 1957. *Science and Hypothesis*. Ithaca, N.Y.: Cornell University Press.

Bogdan, R. ed. 1982. *Henry E. Kyburg Jr. and Isaac Levi*. Dordrecht: Reidel.

Braithwaite, R. B. 1953. *Scientific Explanation*. Cambridge, England: Cambridge University Press.

Carnap, R. 1950/1962. *The Logical Foundations of Probability*. Chicago: University of Chicago Press. 2nd ed. 1962.

———. 1966. *The Philosophy of Science*. Edited by M. Gardner. New York: Basic Books.

Coffa, J. A. 1974. "Hempel's Ambiguity." *Synthese* 28:141–63.

Comte, A. 1970. *Introduction to Positive Philosophy*. Indianapolis: Bobbs-Merrill.

Duhem, P. 1954. *The Aim and Structure of Physical Theory*. Princeton: Princeton University Press.

Fetzer, J. H. 1974. "A Single Case Propensity Theory of Explanation." *Synthese* 28:171–98.

———. 1981. *Scientific Knowledge*. Dordrecht: Reidel.

———. 1983. "Probabilistic Explanations." In *PSA 1982*, edited by P. Asquith and T. Nickles. Vol. 2. East Lansing, Mich.: Philosophy of Science Association.

Fetzer, J. H., ed. 1988. *Probability and Causality*. Dordrecht: Reidel.

———. 1992. "What's Wrong with Salmon's History: The Third Decade." *Philosophy of Science* 59:246–62.

———. 1993. *Philosophy of Science*. New York: Paragon House.

Fetzer, J. H., and D. E. Nute. 1979. "Syntax, Semantics, and Ontology: A Probabilistic Causal Calculus." *Synthese* 40:453–95.

Ford, J. 1983. "How Random Is a Coin Toss?" *Physics Today* 36:40–7.

Gärdenfors, P. 1980. "A Pragmatic Theory of Explanation." *Philosophy of Science* 47:404–23.

Goodman, N. 1955. *Fact, Fiction, and Forecast*. Cambridge: Harvard University Press.

Hacking, I. 1990. *The Taming of Chance*. Cambridge, England: Cambridge University Press.

Hanna, J. F. 1981. "Single Case Propensities and the Explanation of Particular Events." *Synthese* 48:409–36.

Hempel, C. G. 1935. "Über den Gehalt von Wahrschenlichkeitsaussagen." *Erkenntnis* 5:228–60.

————. 1937–38. "On the Logical Form of Probability-Statements." *Erkenntnis* 7:154–60.

————. 1942. "The Function of General Laws in History." *Journal of Philosophy* 39:35–48. Reprinted in Hempel (1965).

————. 1960. "Inductive Inconsistencies." *Synthese* 12:439–69. Reprinted in Hempel (1965).

————. 1962. "Deductive-Nomological vs. Statistical Explanation." In *Minnesota Studies in the Philosophy of Science*, edited by H. Feigl and G. Maxwell. Vol. 3. Minneapolis: University of Minnesota Press.

————. 1965. *Aspects of Scientific Explanation and Other Essays in the Philosophy of Science*. New York: Free Press.

————. 1968. "Maximal Specificity and Lawlikeness in Probabilistic Explanation." *Philosophy of Science* 35:116–33.

————. 1977. "Nachwort 1976." In *Aspekte wissenschaftlicher Erklärung*. Berlin: de Gruyter.

————. 1988. "Provisos: A Problem Concerning the Inferential Function of Scientific Theories." *Erkenntnis* 28:147–64.

————. 1992. "Eino Kaila and Logical Empiricism." In *Eino Kaila and Logical Empiricism*, edited by I. Niiniluoto, M. Sintonen, and G. H. von Wright. Helsinki: Societas Philosophica Fennica.

Hempel, C.G., and P. Oppenheim. 1948. "Studies in the Logic of Explanation." *Philosophy of Science* 15:135–75. Reprinted in Hempel (1965).

Hintikka, J., and I. Halonen. 1995. "Semantics and Pragmatics for Why-questions." *Journal of Philosophy* 92:636–57.

Hitchcock, C. R. 1995. "Salmon on Explanatory Relevance." *Philosophy of Science* 62:304–20.

Humphreys, P. 1989. *The Chances of Explanation: Causal Explanation in the Social, Medical, and Physical Sciences*. Princeton: Princeton University Press.

Jeffrey, R. C. 1969. "Statistical Explanation vs. Statistical Inference." In *Essays in Honor of Carl G. Hempel*, edited by N. Rescher. Dordrecht: Reidel. Reprinted in Salmon et al. (1971).

Keynes, J. M. 1921. *A Treatise on Probability*. London: Macmillan.

Kitcher, P., and W. C. Salmon, eds. 1989. *Scientific Explanation*. Minneapolis: University of Minnesota Press.

Levi, I. 1969. "Are Statistical Hypotheses Covering Laws?" *Synthese* 20:297–307.

————. 1977. "Subjunctives, Dispositions and Chances." *Synthese* 34:423–55.

Lewis, D. 1973. *Counterfactuals*. Oxford: Blackwell.

McCurdy, C. S. I. 1996. "Humphreys's Paradox and the Interpretation of Inverse Conditional Propensities." *Synthese* 108:105–25.

Mill, J. S. 1906. *A System of Logic*. London: Longmans, Green.

Nagel, E. 1939. *Principles of the Theory of Probability*. Chicago: University of Chicago Press.

Nagel, E. 1961. *The Structure of Science*. London: Routledge and Kegan Paul.

Niiniluoto, I. 1976. "Inductive Explanation, Propensity, and Action." In *Essays on Explanation and Understanding*, edited by J. Manninen and R. Tuomela. Dordrecht: Reidel.

————. 1981. "Statistical Explanation Reconsidered." *Synthese* 48:437–72.

————. 1982. "Statistical Explanation." In *Contemporary Philosophy: A New Survey*, edited by G. Fløistad. Vol. 2. The Hague: Nijhoff.

———. 1988. "Probability, Possibility, and Plenitude." In Fetzer (1988).

———. 1993. "Peirce's Theory of Statistical Explanation." In *Charles S. Peirce and the Philosophy of Science,* edited by E. C. Moore. Tuscaloosa: University of Alabama Press.

Niiniluoto, I., and R. Tuomela. 1973. *Theoretical Concepts and Hypothetico-Inductive Inference.* Dordrecht: Reidel.

Peirce, C. S. 1931–35. *Collected Papers.* Vols. 1–6. Edited by C. Hartshorne and P. Weiss. Cambridge: Harvard University Press.

———. 1982–. *Writings of Charles S. Peirce: A Chronological Edition.* Vols. 1–4. Edited by M. H. Fisch et al. Bloomington: Indiana University Press.

Popper, K. R. 1945. *The Open Society and Its Enemies.* London: Routledge and Kegan Paul.

———. 1957. *The Poverty of Historicism.* London: Routledge and Kegan Paul.

Railton, P. 1978. "A Deductive-Nomological Model of Probabilistic Explanation." *Philosophy of Science* 45:206–26.

Reichenbach, H. 1938. *Experience and Prediction.* Chicago: University of Chicago Press.

Rescher, N. 1962. "The Stochastic Revolution and the Nature of Scientific Explanation." *Synthese* 14:200–15.

Salmon, W. C. 1965. "The Status of Prior Probabilities in Statistical Explanation." *Philosophy of Science* 32:137–46.

———. 1970. "Statistical Explanation." In *Nature and Function of Scientific Theories,* edited by R. G. Colodny. Pittsburgh: University of Pittsburgh Press. Reprinted in Salmon et al. (1971).

———. 1983. "Probabilistic Explanation: Introduction." In *PSA 1982,* edited by P. D. Asquith and T. Nickles. Vol. 2. East Lansing, Mich.: Philosophy of Science Association.

———. 1984. *Scientific Explanation and the Causal Structure of the World.* Princeton: Princeton University Press.

———. 1988. "Dynamic Rationality: Propensity, Probability, and Credence." In Fetzer (1988).

———. 1989. "Four Decades of Scientific Explanation." In Kitcher and Salmon (1989). Published also as a monograph. Minneapolis: University of Minnesota Press, 1990.

Salmon, W. C., et al. 1971. *Statistical Explanation and Statistical Relevance.* Pittsburgh: University of Pittsburgh Press.

Schurz, G. 1995–96. "Scientific Explanation: A Critical Survey." *Foundations of Science* 3:429–65.

Sintonen, M. 1989. "Explanation: In Search of the Rationale." In Kitcher and Salmon (1989).

Skyrms, B. 1980. *Causal Necessity: A Pragmatic Investigation of the Necessity of Laws.* New Haven: Yale University Press.

Stegmüller, W. 1973. *Personelle und statistische Wahrscheinlichkeit.* Berlin: Springer-Verlag.

———. 1983. *Erklärung, Begründung, Kausalität.* 2nd ed. Berlin: Springer Verlag.

Suppes, P. 1970. *A Probabilistic Theory of Causality.* Amsterdam: North-Holland.

Tan, Y.-H. 1997. "Is Default Logic a Reinvention of Inductive-Statistical Reasoning?" *Synthese* 110:357–79.

Tooley, M. 1987. *Causation: A Realist Approach.* Oxford: Oxford Universisty Press.

Tuomela, R. 1977. *Human Action and Its Explanation.* Dordrecht: Reidel.

Venn, J. 1888. *The Logic of Chance.* 3rd ed. London: Macmillan.

von Plato, J. 1994. *Creating Modern Probability*. Cambridge, England: Cambridge University Press.

von Wright, G. H. 1941/1957. *The Logical Problem of Induction*. Helsingfors: Acta Philosophica Fennica 3. 2nd ed. Oxford: Blackwell, 1957.

————. 1945. *Über Wahrscheinlichkeit*. Helsingfors: Acta Societatis Scientiarum Fennicae A.3.11.

————. 1971. *Explanation and Understanding*. Ithaca, N.Y.: Cornell University Press.

Williams, D. C. 1947. *The Ground of Induction*. Cambridge: Harvard University Press.

IV

THEORIES AND PREDICTIONS

7

The Symmetry Thesis

PETER ACHINSTEIN

Freud explained slips of the tongue as the outcome of a compromise between an unconscious wish for something and a conscious wish that precludes it. He tells the story of the president of the German parliament who opened the meeting by saying "The meeting is now closed." This slip of the tongue, Freud explained, was the result of a conscious wish to open the meeting and an unconscious wish to avoid the meeting altogether. By using the expression "The meeting is now . . ." the president expressed some element of the conscious wish to open the meeting. But by replacing the word "open" with the word "closed," the slip contains a crucial element of the unconscious wish.

Is this an adequate scientific explanation of why the president said what he did? Carl G. Hempel, the founder of the modern subject of scientific explanation, claims it is not. One of Hempel's most important contributions to this subject is to provide a test of adequacy for explanations such as this. The test is derived from a "symmetry thesis" he suggested (1942, 1948). The symmetry thesis is that a scientific explanation is not adequate unless it could have functioned as a prediction, and a scientific prediction is not adequate unless it could have functioned as an explanation. According to Hempel, to scientifically explain the occurrence of a particular event (e.g., the president's saying "The meeting is now closed") one needs to derive a statement describing that event from statements describing other particular events or facts (e.g., facts about the president's conscious and unconscious wishes) and from general statements or laws relating facts and events of the sort in question (e.g., general laws about conscious and unconscious wishes and slips of the tongue). If one derives a statement in this way about an event that is known to have happened, one has scientifically *explained* that event. If one derives a statement in this way about a future event then one has scientifically *predicted* it. The difference, then, between scientific explanation and prediction is not "structural" (as Hempel puts it) but "pragmatic": it depends not on the content or logical structure of the explanation or prediction but only on the use to which the inference is put, that is, on whether the aim is to derive something about a future event or one known to have happened.

167

Accordingly, the symmetry thesis provides a crucial test for scientific explanation and prediction. Suppose you explain some event *e* by reference to some facts *F*. If you had known those facts before you knew of the event *e*, could you have predicted *e* from those facts? If not, your explanation is not adequate. Suppose, by contrast, you predict some event *e* from facts *F*. If you had known in advance that *e* occurred, could you have explained *e*'s occurrence on the basis of the facts *F*? If not, your prediction is not adequate.

The Freud example, Hempel would say, fails the first test. Suppose before the slip of the tongue one had known that the president had a conscious wish to open the meeting and an unconscious one to avoid it. Using Freud's theory could one have predicted that the president would say "The meeting is now closed"? No, because Freud's theory concerning slips of the tongue does not say that a slip of the tongue always or even usually occurs when one has conflicting wishes. At most, it says that such things can occur. Nor does the theory provide enough detail to infer what type of slips can occur. As far as Freud is concerned, the president might have produced slips of many different kinds, or no slip at all. So, Hempel concludes, at best Freud proposes an "explanation sketch" or "partial" explanation. He suggests some explanatory ideas, but there needs to be a much more fully developed theory before Freud can adequately explain particular slips of the tongue.

Let's briefly look at the second part of the symmetry thesis, namely, the idea that scientific predictions must be potentially explanatory. Astrologers made predictions about events in people's lives from the relative positions of the sun, moon, and stars. These are not adequate scientific predictions, Hempel would say, because even if the events predicted occurred, the relative positions of the heavenly bodies would not provide an adequate explanation for those events. There is no reason to suppose that the relative positions of the heavenly bodies exert any influences on particular human events of the sort astrologers assume.

In what follows I want to examine Hempel's symmetry thesis. I will do so independently of Hempel's two famous models of explanation (the deductive-nomological and inductive-statistical models) that, he believes, satisfy the thesis. The symmetry thesis is of interest whether or not Hempel's favorite models are ours as well.

Prediction: Must It Be Potentially Explanatory?

This part of the symmetry thesis is usually thought to be the more dubious of the two. To begin with, it might be said, a prediction is simply a statement that something will occur (or perhaps that something has occurred that has not been verified). A prediction can be made without being inferred from anything at all, and hence without being inferred from something that potentially explains it. Moreover, such a prediction might turn out to be perfectly correct!

This observation, although true, is not at all damaging to Hempel's claim. Hempel is concerned not just with predictive statements (ones that say that something will occur), but with predictive *arguments* or *inferences*, that is, with cases in which some prediction is made from, or on the basis of, something. It might take this form: given facts *F*, it is reasonable to predict that *p*. And Hempel is claiming that in such cases, to be scientifically adequate, facts *F* must potentially explain *p*.

Are there objections to this? There are, and Hempel (1965, p. 375) is aware of them. Suppose, for example, that a coin has been tossed one hundred times and each time has landed heads. From this fact we might reasonably predict that it will land heads on the 101st toss. No doubt we might explain why *we believe* it will land heads on the 101st toss by saying that it has done so in the first one hundred tosses. But the fact that the coin has landed heads on each of the first one hundred tosses will not satisfactorily explain why heads will result on the 101st toss. Similarly, suppose a drug company tests a drug on one thousand patients with symptoms *S* and discovers that in eight hundred cases the symptoms are relieved, while no one in a control group not taking the drug had relief. This might provide a very sound scientific basis for the prediction that the drug will be effective approximately 80 percent of the time. Yet the explanation for the drug's general effectiveness is not that it was effective in the test cases.

I believe this is a fair objection. Yet I also believe that there may be an important truth in Hempel's claim about prediction. A predictive argument or inference of the sort Hempel has in mind is not just any argument or inference with a prediction as the conclusion. For example, from

(1)   Bill Clinton will smile tomorrow

we can validly infer:

(2)   Tomorrow Bill Clinton will smile.

But if you were to make prediction (2) and claim (1) as your reason for it, I think we would not be impressed with your predictive talents, even if (1) is true.

What Hempel is concerned about are cases in which certain facts provide *a good reason for believing* a prediction, not just with any facts (or statements describing them) that logically entail a prediction. Indeed, even more generally, one might take Hempel to be concerned with cases in which certain facts provide a good reason for believing a hypothesis, whether or not that hypothesis makes a prediction about the future. If you make claim (2), and urge that a good reason for believing this is that (1) is the case, you will convince no one to believe (2). Even those already convinced that (1) is true, and therefore that (2), which is entailed by it, is true, will not believe (2) *for the reason* that (1) is true.

What Hempel is suggesting, or at least what is suggested to me by what he says, is that for some fact *f* to be a good reason to believe an hypothesis *h* there must be some explanatory relationship between *f* and *h*. What explanatory relationship? The most obvious, and the one Hempel himself cites, is that *f* explains *h*, that is, that *f* correctly explains why *h* is true. But there are at least two other possibilities worth mentioning. One is that hypothesis *h* correctly explains why *f* is true. The other is that there is some (different) hypothesis *h'* that correctly explains both why *f* is true and why *h* is true. If any of these three alternatives obtains let us say that there is an *explanatory connection* between *f* and *h*.

Suppose, then, we modify the Hempelian thesis we are now discussing, as follows:

> *f* is a good reason to believe *h* only if there is an explanatory connection between *f* and *h*.

Although this weakens Hempel's thesis in one way, it makes it too strong in another. As can be seen from the definition, an explanatory connection between *f* and *h* requires the truth of both *f* and *h*. (Hypothesis *h* cannot correctly explain why *f* is true unless both *f* and *h* are true; similarly for the other explanatory relationships.) So if one wants to say that *f* can be a good reason to believe *h* even when *h* is false, we need to make a further modification.

To do so I shall borrow some ideas I have proposed for an account of *evidence* (Achinstein 1983, chap. 10; these ideas are further developed in a forthcoming work, *The Book of Evidence*). On my view, if *e* is evidence that *h*, then *e* constitutes a good reason to believe *h*. Two of the conditions I have proposed for evidence require that *e* is evidence that *h* only if

(A) $P(h/e) > k$, where k is some threshold of high probability;

(B) P(there is an explanatory connection between *h* and $e/h \ \& \ e) > k$.

The first condition requires that the probability of *h*, given *e*, be high, say, greater than ½. The second requires that the probability of an explanatory connection between *h* and *e*, given *h* & *e*, be high. Suppose we also take these conditions to be necessary ones for *e* to be a good reason to believe *h*. This allows *e* to be a good reason to believe *h* even if *h* is false (and even if *e* is false).

Now let's look at the sort of example that worries Hempel: the coin-tossing case, where heads outcomes in the first one hundred tosses constitute a good reason to believe that the 101st toss will yield heads. This is so, even though what happened in the first one hundred tosses does not explain what happens on the 101st toss. In this case, however, conditions (A) and (B) are both satisfied. Given heads on the first one hundred tosses, it is highly probable that the coin will land heads on toss 101 (or so we may suppose). And given that the coin landed heads on the first 100 tosses (*e*), and that it will land heads on the 101st toss (*h*), it is highly probable that there is an explanatory connection between the two. This is so in virtue of the fact that given *e* and *h*, it is highly probable that some hypothesis correctly explains both *e* and *h* (e.g., that the coin is weighted so that it always lands heads, or the tossing mechanism is arranged so as to make this happen, or that this is a two-headed coin). Accordingly, conditions (A) and (B), unlike Hempel's, will allow us to claim that *e* is a good reason for believing *h* in this case.

So far so good. What about the case involving Bill Clinton smiling? If we keep Hempel's original condition, namely, that for *e* to be a good reason to believe *h*, *e* must correctly explain *h*, we preclude (1) from being a good reason to believe (2). (We don't want to say that the fact that Bill Clinton will smile tomorrow correctly explains why tomorrow Bill Clinton will smile.) But if we adopt the broader explanatory connection condition (B) together with the high-probability condition (A) we are in trouble, since both conditions are satisfied: P(tomorrow Bill Clinton will smile/Bill Clinton will smile tomorrow) = 1; and given that tomorrow Bill Clinton will smile, and that Bill Clinton will smile tomorrow, it is probable that there is some hypothesis that correctly explains both.

In this case, perhaps what is needed is not a more stringent explanation condition but one of a different sort. The one I impose on evidence (Achinstein 1983) is that for *e* to be evidence that *h*, *e* cannot entail *h*. If we introduce this as a condition for *e*'s being a good reason to believe *h*, we preclude the Clinton example, since (1) entails (2). Nevertheless, this condition seems too strong for our purposes here, since it would preclude the premises of any deductive argument from constituting a good reason to believe the conclusion. But something resembling it may be necessary. It is not the case that in every valid deduction containing true premises, the premises provide a good reason for believing the conclusion. Circular arguments (such as that from [1] to [2]) are valid and may contain true premises, but are not convincing. They fail to provide good reasons for believing their conclusions.

However, the problem with attempting to formulate a condition weaker than nonentailment and stronger than simply precluding cases such as (1) and (2) that are very similar stylistic variants is that there are degrees of circularity. In some deductive arguments the premises, while not quite the same as the conclusion, are sufficiently close to preclude the former from providing a good reason for believing the latter.[1]

It is not my aim here to try to formulate such a condition. In discussing this part of Hempel's symmetry thesis my main purpose is to defend one idea suggested to me by that thesis, namely, the plausibility of some type of explanatory condition for "*e* provides a good reason for believing *h*." The particular one I have proposed allows us to handle one type of case Hempel finds troubling: arguing from particular facts (e.g., about results of tossing this coin) to other particular facts (e.g., about the next toss), where the former does not explain the latter.

It also allows us to preclude certain cases where we obviously do not want to say that *e* provides a good reason for believing *h*, even though the probability of *h*, given *e*, is very high. Let

e = Michael Jordan eats Wheaties

and

h = Michael Jordan will not become pregnant.

Although P(*h*/*e*) is very high, *e* does not provide a good reason for believing *h*. In this case although *e* and *h* satisfy the high-probability condition (A), they fail to satisfy the explanatory connection condition (B). Given the truth of *h* and *e*, there is probably no explanatory connection between Michael Jordan's eating Wheaties and his not becoming pregnant.

Because of examples such as the coin-tossing one, Hempel came to regard this first part of the symmetry thesis with less enthusiasm than he showed originally (see Hempel 1965, p. 376). I recommend restoring some of his original infectious enthusiasm.

Explanation: Must It Be Potentially Predictive?

This second part of the symmetry thesis is one that Hempel never abandoned or doubted. In his most important later work on explanation (1965, pp. 367–8) he expressed the claim as "a general condition of adequacy for any rationally acceptable explanation of a particular event":

> That condition is the following. Any rationally acceptable answer to the question "Why did event X occur?" must offer information which shows that X was to be expected—if not definitely, as in the case of D-N [deductive-nomological] explanation, then at least with reasonable probability. Thus the explanatory information must provide good grounds for believing that X did in fact occur; otherwise, that information would give us no adequate reason for saying: "That explains it—that does show why X occurred.

This claim has generated a good deal of controversy. Various examples have been proposed to refute it (Barker 1961, Scriven 1962, Collins 1966). Since these examples are fairly similar, let me abstract from them and formulate a type of counterexample they represent.

Suppose that some type of state of affairs *S* produces an effect of type *e* once in a while, say 5 percent of the time. Suppose that on a given occasion a state of affairs of type *S* obtained and did in fact produce an effect of type *e*. Since this is so, on that occasion the effect *e* could be explained by citing the fact that *S* obtained. However, since that effect is produced only in 5 percent of the cases when the state of affairs obtains, one could not have predicted the effect from the state of affairs (with any "reasonable probability," to use Hempel's expression). If so, and if the explanation is correct, then a correct explanation need not be potentially predictive, thus violating Hempel's symmetry thesis.

Hempel has a reply to such cases. It is that explanations of this sort are *incomplete*. They are "explanation sketches," not full-blown scientific explanations. Obviously the state of affairs *S* by itself is not sufficient to produce effect *e*. Otherwise it would do so whenever it obtains, not just in 5 percent of the cases. Assuming *e* is caused (and not simply a chance event that occurs 5 percent of the time when *S* obtains), there must be further conditions that together with *S* will yield *e*. An explanation that fails to cite these further conditions is incomplete. If *e* occurs only in 5 percent of the cases when *S* obtains, why did *e* occur on this occasion when *S* obtained when it usually does not occur if *S* obtains? This question needs to be answered by our explanation, and this question calls for citing the further conditions that together with S produce e.

Since I am among those who believe in the efficacy of this sort of counter-example (Achinstein 1971), let me say how I would reply to Hempel.

Hempel Has Changed the Explanatory Question

We began with the question "Why did an event of type e occur?" The answer given was that state of affairs S obtained. Hempel has changed the question to "Why did e occur when S obtained when it usually does not occur when S obtains?" These are different questions. What Hempel needs to show is that you cannot satisfactorily answer the former question without answering the latter. In defending his position he cannot simply invoke the symmetry thesis and claim that an explanatory answer citing S must be potentially predictive. That would beg the question. We can certainly agree that "because the state of affairs S obtained" is not a satisfactory answer to the question "Why did e occur when S obtained when it usually does not?" What Hempel needs to show, independently of the symmetry thesis, is why "because the state of affairs S obtained" is not a satisfactory answer to the question "Why did e occur?"

It is (or can be) a *correct* answer. This is because in the sorts of cases I have in mind, the state of affairs S *caused* the event e. Generally speaking, if S caused e, then the explanation "e occurred because S obtained" is a correct explanation. To be sure, there are cases where explanations of this sort are trivial, or unrevealing, or uninteresting (e.g., "e occurred because the cause of e obtained") But these are not the sort of cases opponents of Hempel have in mind. To invoke a specific example borrowed from Arthur Collins (1966), it is by no means trivial, or unrevealing, or uninteresting (at least not to poor Sam or his doctor) to say that Sam's rash occurred because of his penicillin injection. What makes this explanation correct is that the penicillin injection caused Sam's rash (even though such injections cause rashes infrequently). So I believe that what Hempel must argue is that even if such an explanation is correct as far as it goes, it is not adequate because it does not go far enough. It is incomplete. This charge of incompleteness, a central one for Hempel, must now be addressed.

Incompleteness

In response to Hempel's charge of incompleteness one might be tempted to say simply this. Whether an answer to a question is incomplete depends on the question and on the context in which the question is raised, which determines what sort of answer is appropriate. The answer "because of the penicillin injection" may be perfectly complete if the question is "Why did the rash occur?" and the context is one in which Sam and his doctor simply want to know what external agent or event (e.g., the injection, the heat, something he ate) caused his rash. If the context involves studying physiological conditions under which penicillin causes a rash, the answer would be incomplete. (I return to contextual issues in the section "Pragmatic versus Nonpragmatic Ideas of Explanation.")

However, I believe there is another, perhaps deeper, agenda underlying Hempel's "incompleteness" claim. In addition to his symmetry thesis, Hempel has in mind two requirements that an adequate scientific explanation must satisfy (see Achinstein 1983, chap. 5). To introduce them I will use his terms "explanans" and "explanandum" to refer, respectively, to the sentence(s) giving the explanation and the sentence describing the event to be explained. The first requirement I call *the a priori requirement*. It is that determining whether an explanans, if true, correctly explains an explanandum is an a priori matter. (It involves such things as considering the meanings of words, discerning deductive relationships between sentences, and making mathematical calculations.) The a priori requirement derives from Hempel's more general idea that a priori criteria are possible for metascientific concepts generally, including such concepts as evidence, law, theory, and model, as well as explanation. (In the case of evidence, for example, the idea would be that whether, or the extent to which, *e*, if true, is supporting evidence for *h* is an a priori matter that can be settled by appeal to linguistic rules governing logical and probabilistic relationships.)

The second requirement I call NES, which stands for *no-entailment-by-singular sentences*. It is that no singular sentence in the explanans (no sentence describing *particular* events), and no conjunction of such sentences, can entail the explanandum.[2] There are various reasons Hempel has for the NES requirement; I mention just one here.

Suppose our explanandum is

E: Sam got a rash today,

and suppose our explanans is

Sam's penicillin injection yesterday explains his rash.

The latter is a singular sentence that entails *E*. But for Hempel this trivializes the task of constructing an adequate scientific explanation. What Hempel wants to know is why or how invoking the penicillin injection explains the rash. In effect, Hempel wants to ban from an explanans terms such as "explains" ("because" and "causes"). He wants the explanation to spell out exactly how events cited in an explanans explain the explanandum-event, and not simply to say that they do.

What does all of this have to do with Hempel's idea of "completeness" in explanations? His basic idea is this. The explanans must be complete enough to satisfy the a priori requirement, while not violating NES. So, returning to the explanandum *E* in the previous example, suppose the explanans is

T: Sam had a penicillin injection yesterday.

The NES requirement is satisfied, since even though the explanans *T* is a singular sentence describing a particular event, it does not entail the explanandum

E. However, the a priori requirement is violated, since it is not the case that whether *T*, if true, correctly explains *E* can be determined a priori. Even if *T* is true, the correct explanation of *E* might not be *T*, but something else, for example, some food Sam ate, or the heat he was exposed to.

To be sure, we could satisfy the a priori requirement by changing the explanans *T* to

T': The penicillin injection Sam received yesterday caused (or explains) his rash today.

T', if true, correctly explains *E*, and this is knowable a priori. But now we have violated the NES requirement, since *T'* is a singular sentence that entails *E*.

What must be done, Hempel will say, is to incorporate more information into the original explanans *T*—to complete it—so that whether the explanans, if true, correctly explains the explanandum is knowable a priori. We must do so, however, without violating NES.

Here, for example, is how Hempel's own D-N model would handle this. First, we would attempt to identify some physiological condition *C* that together with a penicillin injection yields a rash. Second, we would expand *T* as follows.

T'': Sam had a penicillin injection yesterday
Sam had physiological condition *C*
Anyone with condition *C* who gets a penicillin injection gets a rash within twenty-four hours.

Now, Hempel would say, we have a "complete" explanation of *E*. Additional information has been incorporated into the explanans so that whether the explanans, if true, correctly explains the explanandum *E* can be determined a priori. (For Hempel's D-N model, this requires determining whether *T'* entails *E* and whether the third sentence is "lawlike"; both are a priori exercises.) Moreover, explanans *T''* satisfies NES, since the singular sentences in *T''* do not entail *E*.

As I said, I believe that Hempel's idea of "completeness" really amounts to "a priori completeness": the explanans should be complete enough so that it becomes an a priori matter to determine whether, if the sentences comprising the explanans are true, they correctly explain the explanandum—provided, of course, that NES is satisfied.

Two questions need answering. First, can there be a priori completeness without violating NES? Second, what is so desirable about such completeness? My answer to the first question is no. (For an extensive discussion, see Achinstein [1983, chap. 5].) Briefly, the problem can be illustrated by invoking cases involving intervening causes. Suppose it is a law that anyone who eats a pound of arsenic dies within twenty-four hours. Suppose poor Ann happens to eat a pound of arsenic at time *T* and dies within twenty-four hours. Our explanandum is

e: Ann died within twenty-four hours of time *T*.

Our explanans is

t: Ann ate a pound of arsenic at *T*.
Anyone who eats a pound of arsenic dies within twenty-four hours.

For Hempel, indeed, *t* is an adequate D-N explanation of *e*, since (we are assuming) *t* is true, the second sentence in *t* is a law, and *t* entails *e*. Moreover NES is satisfied, since the first sentence in *t*—the only singular sentence in *t*—does not entail *e*.

The problem for Hempel is that the a priori condition is violated. It is not determinable a priori whether *t*, if true, correctly explains *e*. Suppose that after taking arsenic Ann was killed not by the arsenic but by a runaway truck, something completely unrelated to the arsenic. Then *t* would not correctly explain *e*. Rather the intervening cause—the truck accident—does. But whether or not there was such an intervening cause is not knowable a priori just by contemplating the explanans *t*. It is knowable only empirically. So the a priori requirement is violated in this example.

We could satisfy the a priori requirement by changing *t* to

T':   Ann's eating a pound of arsenic at *T* caused her death within twenty-four hours.

Whether *t'*, if true, correctly explains *e* is knowable a priori, so the a priori requirement is satisfied. But now NES is violated, since *t'* is a singular sentence that entails the explanandum *e*. In Achinstein (1983) I discuss other unsuccessful attempts to save both the a priori and the NES requirements. More generally, my claim is that if you want to satisfy the a priori requirement you will need to incorporate into the explanans sentences with forms such as these:

C caused *e*.
C explains *e*.
e occurred because of *C*.

These violate NES.

Turning now to the second question, what is so sacred about a priori completeness? Why is this desirable in a scientific explanation? Here is a possible answer. If a priori completeness is satisfied, then whether an explanans, if true, correctly explains an explanandum can be settled with the highest form of certainty, a priori certainty. This has two advantages. Scientists who disagree about whether the sentences of an explanans—that is, those describing particular events and those purporting to express laws—are true, can at least agree on one crucial question, namely, whether if true these sentences would correctly explain the explanandum. Moreover, they can achieve the highest form of certainty about the latter question, a priori certainty.

These alleged advantages are illusory. Making the question a priori does not necessarily mean agreement. Scientists may have different theories of explanation and disagree over the question of whether a given explanans, if true, correctly explains an explanandum. They may be using different a priori criteria. Moreover, rejecting the a priori requirement and allowing the question of whether an explanans if true correctly explains an explanandum to be an empirical question does not necessarily mean disagreement. Indeed, there may be at least as much (if not more) agreement over empirical questions as there is over a priori ones.

Finally, to be sure, if the question of correctness is always a priori, and if there is some unique criterion to be employed, then, for any explanans *T* and any explanandum *E*, whether or not *T*, if true, correctly explains *E* is establishable with certainty and cannot be refuted by experience. To a rationalist seeking certainty in all matters this is an advantage. But why should Hempel, who is an empiricist in other matters, not be one here as well? Hempel does not demand that the explanans *T*, or the explanandum *E*, be establishable with a priori certainty. Why should he insist on such certainty for statements of the form "*T*, if true, correctly explains *E*"? Indeed, if I am right, in view of intervening cause examples such as the previous arsenic example, Hempel will be unable to achieve a priori certainty for statements of the form in question unless he incorporates into the explanans singular sentences that entail the explanandum, that is, unless he violates NES.

In sum, if by "completeness" in explanations Hempel means "a priori completeness," that is, satisfying the a priori requirement, and doing so in such a way as to satisfy NES as well, then I doubt that such completeness is achievable.

Pragmatic versus Nonpragmatic Ideas of Explanation

In opposition to the idea that an adequate explanation must be potentially predictive I have cited cases in which a cause (e.g., the penicillin injection) produced a certain effect (a rash) on a given occasion, even though it does so infrequently. Given the potential cause, we could not predict the effect with high probability. I have also admitted that the cause in such a case could not have produced the effect unless certain other conditions obtained (e.g., unless the person had a certain physiological condition, which we call an allergy to penicillin.)

Now for a fundamental objection. There is no objective, principled difference between what I cited as the cause and the other conditions that obtained and were needed to produce the effect. All of the conditions are part of the cause, and if one is selected that is because of contextual factors having to do with the interests of the investigator. One investigator particularly interested in external agents triggering the rash will select the penicillin injection as the cause. Another investigator interested in the physiological condition that will allow a penicillin injection to result in a rash will select the physiological condition as the cause. There is no one right selection of cause independently of such investigative interests. But the adequacy of a scientific explanation should not depend on what interests particular investigators have. Or at least we should think in terms of an ideal scientific explanation as one that adequately explains independently of particular interests. Accordingly, an ideal causal explanation with this feature will cite all the conditions that were causally necessary on that occasion to produce the effect, together with the laws governing these causes (see Lewis 1986). If this is done, then an adequate explanation will be potentially predictive. From the complete set of conditions, together with the laws, we can infer the effect. This, of course, allows one to select some particular condition as the cause, depending on one's interests. That is a "pragmatic" not a "logical" matter. Really it is the entire set of conditions that is the cause and should be invoked in an ideal causal scientific explanation, where particular interests are irrelevant.

This objection is fundamental because it presupposes a "nonpragmatic" concept of adequate explanation that is divorced from particular interests of investigators. By contrast to Hempel, I have opposed such a divorce (Achinstein 1983). For me, whether an explanation is adequate depends crucially on the interests of the investigator. These interests play a role in determining some particular question the explanation is supposed to answer and the type of answer that is appropriate, which is determined by a set of instructions to be followed in giving the answer. Whether an explanation is adequate depends on whether it answers the question, on whether it follows the instructions, and on whether the instructions are appropriate (which, in turn, depends in part on the interests and knowledge of the investigator and his potential audience).

Suppose that

T: Sam had a penicillin injection yesterday

and

E: Sam got a rash today

are both true, and also that Sam's penicillin injection caused his rash (or, in terms of my opponents, was one of the causal conditions). Is *T* an adequate explanation of *E*? My answer is that it *could be*, depending on the question being raised and the type of answer called for. If the question is "Why did Sam get a rash today?" or "What caused his rash?" and the type of answer called for in the context is simply the citing of an external causal agent, then the explanation may well be adequate. If the question is "Why did Sam get a rash from penicillin?" or "Why did Sam get a rash *today* (rather than yesterday when he had the injection)?" then the explanation provided by *T* is inadequate. Again, if the question is "Why did Sam get a rash today?" but the context imposes instructions to invoke not just an external cause but how that cause operates, then the explanation provided by *T* is also inadequate. Adequacy depends in part on interests. Without contextual considerations there is no answer to the question of whether *T* is an adequate explanation of *E*.

Accordingly, sometimes an adequate explanation will be potentially predictive and sometimes not. There are potential situations in which *T* is an adequate explanation of *E*. In those situations Hempel's symmetry thesis fails to hold. Although *T* correctly and, in those situations, adequately explains *E*, given *T* one could not have predicted *E*. Of course, this conclusion depends crucially on rejecting Hempel's ideas about the nonpragmatic character of explanation. Just as his claims about "completenes" are based on a deeper idea of the a priori char-- acter of explanation, so I think his symmetry claim is based on a deeper idea of a nonpragmatic concept of explanation. If you reject the latter, you are likely to reject the idea that an adequate explanation must be potentially predictive.

Explanation and Probability

Finally, I want to comment on a fundamental dispute concerning explanation and probability that has arisen between Hempel and certain opponents, including Fetzer (1974, 1993), Railton (1978), and Salmon (1971). In accordance with his symmetry thesis, Hempel requires that an explanans make the explanandum at least probable. By this Hempel means that the probability of the explanandum, given the explanans, must be greater than ½, that is, more probable than not. Hempel's opponents say this is not necessary.

Let me select two specific opponents, Railton and Fetzer, and show how the model of explanation each proposes—Railton's deductive-nomological-probabilistic (D-N-P) model and Fetzer's causal-probabilistic model—violates Hempel's symmetry thesis and allows the explanation of events that are extremely improbable given the explanans.

To offer a correct D-N-P explanation of a particular chance event in which some item i acquired a property G at a given time t, we proceed as follows. We begin with some true theory that allows a derivation of a probabilistic law of the form

   (1)   At any time anything that is F has probability p to be G.

Then we state a relevant fact about our item i, namely,

   (2)   i is F at time t.

From (1) and (2) we conclude

   (3)   i has probability p to be G at time t.

We then add, according to how things turn out,

   (4)   i did (did not) become G at t.

Although Railton's model is supposed to be applied to genuinely indeterministic, chance events (e.g., quantum events), it will be useful to cite a simple example involving a deterministic system leading to "chance" events, namely coin tossing. Suppose we toss a coin one hundred times and miraculously it lands heads each time. We want to explain why this coin i had the property G of landing heads one hundred times in a row during some time interval t. Assume that our theory of the coin is that this coin is fair, so that the probability of landing heads on any single toss is ½. Our theory also tells us that the coin tosses are probabilistically independent, so that the probability of landing heads on some toss is not affected by how the coin lands on other tosses. Assume the theory is true. From this theory, plus the mathematical theory of probability, we can derive the following.

(a) During any time interval, if this coin is tossed 100 times in a row it has the probability $(\frac{1}{2})^{100}$ of landing heads all 100 times.

Now we know the following to be true:

(b) This coin was tossed 100 times in a row during interval t.

From (a) and (b) we deduce

(c) This coin has probability $(\frac{1}{2})^{100}$ of landing heads each time during interval t.

We then add that in fact

(d) This coin did land heads each time during interval t.

We may construe (d) as the explanandum, and the basic theory of the coin together with (a)–(c) as the explanans. In this case, according to the D-N-P model, the explanans correctly explains the explanandum event, even though, in accordance with the explanans, the explanandum event is extremely unlikely.

Using his own quantum-mechanical example involving a very improbable alpha-particle decay, Railton asks whether a D-N-P explanation explains the event in question. He writes:

> It does not explain why the decay *had* to take place, nor does it explain why the decay *could be expected* to take place. And a good thing too: there is no *had to* or *could be expected to* about the decay to explain—it is not only a chance event, but a very improbable one. [The explanation] does explain why the event *improbably* took place, which is how it did. [It] accomplishes this by demonstrating that there existed at the time a small but definite physical possibility of decay, and noting that, by chance, this possibility was realized.[3]

Fetzer (1993) introduces what he calls a causal model of explanation in which the explanans may contain either a probabilisitic or universal law. In the probabilistic case, such an explanation takes the form:

For any x, if x has property G, then, with probability p, x has property F.
Item a has property G
$$\overline{}\ [p]$$
Item a has property F

The first sentence in the explanans expresses what Fetzer calls a probabilistic causal conditional. The probability involved is to be interpreted as a single-case physical propensity that is not deterministically reducible. It is the propensity of something with G (at a given time) to be an F (at a given time), and is not to be interpreted as a propensity to be G "in the long run." The symbol $[p]$ represents the "nomic expectability" that item a has property F given the truth of the two sentences in the explanans.

Fetzer imposes several conditions for an explanation of this form to be an "adequate casual explanation of a particular event" (1992, p. 255). Briefly, these are that the explanandum must follow deductively or probabilistically from the explanans; the explanans must contain at least one essential law; the law(s) connot include causally irrelevant factors; and all the sentences must be true. There is no requirements that the probalility value p be high.

Accordingly, we can employ the previous coin example in constructing the following explanation of why this coin landed heads one hundred times in the last one hundred tosses:

Any coin is such that if it is physically balanced ("fair") and randomly tossed (so that the outcomes are probabilistically independent), then with a probability $(\frac{1}{2})^{100}$ it will land heads 100 times in a row.
This coin is physically balanced and was randomly tossed 100 times.
$$\overline{} = [(\frac{1}{2})^{100}]$$
This coin landed heads 100 times in a row.

Assuming there is no deeper deterministic theory (see note 6), Fetzer's conditions are satisfied. On his view this represents an adequate explanation of why this coin landed heads one hundred times in a row, even though, once again, the explanandum event is extremely unlikely.

For Hempel, Railton's D-N-P explanation involving the coin tossing event (or the analogous one involving alpha–particle decay), as well as Fetzer's explanation of this event, would at best count as an explanation of why this coin has a probability of $(\frac{1}{2})^{100}$ of landing heads one hundred times in a row. (In Railton's case the explanation would proceed by deriving this probability from the assumptions of the theory; in Fetzer's case the explanation appeals to the fact that the coin was physically balanced and was randomly tossed one hundred times, and that under these conditions coins have a probability, that is, a physical propensity, of $(\frac{1}{2})^{100}$ to land heads one hundred times in a row.) But it would not count as an explanation of why the coin did in fact land heads one hundred times in a row, since the theory or law in question entails that the probability of this event is so small.

Railton would reply that the explanation explains why the coin landed heads one hundred times in a row because it explains "why the event *improbably* took place." This is a very odd phrase! If it means that the explanation explains why the event, one hundred heads in a row, was so improbable, then Hempel might well agree. But then, referring to the earlier propositions (a)–(d), the explanandum is (C), not (d). What is being explained is why the probability of the event is what it is, not why the event occurred. If it means that it explains why an improbable event did in fact occur, then Hempel would disagree. Here my intuitions are with Hempel. If the event was so improbable, as the probabilistic explanation clearly shows it is, why did it in fact happen? Assuming that there is no deeper deterministic theory underlying this case, my response is to say that there is no explanation. We are dealing here with chance events. The one in question was extremely unlikely. But extremely unlikely events do happen.[4]

Assuming there is no underlying mechanism here, or some cheating going on, there is nothing to be explained, except perhaps why the probability is so small.[5]

To this Railton and Fetzer may reply that the "pure chance" coin tossing event yielding one hundred heads is not an event that is completely incomprehensible. The coin was balanced, it was tossed randomly, and these conditions were "nomically responsible" (Fetzer's term), albeit probabilistically, for the complex event in question. There is a perfectly good sense of explanation that involves this idea of probabilistic "nomic responsibility."

Hempel's response—one I favor—is to deny that there is such a perfectly good sense of explanation. If there is no underlying mechanism, or cheating, we are indeed dealing with an event for which there is no explanation of any kind. The fact that the coin was tossed, we might agree, is responsible (at least partly so) for its landing. But neither the fact that it was tossed randomly, nor the fact that it is balanced, nor both facts together, are responsible, even in part, for its landing heads one hundred times in a row. Nothing was! This is so, despite the fact that under the conditions in question there is a tiny probability that the coin will land heads one hundred times in a row. Is the event therefore "incomprehensible"? No, because in the case of such a chance event there is nothing to comprehend, except why the chance of its happening is so low (but not zero).

By contrast, what happens if the probability of a certain chance event is very high? Borrowing from the previous example, we can illustrate this by choosing as our event one in which the one hundred tosses of the coin do *not* result in all heads. Why didn't the coin land all heads in these one hundred tosses? An explanation of the sort Railton or Fetzer offers seems fine here. Basically, it consists of saying that this is a fair coin and the tosses are probabilistically independent. So the probability of getting one hundred heads in one hundred tosses is $(\frac{1}{2})^{100}$, which means that the probability of not getting this is $1 - (\frac{1}{2})^{100}$, or very close to certainty. Or, to change the example to one involving a "positive" event, suppose there is a lottery consisting of 1000 tickets, one of which will be drawn at random. James, who hates to lose, but who loves at least a slight risk, buys 999 of the tickets. When the drawing occurs James is declared the winner. Why did he win? There is a very simple explanation: he bought all but one of the tickets; so his chance of winning was 999/1000.

Does this mean that Hempel is right in saying that an explanans must make the explananduta probable? No, it does not. The penicillin example, in which we explain why Sam got a rash by citing the penicillin injection, shows that high probability is not necessary. So why allow low probability in this case but not in the case involving one hundred tosses of the coin all resulting in heads? There is a crucial difference here. Sam's rash was *caused* by the penicillin injection; that is what we are assuming. The one hundred heads were not caused, even in part, by the coin's being fair and the tosses being independent. Indeed, we are supposing that *nothing* caused the coin to land heads one hundred times, or even to land heads on any particular toss; it was a matter of pure chance.[6] When we are dealing with a system such as this, in which neither individual simple outcomes (e.g., heads on a given toss), nor compound outcomes (e.g., heads on the next one hundred tosses), are caused, then I think Hempel is right and Railton and Fetzer are not: we can explain very likely outcomes, but not very unlikely ones, by appeal to facts that give those events the probabilities they have. We can explain why in the first one hundred tosses heads did not come up each time by saying that this is a fair coin and the tosses are independent, so that the probability of this outcome is close to one. But if a miracle happens and the coin lands heads 100 times in a row, we cannot explain this by saying that the coin is fair and the tosses independent, so that probability of 100 heads is almost zero. We can explain why James won the lottery by saying that he owned almost all the tickets. But if his brother John, who owned the remaining ticket, happened to win and not James, we cannot explain this fact by saying that John owned one of the 1000 tickets.

It is important to contrast this high-probability explanation involving chance outcomes that are uncaused with inductive-statistical explanations of the sort actually cited by Hempel. There is a crucial difference between these cases. Here is an example used by Hempel (1965, p. 382). (It also involves penicillin, but now we have high, not low, probability.) A certain patient, who had a strepto-coccal infection, was treated with penicillin. The probability of recovery in such cases is close to (but not equal to) 1, let us assume. The patient recovered. To explain why, Hempel constructs the following inductive-statistical explanation:

I-S: This patient, who had a streptococcal infection, was treated with penicillin
The probability of recovery in such cases is close to 1
So (with very high probability)
The patient recovered.

Even if there is what Hempel calls a probabilistic law giving the probability of recovery from a streptococcal infection when taking penicillin, we are not dealing here with what we regard as chance outcomes that are uncaused. In the case of Hempel's patient who took penicillin and recovered, either the penicillin caused the recovery or something else did. If it was the penicillin, then, if Hempel's explanation I-S is correct, it is so in virtue of the fact that the penicillin caused the recovery. If the penicillin did not cause the recovery but something else did, then explanation I-S is incorrect.[7] In either case, *the probabilitic law invoked is irrelevant for the explanation.* If the penicillin caused the recovery, it doesn't matter what the probability is of recovering, given penicillin (as long as it is not zero). And if the penicillin did not cause the recovery, it does not matter either, since the explanation would be incorrect.[8] More generally, suppose the explanandum has the form

item i has property G,

while the explanans has the form

item i has property F
The probability that an item has property G, given that it has property F, is r.

If no matter what probability value r is, such an explanans, if true, correctly explains why the item has G, and does so equally well for any r, then the probability law is doing no explanatory work.

What the probability law (assuming high probability) allows us to do is to infer in Hempel's case that probably the penicillin did cause the recovery. The latter is the crucial fact for the explanation. That is what correctly explains the recovery (if it does), not the law.[9] In such cases, high probability of the explanandum-event, given the explanans-event, is not required for the explanation to be correct.

However, the situation changes for uncaused, chance outcomes. Although uncaused, some of these outcomes are expected. In such cases, explaining why such an outcome occurred is tantamount to explaining why it was expected to occur. And it is possible to explain why it was expected to occur by reference to the chance set-up and probabilities for various outcomes. ("James won the lottery because he owned 999 of the 1000 tickets.") In such cases I suggest that the second part of Hempel's symmetry thesis is correct, namely: "Any rationally acceptable answer to the question "Why did event X occur?" must offer information which shows that X was to be expected" (Hempel 1965, pp. 367–8).[10]

NOTES

Peter Hempel was and remains an inspiration to me both as a teacher and as one of the leading figures in philosophy of science this century. I took two courses from him, one in logic and one in probability, when I was an undergraduate and he was a visitor at Harvard in 1953–54. In my own work I have tried to grapple with issues of explanation and evidence that he introduced and made staples in the literature.

1. Some would claim that Descartes's argument from "I think" to "I exist" is a good example.
2. For a more precise formulation of this requirement, see Achinstein (1983, p. 159).
3. For a recent criticism of Railton, see Gluck and Gimbel (1997).
4. Indeed, frequently! Any particular hand of five cards I receive in poker is very unlikely.
5. Suppose there is a deeper deterministic theory. The result of any particular toss, let us assume, is completely determined by a set of physical variables taking on certain values. We may suppose that heads with the coin does not always require the same values for these variables, but there is some disjunction of values of these variables each disjunct of which will result in heads. For each of the one hundred tosses one of these heads-producing disjuncts obtained. And one could explain why the coin landed heads one hundred times in a row by indicating for each toss which of these disjuncts obtained. Such an explanation, if it could ever be achieved, would be too complex and disunified to be of any interest in most circumstances. If a coin lands heads one hundred times in a row the kind of explanation normally sought is one appealing to some one factor or small set of them present in all the tosses, for example, a weighted coin, a magnetised side, a coin with two heads, and so on. In the absence of a simple, unifying explanation, where there is only an explanation (that we can't even produce) invoking a multitude of physical variables each having a different value for each toss, one might say: there is no explanation of the kind being sought or of a kind that anyone would normally want.

6. For the sake of argument I have been supposing that these are genuinely uncaused events. However, even if each coin-tossing result is determined by some complex set of factors taking on the values they do, these are not the causes in which we are interested, or even know about, when we speak of causes in such a case. There are no causes at the appropriate level; the outcomes are chance events at that level. See note 5.
7. Hempel relativizes inductive-statistical explanations to a knowledge situation. So correctness doesn't enter for him in such cases the way it does in deductive-nomological explanations.
8. This is true even if the probability law is construed causally as implying, for example, that the probability of penicillin *causing* recovery is such and such, or as some type of causal propensity (see Fetzer 1974 and Railton 1978).
9. This is a claim Arthur Collins (1966, p. 133) made more than thirty years ago. "Only if we actually think of a causal factor as a causal factor would we advance it in an explanation. When we do so explain the explanatory force of what we say derives from the fact that we assert that something caused what we explain and not from the strength of the statistical correlation, although correlations and their specific magnitudes *may be* what lead us to think of a factor as a cause."
10. I benefited from the usual scathing comments of my colleague Robert Rynasiewicz. Jim Fetzer's very helpful comments would have been more scathing, but he has mellowed.

REFERENCES

Achinstein, Peter. 1971. *Law and Explanation*. Oxford: Oxford University Press.
———. 1983. *The Nature of Explanation*. New York: Oxford University Press.
Barker, S. F. 1961. "The Role of Simplicity in Induction." In *Current Issues in the Philosophy of Science*, edited by H. Feigl and G. Maxwell. New York: Holt, Rinehart and Winston.
Collins, Arthur. 1966. "The Use of Statistics in Explanation." *British Journal for the Philosophy of Science* 17:127–40.
Fetzer, James H. 1974. "A Single Case Propensity Theory of Explanation." *Synthese* 28:171–98.
———. 1993. *The Philosophy of Science*. New York: Paragon House.
Gluck, Stuart, and Steven Gimbel. 1997. "An Intervening Cause Counterexample to Railton's D-N-P Model." *Philosophy of Science*, 64 (1997), pp. 692–7.
Hempel, Carl G. 1942. "The Function of General Laws in History." Reprinted in Hempel (1965).
———. 1948. "Studies in the Logic of Explanation." Reprinted in Hempel (1965).
———. 1965. *Aspects of Scientific Explanation*. New York: Free Press.
Lewis, David. 1986. "Causal Explanation." In *Philosophical Papers*. Vol. 2. Oxford: Oxford University Press.
Railton, Peter. 1978. "A Deductive-Nomological Model of Probabilistic Explanation." *Philosophy of Science* 45:206–26.
Salmon, Wesley C. 1971. *Statistical Explanation and Statistical Relevance*. Pittsburgh: Pittsburgh University Press.
Scriven, Michael. 1962. "Explanations, Predictions, and Laws." In *Minnesota Studies in the Philosophy of Science*, edited by H. Feigl and G. Maxwell. Vol. 3. Minneapolis: University of Minnesota Press.

8

Hempel and the Problem of Provisos

FREDERICK SUPPE

Carl G. Hempel retired from Princeton in 1973. In 1977 he became University Professor of Philosophy at the University of Pittsburgh.[1] Around that time he widely read papers in which he argued that deductive-nomological explanations were not logically valid deductions because they involved unstated *ceteris paribus* conditions, or as he called them, "provisos." Many of us who heard these presentations marveled how in his later years Hempel was systematically calling into question his earlier work on explanation, theories, and the like. We took it as a mark of an intellectual integrity Hempel shared with Carnap where getting things right was paramount.

There is no doubt that Hempel was a man of great personal and intellectual integrity. But I want to argue here that our perception that Hempel was abandoning earlier views on explanation and deductive inference in science is mistaken. His three publications on "provisos" do not represent a significant change in view. Indeed, essentially the same doctrines (though not the provisos terminology) are found in his and Oppenheim's 1945 "Studies in the Logic of Confirmation" and constitute further development of basic insights found in his earliest English writings done during his 1935–39 Belgium exile.

In the first section herein, I situate Hempel's provisos papers in the larger context of his work on theories and theoretical inference. The second and third sections summarize and interpret Hempel's provisos papers. The fourth section details the continuity of the provisos papers with earlier work going back to the 1930s. The fifth section argues that Hempel was correct that there is an important provisos problem. The sixth section presents a solution to the problem of provisos. That solution is used as a foil in the seventh section to analyze where Hempel went wrong in his unsuccessful attempt to solve the provisos problem. In the eighth section, I conclude with some speculations as to the general influence of Hempel's juvenilia on the confirmation and explanation work done after the war for which he is famous.

186

Hempel's Work on Theories

The provisos papers presuppose, but do not further develop, the positivistic received view analysis of theories in an attempt to explore the nature of theoretical inference in scientific applications such as the prediction and explanation of singular events.

Hempel's contributions to the received view were fairly late in its development and limited. They were modest revisions (focusing on the on the observational/theoretical term distinction and the nature of correspondence rules) of Carnap's 1936–37 "Testability and Meaning" version of the received view: theories can be explicated or rationally reconstructed as partially interpreted axiomatic systems where the nonlogical vocabulary is bifurcated into an *observation vocabulary*, V_O, and a *theoretical vocabulary*, V_T. The V_O terms have standard observational interpretations, and thus V_O sentences have a full semantic interpretation. The *theoretical principles* or laws of the theory are a set of axioms C formulated using just V_T and logical terms. The laws C *implicitly define* the V_T terms by restricting the range of interpretations allowed for V_T terms. Those laws C and their V_T terms are further given an empirical interpretation via *correspondence rules R*, which are "mixed sentences" containing both V_O and V_T terms. Paradigmatic of correspondence rules are operational definitions which may be in the form of explicit definitions of V_T terms or reduction sentences which partially define terms in specific experimental or observational contexts. Each correspondence rule explicitly or partially defines a single V_T term. Correspondence rules R thus combine the specification of meaning for V_T terms with specifying the empirical procedures for testing and applying theories in concrete situations.[2] A theory $T = <C, R>$.

Hempel's 1952 *Fundamentals of Concept Formation in Empirical Science* argued that not all terms individually could be associated with observational circumstances via explicit definitions or reduction sentences. Alleged examples were the Ψ function in quantum theory and various real-valued metrical theoretical concepts such as "mass," "force," and "pressure."[3] Hempel's solution is to expand the range of allowed correspondence rules, R, to include *interpretative system sentences I* that connect the entire C with observable conditions in a manner that does not associate specific V_T terms with specific observable manifestations. Reduction sentences and explicit definitions qualify as degenerate interpretative sentences.

In the 1952 *Concept Formation* monograph, Hempel assumed the received view's observational/theoretical term distinction (1952, chap. 2, sec. 5). However, that distinction was closely associated with the analytic/synthetic distinction and when Hempel abandoned that he replaced the V_T/ V_O bifurcation with an *antecedently available* vocabulary V_A *versus* theoretical vocabulary V_T distinction (Suppe 1977, pp. 66–86, especially p. 79) where the V_A terms are a basic vocabulary of terms that are antecedently understood, but need not be restricted to observational terms.

These changes come out of further work developing the notion of an inter-pretative system.[4] But in many ways this move was anticipated in Hempel's 1935 paper "On the Logical Positivists' Theory of Truth" where he opted for a position where there were no privileged observational or protocol statements. What one took as protocol or basic statements was simply a mater of conven-tion. Since no particular convention is mandated, there is no need to tie the basic vocabulary to V_O terms. Hempel's opting for the requirement that the basic sen-tences be "antecedently available" was based on observations of how theoretical terms in practice are introduced in science where he claims they are partially defined on the basis of terms that are antecedently understood, many of which earlier were introduced as theoretical terms (1965d, especially secs. 7 and 8).

In his later writings, including the provisos papers, Hempel termed his modi-fication $<C, I>$ of the received view where R is replaced by interpretive sen-tences or system I and V_O is replaced by V_A the *standard conception* or the *stan-dard empiricist construal* of theories and he used that standard conception for purposes of analysis.

Around 1965 Hempel began to question the standard conception of theories (1969) and by 1969 abandoned it, offering a replacement analysis wherein theo-ries consist of a set of *internal principles P* associated with V_T but also may con-tain V_A terms and a set B of *bridge principles* connecting V_T terms with V_A terms (1970, pp. 142–5; 1977, pp. 244–6).[5]

On the surface, this seems a superficial change: replacing $<C, I>$ by $<P, B>$. Hempel claims otherwise. For what differentiates $<P, B>$ from $<C, I>$ are the absence from P and B of many of the characteristic features of C and I that were definitive of the standard conception and other versions of the received view: P need not be an axiomatic calculus since Hempel had become convinced that axiomatization and formalization often was unproductive or premature. P is not uninterpreted because the internal principles often contain V_A terms. The B are not definitions or terminological conventions since they often cor-relate theoretical values with the outcomes of specific measurements and thus make empirical assertions that may prove erroneous. Further it is not the purpose of $<P, B>$ to provide an account of how theoretical terms acquire mean-ing on the basis of an observational or antecedently understood vocabulary since that

> problem . . . is spurious because it rests on an erroneous presupposition . . . that if theoretical terms have definite meanings, then it must be possible to construe those terms as introduced by specifiable logical procedures, which as-sign them meanings with the help of terms that are antecedently understood." (1977, p. 253)[6]

Hempel's replacement $<P, B>$ analysis does retain the $<C, I>$ feature that the experimental designs or procedures for applying theories to concrete phenom-ena be incorporated into rules that are proper individuating components of theo-ries. Indeed, since the B no longer are definitional, their primary role appears to be the specification of such procedures. B remains an individuating component of theories <*P, B*> on Hempel's replacement analysis—just as *I* was in the rejected standard conception <*C, I*> analysis.

Twice in his career, Hempel published papers surveying the evolution of key received-view doctrines. The first (1935) charted the evolution of positivist truth notions that ultimately led to a conventionalist construal of the protocol sentences expressing the "observational" basis for theoretical knowledge. Then (1950, 1951) he revisited the issue from the perspective of changes in positivist criteria for cognitive significance of observational and theoretical terms.

However, Hempel's most significant work regarding theories concerned the use of theories in science. First, there are Hempel's many classic papers developing the covering-law model of explanation that all focus on the use of theoretical inference to predict or explain phenomena.[7] His 1988 provisos papers are part of this research enterprise. Second, "The Theoretician's Dilemma" in part is an attack on instrumentalism and other eliminativist programs (e.g., invoking Ramsey sentences or Craig's Theorem) that sought to show that V_T terms and propositions were dispensable from science. In it he argues that an important function of theories is the compact, systematic expression of large bodies of empirical knowledge and that the price of instrumentalisms and eliminativist programs is the loss of this systematicity. His provisos papers further develop the attack against these challenges to realistic construal of theories.

The Problem of Provisos

In 1988 Hempel published two papers on provisos in three places. "Provisoes: A Problem concerning the Inferential Function of Scientific Theories" (hereafter "Provisos") was published in *Erkenntnis* and in the proceedings of a 1980 Pittsburgh conference, "The Limits of Deductivism."[8] He also published "Limits of a Deductive Construal of the Function of Scientific Theories" (hereafter "Limits") in the proceedings of the Israel Colloquium. The two papers are minor variations on each other, though the latter appears to be an earlier, less complete version of the former. I will treat them collectively as articulating his mature provisos position since nothing in "Provisos" contradicts anything in "Limits" though the latter does contain a few things that are not found in "Provisos."

Hempel's focus is "the *hypothetico-deductive* model, according to which, briefly, to explain or describe a phenomenon by means of a theory is to deduce a sentence describing the phenomenon from the theory taken in conjunction with sentences providing certain initial information" ("Limits," p. 1) where "the best known elaboration of this general conception is provided by the so-called *standard empiricist construal*" ("Limits," p. 2; cf. "Provisos," p. 147). He poses the provisos problem in terms of the standard conception despite having rejected it by 1969 (see the seventh section herein).

An application of a theory <*C, I*> begins with a singular descriptive statement S^1_A, which interpretative sentences *I* relates to some theoretical assertion S^1_C. Then theoretical principles ("laws") in *C* yield the theoretical inference S^2_C.

Another application of the interpretative sentences I associates $S^2{}_C$ with another singular description $S^2{}_A$ of a predicted situation. Hempel maintains that such "inferences . . . by way of theoretical principles, from sentences expressing initial and boundary conditions to statements describing the occurrences to be predicted, retrodicted, or explained" ("Provisos," p. 147) are not deductively valid because the mediations via I from $S^1{}_A$ to $S^1{}_C$ and from $S^2{}_C$ to $S^2{}_A$ are not deductively valid. Hempel develops his case using an example from the theory of magnetism in which $S^1{}_A$ is "b is a metal bar to which iron filings are clinging" and $S^2{}_A$ is "If b is broken into two bars, b_1 and b_2, then both are magnets and their poles will attract or repel each other."

The first inference from $S^1{}_A$ to $S^1{}_C$ is not deductively valid because

> the theory of magnetism surely contains no general principle to the effect that when iron fillings cling to a metal bar, then the bar is a magnet. The theory does not preclude the possibility, for example, that the bar is made of lead and is covered with an adhesive to which the filings stick, or that the filings are held in place by a magnet under a wooden board supporting the lead bar. . . .
>
> Hence the transition from $S^1{}_A$ to $S^1{}_C$ is not deductive even if the entire theory of magnetism is used as an additional premise. Rather the transition involves what I will call *inductive or theoretical assent*, i.e., a transition from a data sentence expressed in V_A to a theoretical hypothesis $S^1{}_C$ which, by way of the theory of magnetism, would explain what the data sentences describes. ("Provisos," pp. 149–50; compare "Limits," p. 4)

He tells us this problem has been discussed widely[9] and inductive logics developed to solve it.

The transition from $S^2{}_C$ to $S^2{}_A$ also is not deductive since it tacitly presupposes the absence of other interfering influences such as presence of a stronger magnetic field that would prevent the two magnets b_1 and b_2 from properly orienting themselves in conformity with $S^2{}_A$.

> The theory of magnetism does not guarantee the absence of such disturbing factors. Hence, the inference from $S^2{}_C$ to $S^2{}_A$ presupposes the additional assumption that the suspended pieces are subject to no disturbing influence or, to put it positively, that their rotational motions are subject only to the magnetic forces they exert upon each other. ("Provisos," p. 150; compare "Limits," p. 5)

Hempel terms such "essential, but generally unstated, presuppositions of theoretical inference" provisos ("Provisos," p. 151; "Limits," p. 5).

He next considers whether this problem can be circumvented by letting the interpretative sentences I be probabilistic in form. He rejects this move on grounds that "a probabilistic construal of provisos faces the difficulty that scientific theories do not, in general, provide probabilistic laws that would obviate the need for provisos."[10]

He argues that the problem of provisos has significant philosophical consequences. It precludes a falsifiability requirement for theories, renders irrelevant elimination programs for theoretical terms that rely on Ramsey sentences or Craig's Theorem, "provides a tug away from instrumentalism and in the direction of realism concerning theoretical entities," and shows that the empirical content of theories cannot be identified with the set of V_A sentences entailed by the theory.[11] Curiously he does not stress the point that it also is incompatible with his account of deductive nomological (DN) explanations since it forces violation of the logical adequacy condition that "the explanandum must be a logical consequence of the explanans."[12]

Hempel's argument assumes that the "standard conception" provides an adequate reconstruction of actual theories and that the $<C, I>$ reconstruction is equivalent in theoretical and empirical content to the actual theory of magnetism. Thus the interpretative sentences I is assumed *both* to govern all legitimate applications of the theory to concrete circumstances *and* to add nothing to the theoretical and empirical content of the actual theory of magnetism. Hence,

(1)   If the concrete conditions of applicability (including experimental design, etc.) are not properly part of the theoretical and empirical content of theories, then Hempel's arguments fail to make his antideductive case.

A central contention of most versions of the semantic conception of theories is that such conditions of applicability are not properly part of the theory. Thus the status of Hempel's arguments concerning theoretical inference being nondeductive is problematic. (See the fifth and sixth sections.)

Notice also that the inductive ascent involved in the inference from S^1_A to S^1_C is nondeductive precisely because it crucially depends on provisos. For what, according to Hempel's examples, must be precluded to justify that inference is the presence of contaminating factors the theory does not explicitly take into account. Their absence figures centrally in any inductive ascent from S^1_A to S^1_C and so such inferences encounter the problem of provisos. Thus there are, on Hempel's view, important connections between the problem of provisos and inductive inference.

The Nature of Provisos

Hempel notes that provisos resemble *ceteris paribus* clauses, but does not find that fact helpful since the *ceteris paribus* clause notion is "elusive" ("Provisos," pp. 156–7; "Limits," p. 9).[13] Rather he seeks to understand provisos as *completeness assumptions*:

> The proviso required for a theoretical inference from one sentence, S^1, to another, S^2, asserts, broadly speaking, that in a given case (e.g., in that of the metal bar considered earlier) no factors other than those specified in S^1 are present which could affect the event described by S^2. ("Provisos," p. 156; "Limits," p. 9)

Notice that nothing here requires that the theory must provide the provisos needed for theoretical inference—although that is assumed in his arguments (see the preceding section) posing the problem of provisos.

He goes on to note that provisos concern *ontic completeness*, not *epistemic completeness*, in that they concern "all the factors present in the given case which in fact affect the outcome to be predicted by the theoretical inference," not just those which are known ("Provisos," p. 157; see "Limits," pp. 9–10). Provisos also are to be distinguished from errors of observation, measurement, or deceit whose influences already are precluded by "the premise S^1 itself, which trivially asserts that S^1 is true." Provisos assert that S^1 "states the *whole* truth about the relevant circumstances present." ("Provisos," pp. 158, 159).

Although provisos thus are ontic completeness assertions, theoretical inferences such as in prediction and explanation are epistemic, and so Hempel wrestles with epistemic issues. First, he asks whether provisos can be expressed in the languages of the theories they are used with or even combinations of physical theories. However, he does not immediately answer the question. Instead he first observes:

> At any rate, neither singly nor jointly do those theories assert that forces of the kinds they deal with are the only kinds by which the motion of a physical body can be affected. A scientific theory propounds an account of certain kinds of empirical phenomena, but does not pronounce on what other kinds there are. ("Provisos," p. 158; compare "Limits," p. 10)

Note that Hempel returns here to the key move of his argument against theoretical inferences being deductive—namely, that theories do not ground the provisos required for their application to concrete circumstances—although, as we have seen, nothing in his characterization of provisos requires that they be so grounded. This indicates, I think, how centrally Hempel's thinking was driven by the supposition that applied theories must ground provisos.

He returns to the question whether theoretical language can express provisos in the next paragraph, arguing, via consideration of Newton's second law, that *some* theories do possess the conceptual apparatus to express provisos needed for their inferential application to concrete circumstances. His bottom line seems to be that this happens occasionally, but not generally ("Provisos," p. 158; "Limits," pp. 10–11).

Confining attention to cases where provisos can be expressed in some theoretically relevant language, Hempel asks how one could ascertain that such an inference was *sound*. How can the correctness of provisos be checked?[14] Using Kuhn's normal versus revolutionary science distinction apparatus[15] and considering a case concerning Millikin versus Ehrenhaft over oil-drop experiments, he considers different strategies whereby one might attempt to assess the correctness of provisos. He comes to no particularly interesting insights, and his conclusion is that

> [j]ust, as in the context of theory choice, the relevant idea of superiority of one theory to another has no precise explication and yet its use is strongly affected

by considerations shared by scientific investigators, so in the inferential application of theories to empirical contexts, the idea of the relevant provisos has no precise explication, yet it is by no means arbitrary and its use appears to be significantly affected by considerations akin to those affecting theory choice. ("Provisos," p. 162; compare "Limits," p. 14)

In short, his answer is the same as other empiricist conclusions re theory choice: vague reliance on a host of pragmatic considerations such as simplicity, to mediate inferences that are not deductively sound in such a manner as to achieve unique conclusions. In short, Hempel has no real general answer how to assess the soundness of proviso-based inferences. And that is to say that he has no real answer to how theoretical inferences, including DN explanations, are possible or sound.

In "Limits" he shies away from the full force of his conclusions. "Nothing I have said is meant to imply that elaborate deductively organized theoretical arguments do not play a highly important role in science" (p. 14). Yet if he is right about provisos, then epistemically accessible, deductively sound inference is irrelevant to theoretical prediction, explanation, and inference—and so much of his own work, especially on DN explanations, is irrelevant to real science.

Proviso Antecedents in the Hempel Corpus

A persistent theme throughout Hempel's career has been attempting to reconcile the fact that scientific theories typically employ transfinite concepts but the available evidence for applying those concepts in concrete circumstances always is finite. I argue that Hempel's provisos views are the culmination of that concern.

The issue is a focal concern of Hempel's dissertation (1934).[16] There he presents a reworking of the statistical theory of probability, explores the use of probability in empirical science, comes to the conclusion that the empirical use of probability statements in physics calls for a finitistic construal despite the fact that the corresponding concepts in probability theory are transfinite (see Hempel 1934, chap. 3, especially pp. 46–7), and grapples with how to reconcile the finite with the transfinite (1934, chap. 3).

The same year he completed his dissertation, Hempel left Germany in response to Nazi political developments, and had an intermediate stay in Brussels with Paul Oppenheim as his patron. There he wrote a series of English publications preparatory to his immigration to the United States in January 1939.[17]

The first of these was a 1935 paper in *Analysis*, "On the Logical Positivist's Theory of Truth." There he presents the logical empiricist "coherence" theory of truth as developed by Carnap and Neurath, tracing its evolution as a series of departures from Wittgenstein's notions of truth in the *Tractatus*. Richard Jeffrey has suggested to me that this paper is little more than a reworking for publication of a comprehensive exam answer. I think otherwise—that it is a crucial piece for understanding Hempel's later work and actually rather original.

In it, Hempel first notes Carnap's insight that "in science empirical laws are formulated in the same language as other statements, and that they are combined with singular statements, in order to derive predictions" and thus are "general implicative statements which differ by their form from the so-called singular statements" (1935, pp. 51–2). From this he draws the following strong conclusion:

> A general statement is tested by examining its singular consequences. But as each general statement determines an infinite class of singular consequences, it cannot be finally and entirely verified, but only more or less supported by them: a general statement is not a truth-function of singular statements, but it has in relation to them the character of an *hypothesis*. The same fact may be expressed as follows: a general law cannot be formally deduced from a finite set of singular statements. Each finite set of statements admits of an infinite series of hypotheses, each of which implies all the singular statements referred to. So, in establishing the system of science, there is a conventional moment: we have to choose between a large quantity of hypotheses which are logically equally possible, and in general we choose one that is distinguished by formal simplicity. (1935, p. 52)

He further notes that singular statements are hypotheses with respect to protocol *statements* (p. 52).

The crucial points here are that there is a finitude to singular evidence statements that is compatible with an infinite number of general statements, and that there is deductive failure between finite sets of singular statements and general laws. In the language of his dissertation, evidence statements are finite and general statements are transfinite. In the language of his later writings, quasi-inductive assent is required to move from singular statements to general laws in any attempted theoretical or empirical law-governed inference.

A second thing to note is that he asserts, given the failure of deductive certainty due to the finitude of evidence constraining transfinite theoretical assertions, pragmatic considerations such as simplicity are invoked to pick a unique hypothesis among those logically compatible with the finitude of evidence. In later writings—for example, concerning the nature of mathematical truth and its relations to physical theories (such as geometries) applying such mathematics—Hempel will maintain that the choice of which theoretical hypothesis to link to finite observational evidence is a matter of convention (1945a, 1945b).

In an English *Erkenntnis* paper published in 1938, Hempel revisited the concerns of his dissertation, noting that the statistical theory of probability analyses are in terms of limits of infinite sequences and thus "the probability statement is essentially incomplete" (1938a, p. 158) and therefore mathematical probability statements "do not yet render adequately the logical form of the probability statements established in empirical science" (p. 158) because they do not explicitly characterize the infinite sequences to which the probability statements refer. Thus incorporating such sequences into empirical probability assertion is desirable yet "rather difficult to formulate explicitly" (pp. 158–9).

In a rejoinder to criticisms, Hempel replies:

> The difficulty is that a probability statement about *P*, according to that transfinite definition of probability, is not susceptible of an empirical verification or falsification; for any empirical evidence concerning the frequency of the occurrence of *P* would necessarily be restricted to *finite* sets of events; and whatever the observed frequency of *P* in a finite set may be: it is compatible with whatever limiting value one wants to assume. (1939a, p. 360)

This is simply the focal concern of chapter 3 of his dissertation.

Another 1938 publication, "Transfinite Concepts and Empiricism," joins these two lines of concern, arguing that "one of the problems with which modern empiricism is concerned is to give an adequate account of the transfinite terms which occur in the language of empirical science" (1938b, p. 9) while developing the insight in terms of probability where "the empiricist interpretation of 'probability' is of a transfinite character" and thus is "non-empiricistic; for assertions referring to the outcome of an infinite sequence of events can certainly not be verified by any finite set of observations" (p. 10). He notes that the Vienna Circle long had abandoned the verification criterion in favor of a more liberal requirement of confirmability and grapples with how this can be accommodated via a notion of gradual confirmability admitting of degrees of confirmation (p. 11).[18]

There is a gap in Hempel's publications during World War II.[19] But in his 1945 "Studies in the Logic of Confirmation" we find his earlier concerns over the applicability of theories embodying transfinite concepts on the basis of finite observational evidence culminating in articulation of what is, in substance, his later provisos doctrine without the provisos rhetoric.

In that paper, Hempel considers, and attempts to impeach, a "prediction-criterion of confirmation." He begins by noting that a "general hypothesis . . . entails an unlimited number of observation sentences; thus it cannot be logically inferred from, but at best be confirmed by, a suitable set of observational findings" (1965a, p. 27). From this fact he concludes that "an observation report, which always involves only a finite number of observation sentences, can never provide a sufficiently broad basis for a prediction" (p. 28).

This is the basis for a much stronger conclusion, as follows:

> It is therefore a considerable oversimplification to say that scientific hypotheses and theories enable us to derive predictions of future experiences from descriptions of past ones. Unquestionably, scientific hypotheses do have a predictive function; but the way in which they perform this function, the manner in which they establish logical connections between observation reports, is logically more complex than a deductive inference. . . . In view of the observation report . . . the hypothesis . . . might be accepted as confirmed by, though not logically inferable, from that report. This process might be referred to as a quasi-

induction. From the hypothesis thus established we can then proceed to derive, by means of H, the prediction that a stands in R_2 to at least one object. This . . . is not an observation statement; and indeed no observation statement can be derived from it. . . .

Thus the chain of reasoning which leads from given observational findings to the "prediction" of new ones actually involves, besides deductive inference, certain quasi-inductive steps, each of which consists in the acceptance of an intermediate statement on the basis of confirming, but usually not logically conclusive, evidence. (pp. 28–9)

He concludes that "an adequate analysis of scientific prediction (and analogously, of scientific explanation, and of the testing of empirical hypotheses) requires an analysis of the concept of confirmation" (p. 29).

We find here, in the doctrine of quasi induction, essentially full articulation of the provisos papers' inductive-assent argument why hypothetico-deductive theoretical inference is nondeductive. Such quasi induction–based inductive assent is sufficient to make theoretical inferences applied to concrete circumstances nondeductive. Thus by 1945 Hempel explicitly had embraced positions that precluded deductively valid theoretical inference—including those required by his and Oppenheim's 1948 "Studies in the Logic of Explanation." And such embracement was no incautious slip. It was a natural outgrowth of themes that had exercised him since his dissertation.

At the same time we have to admit that, prior to his provisos papers, Hempel did not *stress* the further deductive failure in the move from theoretical prediction to its application to concrete circumstances. Nevertheless, it is to be found, in passing, in the assertion that "the prediction that a stands in R_2. . . . is not an observation statement; and indeed no observation statement can be derived from it" (Hempel 1965a, p. 29).

Indeed, it is a straightforward consequence of his 1935 realization that "a singular statement which is not a basic statement itself is not a truth-function of basic sentences" or protocol sentences (1935, pp. 52–3). For in that case neither the move from singular V_A statement S^1_A to singular theoretical statement S^1_C nor the move from theoretical prediction S^2_C to singular V_A statement S^2_A can be deductively valid without the addition of explicit provisos. More generally, in the context of his general concern with the finite basis for the application of transfinite concepts, the provisos move is a fairly minor one.

To summarize: Hempel's provisos papers do further strengthen the case that theoretical inference is nondeductive and has inductive elements, offering additional insights as to how this happens. But the basic case was made by 1945 and the key insights go back to his 1934 dissertation and his first English papers of 1935–38.

These continuities from Hempel's early work through his work on confirmation to his mature provisos work indicate that if Hempel is wrong about provisos it is the culmination of basic errors that permeate his thinking about science over some six decades. Thus determining whether Hempel is correct, and if not where he went wrong, promises a revealing assessment of the empiricist approach to understanding science that Hempel championed and practiced. I return to these questions in the seventh section.

Is There a Provisos Problem?

Hempel's proviso doctrines are developed using the standard conception of theories—a statement view wherein theories are construed as deductively connected statements in which V_T theoretical assertions are distinct from observational or other assertions expressed in an antecedently available vocabulary V_A, and these two classes of assertions are connected via interpretative sentences I. I have shown that the heart of Hempel's proviso arguments is that the interpretative sentences I found in actual theories generally do not ground proviso statements. But I established in (1) that his conclusions follow *only* on the further assumption that *all* statements grounding the application of theory to concrete assertions are proper parts of the theories.

The question arises whether Hempel has found some basic truths about scientific inference or whether his conclusions are erroneous artifacts of (a) his reliance on a later version of the received view combined with (b) his assumption that proper content of theories must ground provisos.

Hempel briefly considers (a). I quote his entire discussion.

> Note further that the perplexities of the reliance on provisos cannot be avoided by adopting a structuralist, or non-statement, conception of theories broadly in the manner of Sneed and Stegmüller. That conception construes theories not as classes of statements, but as deductively organized systems of statement functions, which make no assertions and have no truth values. But such systems are presented as having empirical models; for example, the solar system might be claimed to be a model of a structuralist formulation of Newtonian celestial mechanics. But a formulation of this claim, and its inferential application to particular astronomical occurrences, again clearly assumes the fulfillment of pertinent provisos. ("Provisos," p. 159)

Such discussion no way settles the issue whether Hempel's conclusions in part are artifacts of his reliance on the standard conception. For the Sneed-Stegmüller structuralist approach is only one of many nonstatement treatments of scientific theories. Indeed, it is rather anomalous among such views in that it does include analogues to interpretative statements within the content of theories. Most other nonstatement views, the so-called semantic conception ones, part company on exactly this issue, maintaining that descriptions of experimental or observational design mediating the application of theory to concrete circumstances are *not* proper individuating parts of theories (Suppe 1996, p. 521; 1998, sec. 4).

Thus it is a serious blow to Hempel's position if *any* plausible nonstatement analyses of theories, such as semantic conceptions, provide a solution to the problem of provisos. In the sixth section I show that is the case for the quasi-realistic version of the semantic conception I have developed elsewhere (see Suppe 1989, especially pt. 2).

The common core of semantic conception analyses is to identify theories with abstract mathematical *theory structures* such as state spaces, relational systems, or set-theoretic predicates. Such theory-structures precisely determine a family of state-transition model systems where states are characterized by a finite set of parameters such as position and momentum coordinates. Those theory-induced models are asserted to stand in some *mapping relation* to actual systems possessing the same parameters (and others). A theory is *empirically true* or *empirically adequate* precisely if the asserted mapping relationship holds.

This common core of agreement about theories can be developed in realistic, quasi-realistic, or antirealistic versions.[20] *Realistic versions* assert that the class of state-transitions allowed by theory-induced state models are precisely those which are causally possible or could obtain in our universe. Real-world contaminating influences are ignored. The realistic construal thus ignores, indeed rejects, the problem of provisos: if realistic versions of the semantic conception are correct, there can be no problem of provisos.

Antirealistic versions, such as those of van Fraassen (1967, 1970, 1980) restrict the empirical adequacy of theories to just those aspects of theory-induced state-transition models to which one gives ontological assent. For example, one might restrict ontological commitment to just those parameters and aspects that are directly observable under some stipulated criterion of direct-observability. Then the empirical adequacy of theories is limited to an isomorphism between those observational (ontologically countenanced) aspects of theory-induced state-transition models and the corresponding observable aspects of causally possible systems. Antirealism is just the realistic version with truth-relevant scope restricted on grounds of limited ontological commitment. Thus, if antirealistic versions of the semantic conception are correct, there can be no problem of provisos.

Hempel did not go wrong in supposing that there was a problem of provisos. Indeed, his career-long obsession with how the finitude of what we can isolate, measure, and know is compatible with theoretical knowledge and understanding of a world which is unbounded in the range of potentially influences on a given concrete situation is right on target. He had his finger on what I believe to be among the most fundamental epistemological issues in the philosophy of science.

Realistic and antirealistic versions of the semantic conception fail precisely because they do not allow the problem of provisos to emerge. That is why I long have rejected them. Scientific theories *always* can be formulated in terms of relations holding between a finite set of explicitly defined state-variables or parameters plus possibly time. Many other variables can be defined in terms of those explicitly used. But, in general, the set of explicit state variables and those which can be defined in terms of them do not exhaust the range of influences that potentially can impact on the behavior of an actual system as registered in its state-transition behavior as defined in terms of explicit state variables. The number of additional influences not definable in terms of explicit state parameters or variables may or may not be infinite. But in general it is unbounded and not finitely characterizable. Any philosophical analyses of science—whether they be of explanation, or theories, or predictions, or whatever—that assume a fixed finite set of relevant parameters/variables are wrong just because they cannot make sense of the problem of provisos.[21]

So, Hempel is correct that one crucial test of philosophical analyses of scientific practices or artifacts is the ability to embrace and make sense of the problem of provisos. Hempel did not go wrong posing the following problem:

(2)   Scientific theories describe only the influence of a finite set of variables or parameters on the behavior of systems, yet real-world systems potentially are influenced by an open-ended variety of other parameters. Applications of theories to actual systems thus tacitly assume provisos to the effect that such confounding influences are absent. For inferential application of theory to real systems to be deductively valid and sound, provisos must be explicitly formulated and known to be met.

However, in the seventh section I will contend that Hempel's *analysis* of the provisos problem is seriously mistaken in ways that drive his unsatisfactory attempts to solve the problem.

If the semantic conception is to prove Hempel wrong regarding his *analysis* of the problem of provisos, it will have to be some version that is neither realistic nor antirealistic. There is one that I have long championed and developed that has been driven by concern with problems concerning unbounded or infinite possibilities in the real world and the finitude of what epistemically we can expressly know. On my *quasi-realistic* version of the semantic conception, theories do not purport to describe the actual state-transitions that occur, but rather counterfactually characterize those that *would be observed were the system isolated from influences not taken into account in the theory's state variables.* Thus an empirically true theory *literally* describes state transition behaviors of systems *isolated* from outside influences, but only provides *counterfactual* characterizations of *nonisolated* systems.

This is a semantic conception version *driven* by concern with provisos. The concern is that theory-structures *only* take into account an explicit finite set of state variables in determining the theory-induced set of state-transition models, but that the corresponding real-world systems in fact often are contaminated by influence of many other parameters. But it is a version of the semantic conception that does not view experimental design, control, and other concerns collapsed into Hempel's interpretative sentences *I* as proper individuating parts of theories—rather treating them as *extratheoretical.* Thus, if nonstatement construals of theories are to challenge Hempel's specific take on provisos, it most likely is this quasi-realistic version.

A Quasi-realistic Semantic Conception Solution of the Provisos Problem

The quasi-realistic version of the semantic conception embodies an attempted solution to Hempel's problem of provisos.[22] The main question is whether it in fact is a solution to (2). That turns on two questions.

(3) Can provisos be stated in the language of the theory to which they apply?

(4) Can the satisfaction of provisos be known on the basis of the (finite) evidence available in typical scientific experimental and observational circumstances?

Question (3) concerns whether scientific language has resources to fully express the ontic content of proviso conditions. Question (4) concerns the epistemic accessibility of satisfaction of proviso conditions so expressed.

Let T be a theory with deterministic law of succession L[23] whose intended scope is S, and N be a noninterference or isolation condition to the effect that systems are not influenced by parameters not expressed in L. Then on the quasi-realistic version of the semantic conception, T is empirically true if and only if the following *theory hypothesis* is true:

(5) $(x)(t)(t')(Sx \ \& \ Nxtt' \Rightarrow Lxtt')$

where '$\Rightarrow$' is a causal implication operator suitable for expressing counterfactual claims to the effect that L expresses how systems in S would behave were they isolated.[24]

According to Hempel, a proviso "asserts, broadly speaking, that in a given case . . . no factors other than those specified in S^1 are present which could affect the event described by S^2" ("Provisos," p. 157). In the context of (5), that is exactly what N expresses. N is just the proviso clause. Thus (3) becomes the question how to give finite expression to N. It is difficult to express N without making some assumptions about the form of the law L. We will assume that L are deterministic laws of succession since that is the class of theories Hempel was concerned with in his provisos papers.[25]

Let $p_1, \ldots, p_n$ be the state variables in T. Then the state $s_x(t)$ of a system x at t consists of the simultaneous values of $p_1, \ldots, p_n$ at t. Let $e_x(t)$ be all those factors which could affect the values of $p_1, \ldots, p_n$ for any system x within scope S. If e_x is finite and bounded, then all systems in S are governed by an equation of the form:[26]

(6) $F[s_x(t), e_x(t)] = g(s_x(t)) + h(e_x(t)) = s'_x(t')$.

If e_x is unbounded or infinite, then we cannot finitely specify F and h, but we can assume that there is some form-(6) equation that could be expressed in a language with infinitely long expressions which might not be recursively specifiable. Thus we employ (6) in subsequent analysis without regard to whether finitely expressible or not.

Suppose now that *L* is of the form:

(7) $f[s_x(t)] = g(s_x(t)) = s'_x(t')$.

Then system *x* is isolated with respect to of $p_1, \ldots, p_n$ over the time interval [*t*, *t'*] just in case

(8) $(t^*)[t \leq t^* \leq t' \supset [s_x(t^*) \ \& \ e_x(t^*) \ \& \ F[s_x(t^*), e_x(t^*)] = f[s_x(t^*)] = g(s_x(t^*))]]$.

Of course, (8) will not generally be finitely expressible because *F* and e_x may be transfinite. However, the following *always* is finitely expressible:

(9) $(\exists F)(\exists e)(t^*)[t \leq t^* \leq t' \supset [s_x(t^*) \ \& \ e_x(t^*) \ \& \ F[s_x(t^*), e_x(t^*)] = f[s_x(t^*)] = g(s_x(t^*))]]$.

It specifies that no factors other than $p_1, \ldots, p_n$ affect the values of $p_1, \ldots, p_n$ over time interval [*t*, *t'*]. That is precisely the isolation condition theoretical hypothesis (5) requires. Thus the answer to (3) is that the quasi-realistic version of the semantic conception has the resources to express provisos needed to apply the theory to concrete situations. Specifically (5) and (9) together allow deductively valid predictions of $s'_x(t')$.

Before turning to (4), it will be useful to reexamine Hempel's analysis of provisos in light of these developments. First, the problem of provisos arises simply because (6) does not generally admit of finite expression. Second, whenever (6) does not admit of finite expression, then no empirically true theory can ground the satisfaction of its isolation conditions. For, as Hempel observed, theories generally do not exclude forces or other factors not taken into account by the theory. Third, the isolation conditions are not covered by the laws of the theory, but rather concern the mapping relation between the isolated model systems allowed by the theory-structure and actual or possible real-world systems that may or may not be isolated. Differently put, the isolation conditions are not part of the theoretical content of the theory, but are part of what is asserted in claiming the theory is empirically true. Thus Hempel made a fundamental mistake (1) in supposing that theories must ground their own provisos. It further follows that provisos are not an ontic completeness condition for theories. For theoretical inferences based on (5) and (9) generally fail the requirement that "all the factors present in the given case which in fact affect the outcome . . . [can] be predicted by the theoretical inference" ("Provisos," p. 157). Whenever *F* is not finitely specifiable, satisfaction of (9) does not yield ontic completeness.

Hempel was concerned with the epistemic properties of theoretical inferences. Can (4) be answered affirmatively by the quasi-realistic version of the semantic conception? Consider first the case where the system is not isolated—where (9) fails to be met. Knowledge of $s_x(t)$ does enable us to predict what $s'_x(t')$ *would have been* if system *x* *had been* isolated during [*t*, *t'*]. The causal implication operator in (5) allows that inference to be made regardless what is known about the actual state of isolation of *x* during [*t*, *t'*].

Second, consider the case where x is in fact isolated. There we can make predictions about the state $s'_x(t')$ that x *actually* will be in. But such an inference will be sound only if we can know that (9) is satisfied.[27]

Conditions of isolation typically obtain only in contrived experimental circumstances where effective experimental control has been imposed. Such control consists in removing, insulating from, or correcting for contaminating influences within the limits of measurement error. Thus whether (9) can be known to be satisfied becomes the question whether we can know we have effective experimental control. We can assess whether individual anticipated contaminating influences occur. But when (6) is not finitely specifiable, we cannot anticipate all relevant potential contaminants.

Characteristic of good experimental design is that one will get the predicted results under conditions of experimental control *only* if the experimental intervention causes the predicted outcome. Key to experimentation being a source of knowledge is the ability to observe under experimental circumstances whether the intervention *causes* the predicted outcome.

That, in fact, frequently happens. But the philosophical explanation of how that happens and leads to experimental knowledge is complex and only can be sketched here.[28] Briefly it goes as follows: contrary to what Hume supposed, there is mounting evidence that humans directly perceive singular causal events.[29] Thus under good experimental design we should be able to perceive that, hence know that, the intervention caused the predicted outcome. But the intervention can cause the *predicted* outcome *only* if experimental control obtains—that is, if the system is isolated from outside influences. For were there contaminating influences violating isolation, (8) would have to fail and so an outcome other than the predicted one would obtain. Thus whenever we perceive under experimental circumstances that the intervention caused the predicted outcome, (8) and (9) *must* be satisfied and so we can know that (9).

Suppose we have an experiment that is designed to test our theory T. Such an experiment will be designed so that a system b in S is isolated from contaminating influences and that a successful experimental outcome will allow direct causal perception of the following instance of (6):

(10) $(Sb \ \& \ Nbtt' \Rightarrow Lbtt')$

over the time interval $[t, t']$ of the experiment. Hence one will know experimentally that (10). While it generally is fallacious to infer $(\alpha)(\phi\alpha \supset \Psi\alpha)$ from singular instance $(\phi\beta \supset \Psi\beta)$, inferences from $(\phi\beta \Rightarrow \Psi\beta)$ to $(\alpha)(\phi\alpha \Rightarrow \Psi\alpha)$ are valid for a wide range of conditionals $\Rightarrow$ defined in terms of causal necessity modal operators including ones suitable for use in (5).[30]

This result turns on the fact that in possible-world semantics there are deep tradeoffs between quantifiers and necessity operators (Montague 1974). It follows that whenever one can know that (10) one thereby can know that (5).

Thus, under the quasi-realistic version of the semantic conception, experimental circumstances enable us to know both that theories are empirically true and that conditions of isolation obtain. Since we can know that (5) and that (9) holds for specific circumstances b, we can make deductively sound theoretical inferences predicting $s'_b(t')$.

We conclude that the quasi-realistic version of the semantic conception solves proviso problem (2).

Where Hempel Went Wrong

In the previous section, I presented a quasi-realistic semantic conception solution to provisos problem (2). That solution does not involve theories grounding their own provisos. It follows that Hempel was wrong in tying the proviso problem intrinsically to theories grounding their own provisos. For, although that is not characteristic of theories on the quasi-realistic version of the semantic conception, it can pose the problem of provisos and provides a superior—indeed a genuine—solution.

Key to Hempel's failure to solve the problem of provisos was his supposition that theories had to ground their own provisos. That supposition was plausible only in the context of a philosophical analysis of theories which incorporated the conditions of experimental design and application into the empirical content of theories—here the interpretative sentences I. Thus Hempel's analysis of provisos and his attempted solution ultimately fails because of reliance on the received view.

The question arises why Hempel used the standard conception version of the received view when he had rejected it in 1969. Nothing in Hempel's provisos discussion turns on differences between the standard conception $<C, I>$ analysis and Hempel's replacement $<P, B>$ analysis. Further, Hempel's new replacement $<P, B>$ analysis widely was either rejected or, more often, ignored. Thus it was advantageous to make his provisos case using the well-known standard conception. Indeed, beginning with "The Theoretician's Dilemma," Hempel had a history of using the standard conception in the very papers where he would challenge features of it and urge modifications.

Common to the standard conception and its successor was the idea that the I or B were individuating features of theories. Nothing in his rejection of the standard conception called for challenging this feature, which according to semantic conception critiques was perhaps the most fundamental flaw in the received view. Since the incorporation of the conditions of applicability I or B in theories was the driving feature of Hempel's unsuccessful provisos analysis, it made no difference whether he used the $<C, I>$ or the $<P, B>$ construal of theories. If we review Hempel's various emendations of the received view and his retrospectives on truth and cognitive significance, we find a persistent focus on the finite/transfinite question and a commitment to a statement-view of theories in which the grounds for application were individuating components of theories. For all the criticism of the latter in the 1960s and 1970s, Hempel never seriously challenged the latter assumption. He abandoned the idea of correspondence rules being meaning specification rules, but he never could abandon the basic positivistic conception that theories had to carry with them, in correspondence rules, interpretative sentences, or bridge principles, the basis for grounding their application to concrete circumstances.

It was this uncritical commitment to a central received view doctrine that drove Hempel's failed attempt to solve the provisos problem. And it is the abandonment of that commitment coupled with the quasi-realistic interpretation of theories that enables the semantic conception solution given in the previous section.

The inclusion of I or B as individuating elements of theories is central to the positivistic enterprise, being not only crucial to understanding theories but intimately tied to concerns over cognitive significance, testability, explanation, and reduction. It is a central positivistic doctrine which never was questioned or challenged by Hempel, Carnap, or other positivists. Hempel's failure to solve the provisos problem thus rests in a fundamental inadequacy of his and other positivists' empiricisms. That inadequacy precludes solving the provisos problem, and ultimately undercuts Hempel's analyses of theoretical explanation and prediction.

Interpreting the Hempelian Corpus

We saw that the seeds of Hempel's proviso work were found in his dissertation and in his early English papers written during his Belgium exile. The relation between finite empirical concepts and transfinite theoretical ones is an issue that Hempel raised in his dissertation and returned to repeatedly during his career. That issue was the impetus for other work such as his qualitative and quantitative concepts of confirmation[31] and, as noted, his provisos papers.

I also detailed the role of Hempel's 1935 "On the Logical Positivists' Theory of Truth" in developments leading to the provisos paper. But that 1935 paper also can be read as a first approximation to Hempel's 1950 "Problems and Changes in the Empiricist Criterion of Meaning."

Another early work was the monograph *Typusbegriff im Lichte der Neuen Logik (Wissenshaftstheoretische Untersuchungen zur Konstitionsforschung und Psychologie)*, done in collaboration with Paul Oppenheim. Oppenheim was interested in developing a systematic ordering of the sciences (Oppenheim 1926) and sought out Reichenbach for help and possible collaboration. Reichenbach steered him to a graduate student—Hempel—which led to a long collaboration. Initially they focused on investigating the logic and methodology of nonquantifiable ordering concepts and comparative concepts with special reference to the role of such concepts in typological theories of human mental and physical constitution (e.g., ectomorphs, endomorphs, mesomorphs, and their correlates to personality types). These results were presented in several papers and the *Typusbegriff* monograph.

Preliminary examination of the *Typusbegriff* suggests it was seminal for much of Hempel's later work. The covering-law model of explanation is sketched (see

Hempel and Oppenheim 1936, pp. 102–3). The *Typusbegriff* stimulates his development of a purely typological form of non-Aristotelian logic (1937)[32] and his early work on vagueness (1939b). Much of part III of Hempel's 1952 monograph *Fundamentals of Concept Formation in Empirical Science* is derivative from the *Typusbegriff*. Similarly, the taxonomy and typology papers printed in part III of his 1965 *Aspects* collection are derivative from the *Typusbegriff*. I am struck by how rarely philosophers of science consult the early German works in commenting on Hempel.[33]

These considerations prompt me to rethink my understanding of Hempel's work and intellectual development. As I do, curious exegetical issues arise. Consider his work on explanation. His first article on explanation was "The Function of General Laws in History," published in 1942, not the more famous 1948 "Studies in the Logic of Explanation" done with Oppenheim. Yet that 1942 paper contains a clear articulation of the covering-law model, asserts the formal equivalence of prediction and explanation, provides a statement of the DN model, indicates that the DN model does not cover other explanations that make recourse to statistical laws, and introduces the notion of "explanation sketches" (which many think he first introduced in his 1965 "Aspects of Scientific Explanation" only in response to criticisms by Scriven and others). It thus anticipates much of his later work on explanation.

But the question remains why did he *first* focus on historical explanation? The answer in part lies, I think, in the *Typusbegriff*. That work focuses on typological concepts in the study of character, personality, and physique. There Hempel and Oppenheim use the relational resources of the "new" symbolic logic to develop the logic and methodology of comparative type concepts (chap. 3). They then use that analysis to examine and analyze various uses of "extreme," "ideal type," and "empirical type" concepts (chaps. 4, 5). Ideal-type concepts are important because they often are invoked as devices for explaining social, historical, and psychological materials.[34] Although ideal types are thought to be singular notions, analysis of these types using comparative typological concepts shows them to be governed by general hypotheses (chap. 5). In chapter 6 the authors open with a brief statement of the covering-law model of explanation[35] and argue that the development of empirical laws is equally important for the social and the natural sciences because in both cases they are the foundation of every scientific explanation (see Hempel and Oppenheim 1936, especially pp. 102–3).

Hempel thus first examined explanation in the context of sociological, psychological, and historical explanations that often invoked ideal or other types. It is important to note that many of the ideal-type explanations sociology developed were of historical events such as the emergence of capitalism. Hempel and Oppenheim originally introduced what became the covering-law model of explanation as a physical science foil for arguing that social science explanations were no different in kind from those in the hard sciences. Thus Hempel's initial concern with explanation only incidentally concerned the natural sciences. His real focus was the social sciences including historical explanations via ideal types.

Given these facts, it is no surprise that Hempel's first paper on explanation would focus on historical explanation, using natural science explanations as a comparative foil. To be sure, the focus on historical explanation was not mere recycling of the *Typusbegriff* discussions. It was a genuine expansion in focus, extending the analysis of psychological and sociological explanations, which sometimes provided historical explanations, to a *general* analysis of historical explanation. That was a significant stretch from chapter 5 of the *Typusbegriff*. Later he and Oppenheim would do an even greater stretch in their extension of the early covering-law idea to deductive explanations in all of science.

I recall Hempel telling me about his and colleagues' interest in the ongoing mechanism versus vitalism debates during his Berlin student years, how seriously they followed them, and how he often attended presentations. Those debates were part of a larger debate over what has come to be known as the *Verstehen* question—whether the sorts of explanation and understanding suitable for the natural sciences also apply to the social sciences. Hempel's 1942 historical explanation paper can be viewed as a contribution to those *Verstehen* debates—one in which he acknowledges the importance of Weber-like "Ideal-type intentional explanations"[36] but argues that such ideal-type explanations, to the extent availing, can be analyzed in terms of general covering-laws. Thus it may be illuminating to interpret the 1942 historical explanation paper as a contribution to the ongoing *Verstehen* questions that so interested Hempel in their mechanism versus vitalism incarnations.

These speculations suggest readings and interpretations of Hempel quite unlike those in currency when I was a graduate student and ones I have advanced earlier in my career. I offer these observations as tentative interpretative hypotheses. If they are correct, then it means that the Hempel juvenilia are crucial to understanding the mature Hempel's work. It suggests a reading of Hempel where his significant later work was a more dogged and plodding revisiting of his early concerns, with further refinements and embellishments, rather than startling new insights or significant alterations in position.

If these exegetical observations prove out, or even are substantially on target, it follows that keys to understanding Hempel's mature work are his juvenilia and sorting out exactly what the intellectual cross-influences were between Hempel and Oppenheim. Given that Oppenheim was patron-collaborator with the likes of Hempel, Helmer, Putnam, Kemeny, and apparently Grelling, in papers that were definitive of late positivism's treatments of explanation, confirmation, reduction, and so on, perhaps it is time for historical analysis to treat Oppenheim as a serious intellectual and ascertain just how much influence he had in the formation of Hempel's ideas. How much of the intellectual content of the *Typusbegriff* was due to Oppenheim and how much due to Hempel?[37]

I have no firm convictions on the interpretative questions I raise. However, I believe I have made the case that Hempel's provisos papers and his confirmation papers are end-points in the gradual working-out of problems Hempel addressed in his 1934 dissertation concerning how finite empirical concepts relate to transfinite theoretical ones. The later DN and IS models of explanation are the end-points of gradual workings-out of ideas and concerns first addressed in the *Typusbegriff*. Whether such claims can be generalized to the remainder of Hempel's work should be an important research question in the emerging history of the philosophy of science research field.

NOTES

Research presented here was supported in part by the National Science Foundation. I am grateful to Richard Jeffrey, Adolf Grünbaum, and Paul Benaceraff for access to unpublished or rare materials regarding Hempel. Alfred Noordman's comments, during a charming stay with him while lecturing at University of South Carolina, regarding the *Typusbegriff* and its relations to Hempel's later work on explanation were the inspiration for explorations leading to the discussion in the eighth section. Alexander Wörner helped with the German texts.

1. Biographical claims regarding Hempel are based upon two divergent copies of his vita supplied by Paul Benaceraff and Adolf Grünbaum; Oppenheim (1969); oral history interviews of Paul Benaceraff concerning Hempel and Oppenheim done in 1993–94; and Adolf Grünbaum's (1994) remarks which were delivered at Princeton University on 27 May 1994. That event was the last occasion I spent time with Hempel.
2. For details on the received view and its development, see Suppe (1977, pp. 16–61). My discussion here uses Hempel's standard notation, rather than my own from *Structure*.
3. Hempel's arguments do not succeed in making the case. See Suppe (1977, p. 24, n. 48).
4. Hempel (1965d, p. 208); there Hempel refers to V_A as an antecedently understood *basic vocabulary* V_B. He also does so in "Implications of Carnap's Work for the Philosophy of Science" (1963, p. 692). By the late 1960s he had adopted the pretheoretical "antecedently available" terminology (see 1970, p. 143; 1977, p. 245).
5. Hempel uses "*I*" to designate the internal principles, but I use "*P*" to avoid confusion with interpretative systems sentences *I*.
6. The preceding points respectively are made in sections 3–6.
7. Hempel (1942b, 1965a), Hempel and Oppenheim (1965b), and at least a half-dozen other works from 1962 on.
8. Page references herein are to the *Erkenntnis* version. Italics in all quotations from all sources are original.
9. His own major contributions include "The Theoretician's Dilemma" (1965d) and "Studies in the Logic of Confirmation" (1965a).
10. "Provisos," pp. 152–3. In "Limits," p. 6, this is the third of three objections, the other two being that it abandons the idea of a deductivist construal of theory application and that the need for provisos also will arise for probabilistic laws.
11. "Provisos," pp. 153–6. The quote is from p. 156. "Limits" only considers the consequences for eliminability programs and instrumentalism (pp. 7–8).
12. Hempel and Oppenheim, "Studies in the Logic of Explanation," condition (R1) (1965b, p. 247). My recollection is that Hempel's presentations in the latter 1970s of "ur" versions of his provisos papers did focus on the consequences for the DN model.
13. Hempel earlier had deployed the *ceteris paribus* clause notion in discussing theoretical properties of ideal types, so this amounts to a kind of retraction. See 1965e, pp. 167–8.
14. "Limits," p. 11; compare "Provisos," p. 159. "Provisos" and "Limits" diverge here in both organization and specific content. "Provisos" separates out the remaining

discussion in a new section, "Methodological Aspects of Provisos" whereas in "Limits" they are continuation of the previous section, "Further Thoughts on the Character of Provisos" (same title in both). The differences in content do not substantially affect the focus of my discussion.

15. Hempel's reliance on Kuhn here may seem surprising. However, Hempel once told me he found his and Kuhn's positions very compatible, coming to much the same view from different starting points.

   Such an assertion is astounding on standard readings of Kuhn that take the position that his *Structure of Scientific Revolutions* was a sloppy but thereby provocative alternative to positivism, whereas his attempts to respond to his many critics were somewhat lame retreats toward positivism that abandoned much that was most exciting about his original views. I among others have promulgated such a reading. Kuhn always maintained these charges were incorrect and that excepting explicitly acknowledged changes (such as abandoning the notion of a preparadigm period), his later clarifications were just that—*clarifications*, not changes in view. I now am convinced he was right. Kuhn did not retreat toward positivism in *Structure*. For *Structure* is a modest revision of later positivism. His treatment of normal science is an in-house dispute over whether the mediation between theoretical assertions and concrete circumstances can be via an *explicit finite* set of correspondence rules. Kuhn's position is, no. Rather, he suggests, we have a finite set of exemplary concrete applications and open-endedly model new applications on them. Further, the theory-ladenness observation precludes a neutral V_O observation language. His treatment of revolutionary science appears to be an independent reinvention of the basic considerations driving Carnap (1950). And Kuhn comes to much the same conclusions as does Carnap. Based on personal conversations I am convinced that Kuhn was unaware of Carnap's work here (which work was the semantic reworking of the *Aufbau*). Kuhn's overt target is Nagel's views on induction.

   This reading of Kuhn makes sense of Carnap's enthusiasm over Kuhn's *Structure* (which had been commissioned by and appeared first in the *Encyclopedia of Unified Science* coedited by Carnap) and Hempel's observation that he felt that he and Kuhn were coming to much the same position from different starting points. For example, regarding the impossibility of finite specification of correspondence rules, Hempel comes to roughly the same conclusion as Kuhn's in his "Formulation and Formalization of Scientific Theories" (1977) where he questions whether there can be explicit correspondence *rules*, but for different reasons than does Kuhn. Toward the end of Kuhn's tenure at Princeton, he and Hempel cotaught the undergraduate introductory History and Philosophy of Science course and found great affinity in their views. That affinity is evident in the epistemic discussions in Hempel's two proviso papers. While I think these papers provide significant evidence about the convergence of Hempel and Kuhn's thought, such convergence does not affect substantially the issues I focus on here regarding provisos.

16. I am grateful to Richard Jeffrey for providing me with a copy of the dissertation, which, I believe, he found with some effort in Hempel's attic.

17. His Belgium stay was interrupted by a one-year research appointment at University of Chicago during the 1937–38 academic year.

18. This discussion is, to my knowledge, the earliest explicit formulation of the problematic that leads him to develop both a qualitative and a quantitative notion of confirmation in the latter 1940s.

19. Between 1939 and 1945 he published only three entries for the 1942 Runes *Dictionary of Philosophy* and his crucial 1942 "The Function of General Laws in History," which, save hints in the *Typusbegriff*, is his first detailed development of the covering-law model of explanation. By contrast he will publish five papers in 1945, four of which range from significant to landmark.

20. See Suppe (1998, secs. 5 and 6; 1996, pp. 522–3), for expanded discussion.

21. For example, Bromberger's brilliant "Why Questions" improvement on Hempel's DN model of explanation fails for exactly this reason. See Suppe (1977, p. 622).

22. It is appropriate to note that the solution it embodies was developed in my 1967 dissertation, "The Meaning and Use of Models in Mathematics and the Exact Sciences," first published in my 1972 "What's Wrong with the Received View on the Structure of Scientific Theories?" some sixteen years before Hempel published his two provisos papers, and had been in print for some years before Hempel first began presenting his "ur" versions of the provisos papers.

23. On the semantic conception, every theory is equivalent to a theory having only one law. See Suppe (1989, p. 162).

24. Identifying '$\Rightarrow$' with Burks's *nonparadoxical causal implication* **npc** will suffice: ϕ **npc** Ψ iff $\sim<c>\sim(\phi \supset \Psi) \, \& <>(\phi \, \& \, \Psi) \, \& <>(\phi \, \& \sim\Psi) \, \& <>(\sim\phi \, \& \, \Psi) \, \& <>(\sim\phi \, \& \sim\Psi) \, \& <c>\phi \, \& <c>\sim\Psi$, where '$<>$' is the logical possibility operator and '$<c>$' is the causal possibility operator. Intuitively this defines causal implication in terms of material conditionals holding over all causally possible worlds then excludes instances where the conditional holds in virtue of the paradoxes of material implication or logical dependence between ϕ and Ψ. See Burks (1977, p. 428).

25. For detailed analysis of the structure of such laws on the semantic conception, see Suppe (1989, chap. 5).

26. This assumes the systems in S are linear—a condition that will not be met with nonlinear dynamical systems including chaotic ones. The problem of provisos for nonlinear systems has not been investigated and is outside the scope of either Hempel's or my discussions. It is well known that singular predictions from nonlinear dynamical, especially chaotic, systems are problematic. It is unclear how provisos issues bear on that problem. My conjecture is that when the provisos solution presented here fails, *deductive* predictions/inferences fail for nonlinear dynamical systems. If that conjecture is wrong, the solution in this section is not generalizable beyond linear systems. For discussion of deductive difficulties encountered by nonlinear dynamical systems, see Winsberg (1999).

27. This condition is stronger than is required. Hempel ignores issues of measurement error in his provisos discussion, and thus so do I. All that actually is needed is that the influence of contaminating factors be negligible relative to the measurement errors associated with $p_1, \ldots, p_n$.

28. See my "Science without Induction" (1997) for the general treatment. Detailed formal results invoked are in my *Facts, Theories, and Scientific Observation* (forthcoming).

29. See Twardy (1999) for summary and evaluation of the evidence plus discussion of the philosophical significance of direct causal perception.

30. In particular, the result holds for Burks' **npc**. The full proof, which draws on pioneering work by Richard Montague, is in my *Facts, Theories, and Scientific Observation, vol. 1, A Posteriori Knowledge and Truth* (forthcoming, chap. 9, theorem [1-IX-29]). See also my "Science without Induction" (1997).

31. He poses the problems in his Transfinite Concepts and Empiricism (1938b).

32. A German version of this work was published the same year in *Erkenntnis*.

33. I began examining the entire Hempel corpus while at Princeton during the 1993–94 academic year. When I needed to consult the *Typusbegriff* it was in storage and had to be specially requested. I was able to ascertain that the previous time it had been checked out was by Richard Jeffrey early in his career. Hempel's dissertation proved extremely difficult to find. Though published as a book, the Princeton Library does not possess it. I have a copy only because Richard Jeffrey rummaged through Hempel's attic and found a copy. Given that Hempel was at Princeton from 1955 to 1973, where he was much beloved, it seems a safe conjecture to suppose that his early German works are less accessible at other universities and rarely consulted by scholars.

34. Hempel makes the same point in "Typological Methods in the Natural and the Social Sciences" (1965e), pp. 160–1. In the first approximation, this work can be viewed as an updated summary of key ideas in the *Typusbegriff*.

35. "*Die Aufstellung empirischer Gesetze ist* nict etwa ein Spezialproblem der 'exakten Naturwissenschaften', *sondern das zentrale Problem jeder wissenschaflichen Theorienbildung,* denn *die empirischen Gesetze bilden die Grundlage jeder wissenschaftlichen Erklärung.* Ein Ereignis is erkläret, wenn es als 'notwendige Folge' gewisser anderer Ereignisse erwiessen ist, d. h. aber genauer: wenn empirische Gesetze aufgewiesen sind, auf Grund deren sich der Satz, der das zu erklärende Ereignis beschreibt, aus denjenigen Sätzen ableiten lässt, die jene anderen Ereignisse beschreiben.

    "Einer noch recht verbreiteten Meinung zufolge besteht die wissenschafliche Erklärung oder die Aufstellung einer Theorie für eine Gruppe empirischer Befunde in der Einführung eines 'ens', einer 'Kraft', eines allgemeinen 'Prinzips' oder anderer Faktoren, die so zu wählen sind, dass die zu erklärenden Befunde als Wirkungen jenes 'ens' erscheinen oder als Sonderfälle jenes allgemeinen Prinzips 'gedeutet' werden, das als 'das Allgemeine, Konstante, sich Erhaltende im Sinn der *Gestalt,* des *Typus,* des *Charakters . . .* in dehn Besonderen erscheint, sich manifestiert, sich, zum Ausdruck bringt'" (Hempel and Oppenheim 1936, p. 102; the inserted quotation is from Seifert [1931, p. 97]).

36. His explicit focus in discussing "ideal types" is not Weber either there or in the *Typusbegriff.* However, "Typological Methods in the Natural and Social Sciences" (1965e) develops themes from the *Typusbegriif* in such detail that it can be viewed as Hempel's revised summary of what he later viewed as lasting from the *Typusbegriff.* There he develops the themes through a sustained examination of Weber on ideal-type explanations, coming to the conclusion that they invoke general laws.

37. For clues, see the foreword to the (Hempel and Oppenheim 1936, *Typusbegriff* p. vi), where the idea of a general investigation of ordering and "elastic" concepts is attributed to Oppenheim, the logistic analyses and drafting of key text are attributed to Hempel, and collective responsibility taken for the rest.

REFERENCES

Bromberger, Sylvain. 1966. "Why Questions." In *Mind and Cosmos: Explorations in the Philosophy of Science,* edited by Robert Colodny. Pittsburgh: University of Pittsburgh Press.

Burks, Arthur W. 1977. *Cause, Chance, Reason.* Chicago: University of Chicago Press.

Carnap, Rudolf. 1928. *Der Logische Aufbau der Welt*. Berlin, 1928. 2nd ed., Berlin: Felix Meiner. 2nd ed. translated by Rolf George as *The Logical Structure of The World*. Berkeley: University of California Press.

———. 1936–37. "Testability and Meaning." *Philosophy of Science* 3:420–68 and 4:1–40.

———. 1950. "Empiricism, Semantics, and Ontology." *Revue internationale de Philosophie* 11:208–28.

Grünbaum, Adolf. 1994. "Remarks on the Occasion of the Initiation of Professor Carl. G. Hempel as Honorary Fellow of the Center for Philosophy of Science at the University of Pittsburgh, May 27, 1994." Unpublished manuscript.

Hempel, Carl G. 1934. *Beiträge zur logischen Analyse des Wahrscheinlichkeisbegriffs*. Ph. D. thesis. Jena: Universitäts-Buchdruckerei G. Neuenhahn, G. m. b. H.

———. 1935. "On the Logical Positivists' Theory of Truth." *Analysis* 2:49–59.

———. 1937. "A Purely Typological Form of Non-Aristotelian Logic." *Journal of Symbolic Logic* 2–3:97–112.

———. 1938a. "On the Logical Form of Probability-Statements." *Erkenntnis* 7:154–60.

———. 1938b. "Transfinite Concepts and Empiricism." *Synthese* 3:9–12.

———. 1939a. "Supplementary Remarks on the Form of Probability Statements." *Erkenntnis* 7:360–3.

———. 1939b. "Vagueness and Logic." *Philosophy of Science* 6:163–80.

———. 1942a. Articles "Whole," "Carnap," and "Reichenbach." In *Dictionary of Philosophy*, edited by D. D. Runes. New York: Philosophical Library.

———. 1942b. "The Function of General Laws in History." *Journal of Philosophy* 39:35–48.

———. 1945a. "Geometry and Empirical Science." *American Mathematical Monthly* 52:7–17.

———. 1945b. "On the Nature of Mathematical Triuth." *American Mathematical Monthly* 52:543–56.

———. 1950. "Problems and Changes in the Empiricist Criterion of Meaning." *Revue Internationale de Philosophie* 11:41–63.

———. 1951. "The Concept of Cognitive Significance: A Reconsideration." *Proceedings of the American Academy of Arts and Sciences* 80:61–77. This and Hempel (1950) were amalgamated into a successor work, "Empiricist Criteria of Cognitive Significance: Problems and Changes." In Hempel (1965b), with a postscript on pp. 101–22.

———. 1952. *Fundamentals of Concept Formation in Empirical Science*. In *International Encyclopedia of Unified Science*, edited by O. Neurath, R. Carnap, and C. Morris. Vol. 2, no. 7. Chicago: University of Chicago Press.

———. 1963. "Implications of Carnap's Work for the Philosophy of Science. " In *The Philosophy of Rudolf Carnap*, edited by P. A. Schilpp. La Salle, Ill.: Open Court.

———. 1965a. "Aspects of Scientific Explanation." In Hempel (1965b).

———. 1965b. *Aspects of Scientific Explanation and Other Essays in Philosophy of Science*. New York: Free Press.

———. 1965c. "Fundamentals of Taxonomy." In Hempel (1965b).

———. 1965d. "The Theoretician's Dilemma." In *Minnesota Studies in the Philosophy of Science*, edited by H. Feigl, M. Scriven, and G. Maxwell. Vol. 2. Minneapolis: University of Minnesota Press, 1958. Reprinted in Hempel (1965b).

———. 1965e. "Typological Methods in the Natural and the Social Sciences." In Hempel (1965b).

———. 1969. " On the Structure of Scientific Theories." In C. Hempel et al., *The Isenberg Memorial Lecture Series 1965–66*. East Lansing: Michigan State University Press.

———. 1970. On the Standard Conception of Scientific Theories." In *Minnesota Studies in the Philosophy of Science*, edited by M. Radner and S. Winokur. Vol. 4. Minneapolis: University of Minnesota Press.

———. 1977. "Formulation and Formalization of Scientific Theories." In Suppe (1977).

———. 1988a."Limits of a Deductive Construal of the Function of Scientific Theories." In *Science in Reflection*, edited by Edna Ullmann-Margalit. The Israel Colloquium. Vol. 3. Dordrecht: Kluwer.

———. 1988b. "Provisoes: A Problem Concerning the Inferential Function of Scientific Theories." *Erkenntnis* 28:147–164; also in *The Limits of Deductivism*, edited by Adolf Grünbaum and W. Salmon. Berkeley: University of California Press.

Hempel, Carl G., and Paul Oppenheim. 1936. *Die Typusbegriff im Lichte der Neuen Logik (Wissenshaftstheoretische Untersuchungen zur Konstitionsforschung und Psychologie)*. Leiden: Sijthoff's.

———. 1965a. "Studies in the Logic of Confirmation." *Mind* 54(1945):1–26, 97–121. Reprinted with a postscript in Hempel (1965b).

———. 1965b. "Studies in the Logic of Explanation." *Philosophy of Science* 15(1948):135–75. Reprinted with a postscript in Hempel (1965b).

Kuhn, T. 1970. *The Structure of Scientific Revolutions*. Revised ed. Chicago: University of Chicago Press.

Montague, R. 1974. "Logical Necessity, Physical Necessity, Ethics, and Quantifiers." In *Formal Philosophy: Selected Papers of Richard Montague*, edited by R. H. Thomason. New Haven: Yale University Press. Originally published in *Inquiry* 4:259–69.

Neurath, Otto, Rudolf Carnap, and Charles W. Morris, eds. 1938–69 *International Encyclopedia of Unified Science*. 2 vols. in 10 pts. each. Chicago: University of Chicago Press.

Oppenheim, Paul. 1926. *Die naäturliche Ordnung der Wissenschaften*. Jena: Fisher.

———. 1969. "Reminiscences of Peter." In *Essays in Honor of Carl G. Hempel: A Tribute on the Occasion of his Sixty-fifth Birthday*, edited by A. R. Anderson, P. Benaceraff, A Grünbaum, G. J. Massey, N. Rescher, and R. S. Rudner. Dordrecht: Reidel.

Seifert, F. 1931. "Psychologie. Metaphysik der Seele." In *Handbuch der Philosophie*, edited by A. Baeumler and M. Schröoter. Vol. 3, *Mensch und Charakter*. Berlin: Oldenbourg.

Suppe, Frederick. 1967. "The Meaning and Use of Models in Mathematics and the Exact Sciences." Ph.D. dissertation, University of Michigan.

———. 1972. "What's Wrong with the Received View on the Structure of Scientific Theories?" *Philosophy of Science* 39:1–19. Reprinted in Suppe (1989), part of chap. 2.

———. 1977. *The Structure of Scientific Theories*. Urbana: University of Illinois Press. 2nd ed. 1st ed. 1974.

———. 1989. *The Semantic Conception of Theories and Scientific Realism*. Urbana: University of Illinois Press.

———. 1996. "Scientific Theories." In *The Encyclopedia of Philosophy Supplement*, edited by Donald M. Borchert. New York: Macmillan.

———. 1997. "Science without Induction." In *The Cosmos of Science*, edited by John Earman and John Norton. Pittsburgh: University of Pittsburgh Press

———. 1998. "Theories, Scientific." In *Routledge Encyclopedia of Philosophy*, edited by Edward Craig. Vol. 9. New York: Routledge.

———. *Facts, Theories, and Scientific Observation.* 2 vols. Forthcoming.

Twardy, Charles R. 1999. "Causation, Causal Perception, and Conservation Laws." Ph. D. dissertation, Indiana University.

van Fraassen, Bas C. 1967. "Meaning Relations among Predicates." *Noûs* 1:161–80.

———. 1970. "On the Extension of Beth's Semantics of Physical Theories." *Philosophy of Science* 37:325–39.

———. 1980. *The Scientific Image.* New York: Oxford.

Winsberg, Eric. 1999. "Simulations and the Philosophy of Science: Computationally Intensive Studies of Complex Physical Systems." Ph. D. dissertation, Indiana University.

Wittgenstein, Ludwig. 1922. *Tractatus Logico-Philosophicus.* London: Routledge and Kegan Paul.

V

EXPLANATIONS OF BEHAVIOR

9

Explanation in History

WILLIAM H. DRAY

When Hempel's now celebrated essay "The Function of General Laws in History" appeared in 1942, English-speaking philosophy of history was in a somnolent state. There was not much to point to beyond the early volumes of Toynbee's *Study of History*, a chapter in Oakeshott's *Experience and its Modes*, an early work on relativism by Mandelbaum entitled *The Problem of Historical Knowledqe*. and Collingwood's *Autobiography*.[1] Nor did a critical examination of historical knowledge and inquiry have much place in English-speaking philosophy on a longer time-scale. One had to go back through Mill's observations on the social studies generally to Hume's *Essays* to find any English philosopher treating history as a subject of much philosophical interest. What theory of history there was came mainly from historians—Carl Becker and Charles Beard, for example—and its level of philosophical sophistication was not very high. Soon after the end of the Second World War, however, the situation was very different. There was a proliferation of articles and then books on the subject, most of them in the analytic idiom; and by 1960, a new journal, *History and Theory*, was needed to accommodate and monitor the burgeoning discussion. Nothing does more to explain this enormous change than Hempel's article and its reception, especially after its inclusion in a popular anthology by Feigl and Sellars in 1949, and another by Patrick Gardiner ten years later. This single, short piece of writing, on a single problem, by a philosopher who, although already a formidable presence in the philosophy of the physical sciences, gave little indication, either then or later, of being much interested in history for its *own* sake, nevertheless seized and held the attention of a sizeable group of philosophers and their students for more than a generation. It was a remarkable achievement.

Hempel's message to philosophers of history and to historians interested in the theory of their discipline was both simple and tough-minded. While he conceded that the defining interest of historical studies is in the establishment of particular events, not laws or generalizations governing them, he argued that this by no means excuses historians from claiming knowledge of the latter. For laws, he maintained, must have a theoretical function in the explanation of his-

217

torical events which is quite analogous to the one they have in explanation in the natural sciences. To explain an event is to show how from certain antecedent conditions it could legitimately have been predicted. And that will require identifying the law or laws according to which it followed from them.

In his original formulation of this view of explanation—which came to be called *the covering-law model*—Hempel represented the event to be explained as following necessarily from the conditions said to explain it, the relationship between explanans and explanandum thus having to be deductive—a claim reinforced with the observation that in all 'scientific' studies the object of explanation is to exclude chance from the subject matter. Even in his first statement of his position, however, Hempel conceded that explanations meeting such a rigorous demand would not often be found in history; the most one could generally hope for would be approximations in varying degrees to this ideal. But this, he went on to note, is true even in the natural sciences, explanations being routinely accepted there that cite only statistical laws, and thus show no more than the probability of what is being explained. In history, of course, explanations will often be found that state no covering generalizations at all, even statistical ones. With regard to such cases, Hempel maintained, only two kinds of judgments are possible: either the supposed explanations are to be counted as mere 'sketches', becoming full-fledged explanations only when further filled out, or they must be dismissed as mere 'pseudo' explanations.

In a second article, "Explanation in Science and in History," published in 1962, and in subsequent writings, Hempel offered a more elaborate account of the way explanations that mention no covering generalizations can still be regarded as more than pseudoexplanations. An explanation, he points out, can simply be incomplete without also being vague, as in an explanation sketch. It can also be elliptical in the sense that, although formally incomplete, what would complete it could easily be supplied in context, and may therefore be said to be assumed. Or it can be partial, explaining completely some aspect of the explanandum, but not the whole of it as stated—a deviation from his ideal case that Hempel (1965, p. 416) thinks rather common among historians. The most striking change in the second article, however, was Hempel's recognition of probabilistic explanation not just as a widely tolerated way in which actual explanations may sometimes deviate from the deductive ideal, but as a second kind of explanation, with a logical status and logical peculiarities of its own (for example, being subject to degree). His theory of explanation in history thus becomes at this point explicitly dualistic, reference being made thereafter not to the covering-law model, but the covering-law models. I shall argue later that this was a change of great significance for the critical consideration of his theory as it applies to history. For the moment, it is enough to note that it is the second model, not the first, that he would expect most often to find exemplified in history, and even then in a way that still yields no more than incomplete, elliptical, or partial explanations, or explanation sketches.

The discussion of Hempel's position began as early as 1943 with a supportive article by Morton White which went on to consider the question, raised by

Hempel himself and answered negatively by White, whether an explanation can be specifically historical in the sense of applying specifically historical laws. A more nuanced defence of the Hempelian theory was offered by Patrick Gardiner in 1952 in *The Nature of Historical Explanation*, the first philosophical book on history in the analytic idiom—Gardiner being more inclined than Hempel to see the looseness of any laws plausibly ascribed to historians as a virtue rather than a defect. Hempel's most articulate and intransigent critic, Alan Donagan, entered the field in 1957, arguing then and in subsequent writings (e.g., 1964), on the one hand that there are no universal laws of human affairs, none of those which might be extrapolated from historians' explanations being in the least plausible, and on the other that explanations claiming to apply less-than-universal laws are simply bogus, since no alleged explanation which fails to rule out the nonccurrence of its explanandum succeeds in explaining it. Michael Scriven, besides taking issue with covering-law thinking on a number of other grounds, objected, too, that particular events simply "rattle around"in statistical explanations (1959, p. 467). Other authors, like John Passmore (1958, 1962), May Brodbeck (1962), Robert Stover (1967, pp. 38–40), and, more guardedly, Arthur Danto (1965, pp. 206–14), nevertheless continued to defend and develop Hempel's position throughout the 1960s and into the 1970s; and Morton White strengthened his advocacy of it in 1965 with the ingenious argument— he called it existential regularism (pp. 60–78)—that, although the explanations actually offered in history may be nomologically loose, they are at any rate indicators that strict deductive explanations of the same phenomena do exist. Over much the same period, dissatisfactions additional to those aired by Donagan and Scriven were expressed by W. H. Dray (1957), W. B. Gallie (1964, pp. 106–9), L. O. Mink (1966), and others. However, it was a feature of the opposition to the covering(law theory that it was fragmented, never coalescing into a single viable alternative conception of what counts as acceptable explanation in history. Indeed, as Weingartner (1966, pp. 141–2) remarked, Hempel's critics often appeared to differ with each other as much as they did with him.

Not many historians showed much interest in the controversy. A few reacted strongly against any idea of law or predictability being imposed upon their discipline; some objected that the theories of the philosophers made too little contact with the actual practice of history; some criticized the apparent implication that explanation was a matter of special importance to historians—along with a consequent conception of philosophy of history as virtually 'synonymous' with theorizng about it (Ritter 1986, p. 146). Some quite distinguished historians, like J. H. Hexter (1971b, pp. 14–42) and Geoffrey Elton (1970, p. 125) displayed an insecure grasp of the difference between analyzing the basic concepts of a discipline and formulating hands-on rules of research for it. A few, like Perez Zagorin (1959, pp. 249–54), Bruce Mazlish (1963), and Jerry Ginsberg (1975), understood it well, and joined the discussion. But it was noticeable, and sometimes lamented (e.g., by Mink, 1973), that *History and Theory*, which had been conceived as a forum in which historians and philosophers could discuss mutual concerns, performed that function only sporadically.

When the controversy over Hempel's theory began to abate in the mid-1970s, this was due less to a consensus having been reached than to other issues crowding it from center stage: issues like individualism versus holism, constructionism versus realism, and the extent to which historical inquiry can be objective. There was also a sense of ennui; as one Hempel's earlier supporters recently confessed, he simply lost interest in "The World according to Hempel" (Danto 1995, p. 76). An early sign of the change was an increased preoccupation with narrative, first as the vehicle of explanation generally favored by historians themselves, but then for its own sake; and good work was done by Danto (1965, pp. 112–82), Mink (1970), and others in exploring the way narratives can make a human subject matter intelligible, this both supplementing and challenging the view of it as serial covering-law explanation that some of Hempel's remarks had suggested. Reservations about the viability of narrative history expressed by Mandelbaum (1967; 1977, pp. 24–39) only served to fuel the discussion.

However, in the years following the appearance in 1973 of Hayden White's monumental work *Metahistory*, there was a seismic shift in the way historical narrative was discussed by philosophers.[2] The focus of concern moved away from logical and conceptual characteristics of narration toward ideological ones—toward the larger purposes narrative supposedly served in the hands of historians seeking social relevance. In consequence, it came to be viewed as essentially an exercise in rhetoric, as a mode of discourse rather than an instrument of inquiry, or even of understanding. Increasingly, the cognate discipline for philosophy of history was seen as literary theory rather than philosophy of the natural or social sciences. This new interest is typified by the work of Frank Ankersmit (1983), which also clearly exemplifies the exaggerated (and sometimes almost gleeful) historical relativism and presentism that generally went with it. It is rather ironical that, following the sustained argumentation set in motion by Hempel's article, a major trend in English-speaking philosophy of history should amount, in effect, to a reversion to the view of history as an art rather than a science that was common in the 1930s and earlier, and to the relativism that went with it.

What I want to do in what follows is to highlight, and to examine in enough detail to convey some sense of the interest and importance of each, a few of the specific issues raised during the discussion of Hempel's theory of explanation in history. Since I was myself a party to some of the disputes noted, my commentary may not be as evenhanded as would be ideal; but I hope that it will be read as a respectful revisiting of old battlefields rather than as a resumption of hostilities. I shall consider first Hempel's response to two traditional claims about historical inquiry which, long before he wrote, were often considered, especially in German and Italian thought, to indicate a radical difference between the thought-patterns of history and those of the natural sciences: the alleged uniqueness of history's subject matter and its openness to empathetic understanding. I shall then examine two ideas of explanation in history that are still further removed from Hempel's original position than his probabilistic model is: that it may sometimes aim at showing no more than possibility, and that it may sometimes be achieved by subsumption under a concept rather than under a law. I shall then go on to consider what Hempel had to say about two characteristic procedures that historians have generally regarded as explanatory: specifically, causal analysis and narrative. In a final section, I shall summarize briefly what I take to have been Hempel's special importance for English-speaking philosophy of history, and point to what seems to me the most fundamental difference between his own approach and that of most of his critics.

It has often been maintained that historical events cannot be brought under laws or generalizations because they are unique, a well-known example of this view being the characterization of historical inquiry by Wilhelm Windelband, a late-nineteenth-century German philosopher, as idiographic rather than nomothetic. The English philosopher of history who comes closest to maintaining the same position is Michael Oakeshott. According to Oakeshott, historical events are not to be understood by discovering their likeness to events located at other times and places, but by delineating the events themselves in ever-increasing detail. The ideal historical explanation, he maintains, would be an account in which no 'lacuna' is tolerated (1933, p. 143). It is natural to interpret this as meaning that, in history, explanation is equivalent to full description.

Hempel's very salutary response is that, whatever one might hold as a matter of metaphysical principle about the world as it concretely exists, no inquiry can treat its subject matter as absolutely unique (1942, p. 346). For events can only be explained as they are conceived or described, and that involves bringing them under concepts, these having generality. Hempel also puts his point by remarking that, while events may be unique as they actually occur in the sense of having infinitely many characteristics, no attempt to explain them so conceived could possibly succeed: an explanation must always, for this reason, fall short of the full reality of what is explained.[3] But there is no difference, he points out, between natural science and history in this regard: in both cases, inquiry must abstract; in both cases, events will be explained as events of certain kinds—which does not mean, he hastens to add, that what historians explain is kinds of events rather than particular ones (1963, pp. 150–1). What they explain is particulars as instances of kinds—this anticipating an objection to the covering-law approach that both historians and philosophers have sometimes made.

But although Hempel's response here is surely correct as far as it goes, some of his critics have felt that it does not probe deeply enough into the reasons why historians so commonly stress the supposed uniqueness of what they study. In a paper of 1961, C. B. Joynt and Nicholas Rescher took the matter somewhat further, arguing that, although the explanations historians give must apply or assume generalizations, the ones that function in them are often less than universal in a sense going beyond Hempel's concession that they may be merely statistical. For they may be less than universal also, these authors maintained, in the sense of being assertable only of the particular object of interest: for example, they may be generalizations about how nineteenth-century American pioneers behaved, not about how pioneers as such behave. Explanations applying generalizations which thus explicitly incorporate spatiotemporal limitations—'limited' laws, as Joynt and Rescher call them—could at the same time, of course, deviate in other ways from Hempel's original covering-law ideal: for example, they could also be no more than statistical, or the explanations they enter into could be partial, or incomplete, or mere sketches. Historians themselves might put the point in another way. The aim of their explanations, they might say, is often simply to show something to be characteristic of the particular age, culture, movement, institution, or even particular individual they have in view.

In later statements of his position, Hempel (1965, p. 459) himself concedes that spatiotemporally limited generalizations may function in explanations, noting that this sometimes happens even in physical science, where, for example, Kepler's planetary laws are regarded as explanatory even though they refer specifically to our own planetary system. However, there seems to be an important difference between the way such laws are regarded in natural science and the way they are regarded in history. For in science they would not be considered fully satisfactory unless they could be shown to fall under, and ultimately be derived from, corresponding universal laws. In history this is not so: explanations citing limited laws are commonly seen as acceptable whether or not corresponding universal laws can be assumed to hold. Such a stance leaves it open, at least, that what is studied is unique in the sense of not falling under universal laws at all, while at the same time accepting the Hempelian principle that all explanation involves reference to some kind of generality.

There is a further important point to be made. Although Hempel concedes that the laws historians put to explanatory use may be spatiotemporally limited, he does not seem to regard this as a matter of more than passing theoretical interest. Historians, by contrast, will see it as of fundamental significance for their discipline because of its implications for history's relation to cognate studies, especially the social sciences. Hempel began his discussion of explanation in history by conceding that historians do not take as their goal the actual discovery of laws or generalizations. If generalizations are nevertheless needed for their explanations, the question arises where they are to come from. Hempel's own remarks suggest two likely sources. On the one hand, they might be drawn from common knowledge, which his own discussion of cases, however, suggests should be avoided as much as possible. On the other hand, they might be drawn from the findings of the various generalizing sciences—even the physical sciences, at times, but more often social sciences like psychology, sociology, or economics. Hempel's position seems in fact to be that, as far as possible, history should be an application of social science theory to a chosen subject matter. Yet most historians, while not denying that the generalizing social sciences can ever be a useful resource, have denied that they are dependent upon them; they have regarded themselves as able to give viable and relevant explanations on their own authority without falling into an opposite dependence upon unverifiable common wisdom. The doctrine of explanation by limited laws offers a theoretical basis for taking such a position, at the same time qualifying the common view that historians never themselves aim to discover generalizations. For to the extent that the explanations they offer take the limited-law form, they will look in vain to the generalizing social sciences for the laws they need, and they therefore not only may, but must, claim methodological independence of them.[4] To put it another way: no sociologist or psychologist is in a better position than a historian of the period to say what was characteristic of English parliaments in the reign of Elizabeth I, or of Roman senators at the time of the Principate.

The second traditional position to which Hempel responds is that covering-law explanations are offered from the standpoint of an external observer, this being regarded as inappropriate when dealing with a human subject matter rather than a natural one. Historical inquiry, it is argued, should seek to understand what it studies from the inside: it should be empathetic, not nomothetic. As in discussing the uniqueness objection, Hempel identifies no authors who hold this view—he may have had Weber or Dilthey in mind—but he understands the idea of empathy in history as follows (1962, pp. 352–3). Rather than referring past human actions to antecedent conditions and laws, historians are said to be able to understand them by some kind of immediate insight into the minds of the agents. On this view, historical method would consist in a historian's asking what he himself would have thought or felt under the circumstances, and then attributing those thoughts and feelings to the agents in explanation of what they did. Not surprisingly, Hempel insists that empathetic projection, so conceived, is neither a sufficient nor a necessary condition of explaining actions in history. It is not necessary, because we can often understand the actions of agents who were not at all like-minded with ourselves—if need be, with the help of the generalized findings of abnormal psychology. It is not sufficient because the ease with which one may answer the question: How would I have thought or felt in those circumstances? is no guarantee that this particular agent felt the same way. The most that can be allowed to empathy, Hempel observes, is that it may sometimes be heuristically helpful, perhaps suggesting hypotheses about explanatory generalizations that would be worth testing, after which properly warranted covering-law explanations could be offered.

One can hardly object to Hempel's rejection of empathetic understanding as he depicts it. It is unfortunate, however, that what he targeted in this way is so remote from the more considered idea of explanation from the inside that had already entered the literature of English-speaking philosophy of history through the writings of R. G. Collingwood (1936, pp. 213–27; 1939, pp. 107–15). This is the idea that, in historical studies, understanding past actions typically involves critically re-thinking the thoughts which, on the evidence, the historian is prepared to ascribe to the agent, this with a view to discovering whether the action was rationally required by his beliefs about his situation and what he was trying to achieve. Here is no suggestion of projecting upon others thoughts which the historian assumes he would have had himself: the goal is conceived rather as showing why the action performed presented itself as a rational choice, not to the historian, but to the agent. At the same time—and this is implied in the stipulation that the agent's thought be re-thought critically—the historian cannot claim to have shown the action to be understandable unless he can represent the agent's choice as required by that agent's own beliefs and goals. This way of conceiving the historian's approach to understanding action has sometimes been called *rational explanation*. In offering it, historians clearly no more need to assume that all past actions studied are similarly explicable than an advocate of the Hempelian theory needs to assume (and Hempel himself does not) that whatever happens is nomologically explicable. How a given thing is explicable, and even whether it is, is something to be found out in the particular case.

In subsequent writings, Hempel responded in a variety of ways to the arguments of philosophers who regarded something like rational explanation as viable and important in history, thereby enriching the literature on action explanation generally.[5] Here I can consider only what seems to me his chief contention with respect to it, and the special importance which I think accepting this kind of explanation has for historiography. Hempel argued that explanations which show only that agents had good reasons for acting as they did are incomplete, and that when completed, they take on a nomological character (1962, p. 118; 1963, p. 155). Merely indicating such reasons, he maintained, shows only that, if the action was indeed performed, it was rational; it does not show that, given the reasons, it would be performed. Accepting the explanation as stated would thus contravene what Hempel (1963, p. 146) declared to be a fundamental principle of all explanation: that it should give grounds for believing that what is to be explained in fact occurred. With a view to bringing rational explanation into conformity with this principle, he therefore proposed adding to usual statements of it further 'assumed' premises to the effect that the agent was rational, and that the action was the sort of thing a rational agent would do in the circumstances.

In the face of the discrepancy between what Hempel's theory demands and what rational explanation normally offers, two options present themselves. On the one hand, one might judge, as Hempel does, that rational explanation as normally given is simply defective. On the other, one might take the discrepancy to indicate that something is wrong with the principle: that what we have here may not be defective covering-law explanation, but acceptable explanation of another kind, an instantiation of a different concept of explanation. Hempel himself introduced the idea that different concepts of explanation might be at work even in scientific inquiry, when, after his first article, he characterized probabilistic explanation as a second genre, conceptually different from the first in that it renounced the goal of showing that what happened had to happen. It might be claimed that rational explanation, too, applies a distinctive concept of explanation, one different in claims and in goals from either of the nomological kinds. What the latter aim to show is that certain happenings were understandable in the sense of being in some sufficient degree predictable. What rational explanation aims to show is that certain actions were understandable in the sense of being in some sufficient degree choosable, where choosability has a quasi-normative significance.

So conceived, the project of finding rational explanations of actions meshes well not only with a larger goal often ascribed to historical studies, but also with a metaphysical presupposition that many historians carry into their work. The purpose of history, it is often said, if somewhat metaphorically, is to recover the past as something lived. The kind of understanding it seeks is thus understanding from the standpoint of the agents—or perhaps better, from the standpoint of agency—an approach to the past as something to be *re*lived imaginatively or vicariously in the sense of being seen as having offered problems to be solved or opportunities to be seized. Explanation by covering-law seems to be in the wrong universe of discourse for pursuing such an aim: to paraphrase Collingwood (1946, p. 214), it treats human life as a spectacle, as a mere process, not as an activity. It might be added that offering rational explanation is a procedure which is open to those who, like many historians, believe that in human action there is an element of free will, understood in a sense that rules out determinism or any regularized predictability. The question of free will is, of course, a large and controversial metaphysical issue. But it must be a matter of interest for the logical characterization of historical inquiry if explaining actions by reasons is at least compatible, as it appears to be, with the idea of their having no completely determining conditions.

I turn now to consider the objection that Hempel's position, as outlined in his original paper, excludes two further ways of explaining things which are often found in historical studies. The first of these is explanation by reference to conditions deemed necessary but not sufficient for what occurred. As Hempel notes, both Charles Frankel (1957, pp. 411–12) and W. B. Gallie (1955, pp. 387, 402) have put forward this idea, Gallie incorporating it into a larger theory of the nature of explanatory narrative in history, an issue to which I shall return. To illustrate what he has in mind, Gallie points to an explanation offered by the historian Albert Loisy of the rapid expansion of early Christianity throughout the Mediterranean world by reference to its having had the Jewish synagogue as a platform for proselytization. Hempel's response is that an explanation which thus cites only a necessary condition of what is at issue, however useful this may sometimes be in practice, must be judged incomplete, or perhaps elliptical, as stated. Its soundness, as in the case of rational explanation, must depend on whether further conditions can be supplied which would bring it into conformity with one or other of the covering-law models.

Gallie says little about whether he considers any necessary condition of a given result to be explanatory or just some of them; and Hempel has no difficulty in indicating cases where such a condition would not be. If someone wins a lottery, he points out, no one would regard this occurrence as explained by the fact that the winner satisfied the necessary condition of having bought a ticket (1963, p. 149). However, the question of what might make some necessary conditions explanatory and others not was addressed elsewhere by Dray (1954) and later developed further by G. H. von Wright (1971, pp. 84–86). What makes the availability of a condition like the synagogue explanatory, it is argued, is its showing what made the rapid expansion possible, not necessary, or even probable. The need for explanation arises out of the apparent unlikelihood, or even impossibility, of what occurred; the explanation takes the form of a rebuttal of the presumption that it could not occur. The question answered is not why the thing happened, but how it could be that it happened; and the claim would be that such explanation how-possibly rather than why-necessarily (or even why-probably) is not incomplete covering-law explanation, but explanation of a different kind—an application, once again, of a different concept of explanation. Donagan, although agreeing that this is indeed an independent type of explanation, doubts that it is offered very often in history. Von Wright envisages a role for it across the sciences, human and natural.

Hempel's response is not to deny that the indicated presumption-rebuttal pattern characterizes explanation as it is sometimes given, but to insist that the point is one about the pragmatics, not the logic, of explanation—a claim echoed by supporters like John Passmore (1958, pp. 270–1). He therefore dismisses categorically any notion that explanation by necessary condition could constitute a separate kind of explanation in the sense in which the two covering-law models are conceded, in his mature theory, to identify explanations of different kinds. But there is a problem about the way Hempel relegates what is distinctive about this kind of explanation to the realm of pragmatics. What is meant by merely pragmatic aspects of explanation, he quite explicitly says, is aspects that make its acceptability relative not just to what a person believes (which would make the idea of elliptical explanation pragmatic), but also to his intelligence, standards, and personal idiosyncrasies (1965, p. 426). What explanations how-possibly are (or should be) relative to, however, is not persons, but questions and presuppositions; and whether something offered as an explanation does in fact respond to a given question and to what is presupposed is surely a matter to be settled by logical analysis, not psychological preference. As Scriven remarks, in attacking what he considers excessive formalism in explanatory theory, "the territory of logic is not terminated by the period at the end of the sentence"(1966, p. 255).

The idea that mere necessary conditions may sometimes be explanatory—and sometimes completely so, relative to a question posed—has application beyond as well as within historical inquiry. Indeed, one of Hempel's own examples of explanation in a biological or medical setting appears to be most plausibly interpreted as of this kind. In discussing his probabilistic model, Hempel (1942, p. 350) observes that if a child comes down with the measles two weeks after his brother, and has not been in contact with any other children suffering from the measles, we justifiably conclude that he caught the disease from his brother. Since we know no universal law which would allow us to deduce that anyone who has had a measles contact will get the measles, Hempel observes, such an explanation will necessarily be based on a merely statistical generalization linking contacts with cases in a way that merely probilifies the result. But this, besides undervaluing the explanation, surely finds in it something that isn't there. For the explanation would surely be considered a good one even if it were known (as is likely) that in only a small percentage of cases a child comes down with the measles after having had a measles contact, provided it can also be assumed (as Hempel's presentation of the explanation suggests) that a person only gets the measles through a contact. The first generalization, given the fact of contact, warrants the conclusion that getting the measles was highly improbable. The second, given the same fact, shows that, despite this, what happened was quite explicable in the sense of being shown to have been entirely possible in the circumstances. In fact, the necessary condition explanation which is offered in this case is not only a good one, but is complete in a very strict sense (and for that reason a much tighter example of the genre than would often be found in history). For since there were no other contacts, it shows not probably but for certain that the child got the disease from his brother—this despite our still having to say that it was improbable that he would have gotten it at all.

The fact that explanation how-possibly can be found outside as well as inside history prompts von Wright quite rightly to warn that it offers no basis for drawing any fundamental distinction between the natural and the human sciences (as he would accept it that rational explanation does). There is nevertheless a reason for regarding it as a kind of special interest for history. It must be conceded that, although those who give how-possibly explanations do not cite, and may not even know, covering-laws warranting prediction, they would often assume that what they have in view does have a why-necessarily (or why-probably) explanation. This would naturally be assumed, for example, by anyone offering Hempel's explanation of a child's catching the measles. It is true, too, that, as has sometimes been pointed out, when someone sets himself a how-possibly question, he may in fact go on to give a why-necessarily answer.[6] But how-possibly explanations can coherently be offered even under the assumption that what is to be explained had no determining (or highly probilifying) conditions, so that no why-necessarily (or why-probably) explanation remains to be discovered. Since historians, as was noted in considering rational explanation, often carry into their work, implicitly or explicitly, a view of human action as less than fully determined, this should make how-possibly explanation a genre of special interest to them. The issue here (as in the case of rational explanation) is not, of course, whether this controversial assumption is to be accepted. The point is rather that, under an assumption which many historians make, explanation citing only especially significant necessary conditions may be the only kind it makes sense to look for.

The second allegedly non-covering-law way of explaining things, explanation by subsumption under an explanatory concept rather than under a law, was considered briefly in Hempel's first article (1942, p. 350, n. 3) and summarily dismissed. But the examples to which he briefly drew attention there were hardly the sort that any historian would take seriously: explanations by reference to concepts like the historical destiny of a race or the self-unfolding of absolute reason, which he very properly characterized as metaphors without empirical content. Later, however, in considering the claim of the historian Ramsay Muir to explain certain events in nineteenth-century England as a social and not just an economic revolution (an example drawn from Dray [1959]), he also rejected the notion that bringing historical events under empirically respectable concepts could yield explanation, unless at the same time it brought them under empirical generalizations containing the concept (1965, pp. 453–7). Merely bringing a host of details under a concept, he argued, is not explanation but description. And while he did not question that historians needed to spend much of their time describing rather than explaining, he insisted that the two tasks were distinct.

The contention that a concept can only be explanatory if it brings what it applies to under laws needs further explication, however. Hempel offers a biological analogy. A doctor might explain a child's having a sore throat, spots, and a temperature by saying that he has the measles. In applying this diagnostic and admittedly explanatory concept, the doctor clearly brings to bear a whole theory of what is going on which, among other things, permits the likely course of the disease to be predicted. If applying the concept of a social revolution is to be considered explanatory, Hempel maintains, it must similarly license prediction—which in this particular case he thinks the historian must have realized since he went on to recount what, in his judgment, inevitably followed the upheaval. It is an oddity of Hempel's account of explanation by concept, however, that it envisages the explanatory concept as appearing in the apodosis, not the protasis, of the explanatory law it supposedly brings in its train. For if the application of a concept to events makes them nomologically explicable, the explanatory law should surely, on covering-law theory, link them with antecedents from which they, and not their own consequences, can be predicted. In other words, the concept should appear in the protasis of the law. Otherwise, an entirely fresh idea is introduced into Hempel's theory of explanation: that of something being explained by reference to what comes after it rather than precedes it; and this is not easily reconciled with his original position, despite his remark (1965, p. 455) that it at least "conforms in broad outline" to covering-law theory. That is not to say that subsumption under concepts never could entail the application of laws linking an explanandum with antecedent conditions: the Marxist idea of a bourgeois revolution would do this, for example, to the extent that it requires us to think of what it applies to as a kind of thing invariably brought about by determining conditions of a certain sort, which can therefore indeed be retrodicted. The question would then be whether the concepts which historians normally regard as explanatory need to be law-impregnated in this sense.

The concept of a social revolution, at any rate, does not seem to carry such implications, Is its application, then, simply nonexplanatory? The position of a person accepting the idea of explanation by concept would be that it may be explanatory, but in a different sense from explaining why things happened, or even how it could be that they happened, and quite without regard to the Hempelian requirement that an explanation give grounds for believing that what is to be explained in fact occurred. The historian explains a certain group of happenings *as* a social revolution; the explanation proceeds not by relating those events to other happenings, but by finding a pattern in their relationships to each other, a unity in their diversity, which is signified by the concept applied. Following Walsh (1951, pp. 59–64), philosophers of history, and some historians too, have referred to this as colligation, although it has also been characterized in other ways: for example, by Oakeshott (1933, pp. 160–1) as bringing large-scale historical individuals into view; by Goldstein (1976, pp. 83–91) as constituting the historian's true subject matter; by Mink (1966, pp. 41–4) as seeking synoptic or synthetic understanding.

An analogy from music has sometimes been used to clarify the chief point. Grasping a series of notes is not itself recognizing them as together constituting a symphony; but they may together be explained as such; and particular note-sequences may be explained by reference to the way they contribute to the constitution of such a musical whole—an idea given historiographical application by Mandelbaum's contention (1977, pp. 126–7) that, when seeking understanding of a subject matter, historians are far more likely to be concerned with the part–whole relation than with that of antecedent–consequent. It is indicative of the importance that historians themselves ascribe to colligatory or synoptic understanding, so conceived, that some of their fiercest controversies have centered on how given groups of events are most appropriately colligated: events of the mid–seventeenth century in England, for example, as the Puritan Revolution, or as the Great Rebellion, or as the English Civil War, or as the English Revolution. And colligatory understanding is sometimes sought, too, not only of events, movements, or institutions, but of whole periods, which may be characterized, for example, as the Renaissance or the Age of Reason.

Historians, it is true, sometimes call this sort of thing interpretation, not explanation. But Hempel's covering-law theory, as originally presented, was said to apply also to what would ordinarily be called *interpretation* in history, provided it issues from respectable empirical inquiry, which colligation does. It is true, too, that some critics of colligation, like J. W. N. Watkins (1952, p. 733) and G. C. Homans (1961, p. 10), have denigrated it as a procedure which is methodologically weak, a mere placing of things in categories—a judgment with which Hempel agrees (1965, p. 456, n. 11). But it is surely strange to characterize something as a weak method for attaining a goal which is quite other than the one it sets itself. Covering-law explanation might as appropriately be described as methodologically weak where the goal is finding synthetic unity in a subject matter. A further feature of colligatory explanation as historians often give it which will doubtless be looked at askance by Hempelians is that the concepts used, although hardly devoid of empirical content, are sometimes (like Renaissance) partly metaphorical. Their application also commonly requires historians to make value judgments, to distinguish between what is judged more and less important—this being part of the issue, for example, when Marxists and non-Marxist historians argue about whether the English Revolution (which made no large changes in the ownership of property) was really a revolution. As I will note, however, it is far from clear that even causal judgments, as these are routinely made in history, can be said to be value-free.

Since causal analysis and narrative are among the most common procedures of historical inquiry, it is of interest to ask what Hempel had to say about them from the standpoint of the covering-law theory of explanation. With regard to specifically causal explanation, he often gives the impression of believing that the general account he offers of his two explanatory models makes clear most of what needs to be said about it. He does note that not all explanation by reference to laws can properly be called causal. For example, although laws may themselves be explained by reference to further laws, causal explanations must be of particular events. They must also, he says, show necessity, and must therefore be deductive, not probabilistic. And even deductive law–applying explanations, he concedes, are not always causal, since causes must be antecedent to the events they explain, and covering laws may link simultaneous conditions.[7] Within such limits, however, Hempel seems to think it unimportant for philosophical theory, indeed little more than a terminological matter, that conditions regarded as explanatory are sometimes referred to as causes and sometimes not. What matters for an understanding of causal explanation is the underlying notions of necessary and sufficient condition. What is properly called a cause in history, it seems, is either any antecedent necessary condition of an explained event, or an ensemble of such conditions composing a sufficient set.

When historians endeavor to say what they mean by causes, they are notoriously unclear.[8] But representing their causal judgments as simply alternative ways of saying what could have been said more straightforwardly using the language of necessary and sufficient condition is far from reflecting what they generally mean. In particular, it throws no light on what is at issue when, as so often happens, they disagree about which of many antecedent conditions, even if all are considered to have been necessary for what occurred, is properly called its cause—in other words, when they deliberately distinguish between causal and noncausal explanatory conditions. The idea that a causal explanation of some significant historical event should consist, as far as possible, in setting out a sufficient set of antecedent conditions—these perhaps categorized as the economic, the social, the political, the religious, and so on, causes—is not highly regarded by historians. And one reason for this is that explanation, so conceived, remains incomplete in a sense different from the one in which Hempel regards explanation by mere necessary conditions incomplete. For it has not yet reached the stage of determining which of the discovered explanatory conditions were causes and which were not. Nor is it any more satisfactory to maintain that any or all of the necessary conditions of an occurrence can with equal propriety be regarded as its causes: indeed, it invites paradox. Hitler's failure to suffer cardiac arrest just before the Nazi invasion of Poland may well have been a necessary condition of its occurrence, but it would hardly be numbered among its causes. By contrast, the failure of the British and French to oppose his warlike designs in time may plausibly be so regarded.

Hempel occasionally shows awareness of this selective aspect of causal judgment, observing, for example, that, if a venal person succumbs to a bribe, it would ordinarily be the bribe and not his disposition to venality that would be called the cause of his acting as he did, although both may be parts of the explanation. At the same time, he leaves it open that, in certain circumstances, the judgment might properly go the other way (1965, pp. 486–7)—although not asking what might justify its doing so. At another point, he notes the distinction historians sometimes draw between more and less important causes, and refers readers to a discussion of this matter by Nagel (1952, pp. 383–5) which examines various criteria on which this is allegedly done. But the question of the grounds on which some causes can be considered more important than others is not the same as that of how a necessary condition can be regarded as a cause at all. The important difference between these questions is equally obscured by Morton White (1965, chap. 4) when he frames the philosopher's question as discovering the principle on which historians may properly distinguish between a 'contributory' cause, meaning any element in an explanation, and 'the' cause of an event. Collingwood, who, in a much-discussed section (chap. 31) of his *Essay on Metaphysics*, does focus on the difference between causes and mere necessary conditions, unfortunately considers it only with regard to causal judgment in sciences like medicine or engineering, in which, he says, what is typically regarded as the causal condition is the one by means of which some interested party can produce or prevent the phenomenon—a principle of causal selection that Hempel would justifiably call pragmatic. Walsh (1962, p. 236) makes a similarly pragmatic issue of it by suggesting that historians may simply select causal conditions according to their 'interests'.

The account of the cause/condition distinction that has most influenced philosophers of history was offered by H. L. A. Hart and A. M. Honoré (1959, especially pt. 1) in a study stressing similarities between thought patterns in history and in the law. It is not possible here to go into details of their very complex analysis: it must suffice to say that they present impressive evidence that the causal judgments actually made by historians and those working in cognate branches of the human studies apply the principle that explanatory conditions are causal to the extent that they are abnormal in the circumstances or consist of voluntary human interventions. Of special interest here is their contention that the application of these principles is not value-free. Judgments of abnormality, for example, do have a statistical aspect; but they also require choice of a *standard of comparison* considered appropriate in the circumstances, which is not itself a product of statistical analysis. And the idea of actions being voluntary raises questions about how far given agents were forced or obliged to act in the way they did, which involves moral as well as psychological considerations. Philosophers of history who accept the Hempelian account of explanation as far as it goes are unlikely to welcome being led in this direction. Yet analyses in these terms have shed considerable light (see, e.g., Dray 1978) on many actual controversies about causes in history, often finding a stable rationale in what, on the face of it, seem merely arbitrary or pragmatic choices on the part of historians.

Similar considerations arise if one asks how, or indeed whether, causes are to be distinguished from reasons in historical inquiry. Hempel's theory of what was earlier called rational explanation holds, in effect, that if reasons explain actions, they must at the same time be their causes (in the sense of being or completing a set of conditions sufficient for their occurrence). But the need to draw a distinction between causes and noncauses may arise again within the class of reasons. For although it could be said of a threat (at any rate, to what it would be reasonable to regard as vital interests) that it caused a person to respond in a certain way, it would surely be considered, if not a mere joke, then a betrayal of moral flabbiness, to say the same of a mere opportunity to better oneself. Was Hitler caused to invade Poland by the prospect of easy pickings there? Not, surely, in the same sense in which his invasion caused the Poles to undertake their own defense. What is being claimed here is that there can be circumstances which, quite without reference to whether they are (or complete) a set of determining conditions, may rationally compel action, and for this reason be accorded the status of causes. No doubt this is territory which needs to be mapped with circumspection and sensitivity (for a good short attempt, see Donnellan [1967]). The issues involved, however, are simply burked by a covering-law theory of causal explanation.

The other common feature of historiography that was mentioned, narrative, has often been regarded by historians as virtually a defining feature of it. J. H. Hexter (1961, p. 21) calls it "the historian's real business"; and Hempel himself (1962, p. 111) described it as at least an "interesting candidate" for the role of "specifically historical explanation." He doesn't, however, consider the explanatory significance of narrative as such: he attends only to one form of it, which he calls *genetic explanation*, in which a development is traced from a point of origin through a series of stages to a final result; and he endeavors to show that the explanatory force of such reconstructions is fully accounted for by his general theory of explanation. What he says of genetic explanation responds to the analysis of it offered by Gallie (see earlier) when considering explanation by merely necessary conditions. Gallie argued not only that conditions which merely enabled actions to be performed may often be all that explanation requires, but also that the function of citing such conditions in a narrative from time to time is to enable the narrative itself to continue without challenge. Hempel will not allow that a narrative so conceived could be more than sketchily explanatory. Understanding transitions from stage to stage, on his view, requires knowledge of sufficient conditions.

In developing this position, Hempel makes a valid and very important point about the characteristic structure of a developmental narrative that genuinely explains. Some kinds of processes, like the fall of a stone, he notes, consist of stages for each of which what happened at the preceding stage is a sufficient condition. But in tracing developments in human affairs—Hempel's example is changes over time in the Catholic Church's practice of granting indulgences (1962, pp. 111–14; 1965, pp. 447–51)—explaining a change that occurred at a particular stage typically requires reference to something which, as it were, intrudes into the process from outside it. Indulgences were at first issued only to those who actually fought in the Crusades, and when they began later to be offered also to stay-at-homes who contributed financially, this was due partly to the contingent fact that enthusiasm for crusading was waning. As Hempel puts it, a genetic explanation may thus require descriptive additions from time to time, these referring to conditions which are not themselves explained by antecedent states of the process being traced. Hempel had, of course, made the point elsewhere that explanation always requires reference to something which is not itself explained; but new here is the observation that, in genetic accounts, this explanatory surd may be spread across the whole structure.[9] The same structural feature, it might be remarked, will be found in many genetic accounts of natural phenomena: for example, in a tracing of successive physical changes in a coastline, which may have to recognize intrusions ranging from volcanic activity to the impact of tidal waves. And as Hempel rightly says, it will certainly characterize historical accounts in which 'motivational factors' are assigned central roles, whether these are conceived nomologically or along the lines sketched in considering rational explanation.

The kind of narrative Hempel had in view in considering the development of Church policy on indulgences, however, is dissimilar to Gallie's account of the expansion of Christianity in one interesting respect. The historical problem in Gallie's example was to explain a movement from a given point of origin through various stages to a given result. Hempel's historian, by contrast, begins with the question: Where did the practice of granting indulgences come from? and his explanatory account thus has to *find* a point of origin from which a development to the chosen later stage can be traced. Hempel's analysis, although it explicates the idea of a development, says nothing about what counts as a point of origin. And this is not a problem that can simply be brushed aside as a pragmatic matter: no serious historian could get away with saying, when asked why he probed a development back only to a certain point, that he just happened to find that point interesting. And, in fact, historians often find much to argue about, in particular cases, when faced by the question how far back one needs to go to find a point of origin. A prime example is recent disputes about the origins of the English Revolution (see, e.g., Dray 1984), some historians locating it no earlier than the conversion of Charles I to Arminianism, some further back in the arrival of the Stuarts in England, some as far back as the dissolution of the monasteries by Henry VIII, and one at least, in the grip of Marxist theory, holding it necessary to go all the way back to the Norman Conquest. Hart and Honoré (1959, pp. 39–40) have hinted that the ideas of abnormality and voluntary intervention, besides explicating the cause/condition distinction, also throw some light on the idea of points of origin as historians understand them. What is to be stressed, however, is not whether this is the right direction in which to look—although I think it promising—but the fact that a theory of explanation in history which lacks resources for dealing with a structural problem as crucial as this one must be regarded as seriously incomplete.[10]

The larger question, however, is how, if at all, historical narrative can be said to be distinctively explanatory. Morton White (1965, pp. 223–5) expressed a view that seems implicit in Hempel's approach, and is widely shared, when he represented the explanatoriness of a narrative simply as a function of the discrete explanations it contains. But so-called narrativists among philosophers of history have insisted that the narrative form itself introduces a further dimension of explanatoriness. For, besides making discrete connections clear, narratives have holistic characteristics resembling those of what was earlier called explanation by concept. Where the latter aim chiefly at displaying synthetic unity of a cross-sectional sort, however, a narrative may seek to bring into view a temporal whole, a whole of nonsimultaneous parts—whether one as limited as the developing policy implicit in the actions of a government over time or as expansive as "The Waning of the Middle Ages" (on this, see Mink 1970, pp. 547, 553). Narratives have also been depicted as having a distinctive logical structure in that they characteristically make references forward as well as backward, judgments of significance as well as explanatory judgments more narrowly conceived, this often being achieved, as Danto (1965, chap. 8) has pointed out, by a use of language which repeatedly, if often only implicitly, refers to an actual and not just an envisaged future. This, of course, again raises the question whether such ways of making a subject matter more understandable are properly called explanation. Both historians (e.g., Hexter 1971a, pp. 29–30) and philosophers (e.g. Atkinson 1978, pp. 128–33) have spoken of the whole narrative enterprise in such terms. Of course, Hempel may well feel, as he may also in the case of alleged explanation by concept, that to charge covering-law theory with significant omission in this connection would be to blame it for not doing something its advocates never undertook to do. It may nevertheless be regretted that the stress placed upon explanation in the sense of subsumption under laws so long diverted philosophers from giving serious attention to what many historians regard as their most characteristic way of making their subject matter understandable.

In reviewing some of the things Hempel had to say on the six issues considered, I have frequently expressed disagreement with positions he took. I should not want this to obscure my recognition of the tremendous debt that all those working in philosophy of history owe him. Even those most opposed to the main thrust of his account of the way explanation should proceed in history would generally agree that, besides virtually raising English-speaking philosophy of history from the dead and providing it with a widely accepted agenda for over a generation, he challenged it, with some success, to debate the nature of historical knowledge and inquiry at a level approaching the lucidity, economy, and power of his own work. He made it clearer than it had previously been what a thoroughly naturalistic approach to history taking natural science as a paradigm would involve, thereby making it more difficult than it had been before to resist 'scientism' by loose and sometimes condescending talk about history being, in the last analysis, not a science but an art. So far as the clarity of the message is concerned, the writings of Collingwood, a philosopher with a great deal more to say about history and a much deeper, indeed firsthand, knowledge of it, offer a sad and frustrating comparison. It should be mentioned, too, that besides

offering philosophers of history an example of spare and incisive argumentation worth emulating, Hempel's writings set them high standards of civility,
patience, and good humor. Even when dealing hard blows at doctrines he rejected, he rarely failed to find something of value in them, and generally took
the trouble to signal it.[11] He set others a good example, too, in being prepared,
on occasion, to admit that an idea he was pursuing raised problems whose solutions he did not yet know. A case in point is his admission (1965, p. 478) that,
while he regarded it as legitimate from time to time to ascribe explanatory beliefs to people who did not consciously entertain them, on the ground that they
were implied by what they did consciously think, he was not prepared to treat
all the logical implications of what an agent thought in that way, although unable
to say precisely where one should draw the line.

Even those who have most strongly resisted the covering-law centerpiece of
Hempel's account of historical thinking must be grateful, too, for many specific
points of doctrine which they have nevertheless found illuminating for their
own philosophical consideration of history. Somewhat at random, I might
mention his making it clear that, although history is indeed about events, not
kinds of events, it is necessarily about events of certain kinds (1965, p. 423); or
his demonstration that although explanation can be complete so far as its formal structure is concerned, it cannot be so in the sense of taking full account of
concrete happenings (1965, p. 422); or his insistence that accepting the covering-
law theory of explanation carries with it no commitment to explaining in terms
of single overarching laws (1965, p. 346); or his distinction between the epistemological thesis that explanation via universal laws entails a view of an
explanandum as determined, and the metaphysical thesis that all that happens
is determined (1963, p. 150; 1965, p. 425 n.). His work also affords salutary
reading for historians and philosophers of history in its demonstration that,
although explanation often reduces the unfamiliar to the familiar, this cannot
be a defining feature of it (1965, p. 430); in the contrast it stresses between incomplete and partial explanation, the latter being seen as a common but not
always recognized practice in history (1962, p. 106); and in the challenge it
offers to any assumption that nomological explanation in history would need
to be given in terms of specifically historical laws (1942, p. 355). One does
not have to be an Hempelian to be glad to be put straight on such matters,
and on other misunderstandings which have disfigured the literature on
philosophy of history.

But there is a more general and quite crucial point on which Hempel's account
of explanation in history seems to me less clear than one could have wished.
This concerns his view of the relation that ought to hold between a philosophical
theory of history and the actual practice of historians—how the 'job-description'
of a philosopher 'of' should be written. Hempel very properly dismisses the idea
that the philosopher's task is simply to describe practice—much as this may seem
at times to be what his critics among historians (e.g. Elton 1970, p. 153, n. 18)
expect. From the beginning, he concedes that few explanations actually offered
in history come very close to exemplifying his nomological model. At the same

time, he appears often to want to avoid the opposite extreme of taking a straight-forwardly prescriptive approach, which would first say a priori what explanation must only and always be like, and then judge historians' explanatory claims accordingly. What he offers rather, he says (1962, p. 103), is a 'rational reconstruction' of the idea of explanation in history—this suggesting that, in some sense, or to some significant degree, he will work *from* historical practice *to* philosophical theory, although not uncritically.

But that is not what one finds when he cites examples, whether the invented ones with which he began or the ones he later drew from actual historical work. His argument moves not from historical examples, but to them. What it moves from is previously examined cases of explanation in physical science, or, at any rate, of explanation of physical occurrences—for example, the freezing of a car radiator on a cold night (1942, p. 346), or the emission of soap bubbles from a cooling glass (1962, p. 96). In none of his writings on history does he produce a historical example that mentions a law, despite his claim that historians do sometimes explain in an explicitly covering-law way. The example which comes closest to doing so (1942, p. 349; 1962, p. 108) turns out to be irrelevant, since it is drawn from a sociological, not a historical,work, and aims to explain not particular events but a version of Parkinson's law. In fact, although the offering of explanations which mention laws is uncharacteristic of mainstream historiography, genuine instances of it could have been found (see, e.g., Lower 1943, pp. 20–2); and beyond the mainstream, there are, of course, historians who deliberately try to write history as applied social science. But more impressive than pointing to cases of either sort would have been evidence, culled from actual controversy over explanation in history, and preferably innocent of philosophical theory, that when their explanations are challenged, historians tend to fall back willy-nilly into covering-law ways defending them. Alleged evidence of this sort has been cited by Raymond Martin (1989, pp. 27–9); but Hempel does not argue in that way. In all cases, what he shows is only that the explanations historians offer can be added to, or otherwise modified, to make them conform to a standard imposed on them from without.

It is not quite as easy as might be assumed to say where that standard comes from. For Hempel seems to oscillate between two positions. What he says often suggests, despite disclaimers, that his program is really to bring to an examination of explanatory practice in history a conception, or at any rate an ideal, of what it is to explain something which is the fruit of prior philosophical reflection—what Rudolph Weingartner (1961, pp. 146–7), who thinks well of the Hempelian theory, calls an initial 'insight' about the nature of explanation. If that is in fact the case, the proper response of a critic would be to argue in equally a priori fashion that this insight is unacceptable—as Donagan (1964, pp. 132–3) did, for example, with respect to the probabilistic version of the model. But a great deal of what Hempel says suggests something different: that what he is really appealing to, when judging the adequacy of explanations in history, is the authority of natural science (I leave aside the question whether the covering-law model is an acceptable rational reconstruction even of explanatory practice in natural science). It is noticeable, for example, that, when he promoted explanation applying probability hypotheses from being only an approximation to deductive explanation to being a model in its own right (1962, p. 100), what he said justified its new status was not some emendation of an a priori conception of explanation now seen to have been in error, but simply the fact that natural scientists explain in accordance with it. Again, when explanation by spatiotemporally limited laws, of which there was no hint in Hempel's original presentation, are also welcomed into the explanatory fold (1965, p. 459), the argument is simply that, given a second look, many of the most prestigious explanatory laws of physics turn out to have been, at any rate in their first formulation, laws of precisely this kind.

The extent of this scientific prescriptivism is sometimes obscured by a way in which Hempel responds to critics who point to what they regard as nonnomological kinds of explanation in history. His reply is frequently that these can be ignored since his concern is only to show what 'scientific' explanation in that discipline would have to be like, which the proffered kinds are not. But there is a tautological tinge to this apparently conciliatory remark. All it says, taken literally, is that if that historians want to give explanations which are appropriately called scientific, they will have to explain things as scientists do. The point at issue, however, is whether that is the kind of explanation they should always be trying to give. There is a questionably persuasive aspect, too, to Hempel's stating his project in this way. For 'scientific' is a word with a normative as well as a descriptive meaning; and while most historians would probably want their inquiries to be regarded as scientific in the sense of meeting appropriate standards of rational investigation, the question is how far such standards require them to offer explanations like those found in the physical sciences.[12] A further element of persuasion rather than argument appears in Hempel's occasional description of ideal historical inquiry not as 'scientific', but as 'empirical' (1942, p. 352; 1962, p. 123). Most historians would also want to be thought empirical rather than, say, speculative (the contrast which Hempel had in mind when dismissing concepts without empirical content). But whether explanations which are empirically grounded must be nomological in their internal structure is, again, part of what has to be decided. Tautology and persuasion coalesce when Hempel (1962, p. 103) defends the probabilistic model by remarking that it has already enjoyed "extensive and highly successful explanatory use" in natural science—as if the extent of its "success" could be judged independently of determining whether its use was explanatory at all. Indeed, as he at one point hints himself (1962, p. 124), his enterprise often gives the appearance of being simply an application to history of a general doctrine about the conceptual and methodological unity of the empirical sciences, history being assumed to be a candidate science. If historians like D. H. Fischer (1971, p. 128, n. 38) see a looming Procrustean bed here, it is hard to blame them.

Most of Hempel's critics would agree with him nevertheless that philosophy of history should not be uncritical of the discipline which it aims to explicate: that what is needed is indeed not a mere description, but a rational reconstruction of good historical practice. The disagreement is about is what this comes to. As Weingartner puts it, in the course of deploring what he saw as a "stalemate" in the controversy over the covering-law model as early as 1961, the most fundamental difference between Hempel and his critics is the different ideas they have about the 'correct distance' a philosopher of a discipline should keep from the practice of the discipline being examined. Weingartner sees Hempel as having in fact moved appreciably toward a middle position on this point as the controversy progressed, evidence of this being found in his admission of a second, less demanding, model, and his allowing that much of what he originally seemed to reject as pseudoexplanation had value at least as explanation in a pragmatic sense. But, as I noted earlier, what Hempel describes as merely pragmatic aspects of explanation will appear to many of his critics as points of conceptual logic. And his refusal to advance from explanatory dualism to explanatory pluralism will to many of them seem more than a little arbitrary. These are not easy issues to resolve.

Yet despite disagreements that remain about how a rational reconstruction should proceed, Hempel served philosophy of history well in promoting the idea that, in some appropriate sense, such reconstruction is the proper goal of philosophers of history. For, although this may have gone beyond his intention, it has encouraged a number of them (e.g., Murphey 1973, pp. 103–12; Goldstein 1976, pp. 102–24; McCullagh 1984, pp. 91–128; Raymond Martin 1989, chap. 3) to undertake analyses of actual argumentation in history at a level of precision and detail that had not been attempted before—a development which, one hopes, will go some way toward meeting the recurring objection of historians that little is to be learned about their discipline from the analyses of individual sentences torn from their contexts that have so often seemed to them to mark the limits of philosophical interest and expertise. Whether further work of this kind will place the Hempelian theory in a more favorable light, or whether it will give further support to his critics, cannot, of course, be said in advance. And whether enough of it will be done to settle anything will depend at least partly on how much of the available philosophical energy is diverted to the new philosophy of history-as-literature, whose advocates have little interest in clarifying logical structures, whether in Hempel's sense or in some broader one.

NOTES

1. Toynbee's work made only casual observations about historical inquiry; Oakeshott's considered it within a general framework of idealist philosophy; Mandelbaum's dealt mainly with views of nineteenth-century continental thinkers; Collingwood's expounded a theory of historical knowledge already sketched in a public lecture he gave in 1936, and subsequently incorporated into his posthumous book *The Idea of History*. It is indicative of Hempel's impact that his views dominated discussion even after the publication of the latter, arguably the most important book on the epistemology of history ever written by an English-speaking author.

2. For a less monumental but revelatory presentation of his position, see White (1966).

3. As Fetzer (1975, p. 88) points out, in the more usual sense of having a combination of characteristics not in fact found together in any other occurrence—for

example, being a revolution in which a tennis court oath was sworn—there is, in principle, no reason why an explanation of a unique event in terms of laws could not be offered.

4. To the extent that the other social sciences similarly find and use mainly limited laws—an increasingly common view of anthropology and economics at least—they will themselves be history, with no claim to provide a generally necessary support to 'ordinary' historical writing.

5. A position to which he does not respond is the non-covering-law analysis of action explanation offered by Donagan (1957b, chap. 8; 1964, pp. 146–55) and taken further by von Wright (1971, chap. 3) and Rex Martin (1977, pp. 66–73).

6 Passmore (1958, p. 273) maintains, with Hempel's approval (1965, pp.428–9), that unless this is done, a how-possibly explanation must remain a mere guess, but does not say how he justifies this call for explanatory overkill.

7. For all three of these alleged limitations on causal explanation, it is easy enough to think of plausible counterinstances. It might be noted, too, that Hempel himself sometimes uses the term 'cause' in ways not captured by his own theory of the concept, as when he speaks of antecedent conditions 'causing' something to be explained (e.g. 1942, p. 347).

8. See, for example, Social Science Research Council (1946, pp. 136–7).

9. Assuming the acceptability of the analysis of causal selection presented earlier, it might be observed, too, that the cause of a process continuing as it does will sometimes be found in its preceding state, and sometimes in the addition, as pointed out by Danto (1965, chap. 11).

10. There is also the analogous, if murkier, problem of determining endings for narratives which set out to trace consequences from a given point of departure—narratives perhaps bearing titles like "The Legacy of Versailles." Hexter (1961, p. 12) makes it a matter of professional historical judgment that the consequences of the Treaty of Madrid of 1527 have long ago ceased accruing. Philosophers of history have been slow to ask on what basis such judgments can legitimately be made.

11. A good example is his courteous but firm, and certainly justified, correction (1962, p. 159–60) of an ill-considered assertion by me that impulsive or unreflective actions are sometimes explicable by reference to thoughts which the agents would have had, had they not acted "in a flash."

12. Historians themselves, as stressed by Collingwood (1946, pp. 249–66), often claim to be 'scientific' in their own way.

REFERENCES

Ankersmit, F. A. 1983. *Narrative Logic*. Boston: M. Nijhoff.

Atkinson, R. F. 1978). *Knowledge and Explanation in History*. Bloomington: Indiana University Press.

Brodbeck, May. 1962. "Explanation, Prediction, and 'Imperfect' Knowledge." In *Minnesota Studies in the Philosophy of Science*, edited by Herbert Feigl and Grover Maxwell. Vol. 3. Minneapolis: University of Minnesota Press.

Collingwood, R. G. 1936. "Human Nature and Human History." "Reprinted in Collingwood (London, 1936).

———. 1939. *An Autobiography*. Oxford: Oxford University Press.

———. 1940. *An Essay on Metaphysics*. Oxford: Clarendon Press.

———. 1946. *The Idea of History*. Oxford: Clarendon Press.

Danto, Arthur 1965. *Analytical Philosophy of History*. New York: Cambridge University Press.

———. 1995. "The Decline and Fall of the Analytical Philosophy of History." In *A New Philosophy of History*, edited by F. A. Ankersmit and Hans Kellner. Chicago: University of Chicago Press.

Donagan, Alan 1957a. "Explanation in History." Reprinted in *Mind* 64(1957):145–64. Gardiner (1959).

———. 1957b. *The Later Philosophy of R. G. Collingwood*. Oxford: Clarendon Press.

———. 1964. "The Popper-Hempel Theory Reconsidered." *History and Theory* 4, pp. 3–26. Reprinted in *Philosophical Analysis and History*, edited by W. Dray. New York: Harper and Row.

Donnellan, K. S. 1967. "Reasons and Cause." In *The Encyclopedia of Philosophy*, edited by Paul Edward, Vol. 7. New York: Macmillan.

Dray, W. H. 1954. "Explanatory Narrative in History." *Philosophical Quarterly* 4:17–27.

———. 1957. *Laws and Explanation in History*. Oxford: Oxford University Press.

———. 1959. "'Explaining What' in History." In Gardiner (1959).

———. 1978. "Concepts of Causation in A. J. P. Taylor's Account of the Origins of the Second World War." *History and Theory* 17:149–74.

———. 1984. "Conflicting Interpretations in History." In *Hermeneutics: Questions and Prospects*, edited by Gary Shapiro and Alan Sica. Amherst, Mass.: University of Massachusetts Press.

Elton, Geoffrey.1970. *Political History*. New York: Basic Books.

Feigl, Herbert, and Wilfrid Sellars. 1949 *Readings in Philosophical Analysis*. New York: Appleton-Century-Crofts.

Fetzer, J. H. 1975. "On the Historical Explanation of Unique Events."*Theory and Decision* 6:87–97.

Fischer, D. H. 1971. *Historians' Fallacies*. London: Routledge and Kegan Paul.

Frankel, Charles 1957. "Explanation and Interpretation in History." Reprinted in Gardiner (1959).

Gallie, W. B. 1955. "Explanation in History and the Genetic Sciences." *Mind* 64, pp. 160–80. Reprinted in Gardiner (1959).

———. 1964. *Philosophy and the Historical Understanding*. New York:

Gardiner, Patrick. 1952. *The Nature of Historical Explanation*. Oxford: Oxford University Press.

Gardiner, Patrick, ed. 1959. *Theories of History*. Glencoe, Ill.: The Free Press.

Ginsberg, Jerry. 1975. "The Implications of Analytic Philosophy of History for the Practicing Historian." *Historical Methods Newsletter* 8:121–33.

Goldstein, Leon. 1976. *Historical Knowing*. Austin, Tex.: University of Texas Press.

Hart, H. L. A., and A. M. Honoré. 1959. *Causation in the Law*. Oxford: The Clarendon Press.

Hempel, C. G. 1942. "The Function of General Laws in History." Reprinted in Gardiner (1959).

———. 1962."Explanation in Science and in History." In *Frontiers of Science and Philosophy*, edited by R. G. Colodny. Pittsburgh: . Reprinted in *Philosophical Analysis and History*, edited by W. H. Dray. New York: Harper and Row.

———. 1963. "Reasons and Covering Laws in Historical Explanation." In *Philosophy and History*, edited by Sidney Hook. New York: New York University Press.

———. 1965. *Aspects of Scientific Explanation*. New York: The Free Press.

Hexter, J. H. 1961. *Reappraisals in History*. London: Longmans.

————. 1971a. *Doing History*. Bloomington, IN: Indiana University Press.

————. 1971b. *The History Primer*. New York: Basic Books.

Homans, G. C. 1961. *Social Behavior: Its Elementary Forms*. New York: Harcourt, Brace, & World.

Joynt, C. B., and Nicholas Rescher. 1961. "The Problem of Uniqueness in History." *History and Theory* 1:150–62.

Lower, R. M. 1943. "Two Ways of Life." In the *Canadian Historical Association. Report*. Reprinted in *Approaches to Canadian History*, edited by Carl Berger. Toronto: Copp Clark Pitman.

Mandelbaum, Maurice. 1938. *The Problem of Historical Knowledge*. New York: Liveright Publishing Company.

————. 1967. "A Note on History as Narrative." *History and Theory*, 6:413–9.

————. 1977. *The Anatomy of Historical Knowledge*. Baltimore: Johns Hopkins Press.

Martin, Raymond. 1989. *The Past within Us: An Empirical Approach to Philosophy of History*. Princeton: Princeton University Press.

Martin, Rex. 1977. *Historical Explanation: Re-enactment and Practical Inference*. Ithaca, N.Y.: Cornell University Press.

Mazlish, Bruce. 1963. "On Rational Explanation in History." In *Philosophy and History*, edited by Sidney Hook. New York: New York University Press.

McCullagh, C. B. 1984. *Justifying Historical Descriptions*. Cambridge: Cambridge University Press.

Mink, L. O. 1966. "The Autonomy of Historical Understanding." *History and Theory* 5:24–47.

————. 1970. "History and Fiction as Modes of Comprehension." *New Literary History* 1:541–58.

————. 1973. "The Divergence of History and Sociology in Recent Philosophy of History." In *Logic, Methodology and Philosophy of Science*, edited by Patrick Suppes et al. Vol. 4. Amsterdam: North Holland.

Murphey, M. G. 1973. *Our Knowledge of the Historical Past*. Indianapolis: Bobbs-Merrill.

Nagel, Ernest. 1952. "Some Issues in the Logic of Historical Analysis." Reprinted in *Scientific Monthly* 74, March, pp. 162–9.

Oakeshott, Michael. 1933. *Experience and its Modes*. Cambridge: Cambridge University Press.

Passmore, John. 1958. "Review Article: Law and Explanation in History." *Australian Journal of Politics and History* 4:269–75.

————. 1962. "Explanation in Everyday Life, in Science, and in History." *History and Theory* 2:105–23.

Ritter, Harry. 1986. *Dictionary of Concepts in History*. Westport, CT: Greenwood Press.

Scriven, Michael. 1959. "Truisms as the Grounds for Historical Explanation." In Gardiner (1959).

————. 1966. "Causes, Connections and Conditions in History." In *Philosophical Analysis and History*, edited by W. H. Dray. New York: Harper and Row.

Social Science Research Council Committee on Historiography. 1946. *Theory and Practice in Historical Study*. Bulletin 54. New York.

Stover, Robert. 1967. *The Nature of Historical Thinking*. Chapel Hill, N.C.: University of North Carolina Press.

Toynbee, A. J. 1934. *A Study of History*. Vols. 1–6. London: Oxford University Press.

von Wright, G. H. 1971. *Explanation and Understanding*. London: Routledge and Kegan Paul.

Walsh, W. H. 1951. *An Introduction to Philosophy of History*. London: Hutchinson.

———. 1963. "Historical Causation." Reprinted in *Ideas of History*, edited by R. H. Nash. Vol. 2. New York: Dutton.

Watkins, J. W. N. 1952. "Ideal Types and Historical Explanations." Reprinted in *Readings in Philosophy of Science*, edited by Herbert Feigl and May Brodbeck. New York: Appleton-Century-Crofts.

Weingartner, Rudolph. 1961. "The Quarrel about Historical Explanation." Reprinted in *Ideas of History*, edited by R. H. Nash. Vol. 2. New York: Dutton.

White, H. V. 1966. "The Burden of History." *History and Theory* 5:111–34.

———. 1973a. *Metahistory*. Baltimore: Johns Hopkins Press.

———. 1973b. "The Politics of Contemporary Philosophy of History." *Clio* 3:35–53.

White, Morton. 1943. "Historical Explanation." Reprinted in Gardiner (1959).

———. 1965. *Foundations of Historical Knowledge*. New York: Harper and Row.

Zagorin, Perez. 1959. "Historical Knowledge: a Review Article on the Philosophy of History." *Journal of Modern History* 31:243–55.

10

Reasonable People

PHILIP KITCHER

When Charles Darwin was considering whether or not to propose to his cousin Emma Wedgwood, he divided a clean sheet of paper into two columns, noting on one side the benefits of marriage (delight of female society, the regular schedule of domestic life) and, on the other, the costs (loss of freedom to attend meetings of scientific colleagues, time wasted in frivolous family pursuits). Presumably, Darwin believed that noting these points explicitly would enable him to appreciate their relative value. And perhaps it did, for, in a far less careful and restrained hand, he scribbled at the bottom of the page "Marry! Marry! Marry!"

For his presidential address to the Eastern Division of the American Philosophical Association, C. G. Hempel chose the topic of rational action, proposing an explication that might well have been illustrated by Darwin's account of his own decision-making. Hempel's article divided into two parts, corresponding to the two aspects of the notion of rationality, one normative (or, in his terminology, "critical") and concerned with the appraisal of actions, the other focused on the explanation of action. Rational action, according to Hempel, must be understood relative to the agent's ends and to the agent's information: a rational agent is one who maximizes the chances of attaining her ends, given her beliefs about the world.[1] This conception of rationality can play a normative role, in helping us to commend those who "do the best they can" to achieve their goals, and it can also figure in explanations of human behavior that appeal to the fact that the agents are rational. So we can praise Darwin for maximizing his expected utility, and we can view his marriage to Emma Wedgwood as explained in terms of his rationality and the appropriateness of the union as a means for obtaining his ends.

But there is an obvious tension here. Darwin's scribble at the foot of the columns may testify to the fact that his exercise had brought him to act in a way that would maximize his utilities, given his beliefs, but it may signal something quite different, an impatience with—even a revulsion at—the idea of settling the issue in any such way, a response to his love for Emma.[2] Maybe the correct explanation of Darwin's proposal to his cousin is not that he perceived the match as maximizing his chances to attain his ends, but that he was overwhelmed by passions in ways that would have obliterated all other considerations. If that is so, can his action still count as rational? And, if it cannot, does the denial of rationality function here as a kind of criticism, or the attribution of rationality as a form of praise?

The idea that rational action consists in maximizing perceived expected utility[3] has been rich and powerful in many fields, most prominently in economics, political theory, and philosophy. Hempel's career overlapped the modern articulation of the idea, and he was instrumental in its philosophical refinement. Characteristically, his presidential address is a model of lucidity, notable for its attention to philosophical presuppositions and distinctions that are needed to cope with challenging examples of action. Yet, in its double project, its attempt to present as clearly as possible the critical concept and, at the same time, to assimilate rational explanation to psychological explanation (and thus, ultimately, to Hempel's preferred model of scientific explanation), the essay brings to the fore the concerns my example of Darwin's decision-making is intended to dramatize. To put the point simply and crudely, the notion of rational action Hempel reconstructs in the first half of his address is generated by abstracting from certain kinds of questions about the agent; to deploy the notion in the explanation of human action, we are to integrate it with the features of the agent's psychological life that were purposely omitted; nonetheless, it is claimed, the notion serves as a universal standard of commendation; the danger, of course, is that that may seem quite absurd in instances in which there are other kinds of psychological virtues and defects.

My aim in what follows is to explore this theme, and to try to understand what role, if any, a utility-maximizing notion of rationality might play in the explanation of human behavior. I shall start by standing back and asking why we might want any concept of this sort at all.

The point of clarifying normative concepts is that those who study the clarified versions may appreciate the standards that are pertinent to certain areas of conduct and, in consequence, may adjust their actions. This means that, to fulfil its function, the explication of a normative concept should satisfy a condition of *feasibility*:

(1)   An analysis of N is feasible just in case it is possible for individuals to adjust their behavior in ways that increase the probability that it will satisfy the analysans.[4]

I'm going to suggest that the rationality of action emerges as an important normative concept because of the difficulty of providing feasible analyses of more ambitious notions.

Philosophy, in its grandest conception, offers a vision of how to live. Many of the greatest figures in the history of the subject, from the ancient Greeks to the present, have endeavored to provide systematic visions, and, if academic philosophers (particularly, but not solely, in the twentieth century) have been skeptical about such large pretensions, their more particular inquiries are often heir to them. The ultimate normative concept is that of the good life, and it would be a notable achievement if someone could provide an analysis of that concept meeting the feasibility condition (1). Unfortunately, attempts to say what makes for a good life either elicit the criticism that they are parochial and confining or offer such bland accounts that they have no purchase on action. Consider:

(2)   *X* leads a good life just in case *X* has worthy goals and has true beliefs about how to realize them.

Without further advice about what makes a goal worthy and how one obtains true beliefs, this is quite useless, and the feasibility condition (1) exposes just why it is defective.

Of course, many thinkers have been prepared to say more on both these topics. Perhaps the most influential views have been those that ground the worthiness of goals in the ultimate end of the soul's union with a deity, seeing the good life as one involving the pursuit of goals that are given meaning by this end. Contemporary philosophy in the English-speaking world is profoundly suspicious of any substantive account of the worthiness of goals, not only because of widespread skepticism about the existence of a deity, but also because of the legacy of appeals for toleration. From Locke, through the framers of the Constitution, to John Stuart Mill, powerful voices have portrayed the enterprise of trying to specify worthy goals for all as epistemically immodest and inappropriately paternalistic.

In the extreme form, the position is crystallized in a famous passage from Hume's *Treatise*:

> Where a passion is neither founded on false suppositions, nor chooses means insufficient for the end, the understanding can neither justify nor condemn it. 'Tis not contrary to reason to prefer the destruction of the whole world to the scratching of my finger. (Hume/Selby-Bigge 1967, p. 416)

Even those who think that Hume's denial of any constraints on personal goals beyond truth of presuppositions and the commitment of personal passion is an overstatement are likely to believe that the constraints on the worthiness of goals can't be specified without some reference to the agent—that the worthiness of a goal depends on what *an individual* would feel or judge, if that individual were placed in the right circumstances (made vividly aware of possibilities, released from various internal and external pressures, and so forth). This is the Millian strain in our thinking about the worthiness of goals, that we cannot prescribe to others but may only arrange for them to occupy positions from which they may best judge for themselves.[5]

Once we have reached this point, the original enterprise of normative analysis, that of finding a surrogate for (2) that would satisfy (1), looks wrongheaded: either we should simply abandon any general account of the worthiness of goals, simply considering norms for the attainment of whatever goals agents have; or we should divide the project into two parts, one concerned with whatever advice can be given for the setting of goals, the other focused on goal attainment. So we replace the first analysandum, "X leads a good life," with a second, "X is a successful agent." Here, it seems, we can simply retain part of (2), and offer

(3)   X is a successful agent just in case X has true beliefs about how to realize X's goals (whatever those happen to be).

Now there are two very obvious concerns about (3). One is that it seems quite possible for an agent to have true beliefs about which actions will lead to his goals and yet for him to fail to act in the appropriate way.[6] Having knowledge is one thing, using it another. A second worry, in line with the thoughts that prompted the shift from (2) to (3), is that we still haven't satisfied the feasibility condition (1). Advising people to have true beliefs about matters of concern to them is not tremendously helpful, and, as before, the more substantive proposals along these lines are either too vague to overcome the trouble—recall Leibniz's cutting comments on Descartes's rules of method—or else vulnerable to cogent objections.[7] The two points work together to suggest a further bifurcation of the normative enterprise. The first part would assemble standards for the critical assessment of beliefs, providing criteria of confirmation expected to increase the probability that agents acquire and retain correct beliefs. The second would focus on the norms for translation of belief into action. With the latter we come, at last, to the normative project undertaken by Hempel in his presidential address, although, of course, on other occasions, he had made major contributions to the former enterprise (see, in particular, Hempel 1945).

The original grand venture has now divided into three parts, one concerned with whatever may be said (possibly not much, even nothing [Hume]) about the framing of goals, one devoted to the critical evaluation of belief, and a final, rather modest piece about the application of belief in action. With respect to this last project, Hempel offers the following analysis.

(4)   X is a rational agent, relative to X's beliefs and goals, just in case, on the basis of the probability structure derived from those beliefs, and the utility structure derived from those goals, X's actions maximize expected utility. (Alternatively, and more simply: just in case X's actions maximize perceived expected utility.)

Now there are serious and well-known concerns about this analysis, alleging that while we can think of ourselves as having beliefs and goals, those states do not fix unique probability and utility structures. I shall not pursue these here, since I want to press the argument in a rather different direction. Specifically, I want to consider how (4) looks when we regard it in light of the more general normative project from which it descends.

A first and most obvious question results from the fact that our earlier reformulations of analysanda were largely motivated by the difficulties of meeting the feasibility condition (1). How does (4) fare in this regard? At first sight, one might think that the difficulty has been completely overcome, because we envisage a process in which agents identify their probability and utility structures, go through the pertinent calculations, and perform that action which is assigned the greatest expected utility. But (4) doesn't actually commend any such process—indeed it is quite neutral on any psychological implementation.[8] Outside of classes in probability theory and decision theory, cases in which agents actually compute the expected utilities of various outcomes are surely rare—Darwin's account of his premarital musings is quite unusual. So, if the idea is that (4) is feasible because it points to a calculational process, we ought to object that that kind of process isn't present in most agents. If these agents are rational, then there must be some other way in which they satisfy (4). How do they do it? Are there alternative processes that people might follow that would increase the chances of their maximizing expected utility? If so, are these processes best seen as approximations to the ideal of doing the calculation explicitly, so that most of the time we muddle along using heuristics and short-cuts that bring us (with luck) to accord with (4), when we might (at least in principle) be proceeding more systematically in the manner of our decision-theory exercises? Is the explicit calculation always the most reliable way of satisfying (4)? And, finally, does satisfying (4) always fit with the broader aims of the normative project from which (4) derives?

I want to consider these questions by looking at a range of instances. Several of these will raise familiar concerns about the treatment of rational action in terms of maximizing expected utility. I hope, however, that the points will look rather different in the context of the discussion so far.

Let's first imagine Ambrose, who has been placed in a standard decision-theoretic situation. He has a choice between two lottery tickets, one which will pay $50 with probability 0.8, one which will pay $40 with probability 0.9, and he knows these figures and the probabilities. Ambrose's utilities are directly proportional to the dollar values, and there are no interfering effects from risk aversion. Indeed, the expected utilities of choosing the tickets are, as we'd anticipate, 40 for the first, and 36 for the second. The decision theorists who are studying Ambrose are glad to observe that he makes the choice that maximizes expected utility by taking the first ticket, and, since they accept (4), they count Ambrose as acting rationally on this occasion.

However, the decision theorists don't know why Ambrose did what he did. He didn't perform the elementary calculation—Ambrose is dreadful at arithmetic, and, if he'd done so, he might well have reached the wrong answer—but chose the tickets because the first one was blue, his favorite color. If the second ticket had been blue and the first red, then he would have chosen the second. So, even though Ambrose accords with (4), he does so as a matter of luck. Does Ambrose act rationally? I think not. We became interested in the notion of rational action because we recognized that *success* could be a matter of luck, and we wanted to single out those individuals who "do the best they can." Even recognizing Ambrose's flawed arithmetical abilities (he's bad, but his performance is significantly better than chance), he didn't do the best he could to achieve his ends.

It seems fairly clear how we ought to respond to this difficulty. Analysis (4), as it stands, is too weak, and we should amend it to demand that the process that issues in the action be the most reliable way available to the agent of performing an action that would maximize perceived expected utility. So we arrive at

(5) X is a rational agent, relative to X's beliefs and goals, just in case
       X's actions maximize perceived expected utility, and those actions
       result from processes that are, among those available to X, most
       reliable in issuing in actions that maximize perceived expected
       utility.

Notice that this connects directly with our earlier concerns about the feasibility of normative analyses in its assumption that there are processes under agents' control that differ in their reliability with respect to the maximization of perceived expected utility.

The decision-theorists who have been watching Ambrose now learn of the processes that underlie his actions, and, suitably appalled, enroll him in their classes. Although his arithmetic does not improve significantly, he becomes adept at setting up real-life problems in terms of probabilities and utilities. Now, when offered choices between lottery tickets, he conceptualizes the situation in terms of the expected utilities, and often he arrives at the action that maximizes perceived expected utility. Sometimes, however, he makes small arithmetical mistakes and, in consequence, chooses an inferior ticket. According to both (4) and (5), on these occasions Ambrose does not act rationally. This, I submit, should strike us as peculiar, in that Ambrose's rationality shouldn't depend on his flawed mastery of a very particular type of symbolic manipulation, the fact that he sometimes misremembers parts of the multiplication tables or forgets to carry digits. Notice that, in developing the notion of rationality, we've already abstracted from the contents of the agent's beliefs—Hempel is very clear that he wants to separate the issue of the rationality of action from the truth or justification of the beliefs underlying the action. Why, then, do we retain the notion that a rational agent has to be a flawless calculator?

We could avoid this consequence by amending (5), giving priority to the newly added conjunct, and departing further from (4):

(6) X is a rational agent, relative to X's beliefs and goals, just in case
       X's actions result from processes that are, among those available to
       X, most reliable in issuing in actions that maximize perceived
       expected utility.

Analysis (6) stands to (4) somewhat as rule-utilitarianism relates to act-utilitarianism. Now it seems that, even on the occasions when he miscalculates, Ambrose counts as a rational agent. Yet we might have doubts from a different direction. After all, if Ambrose were self-aware (and he knows he has been losing a few points on his decision-theory tests because of arithmetical slips), he'd know that he could do better if he were to invest in a calculator. Indeed, he gets

offered sufficiently many lottery choices that, if we set up the situation properly, the utility-maximizing strategy would be to buy a calculator and use it on
each occasion (the costs of the calculator would be quickly regained through
the reduction in frequency of arithmetical errors). But Ambrose doesn't think
of this. He simply proceeds by doing the computations himself, sometimes reaching the wrong answers. Does this affect his rationality?

According to (6), it does; (6) demands that agents use the best available processes
for performing perceived-utility-maximizing actions, and Ambrose's current
procedure, while good, is suboptimal. Yet we'd do well to reflect on the kind of
cognitive deficiency that Ambrose is exhibiting. Whereas before he was bad at
symbolic manipulation, now he's unimaginative in setting up his options, failing
to see the recurrent decisions as part of a sequence that could be approached in a
systematic way that would lower the number of errors. This is surely a lapse on
his part, but it seems wrong to describe it as a lapse from rationality.

So there are reasons to worry that (6) is too stringent, that it too lumps
together various kinds of cognitive virtues and defects under a blanket heading
of "rationality." Let that pass, for the moment, and suppose that Ambrose is
brought to see the benefits that would accrue from buying the calculator. Having made the investment, he now handles the lottery choices by framing them
in decision-theoretic terms (his forte ever since he took the class) and punching
away at the buttons. Virtually all of the time he reaches the right answer, and
would count as a rational agent according to either (5) or (6). Once in a while
his fingers slip or stick and he comes to faulty conclusions, but, even on these
occasions, (6) tolerates him as a rational agent—as indeed it should since finger
dexterity isn't the sine qua non of rationality. Whatever we say about the early,
precalculator Ambrose, it now appears that (6) is adequate to this phase.

But wait! We haven't yet explored Ambrose's rationale for trusting the calculator or for conceptualizing the lotteries in terms of his decision-theory class.
My description tacitly portrays Ambrose as a sensible fellow doing the best he
can to improve his performance, but that's a far cry from the truth. Ambrose
was converted to taking decision theory because he became besotted with Arabella,
a teacher of probability, on whose every word he hangs, and it's because of her
influence over him that he sets up his decisions in the ways he does and thinks
of the calculator as an advance over his own computations. Were Arabella to
tell him to approach his decision situations by reading chicken entrails, Ambrose
would start raising chickens. In short, although his actions now result from
processes that are optimally designed to maximize his perceived expected utilities, he undergoes those processes as a result of passions that are hard to assimilate to sources of rationality, passions that might easily have led him to
follow quite different decision strategies and to perform quite different actions.

So (6) is also too weak, and it is too weak because it shares a feature that made
(4) vulnerable. Just as we modified (4) to (5) and (6), so too we could make a
parallel move on (6), insisting that the causes of the agent's undergoing processes that would most reliably lead to perceived-utility-maximizing action
themselves be most reliable for producing this effect. It's easy to conceive a

further dialectic of the type in which we've been engaged—we could explore whether we ought to demand reliability at one level if we have reliability at the more fundamental level (as in the move from [5] to [6]) and whether we ought to insist on optimal reliability. But in the end, we'd come back to the possibility that the reliable strategies for pursuing reliable strategies for maximizing expected utility might themselves be fortuitously produced, and that would invite a retreat to a yet more basic level at which we could go through the same considerations, and so, on and on and on.[9]

Enough of scenes from the life of Ambrose. I now want to switch to a different kind of example, and a different range of concerns. Consider Bathsheba, about to go on a long plane journey. She visits her local bookstore to buy something appropriate to while away the tedious hours. As she enters she recalls the name of an author whose past books she has enjoyed, and this leads her to look on the shelves for a new title by the same person. Finding three of the author's books that she hasn't previously read, she quickly scans the brief descriptions on the back cover, finds them all promising and chooses the fattest (on grounds that it will surely last the whole journey).

Bathsheba's action strikes one as completely rational, and yet it probably didn't *maximize* her perceived expected utility. Her tastes are catholic, and many authors whom she admires have books that she hasn't yet read. As we might expect, Hempel was fully aware that there are occasions on which we have many ways to satisfy our ends, but he points out that we must always be careful to consider the situation relative to our *total set of ends*.[10] If we look at a situation from a restricted perspective, focusing just on an agent's current goal, then it may appear that many options are available, even though a more comprehensive view would show that some of the apparent possibilities would tell against the attainment of other ends.

Now if Bathsheba were to try to maximize her expected utility, say by scrutinizing her bookshelves, making an ordered list of the authors she admires, erasing the names of those whom she believes not to have written anything she hasn't yet read, going to the bookstore, assembling all the likely possibilities, reading the first few pages of each, she might expect to do a bit better at the book selection task. But the time she would spend would deprive her of the ability to buy other things she needs for her trip, and, overall, she would be worse off. So, as Hempel suggests, we have to see her actions in a broader context. Book selection is one among a number of tasks Bathsheba has to perform in a limited time. For each task there's a level she'd like to meet, and she wants to perform every task at or above its appropriate level. Hence we might think that *this* is the goal, and Bathsheba's action is rational if she chooses a strategy that maximizes her chances of achieving it.

But maximizing isn't any more appropriate at this level. Proceeding on the basis of her past experience, Bathsheba pursues a strategy that typically gets the job done: she knows herself well enough to understand that she'll usually think of the name of an author when she starts looking at the shelves. She doesn't engage in any systematic assessment of possible strategies (and it may be that to do so would consume time that would detract from her performance) but acts from heuristics. Because those heuristics generally work quite well, she has no reason to reconsider them or to try to refine them. I submit that there's no reason to demand that Bathsheba maximize anything if she is to count as rational.

Bathsheba has a friend, Corinna, who also travels a lot, and whose preparations are a tiny bit more successful than Bathsheba's. Corinna does take a moment before she leaves home to review her bookshelves, and, most of the time, this enables her to make choices that are slightly superior to Bathsheba's. Very occasionally, when the traffic is heavy, the delay is costly, and Corinna fails to complete one of her errands. But this happens so rarely that she does marginally better at satisfying her desires than does her friend. Even Corinna doesn't maximize expected utility (she'd do just a bit better if she tuned in to traffic reports and adjusted her book-buying strategy accordingly), but Bathsheba would improve her goal attainment if she imitated Corinna. Does that mean that Bathsheba is irrational?

I don't think so. We know how to describe the difference between the two women, and it's not in terms of rationality and irrationality: Corinna is more methodical than Bathsheba, that's all. For lots of situations of decision and action, being methodical is a good thing. But not always. One day, Corinna takes her nephew to the beach. As she reclines in her deckchair the surf comes up and she sees, with horror, that her nephew and another child, a little girl, are struggling for their lives. Unlike Bathsheba, who would have plunged in immediately to rescue her nephew, Corinna pauses a moment to take stock, considering whether the fact that the girl is a bit closer to shore ought to make a difference to her action. Her reflection is brief, and she swims quickly and efficiently to her nephew, dragging him from the surf (the little girl, unsupervised, unfortunately drowns). Corinna's "one thought too many"[11] didn't make any difference to the outcome, for she managed to save one child. However, if we suppose that Corinna didn't know that her reflection would make no difference (it's not that she wondered if it wouldn't, but she simply didn't think about the issue) then there's something amiss with her action. I suggest that her behavior on this occasion, in contrast to the way in which Bathsheba would have acted, is irrational and that its irrationality stems from the inappropriateness of Corinna's habit of being methodical in the present context. At present, I simply rest this claim on an intuitive response to the case. Later, I'll try to justify it by developing a broader perspective for appraising actions.

Being imaginative and considering options is a cognitive virtue. Being methodical and trying to stand back from the situation in order to think about what would be best is also a cognitive virtue. But there are occasions on which either virtue can have a paralysing effect on our actions. Part of being rational, or, as I would prefer to say, "being reasonable," is having habits of mind that exercise cognitive virtues within their appropriate limits.

So we return to Darwin. Let's assume that Darwin's account omits some detail, that he really sat down and put numerical values on various outcomes (+30 for the joys of female society and so forth), that he identified point probabilities where the consequences were uncertain, that he did the multiplications and additions, that all the calculations were correct, and that his final scribble is the record of a striking inequality. Does that make Darwin's kneeling at Emma's feet rational? The response that it does not may elicit charges of sentimentality, but I think there are deeper reasons for distrusting a decision-theoretic approach to this particular decision. A person who was self-aware and conscious of the depths of commitment required for a happy marriage would question his own ability to make the numerical judgments and would be profoundly skeptical of attempts to compute the "utility-maximizing action." Yet such a person, Darwin perhaps, might well go through precisely the exercise as Darwin originally described it, noting advantages and disadvantages of marriage, as a way of testing his emotional response to various likely situations in the years to come, and, instead of using these as a prelude to calculation, might see them as eliciting feelings that would express themselves in action. Viewed in this light, Darwin's procedure would not be the detached ratiocination it initially appears, but would be the sounding of his own emotions, and the scribbled decision would embody the successful outcome of that process. This second Darwin, who gives reason and emotion their due in making this particular type of decision, is, I submit, far more reasonable than the decision-theoretic calculator.

There are other occasions on which agents who performed a perceived-utility-maximizing action would not automatically count as rational. Consider Eustace, a college student who perceives himself as having the choice between majoring in biochemistry or majoring in biology, both subjects that bore him. Finding biology the lesser of two evils, he opts for that. Eustace would count as rational according to any of the criteria so far considered: he maximizes his perceived expected utility, and he does so because he pursues a reliable strategy for maximizing perceived expected utility. Yet, as we think more about him, that judgment is less clear, for Eustace assigns fairly large negative utilities to each of the choices he has identified. It would be rational, we feel, for him to think a bit harder about the way in which he has framed the problem. If he were to collect more information, he would come to appreciate other options, recognizing that a major in either philosophy or in music might actually increase his chances of attaining a place in medical school (a long-term goal). The rational thing for Eustace to do is to rethink the problem, not to act on the basis of his current calculation.[12]

Modify the example a bit. Now, given Eustace's goal of becoming a doctor, there really are no other options for him. Even if he were to cast around for a more satisfying course of action, he wouldn't find one. Yet the fact remains that both options look very uninviting. Stoical Eustace may forge ahead, pinching himself during those long lectures on protein–protein interactions, but rational Eustace—or, perhaps, more reasonable Eustace—would reflect on his goals. Is the negative utility of pursuing the means a signal that there are tensions among his preferences? Should Eustace reflect on his goals, asking himself why he is so determined to go to medical school, given that medical schools demand, and build on, training in subjects he detests? In this version of the story, rational Eustace—or reasonable Eustace—takes the marked negative utility of the least worst action not as the basis for gritting his teeth but as the prelude to rethinking his goals.[13]

Hempel's account of rational action appears to be immunized against this kind of example. Recall that we are to assess the rationality of an action relative to an agent's beliefs and desires (or goals). Thus it seems that, in the relative sense of rationality that concerns him, Eustace's stoicism is rational, even though, from a different perspective, the judgments of the last paragraphs would stand. But I think that the immunity has been compromised. Note first that, even given Eustace's current beliefs and desires, it may be rational for him to wonder if what he believes allows further options, that is if his framing of the problem is forced by what he currently believes. Second, if he discovers that his current beliefs do indeed preclude other possibilities, those beliefs may not rule out the possibility that some of the things he believes about his current situation are incorrect.[14] Hence, even relative to his current beliefs, Eustace's most reasonable (or even his rational) action may be to consider whether he is mistaken in those beliefs that seem to deny him a better option. Third, if he should subsequently find that those beliefs are strongly supported by available evidence (including further evidence he has sought out), he may rationally wonder if his goals are coherent, and this question may lead him to reflect carefully on what he really wants. Thus, the Hempelian directive to hold fixed the agent's desires (surely influenced by Hume's skepticism about the rational appraisal of desires) ought to allow for the rationality of self-scrutiny.

All the cases considered in this section point out the same general moral. Hempel's account rests on psychological abstraction, and it seems unclear that we should neglect the things he leaves on one side—the psychological processes that underlie action, the costs of calculation, the role of heuristics some of which reflect aspects of our personalities, the broad range of cognitive virtues, the limits of some kinds of virtues, the possibility of decisions that ought to engage the passions, the desirability of self-scrutiny both of one's options and of one's desires—when we appraise actual agents. The examples I have assembled are intended to show that the ideal we obtain by making Hempel's abstractions is a peculiar one. I now want to try to indicate how we might do better.

Let's return to the general project from which the study of rational action descends. We can envisage an individual agent trying to live well. She forms goals for herself, initially surely by absorbing many of the values of those who teach her, later comparing different approaches to life, critically reflecting on the desires she has and how they hang together. She also acquires beliefs, again initially by relying on members of her society, later evaluating the reliability of various sources and adjusting her judgments accordingly. The explication of rational action does not seek to provide norms for these tasks, but to evaluate the link between beliefs and desires and action. But if we reflect on the stories of the preceding section (particularly on the episodes involving Bathsheba and Corinna), we should appreciate that the same kind of learning goes on in the context of the translation of belief and desire into action as in the other areas. Our agent starts off, perhaps, as an impulsive child, overwhelmed by momentary desires, but she is taught strategies for resisting her urges, she learns to think before she acts, and she develops habits of responding to new decision situations. When things go well, these habits are reliable in prescribing actions that accord with her most stable desires. Reasonable people come to frame the decisions that confront them in ways that reflect their system of beliefs, but they rarely do so by systematically exploring what options their beliefs leave open (although, as we saw in the case of Eustace, there's a place for systematic exploration).

Where is there room in this picture for the notion of rational action? Surely the obvious starting point for considering rational action is in contrast to irrational behavior, and the paradigmatic example of irrational behavior is already present in the behavior of the impulsive child (or, more exactly, since we may well feel that the child can't be expected to do better, in cases where older people behave like the impulsive child). What goes wrong here is that a psychological process sweeps the agent into action that is at odds with long-term preferences: when the job candidate can't resist the offer of a cocktail, even though his background beliefs contain information sufficient to derive the conclusion that the drink would impair his ability to make a good impression, he and we are likely to evaluate the action retrospectively as irrational. Given the long philosophical history of opposing reason to the passions, it's hardly surprising that the notion of irrational action starts from recognizing instances in which passion overwhelms reason (and, as I've suggested, these examples are prominent in our psychological development). One moral of the last section is that the battle ought not always to be decided in favor of reason: passion has its place (as in the examples of Corinna on the beach and Darwin musing on marriage). Another is that the resistance to inappropriate passion is carried out by heuristics which, with luck, work well—however hard he tries Ambrose can't model Arabella's decision theory all the way down, calculating what to do, calculating how to decide what to do, calculating how to decide how to decide what to do, and so on. Even if these heuristics work well, they will have their limits, and an agent can be in the grip of a heuristic just as she can be in the grip of a passion. When Eustace applies his standard devices to generate his options about majors, he's carried along by a habit of thought that often serves him well, but the unattractiveness of his choices ought to lead him to suspend that habit and think more reflectively about his beliefs and desires.

Reasonable people are those who are aware that they may be swept away by momentary impulse, who have developed strategies for coping with that danger, whose strategies are, by and large, put to work in ways that are consonant with the seriousness of the decisions they face, who can stand back and suspend the operation of those strategies when they threaten to sweep them into actions that would realize only poorly their most stable and central desires. Reasonable people aren't always rational agents, although they are subject to the norms of the broader project from which the task of defining rational action descends. If we substituted the ideal of a reasonable person for that of a rational agent, then the psychological abstractions and idealizations that make Hempel's account so clean and compelling would have to be muddied, and the end result would be much messier. But I think we would have a normative concept that was far more valuable in application to most of the decisions we face.

Nonetheless, even in the version I've offered, there's something importantly right about the Hempelian conception of the rational agent, for the standard against which the capacities, dispositions and heuristics are appraised is that of maximization of those utilities with which the person can stably and reflectively identify.[15] My complaint, then, is that the banishment of talk of the psychological springs of action has induced thinkers to apply the idea of maximization too directly. Instead of thinking about general processes that are ultimately judged by their ability to yield actions which maximize (stable) utility—and to understand that in terms of the broader normative project I recalled in section II—the temptation has been to confront the actions themselves with the standard of maximization. To return to a philosophical analogy I employed earlier, we ought to move from act-utilitarianism to rule-utilitarianism . . . and keep going!

I want to support this proposal by looking in a bit more detail at examples of behavior that challenge the importance of rationality. In an important book, the neuroscientist Antonio Damasio describes the case of a patient who had frontal lobe damage that seemed to disrupt his decisionmaking ability.[16] The patient's responses to situations were abnormally dispassionate, and, on occasion, the absence of emotion served him well: on a winter visit to Damasio's laboratory, for example, his sang-froid enabled him to negotiate the icy road, even though a driver in front of him had skidded into a ditch. At the end of that visit, Damasio suggested two alternative dates for the next session, eliciting an extraordinary response.

> For the better part of a half-hour, the patient enumerated reasons for and against each of the two dates: previous engagements, proximity to other engagements, possible meteorological conditions, virtually anything that one could reasonably think about concerning a simple date. Just as calmly as he had driven over the ice, and recounted that episode, he was now walking us through a tiresome cost-benefit analysis, an endless outlining and fruitless comparison of options and possible consequences.[17]

The pathological obsession with considering all possible relevant information is a reminder of two important aspects of our normal decision situations. First, outside the decision-theory classroom, we aren't given a limited set of possible states and possible actions, and we could, in principle, reflect on the varied array of beliefs and goals we have to see how to explore the options and their consequences. Second, in our everyday decision-making, most of us deploy heuristics that shortcut any elaborate survey to highlight some features of our predicaments and ignore others, and, if we do perform anything like a decision-theoretic analysis, it is done against this background.

Damasio cites the examples of various patients and adduces neurophysiological evidence to suggest that the necessary framing of our decisions results from our emotional responses, both to external conditions and to the states of our body. Whether or not his hypothesis is correct in its details, his diagnosis of the case I have cited lends powerful support to the idea that a strategy of detachment, committed to painstaking exploration of all possibilities and consequences, would be pathological in most everyday decision-making, and that some unfortunate people are as much in the grip of that strategy as the chronically impulsive are subject to their momentary passions. Thus his studies reinforce the picture I have been outlining, in which reasonable people need an arsenal of heuristics (quite possibly mediated by their emotional responses in some cases), an arsenal that includes a means of suspending the operation of heuristics in contexts in which they would not prove valuable.

That picture also receives support from quite a different quarter. One obvious aspect of rational action, as we have already seen, lies in the ability of the rational agent to override momentary impulses which would deflect her from her long-term goals. In thinking about that ability, we are naturally encouraged to suppose that the dangerous situations are those constituted by (1) a stable goal G, that the agent would endorse throughout long periods of her life, (2) another goal G' that would be subordinated to G in the agent's preference structure, (3) an option on the present occasion to achieve G', and (4) information available to the agent that has the consequence that exercising that option is either incompatible with or lowers the chances of attaining G. In situations of this type, we suppose that G reflects what the agent *really* wants, and we conclude that exercising the option is irrational.

I think that there is little doubt that situations of this kind arise in virtually everyone's life, and that ascriptions of irrationality are sometimes warranted when people (as we say) "succumb to temptation". However, I also think that the tradition of blaming the passions inclines us to overinterpret the notion of an agent's "real wants," and that, in consequence, we overextend the attribution of irrationality. Thomas Schelling has insightfully commented on the readiness with which we assume that each person has a coherent set of preferences. "[W]e have become convinced (some of us) that it is futile to model collective decision on the analogy of a single individual. I suggest that the ordinary human being is sometimes also not a *single* rational individual."[18] Schelling defends this conclusion by describing a number of instances that one might readily assimilate to our paradigms of irrational behavior, but which raise challenging questions about the identification of the agent's *real* goals. As he notes, many people have conflicting, alternating but *stable* values.[19] Consider, for example, people who undertake programs of self-improvement (whether physical regimes of exercise or intellectual ventures like mastering a new language), pursuing them intermittently. Sometimes, it's fairly clear what the basic preferences are, and we can view occasions on which the person acts contrary to these preferences as involving irrationality (assuming that the person has beliefs that entail, fairly straightforwardly, that there's a conflict). But often it isn't. Often, we may be torn between seeing the desire for self-improvement as primary (so that the agent succumbs when she takes the evening off) and seeing that desire as less central to the agent's preferences (so that she is irrationally obsessive when she pursues the program), but we typically insist that there has to be a right answer, that one or other of the types of decision has to be rational, the other irrational. Schelling's point is that this is unnecessary, a flawed overworking of our notion of rational action. As he wittily puts it, we do not always know "which is Jekyll and which is Hyde."[20]

Our understanding of the complex psychological processes that underlie people's framing of goals, their identifying options, and their responses to and regulation of their emotional states is still in its infancy. I have adduced the work of Schelling and Damasio because I take them to expose, in quite different ways, the shortcomings of the views about human decision-making that lie behind the conception of rational action whose credentials we have been exploring. My own picture of the responsible person draws on their investigations, but it is admittedly vague and embryonic. As we learn more about human psychology, we may hope to remedy these imperfections.[21]

Interestingly, I think that Hempel's account of how the notion of rationality figures in explanations of human behavior anticipates the kind of diagnosis at which I have arrived. The latter sections of "Rational Action" are prompted by William Dray's well-known criticisms of the covering-law model as an account of historical explanation. Dray argued that historical explanations work not by identifying laws that govern an agent's actions, but by revealing the reasons for that action; they show that "what was done was the thing to have done for the reasons given."[22] To this, Hempel responds in a number of ways: (1) by invoking his guiding idea that explanations must make the explanandum expected to contest the view that Dray-style appeals to reasons can do this; (2) by scrutinizing the notion of "*the* thing to do"; and, most important, (3) by presenting a covering-law schema which, Hempel claims, makes better sense of Dray's preferred style of historical explanations. The significant feature of this schema is that it embodies a premise to the effect that the person whose action is to be explained was a rational agent, so that it can then recast the appeal to reasons as a generalization about the kind of action expected of a rational agent in the relevant context. By doing so, Hempel essentially transforms Dray's rational explanations into psychological explanations of a very particular kind.

Consider the kind of explanation that initially seems grist for Dray's mill. Here is a very great historian explaining some of the unsavory behavior of the Byzantine empress Theodora:

> Her rapacious avarice to accumulate an immense treasure may be excused by the apprehension of her husband's death, which could leave no alternative between ruin and the throne; and fear as well as ambition might exasperate Theodora against two generals who, during a malady of the emperor, had rashly declared that they were not disposed to acquiesce in the choice of the capital.[23]

Now we might say, following Dray, that Gibbon has explained Theodora's money-grabbing and political assassination by showing these things to be the "thing to do" (or, more exactly, the thing to do for a rational agent with Theodora's beliefs and desires). Hempel's transformation of this is to recast the explanation roughly as follows:

> Theodora was in a situation in which her own safety, power, and comfort, were threatened by her lack of personal wealth and political enemies in Justinian's court.
>
> Theodora was a rational agent, who desired safety, power, and comfort.
>
> Any rational agent who desires safety power and comfort and whose safety, power, and comfort are threatened by lack of wealth and political enemies will extort money where she can and will eliminate the enemies.
>
> ———————————————————————
>
> Therefore, Theodora extorted money and eliminated her political enemies.

I think it is fairly obvious that this is an improvement over Dray's reconstruction of such explanations, because it brings out the crucial point that Theodora's character traits are quite crucial to the explanatory force of what Gibbon says (he has just lavished several pages on the character of the empress showing her to be clever, unscrupulous, manipulative, calculating, imaginative, seductive, and so on)—there are other women (including some Byzantine women) who would not have done what Theodora did had they been in her place. But it seems to me just as clear that Hempel has not gone far enough. The all-purpose notion of rationality is much too coarse to capture the fine grain of Gibbon's explanation.[24]

Before I develop this point, I want to offer a perspective on what Hempel has achieved in his response to Dray. The situation resembles in important respects the treatment of teleological or functional explanation. If a philosopher of biology were to criticize Hempel on the grounds that explanations can sometimes be given in biology simply by identifying the biological function of an organ or system, it would be legitimate to reply that these identifications stand for a more complex schema. According to the most influential contemporary conception of function,[25] to say that the function of X is F is explanatory because it points to a selective explanation of why X is present. That is, the identification of the function is shorthand for a schema of the following type.

> In the line ancestral to present organisms of type T, there was a first generation in which T-type organisms bearing X arose.
>
> X has the effect F.
>
> T-type organisms which F have selective advantage A over T-type organisms which do not F.
>
> ———————————————————————
>
> Therefore, X spread among T-type organisms and eventually became fixed.

One might view this as a cryptic version of a more adequate schema that would appeal to general principles of evolutionary theory (for example, some principle of natural selection) and thus take it to be in conformity with the covering-law model, but that is not the important issue for this discussion.[26] The main point is that this general schema of evolutionary causal explanation stands behind, and gives explanatory power to, attributions of function. In an exactly similar way, conceding Dray's initial premise, Hempel saw that the explanatory force of invocations of rationality lies in the fact that these point to an underlying schema of psychological explanation.

This is an important insight, but I think that Hempel was misled by Dray into thinking that there was an important general style of historical explanation, comparable in general scope to the biological style of adverting to function. The biological and the historical cases are similar, but they aren't completely parallel. In historical accounts the practice of gesturing toward the rationality of the agents has nothing like the broad applicability of the biologists' invocations of function, because we are primarily interested in the psychological characteristics of past actors that made them conceptualize their options in the ways that they did. Pointing out that Theodora's actions were rational, given her beliefs and desires, takes us only a little way toward understanding her behavior—we learn far more from Gibbon's detailed portrait with its insights about her willingness to override the dictates of conventional morality.[27] Great historians offer compelling delineations of the psychological lives of individuals, and their explanations work by drawing on our expectations about the ways in which people with various kinds of psychological traits would behave.

I suggest, then, that Dray went astray in proposing the "thin" notion of rationality as the historian's analogue of the biologist's concept of function, and that Hempel accepted the centrality of the concept of rationality to historical explanation, but took the important step of seeing that explanations by appeal to rationality were psychological explanations. In light of my earlier proposals about the need to avoid the Hempelian abstractions from individual psychology, a natural moral to draw is that much[28] historical explanation consists in psychological explanation of a more substantive sort, explanation that appeals to a wide variety of cognitive and conative virtues and vices.

However, there is one type of historical explanation for which the notion of rationality might seem especially important. Consider explanations of the activities of scientists and of the growth of scientific knowledge. Here, we might feel, explanations can draw on the rationality of the actors, precisely because rational action is central to the role of scientists. Indeed, the conception of rationality invoked would be somewhat "thicker" because, in their role as scientists, people are dedicated toward particular epistemic ends—most obviously, increasing the stock of true beliefs about the natural world. Hence, we can understand the design and execution of experiments, the proposal and defense of hypotheses, the interchanges and debates among scientists, as expressions of rationality, and offer explanations by pointing out that, for an agent with certain beliefs and in a particular predicament, a specific course of action is the rational thing to do. This will set up a default style of explanation, which can be overridden on those occasions on which scientists lapse from their proper role.

To proceed in this way would resurrect one of the most vilified doctrines of recent years, the alleged asymmetry in philosophical explanations of the growth of science.[29] Now I am not sure that any philosopher has ever claimed either the kinds of asymmetry postulated by defenders of symmetry in the explanation of true and false beliefs—who sometimes appear to think that philosophers explain the growth of science by thinking that the true has a magical attraction for the mind of the scientist—or the version I have just outlined. But, in any event, there are very good reasons for thinking that the notion of rationality should not be built into a default scheme for explaining the growth of scientific knowledge, reasons that recapitulate the points I have made in earlier sections. Scientific inquiry is conducted by people with various cognitive traits, who frame problems more or less imaginatively, draw on the evidence more or less selectively, are more or less cautious, more or less inclined to maintain confidence in the face of problems; who are moved by a variety of goals, including social and moral concerns, considerations of loyalty and friendship, who are worried about their own standing and possibilities for future research; and so forth. Explanation of their activities cannot assume some simple "scientific role," defined by a conception of rationality, "thick" or "thin," but, in line with the suggestions already made, should respond to the full range of psychological capacities and dispositions. This emphatically does not mean that we can't make distinctions among such psychological attributes, that we can't talk of cognitive virtues and vices and judge them in terms of their reliability. The symmetry thesis is right in its counsel to embed the explanation of scientific practice within the framework of psychological explanation, wrong in its claim that this erodes all differences among the processes that engender belief and action.

By a curious irony, some historians who are most influenced by the ideal of symmetry effectively reintroduce the notion of rational explanation to serve as a default in their own narratives. After exploring scientists' religious backgrounds, their political sympathies, the features of the social roles expected of them, they attempt to explain, in these terms, the work they did and the stances they took. The result is a different style of rational explanation, one that identifies an action as rational if it is directed toward achieving religious, political, and social goals. So far as I know, nobody has noted that this creates its own asymmetry, requiring us to explain differently the behavior of those who challenge the constraints of their social milieu, perhaps in the (misguided?) desire to fathom the truth about nature.

The remedy is to follow through on Hempel's insightful assimilation of rational explanation to psychological explanation, recognizing all the cognitive and conative traits at work in scientific activity. Just as we should not fall for the implausible idea that the history of science is the outcome of rational actions, each designed to maximize the chances of obtaining truth, nor should we think that sociopolitical concerns always determine the outcomes. The history of science is not shaped by the ideal agents of decision theory nor by social marionettes. The real actors are those psychologically complex beings, reasonable people.

NOTES

Earlier versions of this essay were presented at the University of Utah and at the University of Vermont, and I am grateful to those who participated in the discussions for suggestions that have led me to make improvements: I am particularly indebted to Peggy Battin, David Christensen, Hilary Kornblith, Arthur Kuflik, Bruce Landesman, Don Loeb, Alan Wertheimer, and Nicholas White. I would also like to thank Steven Yalowitz for helpful written comments.

1. This is an oversimplified version of Hempel's view, since it ignores his insightful remarks about situations of uncertainty. Perhaps some situations of uncertainty can be assimilated to the maximizing formula by considering the ways in which utilities reflect agents' tolerance of or aversion to risk, but I doubt that this will always be the case. However, I don't think that the oversimplification will affect my discussion.

2. There are dangers of sentimentalizing, but, from what we know of the marriage, both parties were devoted to one another.

3. Henceforth I'll take the *perceived expected utility* of an action to be $\Sigma p_i u_i$, where the p_i are the probabilities of outcomes that derive from the agent's beliefs about the world and the u_i are the agent's utilities for those outcomes, and the *expected utility* of an action to be $\Sigma P_i u_i$, where the P_i are the true (objective) probabilities, and the u_i are, as before, the agent's utilities for the outcomes. Sometimes, it will be worth considering other probabilities, for example, the probabilities relative to the set of statements that the agent was justified in believing at the time prior to the action, or the probabilities relative to the set of statements that the agent would have been justified in believing had she put herself in an epistemically superior position prior to the time of decision.

4. Hilary Kornblith has questioned whether the feasibility requirement is appropriate on the grounds that sometimes, by aiming at an unattainable ideal, we do better than we otherwise might have done. There's an obvious response: in such circumstances, we can substitute the end that we actually reach for the unattainable goal. But perhaps this is vulnerable, on grounds that the more limited aspiration doesn't have the same motivational force. I'm inclined to think that there's a general method of substitution in such instances, that where I is unattainable we can conceive agents as being motivated to get as close to I as they can. Nonetheless, Kornblith's question is a fruitful one, since it does need to be shown that people can be spurred on to just the same extent by trying to do as much as possible as by striving for the impossible.

5. See Mill's famous remark in *On Liberty*: "Mankind are greater gainers by suffering each other to live as seems good to themselves, than by compelling each to live as seems good to the rest" (Mill [ed. Shields], Bobbs-Merrill, 1956, p. 17) . Of course, Mill held that parents had a duty to help guide children to a situation from which they could judge for themselves, and that entirely sensible view creates a source of instability within his position, since there will be disagreements among individuals about the appropriate epistemic circumstances from which to make the judgment about what seems worthy. Many contemporary public debates are affected by this instability.

6. We'll return to this topic later in the essay in the context of probing the notion of "the agent's goals."

7. Among important substantive views about the attainment of true belief, empiricist conceptions of methods of discovery stand out. Hempel and Reichenbach are surely the most perceptive critics of such proposals.

8. This is hardly a surprise, given the separation of psychology and philosophy that was characteristic of logical empiricism. As I've argued elsewhere, Fregean scruples about mixing psychology and philosophy had an important influence on much twentieth-century thought, not all of it salutary. (See *The Advancement of Science*, New York: Oxford University Press.)

9. There's a serious issue here about how far the regress runs. The question arises in general for reliabilist accounts of knowledge, justification, and rational decision-making, and it's tempting to think that as we move from more proximal to more distal causes the standard of reliability required decreases. I'm grateful to Hilary Kornblith and especially Nicholas White for discussion of this general topic, and I hope to explore it more systematically in future work.

10. "Rational Action," p. 7.

11. The phrase is Bernard Williams's. See "Persons, Character, and Morality" (Chapter 1 of *Moral Luck*, Cambridge University Press, 1981), where Williams offers a subtle discussion of cases like this, arguing that the calculational delay affects the moral quality of the action. I'm concerned with the rationality of what is done.

12. The point is analogous to one made by Gilbert Harman in his proposal that principles of logic don't offer normative guidance. Just as acceptance of modus ponens doesn't tell you to accept the conclusion, given that you accept the premises (since you might be justified in questioning the premises when you found the conclusion unacceptable), so too, one isn't rationally required to act to maximize expected utility rather than trying to find another course.

13. In my preferred interpretation of this story, Eustace genuinely has an assignment of utilities that fails to accord with his wider preferences: thus he plods ahead maximizing perceived expected utility when he ought to be revising the assignments. Don Loeb suggested an alternative reading, based on the idea that the global preferences actually determine the utility function for Eustace and that, as described, he doesn't maximize perceived expected utility at all. In my judgment, this fails to take into account the power that some motives and aspirations have, even when they are inconsistent with the agent's broader aims, and I'm thus prepared to view actual agents as practically inconsistent. In this I agree with Thomas Schelling (see the discussion in the next section).

14. This point is at the bottom of the paradox of the preface. If Eustace is like most of us, he'll believe lots of statements individually, while believing that at least one of his beliefs is false.

15. I am grateful to Peggy Battin, Bruce Landesman, and especially David Christensen for helping me to become clearer on this point.

16. Antonio Damasio, *Descartes' Error*, New York: Putnam, 1994. The example I discuss is described by Damasio on pp. 192–4.

17. Damasio, *op.cit.* p. 193.

18. Thomas Schelling "Ethics, Law and the Exercise of Self-Command" in *Choice and Consequence*, Cambridge, MA.: Harvard, pp. 83–112. The passage quoted is from p. 93.

19. Ibid., p. 85.

20. "The Intimate Contest for Self-Command" in *Choice and Consequence, op. cit.,* pp. 57–82; the quoted passage is from p. 61.
21. Of course, this is to sound a theme that I've developed in a number of other contexts, namely the importance of a psychologistic approach to human cognition. See, for example, my essays "A Priori Knowledge" (*Philosophical Review,* LXXIX, 1980, 3–23) and "The Naturalists Return" (*Philosophical Review,* 101, 1992, 53–114). Similar points have been developed by others, particularly Alvin Goldman (in his *Epistemology and Cognition,* Cambridge Mass.: Harvard University Press, 1986) and Gilbert Harman (*Thought,* Princeton University Press, 1973 and *Change in View,* Cambridge Mass.: MIT Press, 1987).
22. William Dray, *Laws and Explanation in History* (Oxford University Press, 1957), p. 124. The passage is cited by Hempel in "Rational Action" p. 11.
23. Edward Gibbon, *The Decline and Fall of the Roman Empire,* 3 vols. (New York: The Heritage Press, 1946) p. 1258.
24. Nor is this a peculiarity of this example. I had to search rather hard to find a single instance that would even make a prima facie case for the use of rationality in truly first-rate historical explanation.
25. The approach to functions that I offer here descends from the work of Larry Wright. See, in particular, his *Teleological Explanation* (University of California Press, 1976). A lucid presentation of the approach is provided by Peter Godfrey-Smith in "A Modern History Theory of Functions," *Noûs,* XXVIII, 1994, pp. 344–62. I defend a more eclectic theory in "Function and Design," *Midwest Studies in Philosophy,* XVIII, 1993, pp. 379–97. Of course, Hempel had his own very different view of functional explanation.
26. I'd argue that the schema doesn't require this type of amplification, and that the search for overarching laws of evolutionary biology is misguided. (It has, of course, generated a whole literature designed to explicate the notion of fitness, to identify the [lawlike] principle of natural selection and to solve the "tautology problem." For reasons given in my *Abusing Science* (Cambridge Mass.: MIT Press, 1982, pp. 59–60), I think this is a dead-end. But, for present purposes, my heterodoxies aren't needed.
27. As Steven Yalowitz reminded me, Hempel's schema will accommodate the richer Gibbon story. So, to be completely explicit, the point is not that Hempel can't reconstruct the *good* explanation but that he highlights a part of this account that has no significance for historical explanation.
28. Perhaps not all, since there may be schemata of historical explanation that deploy sociological concepts irreducible to those of individual psychological (think of explanations by appeal to class interactions). I don't think that psychological explanations are restricted to cases in which the historical action is dominated by a "great individual," for there are plenty of instances in which a general trend seems to be explicable by identifying the kinds of decision-making that go in individuals of a particular sort (the actions of seventeeth-century English gentry, eighteenth-century French peasants, or nineteenth-century American slaves are often, it seems to me, explained by constructing a particular account of how typical individuals are led to behave as they do). But, for present purposes, I shall not try to argue that all examples of mass movements are of this type.
29. This asymmetry first came under fire in David Bloor's challenging book *Knowledge and Social Imagery* (London: Sage, 1974), and the "symmetry principle" has become an unchallenged assumption of contemporary sociology (and, more gen-

erally, in sociologically inspired science studies). Many of Bloor's successors are less cautious (and less precise) than he, and the ideal of symmetry is often widely, and wildly, applied. See, for example, Bruno Latour, "One Turn After the Social Turn," edited by Ernan McMullin. In *The Social Dimensions of Scientific Knowledge* (University of Notre Dame Press, 1992).

REFERENCES

Bloor, D. 1974. *Knowledge and Social Imagery* (London: Routledge).

Damasio, A. 1994. *Descartes' Error* (New York: Putnam's).

Dray, W. 1957. *Laws and Explanation in History* (Oxford: Oxford University Press).

Gibbon, E. 1946. *The Decline and Fall of the Roman Empire*, Three Volumes (New York: The Heritage Press).

Godfrey-Smith, P. 1994. "A Modern History Theory of Functions," *Noûs*, XXVIII, pp. 344–362.

Goldman, A. 1986. *Epistemology and Cognition* (Cambridge Mass.: Harvard University Press).

Harman, G. 1971. *Thought* (Princeton: Princeton University Press).

Harman, G. 1987. *Change in View* (Cambridge Mass.: MIT Press).

Hempel, C. G. 1945. "Studies in the Logic of Confirmation", reprinted as Chapter 1 of Hempel (1965).

Hempel, C. G. 1962. "Rational Action," *Proceedings and Addresses of the American Philosophical Associaiton*, XXXV.

Hempel, C. G. 1965. *Aspects of Scientific Explanation* (New York: The Free Press).

Hume/Selby-Bigge 1947. *A Treatise on Human Nature* (Oxford: Clarendon Press).

Kitcher, P. S. 1982. *Abusing Science: The Case Against Creationism* (Cambridge Mass.: IT Press).

Kitcher, P. S. 1992 "The Naturalists Return," *Philosophical Review*, CI, pp. 53–114.

Kitcher, P. S. 1993a. *The Advancement of Science* (New York: Oxford University Press).

Kitcher, P. S. 1993b. "Function and Design," *Midwest Studies in Philosophy*, XVIII, pp. 379–97.

Mill/Shields 1956. *On Liberty*, Indianapolis: Bobbs-Merrill.

Schelling, T. 1984. *Choice and Consequence* (Cambridge Mass.: Harvard University Press).

Williams, B. A. O. 1981. *Moral Luck* (Cambridge: Cambridge University Press).

Wright, L. 1976. *Teleological Explanation* (Berkeley: University of Californai Press).

VI

SCIENTIFIC RATIONALITY

11

Analytic versus Synthetic Understanding

PAUL W. HUMPHREYS

On many accounts of explanation, the purpose of scientific explanations, indeed of explanations of any kind, is to produce understanding. Hempel was sceptical of psychologically oriented accounts of understanding in his early writings on explanation;[1] scientific understanding, on the other hand—which revealingly he identified with theoretical understanding—was the goal of explanatory activity:

> Our main concern has been to examine the ways in which science answers why-questions of the [explanatory] type and to characterize the kind of understanding it thereby affords. . . . The understanding it conveys lies . . . in the insight that the explanandum fits into, or can be subsumed under, a system of uniformities represented by empirical laws or theoretical principles. . . . The central theme of this essay has been, briefly, that all scientific explanation . . . seeks to provide a systematic understanding of empirical phenomena by showing that they fit into a nomic nexus. (Hempel 1965a, p. 488)

Perhaps because nontheoretical modes of understanding seemed to Hempel to be incapable of precise treatment, perhaps because he was sceptical of 'empathic understanding' and the continental tradition of *Verstehen*, Hempel, and almost all of those who wrote after him, approached the concept of scientific understanding indirectly through an analysis of the concept of scientific explanation.[2]

It is useful to see what results when we address scientific understanding rather more directly, using recent work in explanation as an occasional resource. We shall see that scientific understanding provides a far richer terrain than does scientific explanation and that the latter is best viewed as a vehicle to understanding, rather than as an end in itself. My purpose here is primarily to explore what I call 'analytic modes of understanding', although these modes sit uneasily with Hempel's own work, especially with his deductive-nomological model.

Analytic and Synthetic Understanding

In the Port-Royal Logic, Antoine Arnauld and Pierre Nicole wrote:

> there are two kinds of method, one for discovering the truth, which is known
> as *analysis*, or the *method of resolution*, and which can also be called the *method
> of discovery*. The other is for making the truth understood by others once it is
> found. This is known as *synthesis*, or the *method of composition*, and can also
> be called the *method of instruction*. (Arnauld and Nicole 1683/1996, p. 233)[3]

In a similar vein, the seventeenth-century Cartesian Pierre-Sylvain Régis
claimed that there were two methods "of which one serves to instruct ourselves
and is called *analysis* . . . and the other which is used to instruct others is called
synthesis" (Régis 1690).[4]

The central distinction brought out by these writers is one of great importance.[5] Understanding comes initially through discoveries, and the techniques
that science has developed for discovery are not always the same as those it uses
for conveying existing knowledge to subsequent inquirers. At the time that
Hempel formulated his views on explanation, justification was a legitimate topic
of inquiry whereas discovery was less respectable. In both the deductive-
nomological and the inductive-statistical models of explanation there was a parallel, most dramatically exhibited in the symmetry thesis, between the justificatory uses of nomological arguments and their explanatory uses. Because of
this parallel, which I shall examine in greater detail later, it was no accident that
Hempel's model of explanation took on a synthetic rather than an analytic form.
For synthetic arguments and justificatory arguments have the same form in
Hempel's approach, and indeed Hempel frequently views explanations as objects
designed to convey understanding to individuals other than the one providing
the answer to the explanatory why-question. (I do not mean that these were
the primary reasons for Hempel's adopting a synthetic approach, but simply
that by so doing, the resulting apparatus fitted easily into the prevailing views
about discovery versus justification.)

What should we mean by an 'analytic process'? An analytic process resolves
a complex entity into a multiplicity of constituents. Those constituents may or
may not be ultimate, where ultimate constituents are those elements that cannot be further resolved by the methods used in the analysis: ideally an analytic
process does reach such ultimate components. What is ultimate is relative to
the methods used within a field of inquiry. For example, the possibility of the
conceptual division of an elementary particle of physics does not undermine
that particle's claim to be ontologically ultimate, nor does the spatial division
of a syntactically fundamental object destroy that object's primitive syntactic
nature. The constituent elements arrived at by analysis must also be independent. This independence may be logical, causal, statistical, functional, or some
other kind appropriate to the elements involved. There are thus different kinds
of analysis: definitional analysis, causal analysis, statistical analysis, functional
analysis, and so on. A synthetic method, in contrast, is one that produces a given

entity by means of a combination of elements or constituents.[6] With this rough characterization, we can classify the main contemporary approaches to explanation follows:[7]

Analytic	Synthetic
Causal	Covering Law
Functional	Unification

Primary and Secondary Understanding

Many have followed Hempel (and Bromberger) in construing explanation as consisting in an adequate answer to a why-question.[8] Judging from the way that contemporary philosophers write about erotetic issues, it is standard to construe the explanatory dialogue as involving one individual posing the why-question and a different individual providing the answer. Moreover, probably because the need to provide plausible examples requires it, there is a tendency to think of these issues in terms of the answer to the why-question already existing, usually somewhere in the scientific literature.[9] These assumptions are entirely reasonable in most cases, because ordinarily the questioner suffers from an epistemic deficit that the respondent does not, and because almost all of the why-question approaches are linguistically oriented, one instinctively thinks of the answers as being "already on the books."[10] Yet there is nothing in the nature of why-questions themselves that requires the questioner and answerer to be different individuals. Furthermore, the most important kinds of why-questions are those asked at a time when no answer to them is known. Let us then call *primary understanding* the (increase in) understanding that is achieved when an individual or a group discovers at least one previously unknown entity that allows progress toward an (improved) explanation of some phenomenon or, without aid from others, an individual or a group rediscovers the steps made by an earlier discoverer. (This does not include simply looking up an explanation that has been written down.) Primary understanding thus arises at least in part from a method of discovery. We can call *secondary understanding* the (increase in) understanding that occurs when one individual or group is provided by another individual or group with all the items of knowledge that the first needs in order to arrive at some (improved) level of understanding. (A common source of secondary understanding is the scientific literature, where the role of the provider is indirect.) Secondary understanding thus involves a method of instruction.

The distinction between the two types of understanding applies to a wide variety of cases. Primary understanding can be achieved by the first person to carry out a previously undiscovered Hempelian deduction from known laws and facts, by the discovery of a hitherto unknown cause, or by the discovery of a new set of unifying principles in a science (as for example Kepler did by discovering the laws that were later named after him). It is not necessary for the provider of primary understanding to have first asked the associated why-question. Primary understanding can be cooperative in form but its orientation is inward, not outward, in that the understanding desired is initially for the investigator(s) and not for others. Primary understanding is the basis of all secondary understanding in the sense that the latter could not occur without the former but the secondary understanding that builds upon the initial discovery does not always have the same form as the primary understanding that makes it possible. Frequently "textbook" explanations are different from, clearer than, and better than, the explanations given by the pioneers. It is an important question to ask, but one whose answer I shall not explore here, about how primary and secondary understanding are related.

We have already seen from the short list of possibilities that I cited in the previous paragraph that primary understanding need not involve analysis, and secondary understanding need not involve synthesis, as the authors of the Port-Royal suggested. From now on, however, I shall restrict my attention for the most part to analytic primary understanding.

Hempel's own deductive-nomological account is indifferent between primary and secondary understanding; it would count as a deductive-nomological explanation the first time that Newton applied his laws of celestial mechanics to explain the motion of the Moon as it did in subsequent repetitions to eighteenth-century why-questions. The important thing for our purposes is that primary understanding involves a reorientation from the Hempelian emphasis on justifying arguments to a process of discovery. Hempel's emphasis on justification is closely allied with his commitment to synthetic modes of understanding, and to understand how that commitment came about requires a brief examination of Hempel's treatment of why-questions.

Explanation as Discovery

Within Hempel's approach, as we all know, explanation, and hence understanding, were based on the availability of *nomic expectability*, a concept that led to most of the famous features of the covering-law approach—the claim that explanations were arguments, the notorious high probability requirement for statistical explanations, and the thesis of the symmetry of predictions and explanations, to name only three. Much has been made of this symmetry between explanation and predictions, but I want to draw attention to a distinction that was more fundamental for Hempel, but which has been overshadowed by the symmetry thesis.

On the second page of his seminal essay "Aspects of Scientific Explanation," Hempel drew the distinction between explanation-seeking why-questions and epistemic why-questions. The former can be put in the standard form "Why is it the case that p?" where p is some empirical statement specifying the explanandum, whereas epistemic or reason-seeking why-questions have the form "What reasons are there for believing p?" Having contrasted these two types of why-questions, Hempel promised to establish that an answer to one should serve as an answer to the other; "as will be argued later . . . any adequate answer to an explanation-seeking why-question . . . must also provide a potential answer to the corresponding epistemic question" (Hempel 1965a, p. 335). But when one turns to the sections in which this argument is supposed to be given (1965a, secs. 2.4, 3.5), what one finds is an extended discussion of the relations between explanations and predictions instead of a discussion of the relations between answers to the two kinds of why-questions. There is only one sentence[11] about why-questions in the course of eighteen pages of discussion of the symmetry thesis. This leads me to believe that Hempel thought that all Hempelian answers to explanatory why-questions were explanations and vice versa, and that all Hempelian answers to epistemic why-questions were predictions and vice versa. The first of these equivalences is, as we now know, false. The second equivalence is our concern here.

Hempel opens and closes his essay with the contrast between the two types of why-questions, and it seems that for him this was the more important distinction, despite the fact that the explanation/prediction symmetry thesis received so much more attention from him and from his commentators. Yet by requiring explanations to have the same logical form as predictions, explanations were forced to take on a synthetic form that is too narrow to capture all legitimate kinds of scientific understanding. I shall now show that we should, as Hempel intended, take this contrast between the two types of why-questions as the more fundamental distinction, and that we should focus on the differences in the *epistemic* state of the two kinds of inquirers, rather than on the supposed sameness of *logical* structure of the vehicles that convey the requested information.

Restricting ourselves to deductive-nomological explanations of singular events for the moment, Hempel construed the differences between explanation and prediction in such cases as due only to what he called "certain pragmatic respects" (Hempel 1965a, pp. 366–7; see also Hempel 1948, p. 249).

> In one case [i.e., explanations], the event described in the conclusion is known to have occurred and suitable statements of general law and particular fact are sought to account for it; in the other [i.e., predictions], the latter statements are given and the statement about the event in question is derived from them. (Hempel 1965a, p. 367)

But it is very strange to give, as Hempel did, a pragmatic interpretation to these differences because they are clearly epistemic in nature and not pragmatic. Although, for Hempel, the logical form of an explanation is identical to the logical form of a prediction, the epistemic state of an epistemic why-questioner clearly differs from the epistemic state of an explanatory why-questioner. To see this, consider the form of a Hempelian explanation.

Any Hempelian explanation or prediction of a particular fact involves a quadruple, the structure of which is <laws, particular facts, a derivation, a conclusion>. As Hempel's observation just quoted indicates, an explanation seeker knows the truth of the last of these, but is ignorant of at least one of the first three. A prediction seeker, according to Hempel (see the quotation), knows the first two and is searching for the third which will, in the deductive contexts with which we are here concerned, give him the fourth. The situation is quite different with regard to the contrast between the epistemic state of the two kinds of why-questioners. In contrast to prediction seekers (as conceived of by Hempel), those seeking an answer to an epistemic why-question of the form "What reasons are there for believing that p?" will, as well as not yet believing the conclusion, be ignorant of at least one of the first three elements of the quadruple, and often, of at least one of the first two.[12] So the epistemic state of epistemic why-questioners will often be different from the epistemic state of Hempelian prediction seekers and, consequently, how the knowledge state of an epistemic why-questioner is altered by a satisfactory answer to his or her question will frequently be different from the way in which the knowledge state of a Hempelian prediction seeker will be changed. That is, the new knowledge acquired by an epistemic why-questioner will frequently be different from the new knowledge acquired by a Hempelian prediction seeker. But what is more important, the one thing which *always* differentiates explanatory why-questioners from epistemic why-questioners is their epistemic state with respect to the conclusion, which the former always knows but the latter does not know and may not even believe.

Of course, we could just abandon Hempel's restrictive account of prediction seeking—the case where the only thing that is missing is the deductive argument—and allow that a prediction seeker could be in the same kind of broader epistemic deficit as is an epistemic why-questioner, where any of the first three members of the quadruple might be missing. But this then makes it quite clear that what really separates the two kinds of inquirer, the justification seeker from the explanation seeker, is the difference in their status vis-à-vis the last element of the quadruple.

This epistemic asymmetry has consequences, for very often information contained in the explanandum itself provides vital clues for obtaining a primary understanding of that explanandum and these clues can be discovered by analysis of something already in the possession of the explanation seeker. Yet by virtue of providing a counterfactual characterization of the similarities between epistemic and explanatory why-questions ("the explanatory argument might have been used for a deductive prediction of the explanandum event *if* the laws and particular facts adduced in the explanans had been known and taken into account" [Hempel 1965a, p. 366]), this essential epistemic asymmetry was erased, and explanations were forced into the synthetic mode.

So let us take the key feature of explanation seekers to be that they know the truth of the explanandum, that this sometimes means that they have access to the explanandum phenomenon itself, and they are using that as the starting point of their search for understanding.

Analytic versus Synthetic Understanding

Existing accounts of explanation divide into two basic kinds, and our examination of the epistemic differences between answers to the two types of why-questions, explanations, and predictions suggests what they are. In the Hempelian prediction case, the epistemic direction follows a process from the given facts, which in the D-N case are already sufficient for the explanandum sentence's truth, to that conclusion, and the task is to construct an argument that will direct that epistemic process. This is no trivial task of course, but it is essentially synthetic in form, by virtue of its combining already given components to produce a dependent explanandum sentence. But in the case of the explanation-seeking why-questions, the process is initially "backwards" and consists in a process of discovery, seeking which laws and/or specific facts would give rise to the given explanandum. The discovery process is relatively trivial in the case of secondary understanding (you find an expert, or a reliable source of information), but it is crucial in the case of primary understanding. It is here that analytic methods tend to play an important role, although as we have seen they are certainly not the only method of attaining primary understanding.

We can most clearly see how such analytic understanding takes place by looking at some simple cases of causal analysis.

Explanatory Refinement and 'How Exactly' Questions

Within the context of causal explanations it is natural to think of the explanandum event as an effect of some cause, but it is important that we not identify explananda with effects in causal contexts. Recalling that the canonical form of an explanatory why-question was "Why is it the case that p?" the sentence 'p' can have the form "X is the cause of Y" or "X was involved in bringing about Y".[13] Thus, in cases where we have the explanandum itself available, the question could be about a cause, about a process connecting a cause with its effect, or, as we shall see, about entities containing one of these two things.

Understanding is not an all-or-nothing affair and an adequate account of scientific understanding must describe ways in which we can increase that understanding. Analysis then plays an important role in *explanatory refinement*. A common variety of explanatory refinement takes some part of the world that we suspect plays a role in producing a particular phenomenon and identifies the precise etiological agent that caused the outcome. This variety comes in two forms. The first takes a composite object and identifies which substance(s) within it are the 'active ingredients'. Here the analysis separates a compound object into its parts. For example, we say that smoking causes lung cancer. Yet there are known to be more than thirty-eight hundred components of cigarette smoke, and chemical analysis is a first and important step toward identifying the carcinogens among those thousands of components. A historically important example of this use of causal analysis was the discovery by William Withering in 1775 of digitalis as a treatment for dropsy (edema resulting from progressive heart failure). Withering took his cue from a folk remedy administered by an old woman in Shropshire, and from the twenty or so ingredients in her secret recipe, he isolated the foxglove herb as the effective component. (Withering's analysis has since been further refined to identify digitalis glycoside as the active ingredient in foxglove leaves.)

The second kind of analysis identifies which of the many properties possessed by an object are the ones responsible for bringing about an effect. To take a simple example, if a crumbling ledge on a New York City apartment building collapses and a clay flowerpot and a stone gargoyle of identical masses injure separate pedestrians on the street below, it is the kinetic energy transferred from the falling objects to the pedestrians that injures them and not the objects qua flowerpot or qua gargoyle, nor most of the other properties possessed by those objects.

Understanding Does Not Require a Mechanism

A number of authors have suggested that scientific explanation consists, at least in part, in displaying the mechanisms that lead up to the explanandum event. I originally resisted adopting this view because it was clear to me that there were serious difficulties in applying it to quantum systems and, in a quite different way, to economic and social systems. I now believe that there is a persuasive set of more general reasons why being able to display a mechanism should not be a requirement for either understanding or explanations. Consider the case of aspirin. The Assyrians knew that chewing willow leaves produced analgesic effects and Hippocrates used extract of willow bark as a pain reliever. The active ingredient of these folk remedies, salicin, was first isolated in 1828–29 by Buchner and Leroux, with a further refinement to salicylic acid in 1838 by Piria. The discovery and isolation of this material contributed to Felix Hoffman's synthesis of acetylsalicylic acid in 1897, a discovery that led to the first commercial manufacture of aspirin by the Bayer company. For seventy years there was an overwhelming amount of evidence from both scientific trials and everyday usage that acetylsalicylic acid caused relief from headaches and from fever in a wide variety of populations and biological contexts. One thus had exactly the kind of invariant connection between a factor and an outcome that is characteristic of genuine causal relations. Thus it would have been entirely correct to have claimed in say, 1920, that one understood why a particular individual's headache had disappeared, that understanding consisting in the knowledge that the individual had taken some aspirin and that taking aspirin almost invariantly leads to cessation of headaches, even though the mechanism of action between the cause and the effect was unknown at that time. For it was not until the work of the British pharmacologist John Vane in the 1970s that the mechanism of action of aspirin (inhibition of the synthesis of prostaglandins) was discovered.[14]

We have an explanation behind the understanding, too, because a cause of the headache's cessation has been identified, even though the operative mechanism has not. In cases where we have substantial evidence for the invariance of the association between cause and effect, as we do with aspirin, the need for knowledge of a mechanism can be dispensed with.

To take a different example, there is an obvious process connecting smoking and the site of lung cancer, yet the mechanism of carcinogenesis produced by that smoke pathway is still not properly understood at this time, nor is the exact way in which sexual intercourse is linked to an increased risk of cervical cancer in women.[15] Such examples are by no means limited to the life sciences. The initial lack of a known mechanism for gravitation, for heat, and for electricity did not preclude early investigators from acquiring a considerable degree of understanding of the relevant phenomena, and especially of their causal effects.

It is certainly true that knowledge of such mechanisms tends to further our understanding in ways that would be difficult without them. For example, Vane's theoretical work not only allowed separation of aspirin's effects into the analgesic (pain-killing), the anti-inflammatory, and the antipyretic (fever reduction), as well as a certain amount of unificatory understanding of similar analgesics such as ibuprofen through similar modes of action, but it led to the realization that aspirin was also effective against recurrence of strokes by virtue of preventing build-up of prostaglandins at the site of arterial lesions. Equally important, mechanisms are the most important way of ruling out possible confounders (factors that are associated with the effect but are not causally responsible for it).

Carriers and Causes

In many cases of causal discovery, what I shall call the *carrier* of the cause is identified before the cause itself is isolated.[16] Here is one famous example. Between 1849 and 1855 the London physician John Snow identified water contaminated by fecal matter as the carrier for cholera.[17] He had, as he put it, discovered the "mode of transmission" of the disease, but Snow never identified the specific microorganism that was responsible for cholera. That discovery was not made until 1883 when Robert Koch identified the *vibrio cholerae* bacterium as the cause. This kind of situation is different from the one I discussed earlier involving aspirin. There the active causal agent (the acetylsalicylic acid) was known early in the scientific investigation in addition to the carrier. In the cholera cases, Snow had knowledge only of the carrier and not of the causal agent.

In the second kind of situation, we may ask this question: Do we have an explanation of the disease's occurrence when we have identified only the carrier? There is also a different question: Do we have some understanding of how the disease comes about when we have found the carrier? For those of us who adhere to a causal account of explanation, the answer to the first question has to be 'no'. Except in an elliptical manner of speaking, rats do not cause bubonic plague and neither do fleas, and polluted water is not the cause of cholera. It is the *yersina pestis* organism that is the 'active ingredient' of plague transmission, and the rat is no more a cause of an illness than the piece of paper upon which this sentence is printed is a cause of your thinking rather differently about explanation from now on. It cannot be, for the sentence would have had exactly the same effect had you viewed it, as I did, on a computer terminal. A factor, the presence or absence of which makes no difference to an effect, cannot be a cause of that effect.

Yet we do gain some measure of understanding through learning of these vehicles, for the discovery of the carrier has brought us closer to discovering what the explanation of the effect is, even though an explanation is not yet available. *We can thus have an increase in understanding without (yet) having an explanation.* We understand how the disease is transmitted but not what causes it (and thus, at least on the causal accounts of explanation, we have not explained why the individual had it).

It might be argued that polluted water is in fact a cause of cholera.[18] To address this concern, let us clarify the first question that we asked earlier. If the question is one involving a generalization—What, in general, causes cholera?—then the answer to the question is still 'no'. For polluted water is not a general explanation for cholera. There are other carriers, including contaminated shellfish and excreta from infected individuals. What is invariant across all these carriers is the *vibrio* bacterium, and it is that invariance which underpins the causal explanation resulting from Koch's discovery. However, if the question is about whether the carrier is part of the explanation in this particular case, the issue is more complicated, for what constitutes a correct answer to the question requires answers to a collection of other questions involving both factual and conceptual matters.

To argue that in specific cases the carrier plus the agent is a cause of the effect is to resist the persuasive line of argument that supports relevance as a key feature of causation, and hence of causal explanations. The failure of explanatory relevance within Hempel's deductive apparatus was highlighted by Henry Kyburg's hexed salt example.[19] The argument: "All samples of hexed salt placed in warm water dissolve. This sample of salt was hexed and placed in warm water. Therefore, this sample of salt dissolved" satisfied all of Hempel's criteria of adequacy for D-N explanations, yet it is clearly not a explanation. In order to produce an effective example, Kyburg had to explicitly display the irrelevant predicate 'hexed' separately from the relevant predicate so that the syntactic structure of the premises already represented an analysis of factors into those that were relevant and those that were not. It is, needless to say, a much more common situation in science for a factor cited in an explanation to be identified by means of a predicate that does not represent such a separation.

One reason for the difference in views about contaminated drinking water being a cause of cholera doubtless lies in a different choice of contrast cases for the causal analysis. If one contrasts the actual situation containing contaminated water with a situation within which the water plus bacteria is absent, then one arrives at the position that the polluted water is indeed a cause of the disease. If, alternatively, one uses as a contrast the case where the water is still present but the contaminating bacteria are removed, then the water cannot be a cause. Which contrast case is the correct one? Perhaps minimal change semantics for counterfactuals could decide, but a more objective criterion employs experimental analysis on the polluted water itself. Analyze the medium that was present in the case concerned into the carrier and its various pollutants, then see whether the disease occurs in the presence of each single component. Obviously, an inductive inference is required to move from the experimental case to the original case, but with a well-designed experiment this is a safer move than one relying on similarity metrics between possible worlds. (Snow's own use of a naturally randomized experiment, by the way, was incapable of isolating the bacterium, a fact that casts doubt on the ability of many epidemiological trials to identify the cause rather than the carrier.)

I said that Koch discovered the cause of cholera. This is misleading, for current evidence suggests that it is a toxin manufactured by the *vibrio cholerae* bacterium that is actually the cause of the disease. Such cases raise an obvious question: Are the only causes those factors for which no further decomposition into relevant and irrelevant components is possible? My answer is, tentatively, 'yes'. If one is willing to put aside what is ordinarily said, as one should, then the argument from analysis just given surely leads us to that conclusion.[20]

The central issue raised in this section is, I think, one of quite general applicability. Consider just one example pointed out to me by Eric Scerri. A commonly used mechanism for explaining how our olfactory senses detect various smells is the 'lock and key' account of molecular action. Only a small part of the molecule is involved in the detection; is the entire molecule or simply the segment 'actively involved' in the process of smelling a cause of our smelling perfume? More prosaically, with an ordinary key is it the entire key or just the cutouts (or magnetic strip) that explains why the door opened? Our preceding analysis suggests that the key handle or the card is simply a carrier to convey the cause to where it can do its work.[21]

Linguistic versus Material Analysis

A major drawback to any linguistically oriented approach to explanation is thus that it is not effective for the kind of discoveries that material analyses can lead to. Material analysis of objects can reveal hitherto unknown components for which the language as yet has no terms. The analytic decomposition of syntax is a poor cousin of material analysis, for language frequently does not reflect material structure, whereas the system itself trivially does.[22]

It bears noting that the subdivision of reference classes also has a serious defect, for that method never allows us to 'go down' to lower level properties or entities.[23] If we begin with samples of water as the members of the reference class, we shall end with samples of water as members of the reference class, even if the 'relevant' subclass contains samples of water with highly specific characteristics. If the water is simply a carrier, then this method will partially misidentify the explanatory agent.[24]

We can see here one of the major differences between the linguistic approaches to explanation and material approaches. With the examples I have discussed of foxgloves, tobacco smoke, contaminated water, rats, and so forth, the object of potential understanding—the explanandum itself, not the explanandum sentence—is available for analysis whatever its mode of presentation, and this availability is crucial for the discovery process. It is only when one is trapped in a mode of secondary linguistic understanding, where the predicative representation is fixed by the relatively ignorant questioner, that analysis is prematurely blocked.

We can thus see why the knowledge situation of the explanation seeker can be so different from that of the prediction seeker. By virtue of sometimes having the explanandum phenomenon itself available (materially, not just linguistically) operations of analysis and other modes of causal investigation are possible in ways that cannot be carried out in its absence. Moreover, when you have the actual object or process available to you, the modes of possible analysis are determined by the entity itself and not by the often impoverished syntax.

Of course, what one finds by analysis depends upon the structure of the analysandum. Often, analysis is required simply to produce an explanandum and the explanation has to be found elsewhere. For example, in 1963, the astronomer Maarten Schmidt realized that previously unidentified spectral lines from quasar 3C 273 resembled a Balmer series from hydrogen, but one that was greatly shifted toward the red end of the spectrum.[25] This value of the red shift required the quasar to be located 10^9 light-years from Earth. Coupled with its brightness, this indicated that it must be emitting massive amounts of radiation. The spectral analysis thus had led to a why-question that was eventually answered through the theory of the gravitational action of black holes. In this case, the analysis provided the basis for formulating the question, but did not itself provide the answer.

Besides the examples we have already seen, there is a related problem that occurs most often in the social sciences. Here the problem is not one of having available the carrier rather than the cause itself but of using extremely general characteristics in place of the genuine, more specific, causal factors. The almost ubiquitous variables of class, race, and gender, which appear in so many causal models in the social sciences, are usually placeholders for more specific characteristics of individuals. For example, "class" is a cluster term standing for a collection of less abstract properties such as speech characteristics, tastes in music, literature, and food, choice of leisure activities, mode of dress, occupational aspirations, and so on. In any given context, not all of these are likely to be explanatorily relevant to the outcome of interest. More generally, which of them are explanatorily relevant in sociology often turn out to constitute a different subclass from those that are explanatorily relevant in economics, for example.

Analysis Can Provide Unification

But why try to isolate what we usually call the real cause in these situations, the aspect of tobacco that is carcinogenic, the active ingredient in willow bark, the aspects of class that lead to social advancement, and so on? It is because those constituents often occur in other objects or situations and we want to know what those other contexts are. By staying at the level of the object or the process, rather than going down via analysis to the level of the active cause, we restrict the generality of our understanding, as well as the range of our possible interventions, manipulations, and synthetic constructions.

We have seen that the same causal factor can be present in a wide variety of objects or processes. Consider the case of acids. It was once common to characterize acids functionally, as substances that produced carbon dioxide when added to sodium or calcium carbonate, or that turned red phenolphthalein colorless. In contrast to these functional (or operational) definitions, the contemporary Lewis concept of an acid defines it as a species that can accept an electron pair.[26] Here we have a property that is possessed by acetic acid, by sulphuric acid, by hydrochloric acid, and by many others. By virtue of having isolated this common property of acids, it has been possible to unify a wide variety of functionally characterized substances in terms of a single common feature.

This kind of progress by isolating common factors is well known, and I note it only because the explanatory accounts that emphasize unification have focused on synthetic syntactic methods, rather than on analytic material methods. The example of unification through finding a structure common to most substances previously classified as acids was largely the result of theoretical work, but some of the other examples we have seen in which a more general understanding has been achieved are clearly analytic in nature. It is worth exploring the relation of this kind of unification to a more controversial feature that is usually claimed to lead in the opposite direction—to disunification. This is the multiple realizability of most functionally characterized properties.

To arrive at the comparison, we need to be explicit about the ontology and logical form of the realizability relation. Ordinary usage is somewhat flexible about the entities between which the realizability relation holds, and many philosophical treatments are almost as casual. The general form of the realizability relation is that of X being realized by Y in Z. X can be a property (first or higher order), a state type, or an object type; Y can be a property, a state or state type, or an object or an object type; Z is always an object or an object type. Properties and state types are probably the most common subjects of realization; thus pain from ischemia is realized in humans by a specific type of neurophysiological state whereas pain from joint damage is (presumably) realized in iguanas by a distinct type of state. In addition, although only in an elliptical sense as we shall see, object types can be realized: a seat is said to be realized by a box, by a tree stump, by a dining chair, and so on. Frequently, the relation is collapsed by leaving either Y or Z tacit. Thus, the property of serving as money can be realized by banknotes, by electronic transfers, by company store chits, by gold, and so on, but it is assumed that this realization takes place in societies with monetary economies, rather than, say, societies based on barter. Similarly, the example of being a seat must be implicitly relativized to a physical context, such as human societies on Earth, for wicker chairs do not usually function well as seats for elephants.[27] It is not necessary for the first relatum to be functionally characterized: a binomial stochastic process can be realized by the particular sequence HTHHTTTHHTH . . . in a coin tossing setup. There is one kind of case where realization has the form of a two place relation only and that is when the realizer is an abstract entity, as when an abstract group is realized by the group of rotations on two-dimensional Euclidean space.[28]

The apparent looseness of ontology here can be reduced because in any case in which an object type is said to be realized or to be a realizer, reference to the object type can be replaced by reference to an associated property or properties. So, it is the property of being a chair that is realized by properties of a tree stump, for example. In contrast, the third relatum must always be an object or object type.

Because state types are special cases of properties, we then have that when X is realized by Y in Z, X and Y are properties, and Z is an object or object type. This means that an instance of the realized property will be an instance of the realizing property, the instantiator being Z.

Realizability has attracted interest chiefly in the realm of multiply realizable properties. Multiple realizability is often taken to be an argument against the reduction of the multiply realized property to lower level properties. Now, whether or not a given property or other entity is multiply realizable is ordinarily a contingent matter.[29] But so is the antireductionism that is often argued to result from it, for multiple realizability often coexists with unification resulting from a common underlying ontology. Consider the case of doorstops. The property of being a doorstop is functionally characterized and it can be multiply realized by certain properties of bricks, of cast-iron pigs, of wooden wedges, of bean bags, and so on, where all these are tacitly assumed to be located in our gravitational field. Yet there is only one relevant causal property possessed by all doorstops, and that is the ability to exert a counteracting force of magnitude greater than that exerted by the door. The apparent triviality of the doorstop example conceals something of importance, which is that physics discovered an extremely general common factor that is necessarily found in all properly functioning doorstops and, in virtue of separating it from the other properties of doorstops, allows us to understand why they function as they do. This common factor also reunifies the functional type "doorstop" and thus makes its multiple realizability of engineering interest only, and not of physical or of philosophical interest. For a less trivial case, we have already seen the unification that was achieved with the Lewis definition of acids in this way. The dual moral is that property analysis in such cases can provide both understanding and unification. It also serves as a reminder that the connection from multiple realizability to nonreduction is quite shaky and that any appeal to the supposed implausibility of reduction from the existence of multiple realizability in these cases forms, to my mind, an extremely weak general argument against reduction.[30]

Laws Are Not Necessary for Understanding

Consider an utterly simple example of understanding, whereby we understand a phenomenon by showing that it operates as a Poisson process.[31] Suppose we are willing to make these assumptions about the stochastic process:

a) During a small interval of time, the probability of observing one event in that interval is proportional to the length of that interval.

b) The probability of two or more events in a small interval is small and goes to zero rapidly as the length of the interval goes to zero.

c) The number of events in a given time interval is independent of the number of arrivals in any disjoint interval.

d) The number of events in a given interval depends only upon the length of the interval and not its location.

These are informal assumptions, but ones that can be given precise mathematical representations. From those representations it is possible to derive the exact form of the probability distribution covering the output from the process. Such models are of great generality, and can explain phenomena as varied as the rate of light bulb failures and the rate of arrival of cars at a remote border checkpoint. In addition, unlike some models that require severe idealization or simplification, there is good reason to believe that in many applications the Poisson model is true of the processes it represents.

Within the Hempelian approach of nomic expectability, it was necessary to include at least one scientific law in the explanans, whether explaining a particular fact or a general law. In many cases of model construction, laws will enter into the construction process, but in the example just described it is not in the least plausible that any of the assumptions given count as laws. Although one might say that the individual outcomes are explained by virtue of falling under a lawlike distribution, if the fact to be explained is that the system itself follows a Poisson distribution, that fact is not understood in virtue of its being the conclusion in a derivation within which at least one law plays an essential role. Furthermore, even if we consider the distribution that covers the process to itself be a law, that law is not itself understood in terms of further laws, as the D-N account of explaining laws holds, but in terms of structural facts about the system. This, in my view, quite conclusively demonstrates that neither scientific understanding nor scientific explanations require laws.

The last point to note is that although the construction of the model is a synthetic process, it is important to have analyzed the structure of the system into its constituent features. For that analysis allows us to explore what would happen if any of the assumptions were violated in specific ways and understand why the behavior of the actual system deviates in systematic ways from the model. Part of our understanding of systems comes from knowing how they deviate from ideal systems.[32]

Partial Understanding and Truth

One of Hempel's four criteria of adequacy was that the members of the explanans all be true. I believe that Hempel was correct in insisting on the truth of the explanans, but we must accommodate the kind of incompleteness with which science is always faced. There are two objections to the truth requirement that are often made.[33] The first is that an adequate theory of explanation has to accommodate the fact that at least some scientific theories that we now regard as false, such as Newton's gravitational theory, still have explanatory power because they are close to the truth. The second objection is that if we insist that it is necessary for the members of the explanans to be true, it is possible that none of our current 'explanations' are actually explanations at all. (This is the so-called 'pessimistic induction' from the history of science.)

In response to the first objection, one simply has to be explicit about what one means by a theory being close to the truth, or being partially true.[34] There are many sophisticated theories of verisimilitude available, but one rather different way in which an explanation can be partially true is when it postulates that there are multiple causal influences on a phenomenon and the proposed explanation gets some of those factors right but others wrong. Here is one example. In the 1962 Cuban missile crisis, it was said for many years that the Soviets withdrew their missiles from Cuba because (a) Khrushchev had backed down under pressure from a United States quarantine on the island, (b) the United States had provided guarantees that no invasion of Cuba would take place, and (c) the United States had publicly agreed to remove the quarantine measures on Cuba in return for removal of the missiles. It later become known[35] that Khrushchev and Kennedy had a secret understanding, brokered by Robert Kennedy, for the United States to remove its obsolete Jupiter missiles from Turkey in exchange for Khrushchev removing the Cuban missile bases. (a) thus turned out to be false, but (b) and (c) are still true.[36] So the original explanation still has some explanatory power to it, and analysis, by separating independent contributions to the outcome, allows one to see why certain explanations are partially true. It also allows us to retain parts of imperfect explanations rather than rejecting them outright.

In a rather different sense it is claimed that Newton's theory of celestial motion or of bodies falling under gravity would be no explanation at all under the truth requirement. Once we acknowledge that theories and explanations based upon them are composite entities we can see that we can gain understanding from explanations that contain falsehoods because they are correct in part. Take for example Copernicus's explanation of the retrograde motions of the superior planets. Copernicus's theory was false in many respects: it contained compound circular orbits, it misrepresented the size of the universe, it contained only seven planets, it placed the Sun at the center of the universe, and it used crystalline spheres. Yet the basic qualitative features of retrograde motion of the Superior planets have remained explained by the basic geometry of a Copernican arrangement. The Newtonian case can be viewed in the same way. It appeals to an entity, a universal gravitational force, that does not exist in the sense that many Newtonians said it did (instantaneous action-at-a-distance). However, it cannot be a general principle of understanding that if a theory or model makes essential use of a (type of) entity which is such that nothing similar to that exists within the system to be explained, then that account fails to provide understanding, for this would rule out both Copernicus's theory and Newton's theory, as well as many others, as having provided partial understanding. What is needed is a detailed account of how theories and models with both correct and incorrect features provide understanding of different aspects of the world. This is a large task that requires us to separate parts of theories that are construed instrumentally from those that are meant to be taken realistically, the role that idealizations and abstractions play in models, how model refinement is conducted, and so on. But that is a task for another time.[37]

NOTES

This essay is dedicated to the memory of Carl Hempel. His work influenced me when I was an undergraduate and again, many times, when I had become a professional philosopher. Late in his life I had the privilege of discussing philosophy with him personally. I came away, as everyone did, enormously impressed. He was a great philosopher and a wonderful human being. For helpful comments on this essay I am indebted to audiences at the California Institute of Technology and the University of California at Santa Cruz. I particularly benefited from critical responses to section 7 from Fiona Cowie, David Freedman, Christopher Hitchcock, Ric Otte, Eric Scerri, and James Woodward. Not all of them agree with my conclusions. Some of the material in this essay descends, in a much revised form, from an unpublished paper read at the University of Pittsburgh and Johns Hopkins University in the early 1990s. Comments from those audiences were also very helpful.

1. See, for example, Hempel (1942, Sec. 6; 1948, sec. 4). All page references to Hempel's writing cited here refer to Hempel (1965b).
2. A number of philosophers have attempted to capture the process of how scientific explanations provide understanding. For example, Friedman (1974), Achinstein (1983), Salmon (1984), and Kitcher (1989) all recognize the fundamental importance of understanding in the scientific enterprise.
3. For Arnauld and Nicole the synthetic method is the more important of the two "since it is the one used to explain all the sciences" (1683/1996, p. 239).
4. In the case of mathematics, the view that analysis was personal may have arisen from the puzzlement, dating back to Pappus's claims about analysis, concerning how a 'backwards' procedure could yield certain knowledge, or could be a legitimate route to knowledge at all.
5. Arnauld and Nicole identify three things: a method of analysis, a process of instructing oneself, and a method of discovery. The Port-Royal was certainly on the right track, but it is better to keep these three things separate, for self-instruction is not limited to analysis, nor to discovery; analysis can enlighten others, as can a discovery; and analysis does not always lead to discovery, whereas synthesis itself can be a discovery device.

6. Not all synthetic objects, that is objects produced by a synthetic method, can be analyzed, nor can all analytically decomposed objects be (re)synthesized.

7. Examples of the causal approach can be found in Salmon (1984), Humphreys (1989); of the covering law approach in Hempel (1965a); of the functional approach in Cummins (1977) and of the unification approach in Friedman (1974) and Kitcher (1989). I set aside here pragmatic accounts of explanation. In laying out this taxonomy I am in no way denying the validity of the tripartite division used by Wesley Salmon in his 1984 and 1989 works, that division being between the ontic, the epistemic, and the modal conceptions of explanation. That is an extremely important taxonomy and one that is consistent with the one used here. Salmon's classification does, however, divide the conceptual space in a rather different way than does my own.

8. One can do this even when, as I do, the why-question is not the starting point of the explanatory process but is merely a common companion of the process.

9. Why-questions can be viewed as abstract entities. Nevertheless, their role is usually that of one part of a dialogue between epistemically imbalanced agents.

10. Kitcher's (1989) use of the phrase 'the explanatory store' is a reflection of this.

11. Hempel (1965a, p. 368).

12. I do not assume that the set of known sentences is closed under deductive consequence. If it is, and Moore's paradox (I know x but do not believe x) is ill-founded then nonbelief in the conclusion entails the epistemic lack of at least one of the first three.

13. In cases where this is false, and X is actually not involved in bringing about Y, then the presupposition of the why-question is false and suitable corrective answers are in order.

14. This mechanism is at present not fully understood.

15. I owe this last example to David Freedman.

16. When the carrier is a biological agent, it is known as a vector.

17. Snow's treatise *On the Mode of Communication of Cholera* (1855) is a beautiful example of systematic scientific detective work, and the basis of one of the most important public health advances ever made. The full flavor (literally) of the often unspeakably filthy conditions in which most people lived prior to modern public sanitation is vividly conveyed in Snow's essay.

18. I have heard this reaction from a number of different audiences.

19. See also the important examples given in Salmon (1971).

20. I say 'tentatively' here because the decision relies on the acceptance of a considerable number of assumptions about causation, the truth of some of which is not as certain to me as I should like.

21. In other cases, such as the role of "junk DNA," I am not in a position to provide an answer.

22. Understanding why the cat is on the mat is not the same as understanding why the sentence "the cat is on the mat" is true. This is because the answer to material questions such as the first often involve causal antecedents that led up to the state described by the sentence, whereas at least some answers to the second question involve the truth conditions at the time the explanandum sentence is true.

23. How to assign properties or entities to various levels is not straightforward. It is not sufficient for A to be a (proper) part of B for A to be at a lower level than B, because this would consign subareas of plane figures to a lower level than the figure itself. Nor is it necessary, for in some cases of emergent entities, the emergent and higher level entities do not have the lower level entities that generate them as

constituents. (For examples, see Humphreys [1997]). For present purposes, we shall simply take the conventional scientific taxonomy of levels of entities for granted, without endorsing it, and take the level of a property as that of the first level of entities at which it is instantiated. (This means that many lower level properties will be found at higher levels as well.)

24. This puts methodological limitations on such widely used statistical techniques as subclassification, for example, Rosenbaum and Rubin (1983, sec. 3.3).

25. See Schmidt (1963).

26. The two other contemporary concepts of an acid are the Bronsted-Lowry and the Arrhenius conceptions.

27. Alternatively, we could insert the relativization into the functionally defined concept, as in "is a chair on Earth."

28. Because the core usage of 'realization' usually conveys a transition from a more abstract entity to a more concrete entity, this last example could be taken as a courtesy use.

29. Kim (1993, pp. 312–3) suggests that some writers, notably those who construe mental properties as second-order properties, take their multiple realizability as a conceptual fact.

30. Unification and reduction are, of course, different things, but in the kinds of cases I have described with common causal factors, it is plausible to take them as equivalent.

31. For a simple exposition of Poisson processes, see Barr and Zehna (1971). In Humphreys (1995), I describe in detail the construction of models based on the diffusion equation. As a deterministic model, that is closer to the heart of the deductive-nomological approach than is the statistical model described here. However, deductive-statistical explanations were in all essential ways similar to deductive-nomological explanations in Hempel's approach, and the present example has the benefit of being purely structural.

32. For more on this, see Humphreys (1995, sec. 4; 1995–96, sec. 3).

33. I have heard the first from Gary Hardcastle and the second from Stuart Glennan, among others.

34. Hempel's treatment of partial explanations in section 4.2 of Hempel (1965a) does not deal with these issues.

35. See, for example, Hilsman (1996, pp. 129–30; Thompson 1992, pp. 345–6). As with most historical reconstructions, the facts became known only gradually, and some aspects of the development of the crisis and its resolution are still uncertain. Hints of the secret deal were made in Robert Kennedy's memoirs.

36. A matter of considerable interest, although one that is essentially counterfactual in form, is whether President Kennedy would have violated the guarantees against a second invasion of Cuba had he not been assassinated.

37. For first steps toward an answer, see Wimsatt (1998), Humphreys (1995).

REFERENCES

Achinstein, Peter. 1983. *The Nature of Explanation*. Oxford: Oxford University Press.
Arnauld, Antoine, and Pierre Nicole. 1683/1996. *Logic or the Act of Thinking*. 5th ed. Translated and edited by Jill Buroker. Cambridge, England: Cambridge University Press.
Barr, Donald, and Peter Zehna. 1971. *Probability*. Belmont, Calif.: Brooks/Cole.
Cummins, Robert. 1977. "Programs in the Explanation of Behavior." *Philosophy of Science* 44:269–87.

Friedman, Michael. 1974. "Explanation and Scientific Understanding," *Journal of Philosophy* 71:5–19.

Hempel, Carl. 1942. "The Function of General Laws in History." *Journal of Philosophy* 39:35–48. Reprinted in Hempel (1965).

———. 1948. "Studies in the Logic of Explanation." *Philosophy of Science* 15:567–79. Reprinted in Hempel (1965).

———. 1965a. "Aspects of Scientific Explanation." In Hempel (1965b).

———. 1965b. *Aspects of Scientific Explanation and Other Essays in the Philosophy of Science.* New York: Free Press.

Hilsman, Roger. 1996. *The Cuban Missile Crisis.* Westport, Conn.: Praeger.

Humphreys, Paul. 1989. *The Chances of Explanation.* Princeton: Princeton University Press.

———. 1995. "Computational Science and Scientific Method." *Minds and Machines* 5:499–512.

———. 1995–96. "Computational Empiricism." *Foundations of Science* 1:119–30.

———. 1997. "How Properties Emerge." *Philosophy of Science* 64:1–17.

Kim, Jaegwon. 1993. *Supervenience and Mind.* Cambridge, England: Cambridge University Press.

Kitcher, Philip. 1989. "Explanatory Unification and the Causal Structure of the World." In Kitcher and Salmon (1989).

Kitcher, Philip, and Wesley Salmon, eds. 1989. *Scientific Explanation.* Minneapolis: University of Minnesota Press.

Régis, Pierre-Sylvain. 1690. *Système de philosophie, contentant la logique, la métaphysique, la physique, et la morale.* Paris.

Rosenbaum, Paul, and Donald Rubin. 1983. "The Central Role of the Propensity Score in Observational Studies for Causal Effects." *Biometrika* 70:41–55.

Salmon, Wesley. 1971. *Statistical Explanation and Statistical Relevance.* Pittsburgh: University of Pittsburgh Press.

———. 1984. *Scientific Explanation and the Causal Structure of the World.* Princeton: Princeton University Press.

———. 1989. "Four Decades of Scientific Explanation." In Kitcher and Salmon (1989). Reprinted as *Four Decades of Scientific Explanation.* Minneapolis: University of Minnesota Press, 1990.

Schmidt, M. 1963. "3C 273: A Star-like Object with Large Red-shift. *Nature* 197:1040–43.

Snow, John. 1855. "On the Mode of Communication of Cholera." 2nd ed. Reprinted in *Snow on Cholera.* New York: Commonwealth Fund, 1936.

Thompson, Robert. 1992. *The Missiles of October.* New York: Simon and Schuster.

Wimsatt, William. 1998. "False Models as a Means to Truer Theories." Unpublished manuscript.

12

The Objectivity and the Rationality of Science

ROBERT NOZICK

Facts and truths are termed "objective," and so are beliefs. There are three strands to our ordinary notion of an objective fact or truth. First, an objective fact is accessible from different angles. It can be repeated by the same sense (sight, touch, etc.) at different times, and it can be repeated by different senses of one observer, and by different observers. The second mark of an objective truth, related to the first, is that there is or can be intersubjective agreement about it. And the third feature concerns independence. If p is an objective truth, then it holds independently of people's beliefs, desires, hopes, and observations or measurements that p. A fourth and more fundamental characteristic of objective truths underlies and explains the first three features (to the extent that they hold): an objective fact is invariant under all admissible transformations. Which transformations are the admissible ones, for instance, Lorentz transformations, is discovered in the course of the history of scientific investigation.[1]

A judgment or belief is objective when it is reached by a certain sort of process, one that does not involve biasing or distorting factors that lead belief away from the truth. A judge in a courtroom is supposed to be objective and unbiased. If she has particular ties to a party in the case, or a particular interest in the outcome of the case, she must remove herself from participation. For it is difficult to shield from the effects of such factors, and they tend to lead one away from the truth.

A judgment or belief is *rational*, relative to certain epistemic goals, if it is reached or maintained by a process that is effective and efficient at achieving those epistemic goals. It would be too stringent to require that the process be *optimal* in achieving those goals. Perhaps another process is superior, but if this process is not far inferior, then a belief arrived at through it may well be rational. The process need not even be more effective than not. Perhaps no available process is likely to yield true beliefs of a desired degree of specificity, but if the belief is arrived at by (what is close to) the most effective such process it will count as rational, even if the desired result is not more likely than not (see Nozick 1993, pp. 65–6).

On these construals, objectivity and rationality are connected. Nonobjectivity lessens rationality. If a belief is arrived at by a process in which biasing factors that lead one away from the truth play a significant role, then that process will be less effective and efficient in arriving at the truth, and so, to that extent, less rational—at least as judged by a stringent optimizing criterion of rationality.

Whether or not a belief is objective is determined by, and derived from, the nature of the process by which it arises (and is maintained). Just as in the case of justified belief, an objective belief can turn out to be false. What led the person to this false (but objective) belief will not, however, have been the operation of biasing factors. Also, a nonobjective belief may turn out to be true. Though shaped by biasing factors that tend, *in general*, to lead away from the truth, in this case the person happened upon the truth despite the biasing factors.

Being "biasing" is not an intrinsic feature of a factor; it depends upon the role that factor plays in the overall process of arriving at belief. Within one process, a factor may retard finding the truth, within another process that same factor may be neutral or even may aid in discovering the truth.[2] The crucial question is whether the overall process is biased against discovering certain truths, not whether a component is. Under the American system of criminal justice, to convict someone of a crime all twelve jurors must unanimously agree upon a guilty verdict. Any potential juror whose mind is (unalterably) made up, or who is especially likely to favor one verdict, is open to challenge and to exclusion from the jury. Jurors are supposed to be unbiased. Perhaps juries would better arrive at the truth, however, under a system that intentionally admitted two biased jurors, one for each side (who are able to argue their convictions during the jury's deliberations), with the votes of only eleven of the twelve jurors being required for conviction. It is an *empirical* question whether under this alternative system, jurors would more frequently arrive at the truth than in a system where all jurors individually are unbiased.

Since individual biases can be constrained and contained within systems such as the interpersonal system of scientific investigation and (perhaps) the jury system just considered, and since such biases might even perform some positive role there, when bias is unavoidable we can attempt to devise various structures to counteract biases and perhaps even to utilize them, against their own biased wishes, to arrive at the truth. Emotions themselves need not be biasing either, and do not necessarily make judgment subjective. Israel Scheffler has emphasized the useful role certain emotions, such as a passionate concern for the truth, may play in cognition.

Consider this common argument for the claim that science should be value-free:

(1)   Science should be objective.

(2)   Values are not objective.

Therefore:

(3)   Values should not be introduced into science or play a role there.

That is to say, science should be value-free. The truth of this conclusion sometimes is contested by denying the second premiss. Science could contain values, and even make value assertions, and still be objective *if* values themselves are objective. The objectivity of values is a large question; here we are concerned with a smaller point.

This argument for a value-free science based upon the premiss that values are not objective implicitly assumes the following additional premiss which we might call the Contamination premiss:

When something that is not objective is introduced into a subject, or plays a role there, it makes the subject nonobjective.

Yet we have seen that something nonobjective might play a role within a subject or area without making that thing itself nonobjective. It depends on what that role is, and what other structures limit or direct the consequences of such individual instances of nonobjectivity. Hence, the implicit premiss is false as it stands, and needs to be formulated more carefully if the common argument is to be at all plausible.

In saying that an objective belief is one that arises by a process in which biasing factors that tend to lead one away from the truth play no role, I have taken an externalist and an instrumentalist view of the objectivity of belief. Someone might hold that objectivity is an intrinsically valuable characteristic of belief. John Dewey emphasized how starting as instrumentally valuable in reaching end *E*, something can come to be held to be intrinsically valuable. We can add that its being held to be intrinsically valuable can itself be instrumentally valuable, either because holding it thus also is conducive to the particular end E or to some different end. Whether or not one can maintain an instrumentalist theory of all intrinsic value—and it is worth considering the extent to which one can—it is plausible to maintain this in the case of whatever intrinsic value is attributed to objectivity.

Even if the value of an objective belief is instrumental, some will hold that the objectivity of a belief is better defined by its resting upon (objective) *reasons*, rather than by its instrumental connection to the truth. Instrumentality will not thereby be avoided, however, if the reason-relation itself is defined by an instrumental connection to the truth. It seems plausible to think that the fact that *p* is a reason for believing *q* if there is a general type–type *factual* connection (which may be a statistical one) between *p* and *q* (between the truth of facts of some type that *p* falls under and the truth of statements of some type that *q* falls under), so that believing *q* (partly) on the basis of *p* is conducive to believing the truth. The apparent self-evidence and a priori character of the reason-relation might be explained by there having been evolutionary selection for a factual relation coming to seem self-evidently valid (see Nozick 1993, pp. 107–10).

The Objectivity of Science

Let us turn now to the general question of whether science is objective. First, a very brief sketch of the past seventy years or so of the philosophy of science. Karl Popper presents an appealing picture of science as formulating sharp theories that are open to empirical testing and to empirical refutation. Scientific theories are not induced from the data, but are imaginative creations designed to explain the data. Writers in the logical positivist tradition (Hans Reichenbach, Carl Hempel, and Ernest Nagel) elaborated the hypothetico-deductive view of scientific theorizing and testing. Call this (or a combination of these) the standard model of science.[3]

In treating Popper together with the logical positivists, I leave aside his distinctive anti-inductivist position wherein the degree of corroboration of a hypothesis is a purely *historical* description of the severity of the tests that the hypothesis already has undergone and survived, and no justified inference can be made that a better corroborated hypothesis is more likely to survive its next test than a worse corroborated one is, or than it was before it first was tested. It is worth pointing out that Popper cannot consistently combine this doctrine with his acceptance of the standard view that the wider the variety of circumstances under which a hypothesis is tested, the more severely it has been tested—repeating the same test over and over again does not (any longer) constitute severely testing the hypothesis. We severely test a hypothesis H by checking the hypothesis in those circumstances where, if H is false, its falsity is most likely to show itself (and we assess this likelihood according to our background beliefs). After H has passed a test in an area, it would not be as severe a test, not the severest test, to check H again and again and again in that same area. Checking H in another area now becomes its severest test. This can only be because after the initial test has been carried out and passed, the probability that H, if false, will show its falsity in that first area goes down. (It is not that the probability of H's showing falsity in some other area goes up.) This means that:

prob (H passes its next test in area A / H already has passed tests in
   area A) is greater than prob (H passes its next test in area A / H
   has not already passed tests in area A).

Otherwise, repeatedly rechecking H in area A would continue to be the severest test of H. But this means that H's passing severe tests eventually provides some inductive support that H will pass the very next test of that sort. The assessment of H's *past* degree of corroboration, that is, the historical assessment of the severity of the tests that H has passed—a central feature in Popper's philosophy of science—therefore involves some inductive assumption.[4]

Complications of the standard model abounded. (Some of these complications Popper foresaw, and attempted to incorporate within his view.) Here are some of the complications:

1. Isolated statements or even theories, Pierre Duhem claimed, are not subject to refutation by themselves because, by themselves, they do not imply

any particular observational data. Auxiliary hypotheses are needed also to derive observational predictions (for instance, hypotheses about the propagation of light, about the functioning of our measuring instruments, and about how our own perceptual apparatus functions).

2. Theories are not given up unless a better theory is available. Testing might best be seen as differential testing that occurs *between* formulated theories, rather than just one theory being tested alone.

3. Theories might be rendered immune from refutation by ad hoc modifications. Popper formulated a methodological rule barring these, but there is no clear demarcation between a wise modification that reformulates a theory and an ad hoc one that merely preserves it in the face of recalcitrant evidence. Imre Lakatos proposed looking at a series of theories formulated within a research program, and he attempted to formulate criteria to determine if this series was progressive or degenerative.

4. The data itself is not completely solid, and not completely independent of theory. Sometimes it is the data that is dropped or discredited, rather than the theory. And data and observations are shaped by the theories held by the scientist, and are reported in terms of these theories. Such "theory-laden" observations and experimental procedures are used to establish the facts which then are used to test theories, including the very theories they are laden with.

5. There are no rules or algorithms to determine the acceptance of a scientific theory. There are different virtues of a theory which may conflict (fitting data, explanatory power, accuracy, scope, precision, simplicity, theoretical fruitfulness, and so on). There also are different conceptions of each of these virtues; moreover, different weightings can be given to these virtues. No explicitly formulated and accepted rules precisely resolve questions about the acceptance of theories, and there is much leeway for scientists to disagree. Thomas Kuhn sometimes put this more colorfully: accepting a new theory is like a psychological gestalt switch, or (more colorfully still) like a religious conversion.

6. Much scientific work takes place within a tradition of what kind of work is fruitful, what questions are worth asking and working on, what kinds of answers are acceptable, and so on; scientists normally work within a "paradigm."

7. Theories are underdetermined by the data.

There have been two kinds of reactions to these complications for the standard model, a radical reaction and a defensive one.

The radical reaction holds that these features undermine the objectivity of science.[5] The theory-ladenness of observations means that theories cannot (easily?) be refuted, for the theories themselves shape the observational reports, and therefore make it likely that these reports will fit together with the theories. Work within a paradigm makes science "path dependent," in that the past history of science and of what theories have been accepted by scientists partly determines our current formulation and acceptance of theories, which therefore is not simply a function of the data available to us. If different theories had been formulated earlier, science would have taken a different path, with different procedures being invoked and different observations "reported," different theories later being accepted, and so on. The current theories of science are path-dependent historical products. The lack of agreed-upon rules to determine theory acceptance makes such acceptance a matter of subjective judgment, or the product of nonrational social forces, or of other factors not governed by reason such as gestalt switch and conversion. Notice that the radical response frequently accepts the notion of objectivity that went with the standard model, and concludes that since *this* notion is not satisfied, there is no objectivity to science. Another response might be to attempt to formulate a more nuanced notion of objectivity, one according to which science is objective despite the complications.

The defensive reaction follows this path.[6] The theory-ladenness of observation does not guarantee that it will comport with the theory that loads it. People concluded that the Earth revolved around the Sun, despite having previously thought differently and so "observing" the Sun to rise. Proponents of different theories might agree about an observation, or observational report, which differentially tests the theories, and so agree about whether or not a given theory is compatible with the data.

The meaning of scientific terms might vary from theory to theory, but still scientists might be *referring* to the same things in the world, and their different predictions about these things might be comparable and intersubjectively agreed upon, across the competing theories. Although there are not precisely agreed-upon rules of theory choice, rationality does not require such explicit rule-following. (I can add the following point. The literature on parallel distributed processing systems shows how complicated tasks might be accomplished, effectively directed toward a goal, without following any explicitly formulated rules that are adverted to. The activity simply is the result of the weighted connections in the network, which themselves were shaped by some feedback rule.)

Moreover, although there might not be a complete ordering of theory preferability, relative to given data, there might be a partial ordering that is enough to decide the question scientists are facing. One theory might best another according to all the criteria, or it might be that the vague weights that are given to the different criteria are within a range that is precise enough to determine particular theory choices. Hence, science can be rational and objective, *despite* the factors which complicate the standard model.

It seems to me appropriate to place Hempel in this defensive camp, although Hempel was anything but "defensive" in his worrying over, and examination of, the issues raised by Kuhn. In particular, Hempel showed remarkable open-mindedness and intellectual integrity when, already late is his career and having stood for a certain view in the philosophy of science, he acknowledged Kuhn's point that the various desiderata of a scientific theory are not precisely defined or given precise weights in relation to each other. "I think that Kuhn's position on this issue is correct. A formally precise and substantively adequate rational reconstruction of standards of scientific theory choice is not to be expected (Hempel 1984, p. 23). The school of "analytic empiricism" (as Hempel termed it, and of which he had been a leading member) hoped for such formally precise and substantively adequate rational reconstructions of "certain characteristic rules and standards of scientific procedure . . . including criteria for confirmation, explanation and the like" (Hempel 1988, pp. 6, 8), although Hempel notes that the school of analytic empiricism did not attempt to provide such rules for overall theory choice.[7] Hempel did think, however,

> that partial advances will be made, in the spirit of mathematical decision theory, in formulating precise principles of theory choice for more limited purposes and for theories of a less comprehensive kind than the paradigmatic ones Kuhn has in mind. (1979, p. 297)

Hempel sees the objectivity of scientific inquiry as depending upon whether "scientific procedures including theory choice" are "characterized by standards that do not depend essentially on purely idiosyncratic individual factors" (1983, p. 93). In looking back upon the logical empiricist view which he no longer holds, Hempel writes:

> The search for methodological principles that do not refer to psychological or sociological considerations was prompted in part by the ideal of the objectivity of scientific procedures and claims: this would call for methodological norms which determine unambiguous answers to problems of critical appraisal so that different scientists applying them would agree in their verdicts. . . . Such inter-observer agreement concerning observational evidence was seen as safeguarding the objectivity of science at the evidential level. As a result, the methodological norms for the appraisal of scientific claims would then be objective, i.e. intersubjectively binding, since they called for precisely characterized logical relations between a hypothesis under appraisal and a body of evidence sentences that could be established with high intersubjective agreement by means of direct observation. (1988, pp. 3–4)

In the light of criticisms of the logical empiricist view, Hempel proposes "a relaxed but objectivist construal of methodological principles" according to which "science is . . . an objectivist enterprise where claims are subject to a critical appraisal in terms of standards that are not simply subjective and idiosyncratic" (1983, p. 93).

Because the various desiderata of a scientific theory are not precisely defined, or given precise weights in relation to each other, Hempel worried that science does not warrant being termed a rational procedure.

> I argued that a rational procedure consists in the pursuit of a specified goal in accordance with definite rules deliberately adopted on the ground that, in the light of the available information, they offer the best prospects of attaining the goal. I concluded that insofar as scientific procedures are constrained only by considerations of the kind of the desiderata, they should be viewed as arational

(though not as irrational), and I argued further that perhaps they might be qualified as latently functional practices in the sense of functionalist theories in the social sciences.

But, on further thought, Hempel thought this view "does not take sufficient account of the considerable role that precise and rule-governed reasoning does play in the critical appraisal of competing theories," and the desiderata

> are typically perceived, it seems to me, as expressing not just individual taste or preference, but objective, if only roughly specified, traits of the competing theories. Thus, a less rigid construal of rationality may be indicated. (1983, p. 95)

Here we should distinguish three requirements that Hempel, at one time, thought necessary for scientific rationality: first, that the scientific procedures are precise enough to dictate theory choice in all situations; second, that these procedures centrally include the following of explicit precise rules; and third, that these rules themselves are adopted or maintained because they "are judged to specify optimal means of advancing scientific knowledge" (1979, p. 299). If I understand Hempel's "less rigid construal of rationality" correctly, it involves weakening the first requirement so that the scientific procedures need not dictate theory choice in all situations, and they may utilize or refer to notions that are not themselves precisely explicated. It involves weakening the second requirement only in that the rules need not be precise; they still must be explicit and consciously followed. And—here I am less sure—the rules themselves, though weakened in their precision, must continue to be explicitly evaluated and judged as a means of advancing scientific knowledge.

Since Hempel does not require in the case of action that it is rational only if some rule (such as maximizing expected utility) is explicitly followed—it is enough for the agent to have the disposition to behave in accordance with the rule, doing what the rule would call for even though the agent does not explicitly invoke it (1962)—it is not clear why scientific rationality must require the explicit invoking and following of rules. This would follow on the additional assumption that the *only* way to possess the disposition to maximize expected scientific or epistemic utility is to explicitly follow rules directed toward this goal and to adopt these rules *because* they are so directed. (Following Wittgenstein, we can ask whether rationality requires that the adopting of *these* rules also must be done as an explicit application of some *other* rule?)

If science is to be rational, then on Hempel's view it must explicitly follow methodological rules that serve the achieving of its goals. Its rationality is instrumental. What then are its goals? Should one say that its goal is to discover true explanatory theories of (various aspects of) the world? If scientific theory choice is made in accordance with the (sometimes vague) desiderata, then if science is to be rational, there must be some connection between satisfying the desiderata and achieving the goal. Satisfying the desiderata must make it more likely that the goal will be achieved. Hempel came to think that truth could not be the goal of science, because only three of the desiderata (logical consistency, testability, and compatibility with the test data) could be connected with truth. The other desiderata (such as large scope, simplicity) are not so connected.

> I want to claim that most of these desiderata are not logically relevant to the search for true theories. If we regard scientific research as instrumentally rational in a logical way, then its aim cannot solely be seen as the formulation of true theories. We could say instead that pure scientific research aims at the construction of epistemically optimal pictures of the world, i.e. at the most comprehensive, simple and systematically organized theories that are precisely formulated and logically consistent, and are such that their consequences agree well with experimental findings and that they provide the most precise explanations and predictions of empirical events. (Hempel n.d. (2), n.p.)
>
> So, if scientific inquiry is to be viewed as a systematically goal-directed enterprise, its goal surely is not the attainment of true theories. Our considerations about theory choice in the light of the desiderata rather present scientific theorizing as directed towards the construction of well-integrated world pictures that optimally incorporate our experimental data available at the time in to a simply and smoothly cohering and far-reaching conceptual scheme. Scientific theorizing is oriented, we might say, not at the ontological goal of truth, but at the epistemological one of optimal epistemic integration, or at epistemic optimality, of the belief system we hold at any time. (Hempel n.d. (1), n.p.)

On Hempel's view, "the fullest satisfaction of all desiderata is instrumentally rational in the search of [epistemically] optimal pictures of the world," while only two of the desiderata are also instrumentally rational "in the search for true pictures of the world" (n.d. (2), n.p.).

We might see Hempel here as employing some version of a principle of charity, holding that (so far as this is possible) a goal be attributed to an activity so that it comes out as instrumentally rational. It would be clearer, however, that truth is not the goal of science, if there were another, better way, different from science, to pursue the goal of true theories of the various aspects of the world. But if there is no better way than science, then perhaps *true* theories *are* the goal of science. To be sure, a theory of wide scope, a bold theory in Popper's sense, is less likely to be true, is less probable, than a narrower theory. But this does not show that our goal in doing science is not truth, for how else are we to more effectively pursue the truth about the whole world? Perhaps rationality requires that we pursue the most effective means to our goal (although I said earlier that this is too stringent a requirement), but it does not require that we always pursue a goal for which our means are quite effective. A shipwrecked passenger swimming toward a distant shore does not have the goal of exercise, which he is sure to achieve, rather than the goal of saving his life, which he is unlikely to achieve yet is more likely to achieve in this way than by any other means available to him.

The Functional View

Thus ends my sketch of recent philosophy of science, and of Hempel's views in particular. If I had to choose one of these responses—the radical or the defensive—to the complications to the standard model, I would choose the defensive one. However, there is another response that is possible: that science is rational and objective, not despite the complicating factors but (in part) *because* of them. The complicating factors play a role in the advance of science, they contribute to the progress of science, to science's rationality and objectivity. (Note that these are different notions which the literature tends to jumble together. A factor that aids the progress of science might make its objectivity more difficult; there might be trade-offs among these notions, etc.) Let me explain.

It would not be rational to start science from scratch at every moment. Things that have been learned can be built upon, not just to save time and effort but to enable us to get farther, to learn more. This point is not restricted to science but concerns human activities and endeavors in general. In building a brick wall we do not support each layer independently; we let each be supported by what comes below it. In teaching a subject, we do not teach it in a new language unknown to the students, which they must learn; we teach it in a language they already know. We do not start from scratch unless we have to. It would be irrational to always begin at the very beginning.

We can make more, and deeper, empirical predictions by utilizing several theories and assumptions rather than just one. Thereby we learn more things, and also subject our theories to a more severe test, for their inaccurate consequences might be apparent to us only when they are wielded jointly.

Using our already supported theories to make and to report observations, enables us to look farther, at further and deeper consequences. Perhaps only an experimental physicist will see a certain particle in the trail in a Wilson cloud chamber, but given the existence of an evidentially supported theory that tells us this, it would be foolish to report only bare phenomenal seeings, even if such were possible. Only by standing upon our existing theories can we reach to predictions yielded by theories still further from "bare" observations. Similarly, it is rational to work within an existing paradigm that has some successes to its credit. Thereby we build upon its resources as we elaborate it further, and we learn from its further applications in new domains.

We should notice that the notion of observation uncontaminated by theory is, in any case, a pre-evolutionary notion. Consider how we see egg-shaped figures as convex or concave, depending upon the pattern of bright light and shadow (see Churchland and Sejnowski 1992, p. 146). No inference or conscious interpretation takes place. Rather, we see these three-dimensional facts in accordance with the (default) assumption that light comes from above. This is a longstanding and general enough fact (light comes from the sun or from the moon; fires on the ground are a late and relatively infrequent phenomenon) for the evolutionary process to have built it into our very mode of observation, structuring it. If light does come from above, then for a convex figure, the light will be at the top, the shadow at the bottom, while for a concave figure, the darker portion will be at the top, the lighter one at the bottom. When those shading patterns obtain, we automatically see the three-dimensional structure of the object accordingly.

Another way of putting the matter is that evolution has built the equivalent of certain inferences *into* our observations, selecting for structures in our visual system (the pattern of excitations and inhibitions in our neuronal wiring) so that, given certain stimulation of sensory receptors, things are seen a certain way. Those wiring patterns which led our ancestors to see the world (roughly) the way it was, were selected for. We don't need to *infer* from the sensory stimulation that things in the world are a certain way; evolution has made the inference for us. Try as we might, we cannot bring the theoretical content of our observations down to zero, for evolution itself, even if it has not *maximized* the accurate theoretical content of the observations, has placed it at a level much above zero.

Evolution has not produced completely accurate observations though, for interesting reasons. Consider Mach bands, which are lighter and brighter bands seen at the border of a dark and a light surface, or around a dark object against a light background. The gradient of perceived brightness is not proportional to the actual brightness (the intensity of the light reaching the retina), and this difference can be explained in terms of the pattern of neuronal wiring, including adjacent inhibitory connections. Our perceptual experience is *not* linear with the physical phenomenon, but this "distortion" serves the function of accentuating and making more salient the boundaries of an object, which is a useful thing to quickly notice. The particular pattern of neuronal wiring that produces Mach bands leads to an increase of accuracy in one respect, and an inaccuracy in another; there presumably was evolutionary selection for this wiring because the benefits of perceiving boundaries outweighed the costs of the inaccuracy. Evolution seeks to give us a *useful* picture of the world, in preference to a fully accurate one. A similar point applies to the *adaptation* of sensory receptors, where receptor potential declines with a sustained stimulus.

What would observations with zero theoretical content be like? Would there be no internal wiring that recorded things one way rather than another—in the stream of processing of stimulation patterns, would none be taken, automatically in the wiring, as indicating the presence of certain physical phenomenon? Even if we could imagine and state what this would be like, would it be at all desirable? Would it be better to start at (evolutionary) scratch, having learned nothing from the long experiences of our ancestors about what facts typically produce certain stimuli? If so, there is no reason to stop at our human ancestors. How far down the evolutionary scale, and how far back in our origins, should we proceed in search of observations that are uncontaminated by any instilled facts or factual framework? Must uncontaminated science be done only by amoebae? When, or if, we find such primitive organisms, we will not have discovered organisms that know more, and more accurately, about the world than we do. The more evolution has laden our observations with accurate theory, the better.

What of the path-dependence involved in building our current science upon past advances in knowledge? Had we not built upon particular earlier theories and research traditions, and followed the path they most easily led to, we might be accepting very different theories now. (We could not be accepting any very powerful theories unless we had built upon some theories or other—a different path but nonetheless path-dependence.)

However, the existence of Kuhnian revolutions shows that scientists are not *stuck* upon those paths they find themselves upon. They *can* shift to another very different theory, one different enough in its viewpoint to lead some philosophers to hold that the theories (or theorists) cannot even speak to or understand each other. We can leave a previous path for a new one. There may not be precise rules for doing this. (Or there may be rules which are agreed to by proponents of both of the competing theories—a point from the defensive response.) But even if Max Planck is correct that the older generation dies out before it unanimously accepts a theory, the younger generation of new scientists does move almost uniformly in one direction. Presumably they do this because, unburdened by an investment in the old theory, they can more neutrally compare the virtues of the new and the old. (Another explanation, though, is that their incentive is to concentrate upon the new, for it is here that the largest contribution remains to be made.) And individual differences in times of being convinced of a new theory can have positive functions for the institution of science, as Kuhn points out. We can add that gestalt switches may be needed to *understand* a new theory, but that does not show that they play any further role in the decision to *accept* that theory. And if such switches, or even conversions, play a role in individual decisions to accept and work further upon theories, deriving new predictions from them and subjecting them to new tests, still, being impressed and convinced by such results may not be dependent upon any switches or conversions. Perhaps such agreement and conviction comes years later, after all of the interesting choices have been individually made by those willing to run theoretical risks. But who said that the objectively correct choice must be immediately evident? If the owl of objectivity flies only at night, so be it.

If, contrary to fact, all choices about acceptance were made according to given fixed rules, wouldn't this raise the worry that science is strongly path-dependent, dependent upon the particular path *these* particular rules are a part of? That there are not always such rules, and that there is a way of hurtling oneself over to a very different place, one that can rationally be evaluated later, removes some of the sting from the charge of path-dependence. The lack of such fixed and fully determinate rules of acceptance, then, is a virtue, not a defect.

The replacement of an old paradigm by a new one might occur as follows. The old paradigm accepts certain criteria C (e.g., successful precise predictions) for judging a theory, and the theory component of the new paradigm surpasses the theory part of the old paradigm by these very criteria, or by the most important one of them (as judged by the old paradigm). So the old paradigm judges that the new theory is a better theory than the theory associated with the old paradigm itself. Notice that the new paradigm need not give the criteria C as much weight as the old paradigm gave them. It might compliment itself according to different criteria D. Still, the move will be made to the new theory. Once at the new theory, one tends to accept the new paradigm associated with it, and also to accept D, the new criteria for a good theory which are part of the new paradigm, and which that paradigm's new theory satisfies very well (and better than the old theory did).[8] These new criteria D are accepted because the new theory satisfies them. Accepting D is part of the move to a new paradigm. The new criteria D come to seem important when the new theory satisfies them, and the paradigm associated with the new theory, the new paradigm, gives these criteria D importance. An example is the move to the special theory of relativity. This theory satisfies various invariance and symmetry principles, and so criteria giving these great weight in assessing a theory come to seem like good criteria. They emphasize the kinds of features the new theory has, that other theories to be developed also might have. Scientists direct their activities toward searching for new theories that also satisfy these new criteria. A sequence of such changes, each one seen locally as progress, might, bit by bit, alter or even reject all of the initial criteria. By the (perhaps temporary) criteria of the latest stage, its current theory would be superior to each preceding one.

Underdetermination of Theory

The underdetermination of theory seems a different matter, however, serving no apparent function while raising uncertainty about the truth of any theory we accept. Let us look first at *whether* theories are underdetermined by the data, and second at what the implications of this underdetermination might be. To say that theories are underdetermined by the data is to say that more than one theory can explain the data. But we do not yet have an adequate account of explanation, of the explanatory relation E, that enables us to confidently assert such underdetermination. What further conditions, in addition to being Hempelian in form, must our explanations satisfy? Might not these conditions drastically narrow down the range of acceptable explanations, perhaps to just one? Hempel requires that explanations be given in terms of laws. We can add that these laws must satisfy various invariance conditions (or be derivable, via broken symmetries, from statements that satisfy these conditions). Following Wigner's lead, we can add a further requirement, namely, that we formulate a mathematical representation of our fundamental physical theory, and find a set of transformations such that the fundamental properties of entities are the invariants under those transformations of the fundamental theory as so represented. A theory that meets this further desideratum is to be preferred, as is a fundamental theory that is invariant under the widest range of admissible transformations and so itself exhibits a high degree of objectiveness. And if these additional constraints (or desiderata) alone do not reduce the range of theoretical explanations to unity, then perhaps they will do so in combination with further conditions still to be discovered.

We cannot say that theories must be underdetermined by the data (or more strongly, by all possible data), for the conditions that an acceptable theory or explanation must meet are not given a priori but are things that we learn as we go along. There is no reason to believe we know all such conditions already.

Suppose, however, that our theories *are* underdetermined by the data. What are the implications of this? Would we be better off if our theory were *not* underdetermined? This would mean either that our theory did not go beyond our data at all (but then at best it would give us only a compendious repetition of the data) or that it did not step far enough beyond our data to also allow in, as an alternative, another theory.

In that case, for our theory to be a powerful description of the world,

(a)   our data itself would have to be quite robust, matching the robustness of the actual world,

or

(b)   the world itself would have to be quite thin, matching the thinness of our actual data,

or

(c)   theories would have to be quite sparse in the space of possible theories, so that there was only *one* between our thin data and the robust world.

Our actual data, however, is not robust enough to reach almost all of the way to a powerful theory of a thick world. Our observational data is one small consequence of the laws that hold, sometimes quite distant from the most basic processes. For things to be different, our observations and data would have to be "in the round" and deep. In that case, although we could not get very far beyond our observations, we would not need to, for those observations would reach all the way to the basic structure of the world; they would be observations *of* the basic structure of the world, a direct experience of underlying laws, of elementary particles, of the structure of space and time. In that case, science would not exist—it would be unnecessary. We would know its results already, by observation. (And we are fortunate that our ancestors did not face such strong selective pressures against observing merely particular aspects of surface manifestations, for then *those* ancestors would not have survived to successfully give rise to us.)

On the other hand, it the world were (less robust than it is, but) as thin as the observations we actually make, we would not need to risk reaching far beyond our observations, for there would exist nothing robust to reach toward. I shall not pause to discuss what such a thin world might be like—would it be an *objective* world?—or what of value would be absent in it.

The first two alternatives (a) and (b) collapse the distance between our data and the world. The third alternative maintains that distance but leaves the (closed) interval between data and the world underpopulated. Just one possible theory can live there. Strong constraints on what a theory or adequate explanation is could keep that population down to one, as I have noted. If those constraints stem from the nature of our limited powers of understanding, however, they are an uncertain guide to the truth. But suppose that the constraints do reflect a fact F about the actual world, about what in the world is capable of giving rise to (and hence of explaining) what. Still, we might ask whether *that* fact F is entailed by our data or underdetermined by it. There will be *epistemic* underdetermination of theories, even if there is ontological determination, if, so far as we can know, facts incompatible with F also will be compatible with our data and will not necessitate those particular F-based constraints. Even if, in fact, only F is compatible with our data, because F *does* hold and so gives rise to the very constraints which make F the unique choice from our data, and hence, because of F, in general only one theoretical explanation is compatible with any given data (and so ontological underdetermination of theory by data is false), still, perhaps we cannot know all this on the basis of our data (without *already* knowing F), and so epistemic underdetermination holds sway. Over time perhaps we can learn that fact F, but at the present time, data epistemically underdetermine theory.

Epistemic or ontological underdetermination may indeed be an unavoidable fact of life for creatures with thin data in a robust world, but does either have a role or function in propelling scientific progress? They do propel the *existence* of science; we would not need an organized activity of science if our observations reached all the way to basic processes. They do propel the gathering of more data, in an attempt to decide between particular theories, or to test one theory in the area where we believe it is most likely to go wrong.

Perhaps data gathering might go on even without underdetermination of theory. Even if, given data D, only one theory T could explain D, there still would be the possibility that the D are brute facts having *no* explanation, so that further data would have to be gathered to determine if T were true. (And the falsity of T might continue to be a possibility, even though its replacement by another *theory* was not possible.) So continued gathering of data might be spurred, even without underdetermination of theory in the sense of two alternative theories being compatible with the data. Still, there would remain a certain underdetermination, in that compatible with any data D would be the one explanatory theory compatible with that data and *also* the statement (incompatible with the truth of that theory T) that the data D have no correct theoretical explanation. (This will hold if the truth of "everything has some correct theoretical explanation" is itself underdetermined by our data.) Some gap between data and theory spurs the gathering of further data, and thus the gaining of new knowledge about the world.

The fact that our theories reach farther than our data shows how far extended the reach of our theories is—a cause for celebration rather than for lament. To be sure, the further we reach the more our theories become susceptible to being wrong, or overthrown. (Recall, though, that even the observational data presuppose the regularities and incorporate the theories that evolution has instilled.) However, also, the further we reach, the deeper our understanding goes. And this deeper understanding also points toward new obtainable data which, when gathered, make less shaky some previous moves beyond the then existing data.

It might be granted that the complicating factors on the list *do* perform some positive function in the progress and rationality of science, but cannot they, at the same time, also be biasing factors that interfere with science's objectivity? Whether a factor is biasing—we already have seen—is not an intrinsic quality of that factor. It depends upon the nature of the overall system within which that factor operates. Do other factors within the system of science control or counteract (what otherwise would be) the bias of the factor in question? Can some factors on this very list control or counteract other factors on the list?

The theory-ladenness of observation might be counterbalanced by using several distinct theories to derive predictions so that no one theory determines or dominates our observation; by the personal bias of scientists who favor their own new theory, and so do not see the world through the lens of the old theory; and by requiring increasingly greater precision of prediction, a precision beyond what uninstrumented observation can bring. The underdetermination of theory might be counterbalanced by having to construct a theory that can be integrated with (modifications of) past successful theories; also, working within a paradigm will provide additional criteria (beyond compatibility with the data) that constrain new theories. However, the tendency to work within a paradigm also is counterbalanced by the incentive structure that rewards scientists for new breakthroughs, by an insistence on explaining all relevant replicable data so that anomalies cannot persistently be ignored, and by pressing for new integrations of existing theories (e.g. of the four fundamental physical forces), which cannot be done within the existing paradigm. To be sure, that these factors oppose each other does not show that they exactly counterbalance, but such exactness is not necessary to insure that over time no one factor predominates over all the others to push science in the direction of its own particular bias.

We therefore can see the possibility of a third response to the complications of the standard model, a response that is neither radical nor defensive but one that delineates the role of these factors in contributing to the rationality and the objectivity of the scientific endeavor, thereby giving us a better understanding of precisely how science *is* rational. Call this third response the *functional response*.

It is not, of course, necessary to uniformly offer this third functional response for each of the complicating features (theory-ladenness, underdetermination of theory, working within a paradigm, etc.). It is possible to hold a mixed view that combines the second and the third responses. On this mixed view, some features on the list *do* play a positive role, contributing to scientific progress, and other features, while not playing such a role, still do not prevent scientific objectivity. Such a mixed view, nevertheless, might hold that on balance the complicating features do play a positive role in effecting scientific progress.

Rationality, Progress, Objectivity, and Veridicality

We now can sort out and summarize, at least roughly, and keep distinct the notions of the rationality of science, of the progress of science, and of the objectivity of science. Science is *rational* when its processes effectively and efficiently achieve its goals: discovering truths, rejecting falsehoods, uncovering explanations, making precise and accurate predictions, and so forth. (Perhaps we also should add: and its goals themselves also are rational or reasonable.) Science *progresses* when it increasingly achieves its goals, by discovering more truths, accepting fewer falsehoods, uncovering deeper explanations, extending the domain of things that can be explained scientifically, unifying the explanations it offers, making more precise and more accurate predictions, and so forth. Science is *objective* when (differential) human factors do not systematically and irremediably point it away from certain kinds of truths or toward certain kinds of falsehoods. And, we can add, science is *veridical* to the extent that it presents an unadorned description of the world and its processes—nothing but the truth—or (more leniently) to the extent that the adornments of its theories eventually will drop away.

Each of the factors on the complicating list (Duhemian considerations, theory-ladenness of observation, underdetermination of theory, working within a paradigm, etc.) might differently affect the distinct goals of scientific rationality, scientific progress, scientific objectivity, and scientific veridicality. It is worth investigating this in detail. For now, I simply can say that theorists who think the list of complicating factors impugns the objectivity of science owe us an account of objectivity, one that does not demand that science be infallible or omniscient and that does not impugn the objectivity of a system because of the apparent nonobjectivity of one of its component parts, yet according to which such objectivity does stumble before the complicating factors.

Since my argument for the functionalist view thus far has tended to focus upon the progress of science and also, assuming it is rational to organize science so that it does progress effectively, upon the rationality of science, let us say something more about scientific *objectivity*.

Science will be objective when no extraneous factor diverts it from accurately finding out the truth. It might seem that the complicating features on the list do divert it, but we have seen that we cannot determine that a factor is biasing without knowing the role it plays in an overall process. How it strikes us on its face is not enough. Still, doesn't the list of complicating features show that which scientific theories are accepted (at any given time) must depend upon some factors in addition to what the world is like. And doesn't that, all by itself, indicate nonobjectivity?

What root idea of objectivity would this conclusion involve?[9] There are two ways science can deviate from stating all and only the truths, corresponding to the type 1 and type 2 errors discussed by statisticians. Science can accept some false statements, or it can fail to accept some true ones. Since at any time, science is incomplete and nonomniscient, it cannot be that simply failing to accept any particular truth counts as making science nonobjective. Science would be nonobjective if there are some particular truths that must forever be beyond its ken, or if some truths are much harder to discover than others, and not merely because of their greater depth. In such a case, let us say that science is *blinkered*.

Similarly, since science is fallible it will accept some statements that are false; but, again, this alone does not suffice to make it nonobjective. Science will be nonobjective if there are certain false statements that it must accept, or if its falsehoods fit a pattern, if there are certain topics it is more likely to accept falsehoods about, or certain kinds of falsehoods it is more likely to accept, *and* these fall into a pattern of being due to human biases or cognitive limitations.

Since science is not infallible or complete, an objective science cannot be required to make its theories a function only of the world. However, its theories should not be a function also of systematically biasing factors. Science might be (in the phrase of C. S. Peirce) "self-correcting" in overcoming particular biases for particular theories. But if some particular biasing factor continues to operate, now favoring one inadequate theory and next favoring another, or if science continues to maintain some theory because one biasing factor after another favors it, then biasing factors would have more than a temporary influence, and so would interfere significantly with the objectivity of science. Perhaps science is objective when its theories are a function only of the world, of random factors, and (perhaps) also of temporarily biasing factors that do not systematically blind it to certain types of truths or predispose it to certain types of falsehoods. It is far from evident that the list of admitted complicating factors shows that science is biased and so is nonobjective in this sense.

In its broadest form, the question of veridicality asks to what extent our view of the world contains features that are due to our method of knowing or representing the world. Can we disentangle these artifacts from the way the world itself is?

Color phenomena present an illuminating example. There is an objective physical phenomenon, surface reflectance, whose detection is biologically important because of its correlation with other phenomena. Our biological apparatus detects surface reflectance in a particular way that imposes some structural organization upon the information about reflectance that is received. Wavelengths are continuous yet color is psychologically experienced as organized into bands. There is a psychological discontinuity where there is a physical continuity, an experienced psychological categorization where there is a physical continuum.

We have been able, however, to discover this nonisomorphism between the physical continuity of wavelengths and the psychological phenomenon of color bands. By using our senses and our accompanying reasoning power, we have discovered that our sensory organization imposes additional structure. We have thus been able to disentangle the objective nature of what is perceived from the additional structure due to our perceptual apparatus by independently investigating the physical reality, and investigating our perceptual capacities (including their neurophysiological basis), and discovering some lack of isomorphic structure. We could have used different senses (vision, hearing, touch), each with their own special structuring, to discover the special and distinctive structuring of any one sense. And to the objection that this would only identify a sense's distinctive structuring, and not any structuring that was commonly imposed by all the senses, we can point out that even using the same one sense to investigate itself can yield the conclusion that it imposes its own structuring, and also some information about what that imposition is.

Our investigations have used scientific reasoning in addition to perceptual information. So one might wonder whether such reasoning introduces structuring of its own. However, there seems to be no bar in principle to using one component of scientific reasoning to discover artifactual structure introduced by another component, or even to using one component to discovering its very own artifactual structure. For there is no guarantee that a component's artifactual contribution (or that of scientific reasoning as a whole) must remain invisible to itself, especially when that one component (or kind of reasoning) investigates itself from as many angles as it can. To be sure, there does remain the possibility that there is some structural artifactual contribution that it makes which it itself is never able to detect.

"Whoever it is that discovered water, it wasn't a fish," someone once remarked. How can we discover that something is an artifact if it is omnipresent in all of our ways of investigating and representing the world, and present to an equal degree in each so that there are no variations in its character to make it noticeable? What is present everywhere, the thought runs, cannot be discovered because it contrasts with nothing. Even if it could be detected somehow, could it be discovered to be an artifact that was due to the combined operation of scientific method plus our (or every rational being's) cognitive apparatus, rather than being part of the basic fabric of reality?

A clue might exist in its very inescapability. The feature would seem not just universal but *necessary*. Such necessity should raise the strong suspicion that it originates as an artifact of methods of discovery or representation. (I do not say that such a broadly Kantian explanation of necessity is the only possible one, but I do not know of another equally plausible one.)

Once it was held that the domain of necessary statements included central and fundamental truths that provided a structure to which all other truths conformed. It is a task for another time to delineate the waning of the notion of metaphysical necessity in this past century and, despite some encouragement that notion has received recently, to further that implosion. Philosophers might decry this shrinking of (what some think to be) their domain of investigation. And they might mourn, in the loss of necessary statements, what might have seemed the most objective statements there are: statements whose truth is invariant across all possible worlds. However, this cloud of philosophical decline contains a silver lining, for the fewer necessities there are, the more veridical our beliefs can be. We shrink necessity in order to make room for veridicality.

NOTES

1. See Nozick (1998). Substantial portions of this essay also appear in that work.
2. Biasing factors may be only a subclass of the factors that lead one away from the truth. Being nearsighted, or being prone to fallacies of reasoning, may tend to make one's beliefs unreliable but it is not clear that it makes them nonobjective. Further work needs to be done in demarcating *biasing* factors, even among those factors that vary from person to person, and that tend to point away from the truth in a particular direction.
3. Later literature refers to this as "the received view." When I was a graduate student, this was thought of by us—I don't say by Hempel—simply as "the truth." In philosophy, something gets called "the received view" only when it is on the way out, by those attempting to push it out.
4. Couldn't we then continue, in conformity with Popper's methodology, to formulate a general statistical hypothesis about the instance falsification of hypotheses, to the effect that the probability of falsification of a hypothesis H on the *next* test in an area goes down in proportion to the severity of similar tests in that area that the hypothesis already has passed? and couldn't we then go on to severely test *this* statistical hypothesis (where it is most likely to show its falsity), so that it accrues its own degree of corroboration, with the consequence that the probability of falsifying it on the next test in an area where it already has passed tests would have lessened? Thus the inductivist camel takes up residence in the Popperian tent.
5. Under this rubric fall Thomas Kuhn (on the usual interpretation), Paul Feyerabend, Bruno Latour, Andrew Pickering, Barry Barnes, and David Bloor. Note that Hempel dissents from the usual reading of Kuhn. "In view of the considerations presented so far, I think there is no justification for charging Kuhn's account of theory choice, as has been done, with irrationalism and an 'appeal to mob psychology' (referring to the role of the scientific community in theory choice). The charge of irrationalism would have to be supported by showing that Kuhn's account flaunts certain well-established and recognized standards of rationality; and I am not aware of any rule or standard that could be seriously held to be a binding requirement of scientific rationality that has been neglected or rejected by Kuhn" (1979, p. 297).
6. Under this rubric fall Israel Scheffler, Dudley Shapere, Larry Laudan, W. H. Newton Smith, and Philip Kitcher.
7. "It should also be noted here that the analytic empiricist school was not much concerned with the analysis of theoretical *change*; Popper was a notable exception. The main concern of other members of the group was with such topics as induction, confirmation, probability, explanation, concept formation, and the structure and function of theories. There was no general doctrine as to how far the method of analytic explication might eventually reach—especially whether it would or could cover theory choice" (1979, p. 297).
8. If the old theory satisfied D better than the new theory does, we would have oscillation back and forth between the two theories and the two paradigms.
9. Science will be objective, it might appear, (only) when it follows procedures that make its theories (T) and explanations a function of the world, and only of the world (W), and not of any distorting factors: $T = f(W)$. It will not suffice, however, if its theories are a function of the world by providing the negation of truths about the world. The function f must be an accurate one. For an aspect p of the world, the theory about p, term this $T(p)$, must be an accurate function of p alone, stating the way p is:

T(p) = "p". (This notation is, of course, strictly nonsense, since the final p with quotation marks around it refers to the sixteenth letter of the alphabet.) Whenever p is true, the theory says "p". For all p, T(p) if and only if p. So runs the function that the theory must be of the world. This we recognize as Tarski's truth condition, one of his two criteria of adequacy for a definition of truth.

To *prove* that science is objective would be to prove the generalization, or to prove each statement of that form. This would be to offer a Tarski truth-definition. Such a proof cannot be given a priori; it would have to take place *within* science. However, we already know from a theorem of Tarski that this cannot be done without inconsistency. We cannot prove, for each and every p, that T(p) if and only if p. So our ability to prove the objectivity of science must fall short, if objectivity is interpreted as above. The text continues by considering a more attainable notion of objectivity.

REFERENCES

Churchland, P., and T. Sejnowski. 1992. *The Computational Brain*. Cambridge, Mass.: MIT Press.

Hempel, C. G. 1962. "Rational Action." In *Proceedings and Addresses of the American Philosophical Association*. Vol. 35. Yellow Springs, Ohio: Antioch Press.

———. 1979. "Scientific Rationality: Normative vs. Descriptive Construals." In *Wittgenstein, the Vienna Circle , and Critical Rationalism*, edited by H. Berghel et al. Vienna: Hoelder-Pichler-Tempsky.

———. 1983. "Valuation and Objectivity in Science." In *Physics, Philosophy and Psychoanalysis*, edited by R. S. Cohen and L. Lauden. Dordrecht: Reidel.

———. 1984. *Methodology of Science: Descriptive and Prescriptive Facets*. Pamphlet no. IAS 814-84 in series of lecture texts. Mortimer and Raymond Sackler Institute of Advanced Studies, Tel Aviv University.

———. 1988. "On the Cognitive Status and the Rationale of Scientific Methodology." *Poetics Today* 9:5–27.

———. n.d. (1). "The Irrelevance of the Concept of Truth for the Critical Appraisal of Scientific Claims." Unpublished manuscript.

———. n.d. (2). "Science, Induction, and Truth." Unpublished manuscript.

Nozick, R. 1993. *The Nature of Rationality*. Princeton: Princeton University Press.

———. 1998. "Invariance and Objectivity." *Proceedings and Addresses of the American Philosophical Association*. Vol. 72, No. 2, pp. 21–48.

Epilogue

The Spirit of Logical Empiricism: Carl G. Hempel's Role in Twentieth-Century Philosophy of Science

WESLEY C. SALMON

To say that we live in a postpositivist age has been a cliché for decades, often uttered by those who have no understanding of the difference between the logical *positivism* of the Vienna Circle and logical *empiricism*, which originated in Berlin and completely superseded positivism in the second half of the twentieth century. Logical positivism is dead, but logical empiricism, I believe, is still a vital force in philosophy of science. By the middle of the century, logical empiricism had three great leaders, Rudolf Carnap, Carl G. Hempel, and Hans Reichenbach. This essay, which is dedicated to the memory of Hempel, emphasizes his influence on contemporary philosophy of science.

From Positivism to Empiricism

Carnap's *Der Logische Aufbau der Welt* (1928) can be considered the pinnacle of logical positivism.[1] Taking as his point of departure Bertrand Russell's "supreme maxim of scientific philosophizing," namely, "[w]henever possible, logical constructions should be substituted for inferred entities," Carnap mustered enormous ingenuity in his attempt to carry out the construction of the world in terms of private experiences. However, Nelson Goodman's critique in *The Structure of Appearance* (1951) showed convincingly that Carnap's endeavor was hopelessly flawed. Carnap's attempted construction was a magnificent failure. The philosophical labors of Carnap and Goodman did us the invaluable service of showing the futility of the phenomenalistic approach in epistemology.

Long before Goodman's critique, Reichenbach focused his attention on Carnap's *Aufbau*. In an otherwise laudatory review, Reichenbach (1933) complained only that he saw no place for probability in Carnap's approach. Reichenbach's *Experience and Prediction* (1938), which sought to fill that lacuna, can be taken as the first major manifesto of logical empiricism. In this book, Reichenbach invoked probabilistic considerations to make three main points. First, he rejected phenomenalism as an analysis of human knowledge, adopting instead a physicalistic approach in which our knowledge is based upon our admittedly corrigible observations of middle-sized material objects. Thus, Reichenbach explicitly abandoned the quest for certainty that motivated phenomenalism. He denied C. I. Lewis's dictum that "if anything is to be probable, something must be certain" (1946, p.186). He maintained instead that corrigible observation and inductive reasoning yield probabilistic knowledge of the world. Second, like the positivists, Reichenbach advocated a criterion of empirical meaningfulness. Unlike the positivists, however, he required only the physical possibility of positive or negative empirical *probabilistic* evidence, not the possibility of *complete* confirmation or refutation. Third, Reichenbach supported scientific realism, arguing that we can have probabilistic knowledge of unobservable entities.

Reichenbach's *Experience and Prediction* was programmatic; he did not work out the details. To be sure, he had given a much deeper treatment of probability in his *Wahrscheinlichkeitslehre* (1935), but in neither of these books did he show how probabilities could employ uncertain evidence. Nor was this gap filled in *The Theory of Probability* (1949), the enlarged English edition of the 1935 treatise on probability. Moreover, when Carnap turned his attention to probability in the 1940s, the confirmation theory he developed also presupposed evidence statements that are 'given', that is, no probability values could be attached to them. To the best of my knowledge, Richard Jeffrey (1965, chap. 11) was the first philosopher to show precisely how this obstacle could be surmounted. Be that as it may, by 1950 it was clear that the concept of probability was both indispensable and highly problematic.

Reichenbach and Carnap on Scientific Realism

Reichenbach's argument for scientific realism in *Experience and Prediction* consisted of an analogy—his 'cubical world' in which a new 'Copernicus' infers the existence of unobservable birds from bird shadows—along with a passing reference to Bayes's theorem. If one turns to *The Theory of Probability* (which contains material on this topic not contained in *Wahrscheinlichkeitslehre*), one finds an altogether unilluminating explanation of how Bayes's theorem is supposed to enable us to assign probabilities to theories. It seems to me that his argument becomes plausible only by invoking a common cause principle of the sort he later elaborated in *The Direction of Time*, but many gaps need to be filled. His untimely death in 1953 prevented him from elaborating many important themes found in this posthumous publication.

Carnap expounded his views on realism in his justly famous 1950 paper "Empiricism, Semantics, and Ontology." Although this essay deals mainly with questions of existence arising in such fields as mathematics, set theory, and formal semantics, it contains brief references to the same sorts of questions in the empirical sciences. From these remarks we can discern his position on scientific realism.[2] His thesis is that there are two kinds of existence questions, internal and external. Consider some particular linguistic framework, such as Peano arithmetic. If, having adopted it, we ask whether an even prime number exists, this is an internal question to which we can readily give an unambiguous affirmative answer. If, in contrast, we ask whether natural numbers 'really' exist, and thereby question the legitimacy of adopting Peano arithmetic, we are asking an external metaphysical question to which no meaningful answer can be given. According to Carnap, the only legitimate external question that can be raised is whether the framework is a useful one for doing its job, namely, as a foundation for mathematics. This is a pragmatic question, and its answer has no ontological import. The same sorts of considerations apply to linguistic frameworks for empirical science. If we adopt the language of modern atomic physics, then we can answer the question of whether electrons exist in the affirmative without difficulty.

Carnap seems to offer us a choice when it comes to the adoption of a framework for empirical science, for instance, phenomenalism, physicalism (somewhat similar to Bas van Fraassen's [1980] constructive empiricism), or theoretical realism. If we adopt a realistic framework, within which the affirmative answer to the question of the existence of electrons is available, then the only meaningful external question is whether this framework is well adapted to the pursuit of theoretical physics. If, however, we adopt a linguistic framework in which only observables can be said to exist, the question of the existence of electrons receives a negative internal answer. The only meaningful external questions pertain to the utility of the framework itself, not to the question of whether electrons 'really' exist.

Hempel on Scientific Realism

Now, finally, the hero of this story enters the scene.[3] In 1958, Carl G. Hempel published an epoch-making paper, "The Theoretician's Dilemma: A Study in the Logic of Theory Construction." To characterize the purpose of scientific theorizing, he introduces the term "systematization," which is construed broadly enough to cover at least prediction and explanation. He poses the following puzzle.

> If the terms and principles of a theory serve their purpose they are unnecessary, as just pointed out; and if they do not serve their purpose they are surely unnecessary. But given any theory, its terms and principles either serve their purpose or they do not. Hence, the terms and principles of any theory are unnecessary. (1965, p. 186)

He establishes the first horn of this dilemma by means of an elementary logical argument showing that if, through the use of a theory, deductive connections between one set of observables and another can be established (as, for example, in making predictions of observable facts), then it is always possible to invoke a direct relationship among observables without making use of any theoretical terms—that is, terms putatively referring to unobservables. This is not to deny for one moment the heuristic value of theories; it is a question of whether there is any logical necessity of appealing to a theoretical vocabulary. The second horn of the dilemma is trivial.

In the end Hempel argues that there are two types of scientific systematization, deductive and inductive.[4] For purposes of deductive systematization, he admits, theoretical terms are dispensable, but he maintains that they are indispensable for inductive systematization. Given the pervasive character of inductive (i.e., nondemonstrative) arguments in science, he concludes that theoretical language is essential. Although I may be carrying the argument a bit beyond Hempel's own view, it seems to me that he presents a pretty strong case for saying that, given the indispensability of the theoretical vocabulary, it is reasonable to conclude that theoretical terms denote unobservable entities.[5]

Hempel offered essentially the same argument in his contribution to the volume on Carnap in *The Library of Living Philosophers* (1963). In his response, Carnap accepts Hempel's point about the indispensability of the theoretical vocabulary for inductive systematization (1963, p. 960). Applying this consideration to Carnap's own position, we may say that the inadequacy of a phenomenalistic language was shown by Goodman; Carnap did not try to rehabilitate it. Moreover, he agrees with Hempel that a physicalist language that refers only to observables is inadequate to the purposes of modern science. It would seem that powerful negative arguments have been given to the *external* questions about the adequacy of those languages. That leaves us with the theoretical language as the only adequate alternative. When we ask the *internal* questions about the existence of such unobservables as atoms and electrons, we obviously get the scientific realist's answer. In addition, correctly or incorrectly, Carnap classifies the result of Reichenbach's cubical world argument as an answer to an internal scientific question. Although there are many subtle issues I have not taken up here, there seems to be a high degree of convergence of opinion among the three great leaders of logical empiricism on the doctrine of scientific (theoretical) realism.[6]

Hempel and Oppenheim on Scientific Explanation (1948)

As already noted, when Hempel refers to scientific systematization, he explicitly includes both confirmation and explanation.[7] Carnap and Reichenbach wrote major treatises on probability and confirmation. Although their viewpoints differed enormously, both of them made contributions of striking importance. Hempel also contributed significantly to this subject, but not to the degree of the other two.[8] Carnap and Reichenbach, however, found little to say about scientific explanation. I have found fruitful suggestions on causality and explanation in Reichenbach's *Direction of Time*, but by no stretch of the imagination could Reichenbach be said to have offered any explicit account of explanation. To the best of my knowledge, Carnap did not contribute constructively to this subject.[9] This is the area in which Hempel's work is preeminent.

To put things in perspective, let's look at the dominant attitude of scientifically oriented philosophers and philosophically inclined scientists at the beginning of the twentieth century. By and large, they held that there is no such thing as scientific explanation—explanation lies beyond the scope of science, in such realms as metaphysics and theology. Karl Pearson stated it concisely: "[n]obody now believes that science *explains* anything; we all look upon it as a shorthand description, as an economy of thought." (1911/1957, p. xi, emphasis in original.) For a sharp contrast, consider the following statement, published in the final decade of this century, by the Nobel laureate physicist Steven Weinberg: "[w]hether or not the final laws of nature are discovered in our lifetime, it is a great thing for us to carry on the tradition of holding nature up to examination, asking again and again why it is the way it is" (1992, p. 275). His view on this matter is shared by large numbers of philosophers and scientists. In fact, I cannot think of any contemporary philosopher of science who denies the possibility of scientific explanation. While I cannot claim any comprehensive knowledge of the attitudes of contemporary scientists on this subject, I do feel confident that Weinberg speaks for a substantial group.[10] What happened to bring about this remarkable reversal of attitude?

Part of the answer, I think, hinges on an issue I have already touched upon. A large proportion of the philosophers and scientists who, at the beginning of the century, denied the possibility of scientific explanation, also denied the existence of such unobservables as molecules, atoms, and electrons. Pearson warns: "may there not be some danger that the physicist of to-day may treat his electron, as he treated his old unchangeable atom, as a reality of experience, and forget that it is only a construct of his imagination?" (1911/1957, p. xii).

When Hempel wrote the two essays on scientific realism already mentioned, I think that the issue had already been settled, but that philosophers were slow to perceive the import of certain scientific developments. The two crucial and profoundly related events occurred during the first decade of this century. The first is the theoretical explanation of Brownian motion by Albert Einstein and Maryan Smoluchowski; the second is the experimental determination of the value of Avogadro's number by Jean Perrin. In the first place, Perrin's work, as Einstein noted with pleasure, was the experimental verification of the Einstein-Smoluchowski theory. In the second place, Avogadro's number is *the link between the macrocosm and the microcosm*. Given the values of macroquantities, values of related microquantities can be computed, and vice versa. In the third place, the value of Avogadro's number established by Perrin on the basis of Brownian motion agreed within experimental error with determinations based on a wide variety of completely distinct physical phenomena. Perrin says it beautifully:[11]

Our wonder is aroused at the very remarkable agreement found between values derived from the consideration of such widely different phenomena. Seeing that not only is the same magnitude obtained by each method when the conditions under which it is applied are varied as much as possible, but that the numbers thus established also agree among themselves without discrepancy, for all the methods employed, *the real existence of the molecule is given a probability bordering on certainty.* (1913/1923, pp. 215–6, emphasis added)

The philosophical importance of Perrin's work was not widely appreciated until relatively late in the century. Philosophers interested in the issue of scientific realism should consult, in addition to Perrin's *Atoms*, Mary Jo Nye's philosophically sophisticated historical account in her *Molecular Reality*. As I have explained elsewhere (Salmon 1984, pp. 213–27), I find in this scientific development a stronger argument for scientific realism than any philosophical account of which I am aware.

Returning now to scientific explanation, it seems to me that the key development stems from the classic Hempel-Oppenheim essay of 1948, in which what came to be known as the deductive-nomological (D-N) explanation of particular facts was first presented with an unprecedented degree of precision. The authors of this article state explicitly that the account they offer is not novel; they cite a number of nineteenth- and twentieth-century authors, including John Stuart Mill and Karl R. Popper, as anticipators. However, even though the basic idea is not new, this 1948 article is the fountainhead from which practically all subsequent philosophical work on scientific explanation flowed, either directly or indirectly. My personal historical slant is that philosophers in roughly the first half of the twentieth century who wondered about scientific explanation may have had no clear idea of what it might be. "Explanation" (especially without the qualifier "scientific") seems so vague and ambiguous, with so many subjective overtones, that it is hard to see what sense can be made of it.

Hempel and Oppenheim gave a clear model. It had two stages. In part 1, the preliminary considerations are set forth, including four specific criteria of adequacy. These criteria provided a target. Arguments could be offered attacking or defending any or all. A strange temporal gap appears in the history. For about ten years this article attracted virtually no attention. Then, beginning in the late 1950s a huge literature began to emerge.[12] The crucial point is that virtually nobody argued that there can be no such thing as scientific explanation. They argued, for instance, whether every scientific explanation must include at least one law. They argued about the explanation/prediction symmetry thesis—that is, whether every scientific explanation could, under suitable circumstances, have been a prediction, and whether every prediction, under suitable circumstances could have been an explanation. They argued whether the statements in the explanandum must be true, or whether high confirmation would be a more appropriate requirement.

The upshot is that, rightly or wrongly, Hempel and Oppenheim gave us a general idea of what a scientific explanation might consist in. Maybe they got it wrong, but if so, the aim is to formulate a correct analysis, not to banish the very idea. For reasons I go into hereafter, this is, I believe, one of the most significant philosophical achievements of the twentieth century.

We should note with care that part 3, not part 1, contains the precise analysis. Here we find an attempt to characterize lawlike statements and laws of nature. Philosophers the world over are still wrestling with that problem.[13] Hempel and Oppenheim found that laws are not necessary for explanation; the formal requirement is for theories. It turns out, however, that theories are simply generalizations that may, but need not, contain existential quantifiers. Most of us would have called them laws. So the informal clarification of the explicandum mentions laws, but the formal explication makes matters precise by distinguishing laws from theories in this special sense. This terminological decision has absolutely no bearing on the problem of theoretical realism I have already discussed. Hempel and Oppenheim found (as they explain in note 33) that, although the informal clarification of the explicandum discusses explanations of laws as well as explanations of particular facts, the formal explication covers only explanations of particular facts. This resulted from a fundamental logical difficulty Hempel and Oppenheim were unable to overcome, and, to the best of my knowledge, Hempel never returned to that problem.[14]

To top this all off, the logicians Rolf Eberle, David Kaplan, and Richard Montague (1961) showed, to put it roughly, that according to the formal explication, almost any law could explain almost any fact. They did this essentially by exploiting the paradoxes of material implication. Then Kaplan (1961)[15] and Jaegwon Kim (1963) showed two different ways in which this formal difficulty could be avoided by means of a little patchwork. To those of us (and there were many) who were enamored of formal logic, these exercises proved extremely exciting.

We can thus see that, for many reasons, the Hempel-Oppenheim 1948 article forced scientific explanation onto the attention of a wide class of logicians and philosophers of science. There was an explicit proposal regarding the nature of scientific explanation on the table, and it challenged philosophers to respond either positively or negatively. It elicited alternative analyses. The temptation to say that there is no such thing as scientific explanation seems to have vanished.

Hempel on Scientific Explanation (1965)

The largest piece of business left unfinished in the 1948 essay was the characterization of statistical explanation. In a 1962 essay, Hempel dealt at length with this topic, but, dissatisfied with the results, he reexamined the whole subject of scientific explanation—including many of the criticisms that had been leveled against the 1948 account. The fruit of his further work was a monographic essay, "Aspects of Scientific Explanation," which appeared in his 1965 book *Aspects of Scientific Explanation and Other Essays in the Philosophy of Science*. Here, in a large and detailed section (sec. 3), he laid out two models of statistical explanation, namely, the *deductive-statistical* (D-S), in which statistical generalizations are explained by derivation from other statistical laws, and the *inductive-statistical* (I-S), in which particular facts are explained by subsumption under statistical laws. It seems to me that there is no important distinction between the two kinds of explanations of laws, be they explanations of universal laws (D-N) or statistical laws (D-S). The problem that precluded explanations of generalizations in the 1948 paper is inherited by the D-S model. However, Hempel explicitly expressed his view that I-S explanation is more important than D-S explanation, and he devoted a great deal more attention to I-S explanation.[16]

It is simple to say that the I-S model is analogous to the D-N model of explanation of particular facts, in that each is an argument that must exhibit correct logical form, each explanans must contain a law statement essentially, and the explanans must be true. The difference is that one argument is deductive, while the other is inductive because of its use of a statistical law.[17] Hempel realized that this difference raised philosophical problems of the most serious sort. They arise because inductive arguments, in contrast to deductive arguments, are not erosion-proof.[18] This means that a valid deductive argument remains valid (its validity cannot be eroded) by the addition of new premises as long as none of the original premises is removed, while a strong inductive argument can be rendered weak or worthless (its strength can be eroded) by the addition of new premises. The immunity of deduction to erosion is reflected in a principle of weakening, namely, if p entails q, then $p.r$ entails q, for any arbitrary choice of r. The susceptibility of inductive arguments to erosion is mirrored in the probability calculus, where a high value of $P(G|F)$ does not entail that $P(G|F.H)$ will be high; indeed, the addition of H to the specification of the reference class may render the latter probability zero. Thus, I-S explanation raises the notorious reference class problem, a problem that does not exist for D-N or D-S explanations. Hempel recognized the problem and articulated it as the doctrine of *essential ambiguity of inductive-statistical explanation*. He introduced the *requirement of maximal specificity* to deal with it.

His accomplishment in this essay was no less than a formulation of the *received view* of scientific explanation that was to dominate discussions of the topic for about two decades.[19] Its importance is twofold, namely, in the issues that are raised and clarified, and in its power to engender a vast and fruitful literature devoted to the nature of scientific explanation. I believe it is fair to say that the received view of "Aspects" is no longer received; indeed, it seems to me that none of the leading contributors to this subject any longer holds that all and only explanations that conform to Hempel's models are legitimate scientific explanations. It provoked various alternative models or conceptions of scientific explanation. This fact in no way diminishes the fertility and importance of Hempel's work. Going beyond the limited goals of the 1948 article, it opened up an even broader target for philosophers to contemplate and at which they could take aim.[20] It is noteworthy that by 1965 Hempel had given up on the attempt, which we saw in the 1948 essay, to provide an explication of scientific explanation in terms of formal syntax and semantics alone. I take this to be a large step forward, not a retreat.

I remarked earlier that an awareness of the possibility of scientific explanations of natural phenomena is one of the most significant pieces of philosophical progress in the twentieth century. The bases of this claim are both intellectual and practical. Philosophers from Aristotle onward have observed that we want to know not only *what* but *why*. The same sentiment is expressed by Weinberg in the passage quoted. The why-questions he poses are obviously requests for intellectual satisfaction. The crucial point is that we now believe that *scientific* knowledge can provide the answers. Going back to pre-Newtonian times, we find that mariners knew *that* there was a correlation between the tides and the position and phase of the moon. In answer to the *why* question, they might have said that divine providence, in its goodness, had provided a sign to guide the sailors. (A similar guide to longitude would have been greatly appreciated; see Sobel (1995) for a fascinating account.) Newton, in contrast, provided a *scientific* explanation of the phenomenon. It is intellectually satisfying to identify a mechanism that ties the behavior of the tides to many other diverse phenomena such as the appearance of comets, the falling of apples, and the motions of planets. And it is significant that the Newtonian explanation relies on a theory that is amenable to extensive testing. In the twentieth century, we find it intellectually satisfying to realize that the anomalous precession of the perihelion of Mercury can be explained by general relativity on the basis of the fundamental character of universal spacetime. Although this explanation has no known practical utility—general relativity is not required for management of space vehicles—it satisfies a deep desire to understand the nature of our universe and how it came to be as it is.

But there is also a major practical consequence of the view that science can provide explanations of natural phenomena. As we enter the twenty-first century, we know that we will face enormous global problems—for example, overpopulation, famine, pandemic diseases, inadequate supplies of safe water, global climate change, pollution of air and water, reduction in biodiversity, and . . . the list goes on. The challenge is to arrive at scientific understanding of the problems, based on hard scientific evidence. We need to know how and why these problems arise. When we have explained the nature of the problems, we may be able to summon resources to combat them. Again, we need scientific understanding of the consequences of whatever means may be undertaken. The point is clearly illustrated by attempts—not always successful—to explain why a particular airplane crashed, in order to try to eliminate the causes and prevent similar accidents in the future.

I certainly am not suggesting that we can come to complete scientific understanding of all the just-mentioned problems and find the means to solve them. What matters is the realization that scientific explanations are possible to some degree in some cases. It does not suffice, I think, to say with Pearson that science can be regarded merely as an instrument of prediction and control. Consider a couple of examples. First, it seems to me that considerable understanding of complex factors is required to ascertain whether recent apparent trends in the climate of Earth are results of human activities or merely natural fluctuations that would occur even in the absence of human intervention. Even to trace global temperature fluctuations over many millennia in the past requires theoretical knowledge of the mechanisms by which the records have been laid down. Second, I think that genuine understanding of physico-chemical mechanisms—many of which are not directly observable—is required to determine the relationships among the human use of fluorocarbons, the depletion of the ozone layer, and the incidence of skin cancer. The examples are numerous, and the complexities are extreme, but these cases should serve to illustrate the crucial practical importance of scientific understanding of nature. They show that scientific explanations are essential even when the goals are *entirely* practical; these needs exceed by far the instrumentalist rubric of prediction and control.

I certainly am not suggesting that science holds the keys to all policy decisions. What matters is that policy makers should have available to them the scientific understanding to make wise policy decisions. I certainly am not suggesting that everyone who is scientifically informed will make wise policy decisions. But decision makers should understand the consequences of their choices. *The point is to compare this situation to that at the beginning of our century, when scientific explanation and understanding were widely considered to be impossible.* One can hold out the hope, limited though it may be, that science *can* supplant superstition to some extent as scientific understanding becomes more widely available.[21]

The Spirit of Logical Empiricism

Let me now turn from Hempel's specific work on scientific explanation to the more general question of the status of logical empiricism at the close of the twentieth century. If one should ask which book, among all treatises in philosophy of science, gives the finest introduction to logical empiricism, I would answer, without hesitation, *Aspects of Scientific Explanation.* It treats all of the *core* issues in scientific methodology. It deals profoundly with theoretical realism, scientific explanation, confirmation, concept formation,[22] and scientific meaning. Under the latter heading we find an essay on operationism and one on the empiricist criterion of cognitive significance.[23] These are the issues that extend into all of the empirical sciences. Reichenbach never gave up on his probabilistic version of the verifiability criterion, and Carnap (1956) attempted to reformulate the criterion in terms of meanings of theoretical concepts, but today logical empiricists and their direct descendants seem largely to have abandoned the effort to formulate such criteria. Hempel's "Empiricist Criteria of Cognitive Significance: Problems and Changes" (1965, pp. 101–22) played a crucial role in this development.

In commenting on Hempel's work on the 'core issues' in philosophy of science, I am not suggesting that logical empiricists do or should confine their philosophical efforts to these issues. Reichenbach, who wrote classic works on philosophy of space and time, was a member of Einstein's department prior to Hitler's rise in 1933, and he had a deep understanding of the theory of relativity. In addition, he addressed problems in quantum mechanics and thermodynamics extensively. As already mentioned, he also made monumental contributions to probability and induction. Carnap, in addition to his equally monumental contributions to confirmation and probability, contributed profoundly to formal logic and semantics. We must keep in mind that logical empiricism embraces logic, and not only such simple systems as first-order predicate logic. In their approach to empirical science, logical empiricists employ the most sophisticated logical and mathematical systems available at any given time.

It is well known that many philosophers with extensive training in physics are presently dealing with a plethora of issues in general relativity and quantum mechanics. Although many of them would decline to be listed as adherents of a philosophical movement such as logical empiricism, a great number of them are doing exactly the sort of work that Carnap, Hempel, and Reichenbach would applaud. As physical science progresses, new philosophical problems and perspectives arise. Philosophy of biology, as we understand it today, did not exist when these three great philosophers did their most significant work. Nevertheless, much recent and contemporary work on evolutionary and molecular biology is equally well grounded in the scientific subject matter and would be gratefully accepted by logical empiricists as a growth in scope of their point of view. Similar comments could be made with respect to the social sciences. A striking case in point is the great import of Hempel's models of explanation in recent archaeology (see M. Salmon 1982, chap. 6). Advances in neurophysiology offer major challenges to philosophy of science. Moreover, some serious work on psychoanalysis falls entirely within the scope of logical empiricism.[24] Although, as noted, many of the practitioners of these philosophical endeavors would decline classification as logical empiricists, *the spirit of logical empiricism* deeply pervades their work. This *spirit* is very much alive today.

The question is bound to arise whether Thomas Kuhn killed logical empiricism with the publication of *The Structure of Scientific Revolutions*. The answer is unambiguously negative, as George A. Reisch (1991) has pointed out. Kuhn's work was, after all, first published in the *International Encyclopedia of Unified Science*, a compendium that was to encapsulate the results of logical positivism and logical empiricism. Carnap was one of the editors of the *Encyclopedia* when Kuhn's book was accepted for publication, and in Carnap's papers Reisch found correspondence between Carnap and Kuhn, and between Carnap and the other editors, which shows unequivocally that Carnap thoroughly approved of the work Kuhn had submitted.[25]

Kuhn deplored the degree to which the history of science was ignored or misused by scientists and philosophers. Logical empiricism in no way precludes history. It has no call to hold onto history badly done, though logical empiricists have sometimes been guilty of doing it badly. My commitment (as a logical empiricist) to the importance of the history of science is illustrated in my invocation here of turn-of-the-century work on Brownian motion and Avogadro's number in the discussion of scientific realism.

In 1983 a symposium on Hempel's philosophy was held at the Eastern Division meeting of the American Philosophical Association. I had the honor to share the floor with Hempel and Kuhn. Inasmuch as Hempel and Kuhn had been engaged for some time in a discussion of scientific rationality, that was the topic Kuhn chose to address. I was happy to go along with that decision. The first point I should mention is that the three of us were able to discuss the topic without breakdowns of communication. We found that our profound agreements far outweighed our differences.[26]

The second point has to do with our audience. After Kuhn and I had given our initial papers, Hempel responded incisively to the issues that had been raised. The room in which the symposium was held was large, but all of the seats were occupied and many listeners stood in the back. When Hempel finished his comments, the audience gave him a standing ovation that endured for an unprecedented period of time. At the close of the symposium, after Kuhn and I had made our responses and dealt with questions and comments from the floor, Hempel briefly summarized his reactions to the discussion. When he finished, the audience repeated its standing ovation, with even greater enthusiasm. Never have I ever witnessed such a response from any audience at any philosophical gathering. It was a most beautiful expression of the respect and affection in which he was held by this large group of philosophers. While I cannot say what feelings motivated various members of the audience, I vividly recall my sense of the overwhelming vitality of Hempel's presence—his incisive articulation of his views without the slightest trace of dogmatism, his eagerness to know and appreciate the views of others without compromising the clarity of his own, his forward-looking problem-solving perspective, his intellectual integrity, and his personal warmth. These are characteristics of his life and his work; they were celebrated in this symposium. My heart is filled with joy whenever I recall this moving occasion.

NOTES

This article was originally published in *Philosophy of Science* 66 (September 1999). Reproduced by permission of the University of Chicago Press. I am extremely grateful to Philip Kitcher and Peter Lipton for many helpful comments on earlier drafts of this essay.

1. Clearly the transition from logical positivism to logical empiricism is a complex historical matter, but a few central points are essential to our story.
2. Although he made some confusing statements on this issue in later works, he never actually changed his mind. See Paolo Parrini (1994) and my comment immediately following his essay.
3. Obviously, I do not intend to imply that this essay is Hempel's earliest important contribution; it is simply the first piece in the story I am trying to tell.
4. Hempel's commitment to inductive systematization may have been an important motivating consideration for his attempt to deal with statistical explanation a few years later (Hempel 1962).
5. In drawing this conclusion, I am relying heavily upon three paragraphs in *Aspects* (1965), beginning on the bottom of page 219 and continuing on page 220. Here, I think, Hempel is expressing his own views. When he continues, in the last paragraph of page 220, to offer alternatives to those who are unwilling to accept his

account of the status of sentences in partially interpreted theories, I take him to be suggesting lines of argument (which he ultimately finds unsatisfactory) to those who take a different view of theoretical significance. In these passages he refers to a basic vocabulary V_B, consisting of antecedently understood terms from other theories, as well as the observational vocabulary, but this move involves no difficulties for his fundamental thesis.

6. See Salmon (1994) for a more detailed examination of the views of Carnap, Hempel, and Reichenbach on this issue.

7. It is plausible to suppose that Hempel's commitment to explanation as one form of systematization, along with his doctrine that theories explain and explanations must be true, provides a strong motive for his realistic interpretation of theories.

8. It is worth remarking that Clark Glymour's bootstrapping account of confirmation is heavily indebted to Hempel's satisfaction criterion. See Glymour (1980) and Hempel (1945).

9. Carnap (1966, p. 7) states explicitly that all scientific explanation conforms to the deductive-nomological model, and on the very next page he says that some explanations are statistical and therefore do not conform to the schema offered on the previous page. This error was corrected when the book was reissued under a different title in 1974.

10. I should emphasize that I am referring only to his views on the importance of scientific explanation, not to his views on the nature of explanation, on the existence of a "final theory," or on the enormity of abandoning the Superconducting Supercollider (SSC) project. I happen to agree with him on this final matter, but that is beside the point.

11. Just before this passage, Perrin furnishes a table of thirteen distinct ways of ascertaining Avogadro's number. The table contains the results of each method.

12. Details of the historical developments are given in Salmon (1990a, pp. 11–50).

13. In attempting to clarify the nature of lawlike statements, Hempel and Oppenheim introduce the concept of a purely qualitative predicate. This concept arose in Carnap's earlier attempt to resolve Goodman's "grue-bleen" paradox.

14. A 1974 attempt by Michael Friedman to circumvent the difficulty was unsuccessful (Salmon 1990a, sec. 3.5).

15. This paper follows immediately after Eberle et al. (1961) in the same issue of the same journal.

16. More recently, a number of philosophers have claimed that I-S explanations do not exist. They hold that only statistical regularities, not individual events, are amenable to statistical explanation. For details, see Salmon (1988).

17. In the deductive case, the truth of the explanans entails the truth of the explanandum, whereas, in the inductive case, no such guarantee exists. Nevertheless, we presuppose the truth of the explanandum, since we do not try to explain facts that do not obtain.

18. Logicians characterize the difference by calling deduction *monotonic*, while induction is *nonmonotonic*.

19. Any reader who is unfamiliar with "Aspects of Scientific Explanation" should at least examine the detailed table of contents of the essay in Hempel (1965, pp. 331–2) to gain an appreciation of its scope.

20. My personal intense interest in scientific explanation was sparked by Hempel's 1962 article on statistical explanation.

21. The organization formerly known as the International Council of Scientific Unions but recently renamed as the International Council for Science (but retaining the

acronym ICSU), is a scientific organization formally connected to UNESCO. It has seventy-five national members (represented by National Academies of Science or similar organizations) and twenty-five scientific unions as members, ranging from the International Mathematical Union and the International Union of Pure and Applied Physics to the International Union of Food Science and Technology. It is the largest nonpolitical and noncommercial scientific organization in the world. Through its Committee on Capacity Building in Science, it has undertaken a massive effort to make relevant scientific knowledge available throughout the world. These efforts are specifically designed to deal with the kinds of global problems to which I have referred. The Internation Union of History and Philosophy of Science is a member of ICSU.

22. Hempel's contribution to the *International Encyclopedia of Unified Science* was his 1952 monograph *Fundamentals of Conception Formation in Empirical Science.*

23. This essay is an artful combination of two previously published essays, Hempel (1950, 1951). A 1964 postscript is added.

24. As a matter of fact, I had serious discussion with Reichenbach shortly before his death in 1953 about the possibility of applying philosophy of science to psychoanalysis. He was enthusiastic and supportive. Although, for personal reasons, I did not pursue this line of research, it has been taken up by Adolf Grünbaum with extremely fruitful results.

25. Carnap (1949, p. 126) writes: "In translating one language into another the factual content of an empirical statement cannot always be preserved unchanged. Such changes are inevitable if the structures of the two languages differ in essential points. For example: while many statements of modern physics are completely translatable into statements of classical physics, this is not so or only incompletely so with other statements. The latter situation arises when the statement in question contains concepts (like, e.g., 'wave function' or 'quantization') which simply do not occur in classical physics; the essential point being that these concepts cannot be subsequently included since they presuppose a different form of language. This becomes still more obvious if we contemplate the possibility of a language with a discontinuous spatio-temporal order which might be adopted in a future physics. Then, obviously, some statements of classical physics could not be translated into the new language, and others only incompletely. (This means not only that previously accepted statements would have to be rejected; but also that to certain statements—regardless of whether they were held true or false—there is no corresponding statement at all in the new language.)" The similarity of this statement to some of Kuhn's views is striking. I am grateful to John Earman for calling this passage to my attention.

26. I have discussed this point in detail in (Salmon 1990b). To strengthen the bridge between logical empiricism and Kuhn I invoke Bayes's theorem.

REFERENCES

Carnap, R. 1928. *Der Logische Aufbau der Welt.* Berlin: Weltkreis.
———. 1949. "Truth and Confirmation." In *Readings in Philosophical Analysis,* edited by H. Feigl and W. Sellars. New York: Appleton-Century-Crofts.
———. 1950. "Empiricism, Semantics, and Ontology." *Revue Internationale de Philosophie* 4:20–40.

————. 1956. "The Methodological Character of Theoretical Concepts." In *Minnesota Studies in the Philosophy of Science*, edited by Herbert Feigl and Michael Scriven. Vol. 1. Minneapolis: University of Minnesota Press.

————. 1963. "Carl G. Hempel on Scientific Theories." In Schilpp (1963).

————. 1966. *Philosophical Foundations of Physics*, edited by Martin Gardner. New York: Basic Books.

————. 1967. *The Logical Structure of the World*. Berkeley: University of California Press. Translation of Carnap (1928) by R. A. George.

————. 1974. *An Introduction to the Philosophy of Science*. New York: Basic Books. Reissue, with modifications, of Carnap (1966).

Eberle, R., et al. 1961. "Hempel and Oppenheim on Explanation." *Philosophy of Science* 28:418–28.

Friedman, M. 1974. "Explanation and Scientific Understanding." *Journal of Philosophy* 71:5–19.

Glymour, C. 1980. *Theory and Evidence*. Princeton: Princeton University Press.

Goodman, N. 1951. *The Structure of Appearance*. Cambridge: Harvard University Press.

Hempel, C. G. 1945. "Studies in the Logic of Confirmation." *Mind* 54:1–26, 97–121. Reprinted in Hempel (1965).

————. 1950. "Problems and Changes in the Empiricist Criterion of Meaning." *Revue Internationale de Philosophie* 11:41–63.

————. 1951. "The Concept of Cognitive Significance: A Reconsideration." *Proceedings of the American Academy of Arts and Sciences* 80:61–77.

————. 1952. *Fundamentals of Concept Formation in Empirical Science*. Chicago: University of Chicago Press. (*International Encyclopedia of Unified Science*, vol. 2, no. 7.)

————. 1958. "The Theoretician's Dilemma: A Study in the Logic of Theory Construction." In *Minnesota Studies in the Philosophy of Science*, edited by H. Feigl, M. Scriven, and G. Maxwell. Vol. 2. Minneapolis: University of Minnesota Press. Reprinted in Hempel (1965).

————. 1962. "Deductive-Nomological vs. Statistical Explanation." In *Minnesota Studies in the Philosophy of Science*, edited by H. Feigl and G. Maxwell. Vol. 3. Minneapolis: University of Minnesota Press.

————. 1963. "Implications of Carnap's Work for the Philosophy of Science." In Schilpp (1963).

————. 1965. *Aspects of Scientific Explanation and Other Essays in the Philosophy of Science*. New York: Free Press.

Hempel, C. G., and P. Oppenheim. 1948. "Studies in the Logic of Explanation." *Philosophy of Science* 15:135–75. Reprinted, with a 1964 postscript, in Hempel (1965).

Jeffrey, R. C. 1965. *The Logic of Decision*. New York: McGraw-Hill.

Kaplan, D. 1961. "Explanation Revisited." *Philosophy of Science* 28:429–36.

Kim, J. 1963. "Discussion: On the Logical Conditions of Deductive Explanation." *Philosophy of Science* 30:286–91.

Kuhn, T. 1962. *The Structure of Scientific Revolutions*. Chicago: University of Chicago Press.

Lewis, C. I. 1946. *An Analysis of Knowledge and Valuation*. La Salle, Ill.: Open Court.

Nye, M. J. 1972. *Molecular Reality*. London: Macdonald.

Parrini, P. 1994. "With Carnap, beyond Carnap: Metaphysics, Science, and the Realism/Instrumentalism Controversy." In Salmon and Wolters (1994).

Pearson, Karl. 1911/1957. *The Grammar of Science*. 3rd ed. New York: Meridian Books.

Perrin, J. 1913. *Les Atoms*. Paris: Alcan.

———. 1923. *Atoms*. New York: Van Nostrand. Translation of Perrin (1913) by D. L. Hammick.

Reichenbach, H. (1933). "Rudolf Carnap, *Der Logische Aufbau der Welt.*" *Kantstudien* 38:199–201.

———. 1935. *Wahrscheinlichkeitslehre*. Leyden: Sijthoff's Uitggeversmaatschappij.

———. 1938. *Experience and Prediction*. Chicago: University of Chicago Press.

———. 1949. *The Theory of Probability*. Berkeley: University of Chicago Press. Translation of Reichenbach (1935) by E. H. Hutten and M. Reichenbach. 2nd enlarged ed. of Reichenbach (1935).

———. 1956. *The Direction of Time*. Berkeley: University of California Press.

Reisch, G. A. 1991. "Did Kuhn Kill Logical Empiricism?" *Philosophy of Science* 58:264–77.

Salmon, M. 1982. *Philosophy and Archaeology*. New York: Academic Press.

Salmon, W. 1988. "Deductivism Visited and Revisited." In *The Limitations of Deductivism*, edited by A. Grünbaum and W. Salmon. Berkeley: University of California Press.

———. 1990a. *Four Decades of Scientific Explanation*. Minneapolis: University of Minnesota Press.

———. 1990b. "Rationality and Objectivity in Science, or Tom Kuhn Meets Tom Bayes." In *Minnesota Studies in the Philosophy of Science*, edited by W. Savage. Minneapolis: University of Minnesota Press.

———. 1994. "Carnap, Hempel, and Reichenbach on Scientific Realism." In Salmon and Wolters (1994).

Salmon, W., and G. Wolters, eds. 1994. *Logic, Language, and the Structure of Scientific Theories*. Pittsburgh: University of Pittsburgh Press.

Schilpp, P. A., ed. 1963. *The Philosophy of Rudolf Carnap*. La Salle, Ill.: Open Court.

Sobel, D. 1995. *Longitude*. New York: Walker.

van Fraassen, B. 1980. *The Scientific Image*. Oxford: Clarendon Press.

Weinberg, S. 1992. *Dreams of a Final Theory*. New York: Vintage Books.

A Bibliography of Carl G. Hempel

Editor's note: Special thanks to Richard Jeffrey for providing the editor with a bibliography of Hempel's work, which has been slightly revised for publication here. Those pieces reprinted in *Aspects*, the Jeffrey collection (which is entitled *Selected Philosophical Essays*, from Cambridge University Press), and my *Philosophy of Carl G. Hempel: Studies in Science, Explanation, and Rationality* (New York, N.Y.: Oxford University Press, 2001) have been identified to facilitate cross-reference.

1. *Beitraege zur logischen Analyse des Wahrscheinlichkeitsbegriffs.* Ph.D. thesis. University of Berlin, June 1934. 72 pp. [Subsequently translated into English by the author as "Contributions to the Logical Analysis of the Concept of Probability."]
2. "On the Logical Positivists' Theory of Truth," *Analysis* 2 (1935), pp. 49–59. [Reprinted in Jeffrey.]
3. "Analyse logique de la psychologie," *Revue de Synthese* 10 (1935), pp. 27–42. (English translation, under the title "The Logical Analysis of Psychology," in H. Feigl and W. Sellars, eds., *Readings in Philosophical Analysis* (New York: Appleton-Century-Crofts, 1949), pp. 373–384). [Reprinted in translation in Jeffrey.]
4. "Zur Frage der wissenschaftlichen Weltperspektive," *Erkenntnis* 5 (1935–36), pp. 162–4.
5. "Ueber den Gehalt von Wahrscheinlichtkeitsaussagen," *Erkenntnis* 5 (1935–36), pp. 228–60. [Reprinted in translation, under the title "On the Content of Probability Statements," in Jeffrey.]
6. "Some Remarks on 'Facts' and Propositions," *Analysis* 2 (1935), pp. 93–6. [Reprinted in Jeffrey.]
7. "Some Remarks on Empiricism," *Analysis* 3 (1936), pp. 33–40. [Reprinted in Jeffrey.]
8. (With P. Oppenheim.) *Der Typusbegriff im Lichte der Neuen Logik* (Leiden: Sijthoff, 1936.) (Wissenschaftstheoretische Untersuchungen zur Konstitutionsforschung und Psychologie.)
9. (With P. Oppenheim.) "L'importance logique de la notion de type," *Actes du Congrés International de Philosophie Scientifique*, Paris, 1935, vol. 2 (Paris: Hermann, 1936), pp. 41–9.
10. "Eine rein topologische Form nichtaristotelischer Logik," *Erkenntnis* 6 (1937), pp. 436–42.

11. "A Purely Topological Form of Non-Aristotelian Logic," *Journal of Symbolic Logic* (1937), pp. 97–112.
12. "Le problème de la verité," *Theoria* (Göteborg) 3 (1937), pp. 206–46. [Reprinted in translation, under the title "The Problem of Truth," in Jeffrey.]
13. "Ein System verallgemeinerter Negationen," *Travaux du 19e Congres International de Philosophie*, Paris, 1937, Vol. 6 (Paris: Hermann, 1937), pp. 26–32.
14. "On the Logical Form of Probability-Statements," *Erkenntnis* 7 (1938), pp. 154–60. [Reprinted in Jeffrey.]
15. "Transfinite Concepts and Empiricism," *Unity of Science Forum, Synthese* 3 (1938), pp. 9–12.
16. "Supplementary Remarks on the Form of Probability Statements," *Erkenntnis* 7 (1939), pp. 360–3.
17. "Vagueness and Logic," *Philosophy of Science* 6 (1939), pp. 163–80.
18. Articles "Carnap," "Reichenbach," "Whole," in D. Runes, ed., *Dictionary of Philosophy* (New York: Philosophical Library, 1942), pp. 45, 268, and 335–6.
19. "The Function of General Laws in History," *Journal of Philosophy* 39 (1942), pp. 35–48. [Reprinted in *Aspects*.]
20. "A Purely Syntactical Definition of Confirmation," *Journal of Symbolic Logic* 8 (1943), pp. 122–43.
21. "Studies in the Logic of Confirmation," *Mind* 54 (1945), pp. 1–26 and 97–121. [Reprinted in *Aspects*.]
22. "Geometry and Empirical Science," *American Mathematical Monthly* 52 (1945), pp. 7–17. [Reprinted in Fetzer.]
23. Discussion of G. Devereux, "The Logical Foundations of Culture and Personality Studies," *Transactions of the New York Academy of Sciences*, ser. II, vol. 7, no. 5 (1945), pp. 128–30.
24. (With P. Oppenheim.) "A Definition of 'Degree of Confirmation,'" *Philosophy of Science* 12 (1945), pp. 98–115. [Reprinted in Jeffrey.]
25. "On the Nature of Mathematical Truth," *American Mathematical Monthly* 52 (1945), pp. 543–56. [Reprinted in Fetzer.]
26. "A Note on the Paradoxes of Confirmation," *Mind* 55 (1946), pp. 79–82.
27. (With P. Oppenheim.) "Studies in the Logic of Explanation," *Philosophy of Science* 15 (1948), pp. 135–75. [Reprinted in *Aspects*.]
28. (With P. Oppenheim.) "Reply to David L. Miller's Comments," *Philosophy of Science* 15 (1948), pp. 350–2.
29. "Problems and Changes in the Empiricist Criterion of Meaning," *Revue Internationale de Philosophie* 11 (1950), pp. 41–63.
30. "A Note on Semantic Realism," *Philosophy of Science* 17 (1950), pp. 169–173.
31. "The Concept of Cognitive Significance: A Reconsideration," *Proceedings of the American Academy of of Arts and Sciences* 80(1)(1951), pp. 61–77.
32. "General System Theory and the Unity of Science," *Human Biology* 23 (1951), pp. 313–22.
33. *Fundamentals of Concept Formation in Empirical Science* (Chicago: University of Chicago Press, 1952), 93 pp. Volume II, No. 7 of the *International Encyclopedia of Unified Science*, vol. 2, no. 7. Spanish edition: *Fundamentos de la formación de conceptos en Ciencia empirica* (Madrid: Alianza Editorial, 1988).
34. "Problems of Concept and Theory Formation in the Social Sciences," in *Science, Language, and Human Rights*, American Philosophical Association, Eastern Division, vol. 1. (Philadelphia: University of Pennsylvania Press, 1952), pp. 65–86.

German translation, "Typologische Methoden in den Sozialwissenschaften," in E. Topitsch, ed., *Logik der Sozialwissenschaften* (Köln: Kiepenheuer und Witsch, 4. Auflage 1967.) [Reprinted, under the title "Typological Methods in the Natural and the Social Sciences," in *Aspects*.]

35. "Reflections on Nelson Goodman's *The Structure of Appearance*," *Philosophical Review* 62 (1952), pp. 108–16.

36. "A Logical Appraisal of Operationism," *Scientific Monthly* 79 (1954), pp. 215–20. [Reprinted in *Aspects*.]

37. "Meaning," *Encyclopedia Britannica*, vol. 15 (1956 ed.), p. 133.

38. "Some Reflections on 'The Case for Determinism,'" in S. Hook, ed., *Determinism and Freedom in the Age of Modern Science* (New York: New York University Press, 1958), pp. 157–63.

39. "The Theoretician's Dilemma," in H. Feigl, M. Scriven, and G. Maxwell, eds., *Minnesota Studies in the Philosophy of Science*, vol. 2 (Minneapolis: University of Minnesota Press, 1958), pp. 37–98. [Reprinted in *Aspects*.]

40. "Empirical Statements and Falsifiability," *Philosophy* 33 (1958), pp. 342–8.

41. "The Logic of Functional Analysis," in L. Gross, ed., *Symposium on Sociological Theory* (Evanston, Ill.: Row Peterson, 1959), pp. 271–307. Italian translation published as a monograph: *La logica dell'analisi funzionale* (Trento: Istituto Superiore di Scienze Sociali, 1967). [Reprinted in *Aspects*.]

42. "Science and Human Values," in R. E. Spiller, ed., *Social Control in a Free Society* (Philadelphia: University of Pennsylvania Press, 1960), pp. 39–64. [Reprinted in *Aspects*.]

43. "Inductive Inconsistencies," *Synthese* 12 (1960), pp. 439–69. Also included in B. H. Kazemier and D. Vuysje, eds., *Logic and Language: Studies Dedicated to Professor Rudolf Carnap on the Occasion of His Seventieth Birthday* (Dordrecht: Reidel, 1962). [Reprinted in *Aspects*.]

44. "Introduction to Problems of Taxonomy," in J. Zubin, ed., *Field Studies in the Mental Disorders* (New York: Grune and Stratton, 1961), pp. 3–23. (Also contributions to the discussion on subsequent pages.)

45. *La formazione dei concetti e delle teorie nella scienza empirica* (Milan: Feltrinelli, 1961). (Contains items 33 and 39, translated and with an introduction by Alberto Pasquinelli.)

46. "Meaning," *Encyclopedia Americana*, vol. 18 (1961 ed.), pp. 478–9.

47. "Deductive-Nomological vs. Statistical Explanation," in H. Feigl and G. Maxwell, eds., *Minnesota Studies in the Philosophy of Science*, vol. 3 (Minneapolis: University of Minnesota Press, 1962), pp. 98–169. Czech translation in K. Berka and L. Tondl, eds., *Teorie modelu a modelování* (Prague: Nakladatelství Svoboda, 1967), pp. 95–172. [Reprinted in Fetzer.]

48. "Explanation in Science and in History," in R. G. Colodny, ed., *Frontiers of Science and Philosophy* (Pittsburgh: University of Pittsburgh Press, 1962), pp. 9–33. [Reprinted in Fetzer.]

49. "Rational Action," *Proceedings and Addresses of the American Philosophical Association*, vol. 35 (Yellow Springs, Ohio: Antioch Press, 1962), pp. 5–23. [Reprinted in Fetzer.]

50. "Carnap, Rudolf," *Colliers Encyclopedia*, vol. 5 (1962 copyright), pp. 457–8.

51. "Explanation and Prediction by Covering Laws," in B. Baumrin, ed., *Philosophy of Science: The Delaware Seminar*, vol. 1, 1961–62 (New York: Interscience, 1963), pp. 107–133. [Reprinted in Fetzer.]

52. "Reasons and Covering Laws in Historical Explanation," in S. Hook, ed., *Philosophy and History* (New York: New York University Press, 1963), pp. 143–63. [Reprinted in Fetzer.]

53. "Implications of Carnap's Work for the Philosophy of Science," in P. A. Schilpp, ed., *The Philosophy of Rudolf Carnap* (La Salle, Ill.: Open Court; London: Cambridge University Press, 1963), pp. 685–709.

54. *Aspects of Scientific Explanation and Other Essays in the Philosophy of Science* (New York: Free Press; London: Collier-MacMillan, 1965). [*Aspects.*]

55. "Empiricist Criteria of Cognitive Significance: Problems and Changes," in C. G. Hempel, *Aspects of Scientific Explanation and Other Essays in the Philosophy of Science* (New York: The Free Press; London: Collier-MacMillan, 1965), pp. 101–19. [This is a conflation, with certain omissions and other changes, of items 29 and 31. First published in *Aspects.*]

56. "Fundamentals of Taxonomy," in C. G. Hempel, *Aspects of Scientific Explanation and Other Essays in the Philosophy of Science* (New York: Free Press; London: Collier-MacMillan, 1965), pp. 137–54. [This is a revision of item 44. First published in *Aspects.*]

57. "Aspects of Scientific Explanation," in C. G. Hempel, *Aspects of Scientific Explanation and Other Essays in the Philosophy of Science* (New York: Free Press; London: Collier-MacMillan, 1965), pp. 331–496. Japanese translation of the title essay published as a monograph by Bai Fu Kan, Tokyo, 1967. [First published in *Aspects.*]

58. "Coherence and Morality," *Journal of Philosophy* 62 (1965), pp. 539–42.

59. "Comments" (on G. Schlesinger's "Instantiation and Confirmation"), in R. S. Cohen and M. W. Wartofsky, eds., *Boston Studies in the Philosophy of Science*, vol. 2 (New York: Humanities Press, 1965), pp. 19–24.

60. "Recent Problems of Induction," in R. G. Colodny, ed., *Mind and Cosmos* (Pittsburgh: University of Pittsburgh Press, 1966), pp. 112–34. [Reprinted in Fetzer.]

61. *Philosophy of Natural Science* (Englewood Cliffs, N. J.: Prentice-Hall, 1966). Translations: Japanese, 1967; Italian and Polish, 1968; Swedish, 1969; Portuguese and Dutch, 1970; French, 1972; Spanish, 1973; German, 1974; Chinese, 1986.

62. *Philosophy of Natural Science* "On Russell's Phenomenological Constructionism," *Journal of Philosophy* 63 (1966), pp. 668–70.

63. "Scientific Explanation," in S. Morgenbesser, ed., *Philosophy of Science Today* (New York: Basic Books, 1967), pp. 79–88.

64. "Confirmation, Qualitative Aspects," in *The Encyclopedia of Philosophy*, vol. 2 (New York: MacMillan and Free Press, 1967), pp. 185–87.

65. "The White Shoe: No Red Herring," *British Journal for the Philosophy of Science* 18 (1967–68), pp. 239–40.

66. "Maximal Specificity and Lawlikeness in Probabilistic Explanation," *Philosophy of Science* 35 (1968), pp. 116–33. [Reprinted in Fetzer.]

67. "On a Claim by Skyrms Concerning Lawlikeness and Confirmation," *Philosophy of Science* 35 (1968), pp. 274–78.

68. "Logical Positivism and the Social Sciences," in P. Achinstein and S. F. Barker, eds., *The Legacy of Logical Positivism* (Baltimore: Johns Hopkins University Press, 1969), pp. 163–94. [Reprinted in Fetzer.]

69. "Reduction: Ontological and Linguistic Facets," in S. Morgenbesser, P. Suppes, and M. White, eds., *Philosophy, Science and Method: Essays in Honor of Ernest Nagel* (New York: St. Martin's Press, 1969), pp. 179–99. [Reprinted in Fetzer.]

70. "On the Structure of Scientific Theories," R. Suter, ed., *The Isenberg Memorial Lecture Series 1965–1966* (East Lansing: Michigan State University Press, 1969), pp. 11–38. [Reprinted in Fetzer.]

71. "On the 'Standard Conception' of Scientific Theories," in M. Radner and S. Winokur, eds., *Minnesota Studies in the Philosophy of Science*, vol. 4 (Minneapolis: University of Minnesota Press, 1970), pp. 142–63. Also some contributions to "Discussion at the Conference on Correspondence Rules," pp. 220–59. [Reprinted, without the additional comments, in Fetzer.]

72. "Formen und Grenzen des wissenschaftlichen Verstehens," *Conceptus* 4 (1–3) (1972), pp. 5–18.

73. "Rudolf Carnap, Logical Empiricist," *Synthese* 25 (1973), pp. 256–68. [Reprinted in Jeffrey.]

74. "Science Unlimited?" *Annals of the Japan Association for the Philosophy of Science* 4 (1973), pp. 187–202. [Reprinted in Fetzer.]

75. "The Meaning of Theoretical Terms: A Critique of the Standard Empiricist Construal," in P. Suppes et al., eds., *Logic, Methodology and Philosophy of Science 4* (Amsterdam: North Holland, 1973), pp. 367–78. [Reprinted in Fetzer.]

76. "A Problem in the Empiricist Construal of Theories" (in Hebrew, with English summary), *Iyyun, A Hebrew Philosophical Quarterly* 23 (1972), pp. 68–81, and 25 (1974), pp. 267–8.

77. "Formulation and Formalization of Scientific Theories: A Summary-Abstract," in F. Suppe, ed., *Structure of Scientific Theories* (Urbana: University of Illinois Press, 1974), pp. 244–54.

78. "Carnap, Rudolf," *Encyclopedia Britannica*, 15th ed. (1974); *Macropedia*, vol. 3, pp. 925–6.

79. *Grundzüge der Begriffsbildung in der empirischen Wissenschaft* (Dusseldorf: Bertelsmann Universitatsverlag, 1974), 104 pp. German translation of item 33, but enlarged by an additional chapter, not previously published, on theoretical concepts and theory change titled "Theoretische Begriffe und Theoriewandel: ein Nachwort (1974)," pp. 72–89 and 97–8.

80. "The Old and the New 'Erkenntnis,'" *Erkenntnis* 9 (1975), pp. 1–4.

81. "Dispositional Explanation and the Covering-Law Model: Response to Laird Addis," in R. S. Cohen, C. A. Hooker, A. C. Michalos, and J. van Evra, eds., *PSA 1974: Proceedings of the 1974 Biennial Meeting of the Philosophy of Science Association* (Dordrecht: Reidel, 1976), pp. 369–76.

82. "Die Wissenschaftstheorie des analytischen Empirismus im Lichte zeitgenössischer Kritik," *Kongressberichte des XI. Deutschen Kongresses für Philosophie, 1975* (Hamburg: Felix Meiner Verlag, 1977), pp. 20–34.

83. *Aspekte wissenschaftlicher Erklärung* (Berlin: de Gruyter, 1977). (Revised translation of item 57 of this list, with a new section on statistical explanation). [Translation of this new section on statistical explanation (by Hazel Maxian), under the title, "Postscript 1976: More Recent Ideas on the Problem of Statistical Explanation." First published in Fetzer.]

84. "Dispositional Explanation," in R. Tuomela, ed., *Dispositions* (Dordrecht: Reidel, 1978), pp. 137–46. (This is a revised version of section 9 of item 57.)

85. "Selección de una teoría en la ciencia: perspectivas analíticas vs. pragmáticas," in *La filosofía y las revoluciones científicas. Segundo Coloquio Nacional de Filosofía, Monterrey, Nuevo Leon, México* (Mexico City, D.F.: Editorial Grijalbo, 1979), pp. 115–35.

86. "Scientific Rationality: Analytic vs. Pragmatic Perspectives," in T. S. Geraets, ed., *Rationality To-Day/La Rationalité Aujourd'hui* (University of Ottawa Press, 1979), pp. 46–58. Also remarks in the discussion, pp. 59–66, passim.

87. "Der Wiener Kreis-eine persoenliche Perspektive," in H. Berghel, A. Huebner, and E. Koehler, eds., *Wittgenstein, the Vienna Circle, and Critical Rationalism.* Proceedings of the Third International Wittgenstein Symposium, August 1978 (Vienna: Hoelder-Pichler-Tempsky, 1979), pp. 21–6.

88. "Scientific Rationality: Normative vs. Descriptive Construals," in H. Berghel, A. Huebner, and E. Koehler, eds., *Wittgenstein, the Vienna Circle, and Critical Rationalism.* Proceedings of the Third International Wittgenstein Symposium, August 1978 (Vienna: Hoelder-Pichler-Tempsky, 1979), pp. 291–301. [Reprinted in Fetzer.]

89. "Comments on Goodman's 'Ways of Worldmaking,'" *Synthese* 45 (1980), pp. 193–9.

90. "Turns in the Evolution of the Problem of Induction," *Synthese* 46 (1981), pp. 389–404. [Reprinted in Fetzer.]

91. "Some Recent Controversies Concerning the Methodology of Science" (in Chinese translation), *Journal of Dialectics of Nature* (Peking), 3 (5) (1981), pp. 11–20.

92. "Der Wiener Kreis und die Metamorphosen seines Empirismus," in Norbert Leser, ed., *Das geistige Leben Wiens in der Zwischenkriegszeit* (Vienna: Oesterreichischer Bundesverlag, 1981), pp. 205–15. [Reprinted in translation, under the title "The Vienna Circle and the Metamorphoses of Its Empiricism," in Jeffrey.]

93. "Analytic-Empiricist and Pragmatist Perspectives on Science" (Chinese translation of a lecture given in Peking), *Kexue Shi Yicong* [Collected Translations on History of Science], no. 1 (1982), pp. 56–63, 67.

94. "Logical Empiricism: Its Problems and Its Changes" (Chinese translation of a lecture given in Peking), *Xian Dai Wai Guo Zhe Xue Lun Ji* (Contemporary Foreign Philosophy; People's Publishing House), vol. 2 (1982), pp. 69–88.

95. "Schlick und Neurath: Fundierung vs. Kohärenz in der wissenschaftlichen Erkenntnis," in *Grazer Philosophische Studien*, band 16/17 (for 1982, but published in 1983), pp. 1–18. [Published in translation, under the title, "Schlick and Neurath: Foundation vs. Coherence in Scientific Knowledge," in Jeffrey.]

96. "Valuation and Objectivity in Science," in R. S. Cohen and L. Laudan, eds., *Physics, Philosophy and Psychoanalysis: Essays in Honor of Adolf Grunbaum* (Dordrecht: Reidel, 1983), pp. 73–100. [Reprinted in Fetzer.]

97. "Kuhn and Salmon on Rationality and Theory Choice," *Journal of Philosophy* 80 (1983), pp. 570–2.

98. *Methodology of Science: Descriptive and Prescriptive Facets,* Pamphlet number IAS 814-84 (in series of lecture texts published by the Mortimer and Raymond Sackler Institute of Advanced Studies, Tel Aviv University, 1984), 30 pp.

99. "Der Januskopf der wissenschaftlichen Methodenlehre," in Peter Wapnewski, ed., *Jahrbuch 1983/84, Wissenschaftskolleg—Institute for Advanced Study—zu Berlin* (Siedler Verlag, 1985), pp. 145–57.

100. "Wissenschaft, Induktion und Wahrheit," in brochure published by Fachbereich Wirtschaftswissenschaft der Freien Universität Berlin: "Verleihung der Würde eines Ehrendoktors der Wirtschaftswissenschaft an Prof. Dr. Phil. Carl G. Hempel (University of Pittsburgh) am 10. Dezember 1984." Published 1985. (Translated into English under the title, "Science, Induction, and Truth.")

101. "Thoughts on the Limitations of Discovery by Computer," in K. F. Schaffner,

ed., *Logic of Discovery and Diagnosis in Medicine* (Berkeley: University of California Press, 1985), pp. 115–22.

102. "Prova e verità nella ricerca scientifica," *Nuova Civiltà Delle Macchine*, anno 4, nos. ¾ (15/16), 1986, pp. 65–71 (Roma). (Translation by Patricia Pincini of lecture given in June 1986 at Locarno Conference under the title "Evidence and Truth in Scientific Inquiry.") English summary p. 149.

103. "Provisoes: A Problem Concerning the Inferential Function of Scientific Theories," *Erkenntnis* 28 (1988), pp. 147–64. Reprinted in A. Grünbaum and W. C. Salmon, eds., *The Limitations of Deductivism* (Berkeley: University of California Press, 1988), pp. 19–36. [Reprinted in Jeffrey.]

104. "Limits of a Deductive Construal of the Function of Scientific Theories," in E. Ullmann-Margalit, ed., *Science in Reflection. The Israel Colloquium*, vol. 3 (Dordrecht: Kluwer, 1988), pp. 1–15. [Reprinted in Fetzer.]

105. "On the Cognitive Status and the Rationale of Scientific Methodology," in *Poetics Today* 9 (1) (1988), pp. 5–27. [Reprinted in Jeffrey.]

106. "Las facetas descriptiva y valorativa de la ciencia y la epistemología," in E. Villanueva, compilador, *Segundo Simposio Internacional De Filosofía* (1981), vol. 1 (Mexico City, 1988), pp. 25–52.

107. *Oltre il Positivismo Logico: Saggi e Rícordi. A cura di Gianni Rigamonti* (Rome: Armando), 1989. Italian translations of twelve selected essays and of a recorded interview with Richard Nollan, 1982. [The interview is published in this book under the title "An Intellectual Autobiography."]

108. "Ernest Nagel," memorial note, *1989 Year Book of the American Philosophical Society* Philadelphia: The American Philosophical Society, 1990, pp. 265–70.

109. "Il significato del concetto di verità per la valutazione critica delle teorie scientifiche," *Nuova Civiltà delle Macchine*, anno 8, n. 4 (32) (1990), pp. 7–12. (English text, "The signification of the concept of truth for the critical appraisal of scientific theories," pp. 109–13. (The second word in the submitted typescript, however, was "significance.") [Reprinted, under the title "The Irrelevance of the Concept of Truth for the Critical Appraisal of Scientific Claims," in Jeffrey.]

110. "Hans Reichenbach Remembered," *Erkenntnis* 35 (1991), pp. 5–10. [Reprinted in Jeffrey.]

111. "Eino Kaila and Logical Empiricism," in I. Niiniluoto, M. Sintonen, and G. H. von Wright, eds., *Eino Kaila and Logical Empiricism*. (Helsinki: Philosophical Society of Finland, 1992), pp. 43–51. (*Acta Philosophica Fennica* 52.)

112. "Empiricism in the Vienna Circle and in the Berlin Society for Scientific Philosophy: Recollections and Reflections," in Friedrich Stadler, ed., *Scientific Philosophy: Origins and Developments* (Dordrecht: Kluwer, 1993), pp. 1–9. [Reprinted in Jeffrey.]

Index of Names

Index of Subjects

Printed in the United States
47928LVS00003B/240